What is the place of the  t
we rethink world history

This is the first comprehensive volume to bring together the histories of the Pacific Islands, the Pacific Rim and the Pacific Ocean. A distinguished international team of historians provides a multidimensional account of the Pacific, its inhabitants and the lands within and around it – from the first human migrations to the present.

The book covers the Pacific from Russia to Antarctica and from Southeast Asia to Central America, with focused attention on the peoples of Oceania. It introduces the Pacific's multiple pasts, before examining major themes in Pacific history: the connections created by the environment, migration and the economy; religious, legal and scientific ways of knowing; and the identities expressed in ideas and practices of race, gender and politics.

This is essential reading for anyone wishing to explore the Pacific and its place within global history.

Introduction by David Armitage and Alison Bashford. Essays by: Damon Salesa, Joyce E. Chaplin, Nicholas Thomas, Akira Iriye, Ryan Tucker Jones, Adam McKeown, Kaoru Sugihara, Bronwen Douglas, Lisa Ford, Sujit Sivasundaram, James Belich, Patricia O'Brien and Robert Aldrich. Afterword by Matt K. Matsuda.

David Armitage is the Lloyd C. Blankfein Professor of History at Harvard University.

Alison Bashford is the Vere Harmsworth Professor of Imperial and Naval History at the University of Cambridge.

*Other books by the editors*

David Armitage, *Foundations of Modern International Thought* (2013)

Alison Bashford, *Global Population: History, Geopolitics, and Life on Earth* (2014)

# Pacific Histories

## Ocean, Land, People

*Edited by*

DAVID ARMITAGE

*and*

ALISON BASHFORD

First published 2014 by
PALGRAVE MACMILLAN

Palgrave Macmillan in the UK is an imprint of Macmillan Publishers Limited, registered in England, company number 785998, of Houndmills, Basingstoke, Hampshire RG21 6XS.

Palgrave Macmillan in the US is a division of St Martin's Press LLC, 175 Fifth Avenue, New York, NY 10010.

Palgrave Macmillan is the global academic imprint of the above companies and has companies and representatives throughout the world.

Palgrave® and Macmillan® are registered trademarks in the United States, the United Kingdom, Europe and other countries.

ISBN: 978–1–137–00165–8 hardback
ISBN: 978–1–137–00163–4 paperback

This book is printed on paper suitable for recycling and made from fully managed and sustained forest sources. Logging, pulping and manufacturing processes are expected to conform to the environmental regulations of the country of origin.

A catalogue record for this book is available from the British Library.

A catalog record for this book is available from the Library of Congress.

Printed in China

# Contents

## Part IV: Identities

# List of Maps, Illustrations, Figures and Tables

**Figures**

**Tables**

# Acknowledgements

This volume emerged from a series of trans-Pacific, indeed genuinely global, conversations among the editors, the contributors and many other scholars with an interest in the Pacific and its histories. Noelani Arista and Iain McCalman offered particular early inspiration and encouragement for the project.

Drafts of the chapters were presented at a conference held at Harvard University on 16 and 17 November 2012. We are very grateful to the generous funders at Harvard who made that event possible: the Australian Studies Committee (especially David Haig), the Edwin O. Reischauer Institute of Japanese Studies (especially Andrew Gordon and Ted Bestor) and, above all, the Weatherhead Center for International Affairs (especially Beth Simmons and Steve Bloomfield), which provided the bulk of our support. Special gratitude goes to Marina Ivanova and her team at the Weatherhead Center for making the complex arrangements that brought everyone together for the workshop.

Elizabeth Solomon, representative of the Massachusett at Ponkapoag, offered a moving welcome from the traditional owners of the land on which the conference took place: 'May you hear each other's stories'. We are grateful to Bernard Bailyn, Andrew Gordon, Arthur Kleinman, Francine McKenzie, Micah Muscolino and Christina Thompson for chairing sessions and contributing to our discussions, to Maria John for making an admirably comprehensive and accurate record of the proceedings, and to Matt Matsuda for delivering the closing remarks published here as the afterword to the volume. Finally, David Armitage warmly acknowledges the undergraduate and graduate students in his Fall 2012 seminar on Pacific History for reading the drafts and for putting so much energy into thinking about models for the field: Michael Thornton's help with recent literature in Japanese was especially important in this regard.

At Palgrave Macmillan, Jenna Steventon has been an outstandingly supportive editor. She grasped the potential of this project immediately and went well beyond the call of editorial duty to propel and promote it, along with her colleagues Jenny McCall and Felicity Noble. Palgrave's outside readers offered immensely helpful comments on the original proposal and on the text of the volume. Paul D'Arcy, Kate Fullagar and David Hanlon generously commented on the Introduction, which also benefited greatly from the exacting scrutiny of the Atlantic World Workshop at New York University. In Sydney,

Chris Holdridge provided exemplary research assistance and in Cambridge, Massachusetts, Bina Arch helped with the illustrations.

Most of all, we are grateful to our distinguished contributors for the promptness and alacrity with which they wrote and then revised such ambitious and original chapters. Their willingness to rise to the many challenges presented by the Pacific and its histories, and their eagerness to embrace the opportunities it offers, has been inspiring and exhilarating. We hope our readers will share the sense of excitement and satisfaction we have felt in opening up so many possibilities for Pacific histories in the future.

David Armitage, Cambridge, MA
Alison Bashford, Sydney

# Notes on the Contributors

**Robert Aldrich** is Professor of European History at the University of Sydney. He has published works on France in the Pacific and French colonialism in general, most recently *Vestiges of the Colonial Empire in France: Monuments, Museums and Cultural Memory* (2005), as well as on the history of sexuality. He is the editor of *The Age of Empires* (2007) and, with Kirsten McKenzie, of *The Routledge History of Western Empires* (2014). His current research concerns the deposition and exile of indigenous rulers by British and French colonialist authorities.

**David Armitage** is the Lloyd C. Blankfein Professor of History at Harvard University and an Honorary Professor of History at the University of Sydney. Among his publications are *The Ideological Origins of the British Empire* (2000), *The Declaration of Independence: A Global History* (2007), *Foundations of Modern International Thought* (2013) and, as co-editor, *The British Atlantic World, 1500–1800*, 2nd edn (2009) and *The Age of Revolutions in Global Context, c. 1760–1840* (2010).

**Alison Bashford** is the Vere Harmsworth Professor of Imperial and Naval History at the University of Cambridge. She was Visiting Chair in Australian Studies at Harvard University in 2009–10. Her most recent book is *Global Population: History, Geopolitics, and Life on Earth* (2014). Amongst her co-edited books are *The Cambridge History of Australia*, 2 vols (2013) and *The Oxford Handbook of the History of Eugenics* (2010), which won the Cantemir Prize.

**James Belich** is the Beit Professor of Commonwealth and Imperial History at the University of Oxford, Director of the Oxford Centre for Global History and a Fellow of Balliol College. He taught in New Zealand for many years and has published several books on New Zealand history. His most recent book is *Replenishing the Earth: The Settler Revolution and the Rise of the Anglo-World, 1783–1939* (2009).

**Joyce E. Chaplin** is the James Duncan Phillips Professor of Early American History at Harvard University. Her most recent books are *Round about the Earth: Circumnavigation from Magellan to Orbit* (2012) and *Benjamin Franklin's Autobiography: A Norton Critical Edition* (2012). She has taught at six different universities on two continents, a peninsula, and an island and in a maritime studies programme on the Atlantic Ocean.

**Bronwen Douglas** is an Adjunct Senior Fellow in Pacific and Asian History in the College of Asia and the Pacific at the Australian National University. Her present research interests are race, geography and encounters in greater Oceania; indigenous imprints on European representations; and maps as ethnohistorical texts. Her most recent books are *Foreign Bodies: Oceania and the Science of Race 1750–1940* (co-edited, 2008) and *Science, Voyages and Encounters in Oceania, 1511–1850* (2014).

**Lisa Ford** is Senior Lecturer in the School of Humanities and Languages at the University of New South Wales. She is the author of the prize-winning *Settler Sovereignty: Jurisdiction and Indigenous People in America and Australia, 1788–1836* (2010) and co-editor of *Between Indigenous and Settler Governance* (2013). She is now completing two major projects spanning the relationships among convict, slave and indigenous legal status and ideas about British imperial jurisdiction in the eighteenth and nineteenth centuries.

**Akira Iriye** is the Charles Warren Professor of American History, Emeritus, at Harvard University and was president of the American Historical Association in 1988. He is the author most recently of *Global and Transnational History: The Past, Present, and Future* (2013) and he is the co-editor of *The Palgrave Dictionary of Transnational History* (2009) and, with Jürgen Osterhammel, of *A History of the World*, 6 vols (2012– ).

**Ryan Tucker Jones** is Assistant Professor of History at Idaho State University. Among his publications are *Empire of Extinction: Russians and the Strange Beasts of the Sea in the North Pacific, 1709–1867* (2014) and articles on Russian and Pacific environmental history. He is currently working on a global history of the Russian whaling industry.

**Matt K. Matsuda** is Professor of History at Rutgers University, New Brunswick, where he teaches modern European and Asia–Pacific/global-comparative histories. His publications include *The Memory of the Modern* (1996), *Empire of Love: Histories of France and the Pacific* (Oxford, 2005), the essay on the Pacific in the *American Historical Review* forum, 'Oceans of History' (2006) and *Pacific Worlds: A History of Seas, Peoples, and Cultures* (2012). He is the series editor of *Palgrave Studies in Pacific History*.

**Adam McKeown** is Professor of History at Columbia University, where he offers courses on the histories of world migration, globalisation and drugs. Among his publications are *Chinese Migrant Networks and Cultural Change: Peru, Chicago, Hawaii, 1900–1936* (2001), *Melancholy Order: Asian Migration and the Globalization of Borders* (2008) and 'Chinese Emigration in Global Context, 1850–1940', *Journal of Global History* (2010).

**Patricia O'Brien** is Associate Professor in the Center for Australia, New Zealand and Pacific Studies at Georgetown University. She is the author of *The Pacific Muse: Exotic Femininity and the Colonial Pacific* (2006). She is currently working on interwar histories of Australia's colonies of Papua and New Guinea and New Zealand's colony of Sāmoa, in addition to a study of British colonialism, privateers and indigenous contact in the Caribbean.

**Damon Salesa** is Associate Professor in the Centre for Pacific Studies at the University of Auckland. He is the author of *Racial Crossings: Race, Intermarriage, and the Victorian British Empire* (2011), which won the Ernest Scott Prize, and co-editor of *Tangata o le Moana: New Zealand and the People of the Pacific* (2012). He is currently completing *Empire Trouble: Sāmoans and the Greatest Powers in the World*.

**Sujit Sivasundaram** is Lecturer in World and Imperial History since 1500 at the University of Cambridge and a recent recipient of the Philip Leverhulme Prize for History. Among his publications are *Nature and the Godly Empire: Science and Evangelical Mission in the Pacific, 1795–1850* (2005) and *Islanded: Britain, Sri Lanka, and the Bounds of an Indian Ocean Colony* (2013).

**Kaoru Sugihara** is Professor at the National Graduate Institute for Policy Studies (Tokyo). He is the author of *Patterns and Development of Intra-Asian Trade* (1996) and *The Rise of the Asia-Pacific Economy* (2003), both in Japanese, the editor of *Japan, China and the Growth of the Asian International Economy, 1850–1949* (2005) and co-editor of *Labour-intensive Industrialization in Global History* (2013).

**Nicholas Thomas** is Professor of Historical Anthropology and Director of the Museum of Archaeology and Anthropology at the University of Cambridge. He first visited the Pacific Islands in 1984 to research his Ph.D. thesis on the Marquesas and later worked in Fiji and New Zealand. His books include *Entangled Objects: Exchange, Material Culture, and Colonialism in the Pacific* (1991), *Oceanic Art* (1995), *Discoveries: The Voyages of Captain Cook* (2003) and *Islanders: The Pacific in the Age of Empire* (2010), which won the Wolfson History Prize.

# 1

# Introduction: The Pacific and its Histories

## David Armitage and Alison Bashford

*Oceania is humanity, rising from the depths of brine and regions of fire deeper still. Oceania is us.*

Epeli Hau'ofa, 'Our Sea of Islands' (1993)

*... this mysterious, divine Pacific zones the world's whole bulk about; makes all coasts one bay to it; seems the tide-beating heart of earth.*

Herman Melville, *Moby-Dick* (1851)

The Pacific Ocean is often thought of as a centre. For its inhabitants – like the Tongan-Fijian intellectual Epeli Hau'ofa – it was cultural, physical and political home.[1] For those imagining the Pacific from without – such as the American novelist Herman Melville – this heart-shaped ocean was the very heart of earth itself. For the Islander, the Pacific was the centre of *his* world; for the American, it was the centre of *the* world. What, then, is the history of this ocean that is so often perceived as a fulcrum? If it is a pivot around which various worlds turn, what is its place in world history?

Pacific History entails the past of 'a water hemisphere' in itself.[2] More than any similar oceanic region the Pacific has a fundamental physical unity. It is a geological entity, comprising the globe's largest basin, created by tectonic movements that in turn generate circum-Pacific zones of volcanic and seismic activity collectively known as the 'Ring of Fire'.[3] These underlying physical features form linkages, both destructive and productive, that have joined the destinies of peoples in the lands around and within the Ocean. Earthquakes in this fragile region whip up the hemisphere-spanning tsunamis that lend the Pacific basin an intermittent catastrophic unity. As Ryan Jones notes in this volume, 'Tsunamis are a useful example and metaphor for the environmental history of the Pacific Ocean,

1

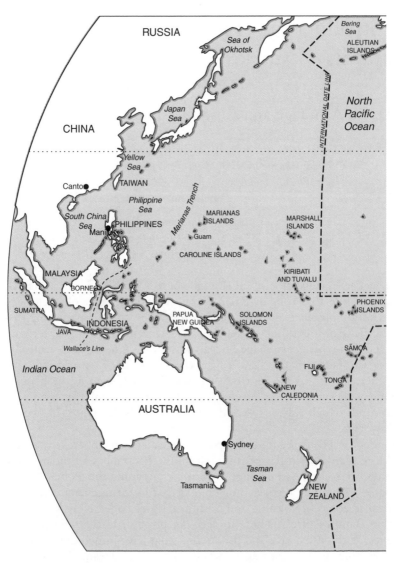

*Map 1*   The Pacific world

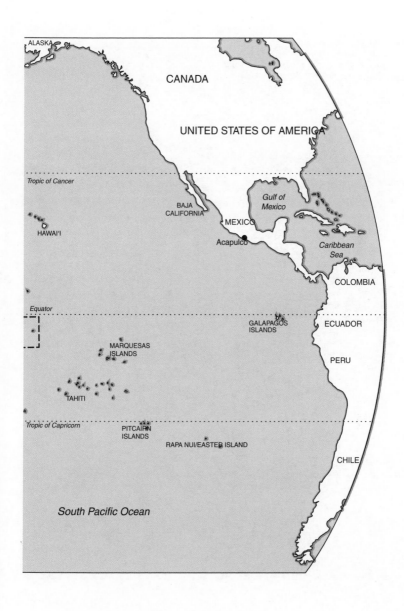

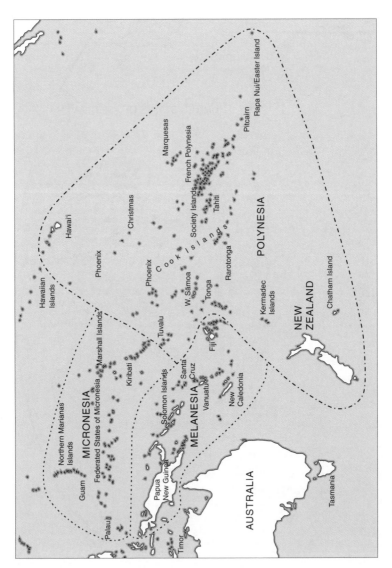

*Map 2* Oceania

pointing as they do to the connective force that the ocean itself has projected on humans over long distances'. The same seismic forces that produce these surging waves of energy also gave rise to the precious minerals that sparked the gold rushes around the Ocean's rim in the mid-nineteenth century. The Pacific also has distinct hydrographic and climatic patterns that make it 'a uniquely coherent oceanic space', as warm water and cool air circulate across it in the system known as the El Niño/Southern Oscillation (ENSO), which also has climatic effects in the Indian and Atlantic Oceans, as well as in Africa: an apt metaphor for the Pacific as integrated but connected to the world.[4]

Unified and coherent though the Pacific basin is, its history remains undeniably divided in complex ways. Great lines cross and bisect it. The Equator divides it cartographically in one direction. The International Date Line snakes across it in another, more arbitrary manner, much like the line drawn between the Spanish and Portuguese empires in the Treaty of Tordesillas (1494) more than five centuries ago. The Tropics of Cancer and Capricorn define the characters of land, sea and people; in bio-geographical terms, even Wallace's Line, running through the middle of Indonesia, delineates the ecological and faunal barrier between Asia and Australia, marking the border between the ancient continents of Sunda (what is now Southeast Asia and Indonesia) and Sahul (the once-joined lands of New Guinea and Australia).

For centuries called by Europeans the 'South Sea' – *mar del sur* – the Pacific (as Europeans were the first to term it) reaches from the Arctic to the Antarctic, and straddles the 180th meridian, or what came to be seen as the eastern and western hemispheres.[5] Within its bounds are the three 'nesias' – Micronesia, Melanesia and Polynesia – which together make up 'Oceania' (now sometimes subdivided into 'Near Oceania' and 'Remote Oceania'), an originally racialised set of European desig-nations that the peoples of the region themselves have adopted.[6] More than any other ocean, the Pacific is thus a region where worlds meet and pulse together, much as Melville imagined it in the mid-nineteenth century.

The Pacific invites extreme assessments. In the early 1920s, the German writer on geopolitics Karl Haushofer saw the Ocean, much like Melville, as alive, constantly criss-crossed by the agents of competing polities and empires: 'It is … in its gigantic triangular shape absolutely the largest unified living space on earth'.[7] Yet in exactly the same years, the novelist D. H. Lawrence looked out at the Ocean from Southern California and saw only emptiness, 'the void Pacific'. No one would now write of the region as the 'earth's empty quarter', and such appellations were always nonsensical to those living on and in the great ocean.[8] Both assessments, however, were a response to the Pacific's hemispheric scale. This Ocean suggests a whole globe in a way that other oceans do not.

In the past generation, historians have tried with accumulating energy and success to construct accounts of the human past that fully encompass its mobility, hybridity and interconnectedness across geographies and polities. Those efforts go under various names, including international history, transnational history, global history and world history.[9] They now strive to encompass the histories of overlapping worlds, often those centred on seas and oceans. The Mediterranean came first, figured as a cradle of civilisations and as an environmental unity, if not a cultural one.[10] The Indian Ocean has been analysed as a conduit of commerce, migration and religious syncretism.[11] Atlantic history, also, has linked and transformed understandings of littoral Europe, the Americas, the Caribbean and Africa.[12] These novel histories – some with ancient lineages – have been collectively termed 'the new thalassology': that is, the turn towards the waters of the world, the dwellers on their shores and islands, and the modes of interaction across maritime spaces.[13]

All along, the Pacific has been historicised too, although its scholars have generally stood to one side of this new thalassology, and so have sometimes been perceived as absent altogether. On this view, the Pacific is a relative latecomer to these new oceanic approaches to supranational history: 'Despite its size, the Pacific has received only scant historical attention when compared to the Atlantic and the Indian Oceans'.[14] As a result, one global historian has remarked, 'there has not yet emerged an organized scholarly community focused on Pacific history' comparable to the one working on Atlantic history; another argues that '[t]he Spanish American and Pacific Ocean worlds remain, for many historians, part of separate historiographies', outside the mainstream of global history.[15] The historical importance of the Pacific, it seems, has not been matched by its place in contemporary historiography. Despite its economic, demographic and strategic centrality in the present, the Pacific and its historians have not been prominent in the various recent attempts to expand our sense of the past beyond the histories of nations and states. This suggests we need new models and new narratives for writing the history of the Pacific. As Akira Iriye argues later in this volume, Pacific history can be a leading model for transnational history more generally, as well as means to reconstruct historical memory across a once-conflicted region.[16]

The changing history of the Pacific has evidently not kept pace with the Pacific's shifting place within history itself. Those who identify themselves most squarely as Pacific historians – island historians of Oceania – protest that decades of scholarship and myriad professional journals and centres devoted to Pacific history are overlooked. Yet even they admit that the Pacific remains historiographically underrepresented: 'somewhere along the way, the dialogue between studies of the Pacific and studies of humanity [has] broken down', so that the Pacific has become historically invisible amid surveys focused on other world regions: 'outside of its bounds... [the Pacific] is little known, marginalized, disavowed or excised'.[17]

On another view, however, the long tradition of Pacific island histories might better be seen as an original model, if a generally unacknowledged one, for the new thalassology itself. Historians of Oceania have long linked continents, islands, seas and peoples as standard fare: the nation-state never figured as the central driver for explaining the past of this region of the world. This necessarily troubles a 'northern hemisphere' self-conception as the point of origin for successful transnational history. We might even figure this – to cut the world, the oceans and communities of historians another way – as an historiographic north/south divide. But such a divide has also troubled and limited Pacific history itself. It is a line that has produced hemispherically separate traditions. How does the North Pacific relate to the South? How does the sea of islands relate to the Pacific Rim or to conceptions of an Asia-Pacific? Or the history of Oceania to the history of the Ocean writ large? These questions are still very much alive.[18] By bringing them all within the same frame, this book marks a step-change towards the creation of integrated and dialogic pan-Pacific histories.

Perceptions about, and assessments of, the absence or presence of Pacific historiography seem to be dependent, unsurprisingly, on whether that history-writing is viewed from the Pacific itself, or from other parts of the globe. There is a cartographical analogy to be made about this geography and the perspectives it affords. The whole Pacific has been made hard to grasp by maps centred on the Atlantic, and ordered around the Greenwich Meridian. Yet those educated from bases in the Pacific have, as often as not, viewed differently configured maps of the world, which centre on the Pacific Ocean, which represent it as a whole, and which split other oceans down arbitrary longitudes. It is clear that world history has been envisaged far more often from the perspective of the 'standard' map, with the Atlantic Ocean intact, than from the 'deviant' map that ensures the integrity of the Pacific and the visibility of its rim. This volume seeks to adjust this imbalance of perspectives.

★ ★ ★

One obvious reason for the Pacific's relative lack of integration is the difficulty of comprehending its immensity. Its scale and scope challenge history and they challenge historians. The Pacific is the world's largest natural feature. It covers roughly 165 million square kilometers (*c*.63 million square miles), occupying an area twice the size of the Atlantic Ocean and greater than all the world's land surfaces taken together. At its extremes, it extends from the Arctic to the Antarctic and from Southeast Asia to Central America. Five continents abut and encircle the Pacific – Antarctica, Asia, Australasia, North America and South America – and more than 25,000 islands punctuate it, making it unique among the world's oceans in being a sea of islands. Yet its outer boundaries are unclear. Where does the Pacific begin and end? What marks the boundary between the Pacific and Indian Oceans, or between the Pacific and the Atlantic? Does it include Indonesia or the Philippines? Is it not simply part of one, arbitrarily divided, world ocean?[19] The range of climatic regions along its shores also defies easy assimilation. Even its profundity beggars the imagination, as it descends more deeply than any other ocean, to more than 11,000 meters in the Challenger Deep off the coast of Guam.

The huge reach of Pacific geography means that the region's past and present are characterised by great diversity, both human and environmental. It has been difficult, perhaps impossible, to encompass the range of its environments and the variety of its inhabitants – human and non-human, long-settled and more recently arrived – within a single historical frame. The inhabitants of the Pacific now speak about one-third of the world's languages, English, Chinese and Spanish most prominent among them. The expansive spectrum of human communities within and around the Pacific – among them, the Islanders of Oceania, the settler societies of Siberia, the Americas and Australasia, and the long-established polities of East Asia – has proven almost impossible to survey synoptically. Surely a single history of the Pacific, written from a supramundane vantage point, could only be artificial: as the ethnographic historian Greg Dening ironically put it, 'The Pacific is...a hard place to identify with – so much ocean, too many islands'.[20] As a result, historical writing on the Pacific has been kaleidoscopic, if also somewhat episodic: 'the

"Pacific" has been historically reimagined many times', Matt Matsuda has noted: 'from an ancient Polynesian and early modern Magellanic space of transit, to an Enlightenment theater of sensual paradise, to a strategic grid of labor movements and military "island-hopping," to a capitalist basin'.[21] These multiple visions of the Pacific have not settled into a distinct narrative or defining historical trajectory within the telling of world history.

Atlantic history, to take the most obvious comparison, does possess such a narrative, a story of discovery, migration and settlement, of indigenous dispossession, of the proliferation of unfreedom (through the Atlantic slave trade and the creation of plantation societies) and the securing of freedom (in movements for political independence and the emancipation of the enslaved), that runs from the late fifteenth century to the late nineteenth century.[22] Pacific parallels with these Atlantic episodes are bound to be inexact and misleading. The greatest navigations of the Pacific were those of the Polynesians – 'the most extensive nation upon earth', in James Cook's admiring words – not those of the Europeans, who bumbled their way through the Ocean, missing almost all its islands except Guam until the last third of the eighteenth century, as Joyce Chaplin shows in her chapter.[23] J. R. McNeill also sees a distinction: 'There was no great and sudden "Magellanic exchange" across the Pacific, let alone one involving the islands' after 1521, comparable to the Columbian exchange of biota across the Atlantic after 1492.[24] The Pacific labour trade was violent and disruptive, to be sure, but its scale was not comparable to that of the Atlantic slave trade, much of the migration was voluntary, servitude was not heritable and there was no concerted movement for emancipation to remedy its iniquities as there was in the Atlantic world.[25] (The Pacific, like the Atlantic, was nonetheless a forcing-house for modern conceptions of race, as James Belich shows in his chapter.)[26] Similarly, the processes of decolonisation and independence in the Pacific were comparatively rapid yet remain incomplete even now, as the region retains some of the world's last vestiges of formal empire in French Polynesia and in Pitcairn Island, for example.[27] For all these reasons, 'Pacific history does not represent an obvious rival paradigm to Atlantic history', in part because there is as yet no integrated field of 'Pacific World' history to stand alongside the histories of other oceanic 'worlds'.[28] It may be comparable in producing multicoloured Pacifics – brown, black, white and yellow – like the variegated black, white, green and red Atlantics.[29] These are among the histories of multiple 'translocal' and contested Pacific worlds, sometimes overlapping and often intersecting but always plural.[30]

At the same time, the histories of the Atlantic and the Pacific were connected: the American War of Independence spurred the great 'swing to the East' and the colonisation of the Australian continent and then New Zealand; with the abolition of slavery, other kinds of unfree labour emerged in the nineteenth century, convict and indentured. And the postcolonial literacy of much Pacific historiography stands as one model for Atlantic history's less thorough investigation of indigenous questions: indeed major thinkers from and about Oceania could well have been integrated into Atlantic history decades ago, as they might also be better known to postcolonial theorists more generally.[31]

If the Pacific has been 'usually treated more as a zone of fragmentation than of interaction', in Adam McKeown's words, that is in part because Pacific history itself – including in that term all those who would identify themselves as working on the Pacific, insular and littoral, south and north, east and west – has been diverse and divided.[32] Histories of the Pacific have been constructed variously by geographers and anthropologists, geologists and oceanographers, literary scholars and art historians, as well as by those who identify themselves professionally as historians of one kind or another. Their framings of the Pacific are so different, and their points of reference so divergent, that they have not always been in dialogue with one another, even as each group of scholars and thinkers has produced its own distinguished understanding of the Pacific. Accordingly, when Lisa Ford describes the legal histories of the Pacific as 'many and disconnected', she could be referring to other potential histories of the region.[33]

This fragmentation may be a leading reason why, until the last decade, there have been few works of synthesis that draw upon all these various strands of history-writing. From an outsider's perspective this is what Damon Salesa calls the 'nearly universal absence of such a large presence'.[34] Nonetheless, a recent series of pan-Pacific surveys produced in quick succession from Japan, France, the USA and Britain suggests that some of the barriers between various Pacific histories are already breaking down.[35] They have also been accompanied by histories of sub-oceanic regions within the Pacific: the native seas of Oceania, the north Pacific and the increasingly American-inflected eastern Pacific, for example.[36] This activity is creating a holistic field of 'Pacific History', on the analogy of other oceanic histories. The fruits of the various Pacific historiographies that have developed over the past half-century and more are turning into something else; something much larger. And they in turn often depended upon sources created hundreds of years before that.

Pacific history itself has multiple histories that are gradually coalescing in the early twenty-first century.

★ ★ ★

Three institutional genealogies of Pacific history can illustrate the diversity and fertility of the field, but also its disaggregation, in recent decades. Each emerged from a different position within the Pacific – from its northeastern edge at the University of California, from its southwestern corner at the Australian National University and from close to its centre at the University of Hawai'i – and at distinct moments, in the 1930s, the 1950s and the 1960s. These three species of Pacific History have each flourished independently, the first as a national history in Pacific context, the second as transnational and largely postcolonial historiography and the third as a trading zone between histories, Pacific and otherwise. They emerged successively and competitively, not with one another but ranged against other national historiographies. Each therefore models Pacific history as a key intellectual space where national certainties have long been questioned, and where connections between imperial and world history were early integrated.

In 1932, the University of California Press published the first issue of the *Pacific Historical Review*. A quarterly for the Pacific Coast branch of the American Historical Association, the journal opened tellingly with the Western historian Dan E. Clark's address, 'Manifest Destiny and the Pacific'. He announced that the journal would be 'devoted to the history of the entire basin of the Pacific', but there was not much 'basin' in that first issue, it was all 'rim': articles dealt with Australasia, with Sino-Japanese relations and with links between California and Japan.[37] Over time, the *Pacific Historical Review* came to double as a publishing outlet for West Coast historians on any topic, and for historians of the American West and of the Pacific basin. Even today it remains defined by its original manifest destiny tradition: as the masthead puts it, the journal's remit is 'devoted to the history of American expansion to the Pacific and beyond, to the post-frontier developments of the twentieth-century American West, and to the interconnections between American overseas expansion and the recent West'.[38]

Despite this, its recent content in fact has a greater reach, incorporating significant transnational studies. Nonetheless, this self-definition is an honest declaration of a US-oriented 'Pacific', and of a particular kind of northern-hemisphere Pacific-oriented US history. The Californian coast links the long history of continental expansion with the extension of a 'frontier' into the Pacific Ocean; the annexation of Hawai'i; the mid-twentieth century geopolitical encounter with Japan; and the later-twentieth-century economic encounter with China. This approach marks the leading edge of a movement to transform one of the most inward-looking of national historiographies into one oriented towards the Pacific, a trend that has produced many distinguished manifestoes, monographs and surveys in recent years as American history has begun to take a Pacific turn.[39]

An alternative vision of the Pacific, as a vibrant region that was vast and expanding not fragmented and virtually empty, informed the second genealogy of Pacific history. This emerged more than a generation later in Canberra at the Australian National University during the era of decolonisation. This was a place where the independence of Pacific island states was high on political agendas and, accordingly, this particular Pacific historiography was steeped in emerging postcolonial politics with the ambition to produce an 'island-centred' history. (It was no coincidence that this strain of Pacific history emerged at the same time as African history, or that many early Pacific historians had been trained as Africanists.)[40] The historian Jim Davidson, for example, was simultaneously foundation professor of Pacific History at the Australian National University, author of *Samoa mo Samoa* [*Sāmoa for the Sāmoans*] (1967) and advisor in the drafting of constitutions for the newly independent Cook Islands, Nauru, Micronesia and Papua New Guinea. Under his watch, the *Journal of Pacific History* commenced publication in 1966, announcing Australia, at the far southwest of the Ocean, as a major centre for Pacific scholarship.[41] From that corner of the Ocean, Pacific history was also conceptualised through different disciplinary prisms. At the Australian National University, the art historian Bernard Smith composed his *European Vision and the South Pacific* (1960);[42] the geographer Oskar Spate wrote his magisterial three-volume history of the Pacific (1979–88);[43] and the former ANU student Greg Dening, then teaching at Melbourne, revised his Harvard doctoral dissertation as *Islands and Beaches* (1980), one of a generation of anthropologically-inclined histories and historically-inclined anthropologies of the Pacific from this period.[44]

The *Pacific Historical Review* (1932– ) created a forum from the north Pacific for the north Pacific; with the *Journal of Pacific History* (1966– ), there emerged one for the history of the South Pacific and the Islands. The US-based journal's intellectual provenance was diplomatic history; the Australia-based journal was rather more anthropological and ethnohistorical, implicitly and sometimes explicitly postcolonial. In between, a third centre for Anglophone scholarship was founded that served to connect the west coast of the USA and the east coast of Australia. At the University of Hawai'i, Pacific history thrived, shaped both by local Indigenous and Polynesian studies, and by a tradition of world history-writing. The University of Hawai'i Press has hosted an important *Pacific Islands Monograph Series* since 1983, fostering significant studies of Hawai'i, its region and its indigenous and US history.[45] This has itself exemplified the reach of Pacific identity amongst scholars, functioning as an important publishing outlet for Australian, New Zealand and Islander historians, for example – writing from thousands of miles away but nonetheless writing from and about Pacific history. This intellectual and publishing hub represents an epistemological as well as a geographical centre for Pacific history, combining Indigenous scholarship with work on East Asia and North Asia (including significant studies on Korea) and Oceania. It is from monographic work such as this that synthetic histories of the Pacific might be constructed in a 'collective effort to develop Pacific history as a key example of how transnational history may be studied in a regional framework'.[46]

As these genealogies suggest, Pacific historiography possesses an idiosyncratic geography that distinguishes it from other oceanic and transnational histories. It is a geography of history-writing that neatly inverts the standard evaluation of edge and centre: in the Pacific, and in Pacific history, the islands are at the centre while the edge comprises the more economically and political powerful 'rim'. For this reason, the 'centre' in the Pacific – that sea of islands – can be simultaneously indigenous and postcolonial.[47] But the postcolonial history of the Pacific, drawing equally on the epistemological and political perspectives of both indigenous peoples and incomers, can now be written from imperial records and in imperial centres.[48] This work has dovetailed with recent scholarship on the history of settler colonialism, a literature whose critical perspective has become almost orthodox in many Pacific-centred communities of historians and has strongly shaped some national histories.[49] This has made the Pacific a vital site for the development and practice – even the normalisation – of postcolonial history more broadly.

★ ★ ★

If the Pacific Ocean is a terraqueous hemisphere unto itself, and thus suggestive of a global Earth, how has this translated into the temporal axis of world history, its periodisation? A vast range of temporalities and great depth of time accompany the Pacific's geographical scale and environmental variety, and in ways that productively challenge received historical divisions. The first human migrations into the Pacific sprang from Southeast Asia over 50,000 years ago into the Australian continent via New Guinea. Diverse Aboriginal societies have lived along the Pacific edge of that continent as a continuous culture from then until now. The connection from deep time to modernity, the alternative cosmologies, and the sustained non-agricultural economies of these Pacific Ocean-dwellers reveal the partiality and particularity of the history of humanity and of 'civilisation' that privilege agricultural revolutions, whether Neolithic or modern. Efforts to fit this particular Pacific history into a world history told through agricultural or industrial 'breakthroughs' are confounded. So are distinctions between 'prehistory' and 'history'.

Other migrations of 'Austronesian' speakers from present-day Taiwan, successively occupied Melanesia, Micronesia and Polynesia as far east as Rapa Nui (Easter Island). This migration was sustained until the middle of last millennium, when the great Polynesian navigator-farmers ceased their voyages, at much the same time as China's great exploratory fleets – which had reached the coast of Africa in the early fifteenth century – retreated. The Polynesian migrants likely found South America (where the bones of their chickens have been identified),[50] and their descendants inhabit the islands and continents of the Pacific to this day. 'Indigenous time', then, as one chapter is titled, signals a different periodisation altogether, even different temporalities. The Pacific in indigenous time covers millennia but defies any narrative of 'prehistory to modernity'; it stands independently of other currents in world history, but is also part of it and needs to be accounted for.

Recent indigenous and postcolonial studies of Pacific history lie over and respond to extensive earlier analyses of European exploration and colonisation emerging from conventional traditions of imperial history. This presents challenges for historians attempting to relate what Bronwen Douglas here calls 'the highly uneven chronologies of evangelism, colonialism and decolonisation in this vast, disparate region' since the sixteenth century.[51] Early modern European maritime journeys into the Pacific coincided – more or less – with Spanish, Portuguese and British colonisation of the Americas. But the outcome and impact was altogether more minimal in the sixteenth and seventeenth centuries. The Spanish established a galleon route between South America and China, with a main port in Manila and a stopping-point in Guam. Otherwise, the mariners who journeyed – typically with great difficulty – across the Pacific, did so and left it alone. By and large, the Pacific as a 'new world' from the European perspective was a late eighteenth- and nineteenth-century phenomenon.[52] It coincided with European modernity, emerging out of the Enlightenment. The Pacific in the 'age of Empires' coincided with 'the birth of the modern world'.[53]

James Cook's three Pacific journeys (1768–71, 1772–5, 1776–9) have attracted vast scholarly inquiry and exemplify this new European vision of the Pacific as an Enlightenment project and space, as well as the hemispheric scale of the Ocean. Commissioned originally to observe from Tahiti the transit of Venus across the Sun, Cook was also charged in his first journey to search for and, if possible, chart the mysterious southern continent, Terra Australis. In the process he circumnavigated the New Zealand islands and the Pacific coastline of Australia. His second journey travelled much further south, into the Antarctic Circle. His third journey ranged from the southwest Pacific, via Hawai'i to the far northeast, along the North American coastlines and the Bering Strait, in search of a northwest passage. These explorations have rightly become the focus of extensive scholarship on eighteenth-century sciences, maritime and navigational history.[54] Richly detailed readings of encounter between the British and Indigenous people across the Pacific have emerged;[55] accounts of Indigenous men who travelled on European ships – most notably the Polynesian navigator Tupai'a who travelled with Cook and drew charts of islands to several thousand miles' circumference; and studies of Indigenous people who returned to Britain.[56] Some scholars focused on the violence of encounters – their immediate human and natural damage;[57] others stress expediency and exchange, especially when using the tools of gender history that, as Patricia O'Brien notes, began 'transforming Pacific history from the 1970s'.[58] Some treat the famous voyagers; others examine the more enduring Islander engagement with the lesser-known 'beachcombers', the traders, and slightly later the missionaries.[59] From these analyses of Pacific encounters emerged one of the most distinctive and influential strains of Pacific history – the history of the beach as the meeting place of cultures and selves, later extended to include encounters on ships and other liminal spaces.[60]

Similar patterns of cross-cultural analysis have been pursued for all of the extraordinary eighteenth-century and early nineteenth-century European voyages: the navigators and explorers whose personal names are now place-names across the Ocean's islands and coastlines: Bougainville, La Pérouse, Vancouver. Slightly later, the one Pacific voyage that perhaps rivals Cook's for fame – that of the *Beagle* (1831–6) – was germinal for Charles Darwin's theory of evolution by natural selection. Arguably, the idea was born in the Pacific Islands, 'Darwin's laboratory' as a generation of historians of science have dubbed it. However, as Sujit Sivasundaram argues, the idea of the Pacific as 'laboratory' may drain the Ocean of agency and life and overestimate the capacities of incomers at the expense of indigenous knowledges. Europeans and Pacific Islanders both possessed cosmologies that oriented their sense of the world and its origins: out of these emerged hybrid forms of knowledge, such as Darwin's theory of the formation of coral reefs, which echoed indigenous conceptions of cosmogenesis.[61] Recognition of, research on, and integration into other knowledges and cosmologies is expected, if not always successfully or fully implemented. This awareness of other epistemologies is most clear perhaps in histories of Pacific politics on the one hand, and of maritime journeying and navigation on the other.[62] The result of this awareness is an unsettling of conventional teleologies of political and scientific progress and a determination among Pacific historians not to follow narratives of world history derived from other spaces and alternative traditions.

The history of the Pacific resists such extraneous narratives, drawn from the histories of distant oceans and regions, but that is not to say that there have not been – or could not be – global histories structured around processes and experiences that began in the Pacific Ocean. For example, the Pacific was a primal site of early globalisation, as the trans-Pacific silver trade linked continents and economies for the first time into an intercontinental, even global, system of exchange. It was after all a Spanish–China connection that originally put Europeans into the Pacific, travelling westwards from Acapulco to Canton via the port of Manila in the Philippines. After 1571, the Spanish galleons crossed and returned for centuries, part of a Canton-driven economy that drew in the Dutch, the Portuguese and the English as well.[63] And that economy also functioned outside European economies altogether: a *bêche-de-mer* trade linked Aboriginal people in the north of Australia, fishers from islands in the present-day Indonesian archipelago, and Chinese in Canton, arguably from the mid-seventeenth century.[64]

The significance of Chinese markets, tastes, demands and commodities has endured, analysed by generations of economic historians of the Pacific. In the process, these histories have affirmed the idea of an economically-linked 'Pacific Rim' whose roots lie in sixteenth-century Spanish visions of the Ocean, even if the term itself would not emerge until the late nineteenth century.[65] This was to some extent a 'just-so' story of how the world became economically globalised, projected back onto earlier periods. But it is nonetheless clear that early modern economies already functioned across vast maritime as well as continental spaces. Between galleons and caravans the world was being encircled as part of the processes historians now call 'archaic' and 'proto-globalisation'.[66]

Economic histories look for, and often find, connections, exchange and unities where other kinds of history tend to see irreducible difference. Two chapters, by Adam McKeown and Kaoru Sugihara, focus on mobility, flows and exchanges across the Pacific, of people, goods and capital. McKeown argues that the middle of the nineteenth century was 'the apex of Pacific integration' up to that point.[67] This means that Melville's vision of the Pacific as the heart of earth, the fulcrum of world history, was fleeting even at the time he pronounced it in 1851. Major commercial flows were peaking, among them the trans-Pacific trade with China, the export of sandalwood from the Pacific Islands and the global whaling industry that inspired *Moby-Dick* itself. The California gold rush of the 1840s and the Australian gold rushes that began in the year that Melville's novel first appeared accelerated migration around the rimlands of the Pacific. They also helped inspire Karl Marx to study political economy at the British Museum in order to understand 'the new stage of development which [bourgeois] society seemed to have entered with the discovery of gold in California and Australia': *Das Kapital* was one result of these prompts from the Pacific.[68]

The decades on either side of 1850 witnessed an unprecedented boom in mobility linking Asia, the Americas and Australasia via multiple island ports: the white folk who moved in this period even imagined themselves as 'Pacific Man'.[69] Yet this upsurge would be short-lived. By the end of the nineteenth century, a downturn in the global economy coincided with the greater penetration of states and empires – European, American and Asian – into the Pacific. States were more directly controlling the movement of peoples and empires carved out ever greater, and ever more competitive, spheres of influence. Their actions pushed Pacific integration into reverse and disengaged it from broader currents of what would later be called 'globalisation'. Nicholas Thomas reminds us that the transformations of the nineteenth century were like a tattoo, 'at once permanent and skin deep. What we don't know is whether "skin deep" means merely superficial, or in fact profound.'[70] The economic prominence of the Pacific in the mid-nineteenth century proved to be temporary. In the long run, its centrality would return.

If we fast-forward to our own time, in the early twenty-first century, the Pacific seems by many measures to be once again 'the tide-beating heart of earth', while it never stopped being 'our sea of islands' to its inhabitants. One-third of the world's population inhabits its islands and the continents around its shores. The region produces roughly 60 per cent of global GDP and nearly 50 per cent of world trade crosses the ocean – that is, three times the amount now trafficked across the Atlantic.[71] The demographic and economic rise of China in the last generation – although a reversion to historical patterns of power and prosperity – has also redirected the focus of global geopolitics back to the Pacific.

Discourses of the Pacific Rim privileged East Asia and its economies – Japan, China, Korea, Hong Kong and Singapore – but saw them as connected to North America in the main, as well as to Australasia, and to some extent to South American economies, although the latter with nowhere near the same clarity as in the early modern period.[72] As historian Bruce Cumings noted in 1998, the late twentieth-century talk of a 'Pacific Rim' was oriented to the future rather more than to the past. He linked the idea to its earlier use in a tradition of Manifest Destiny, dubbing the Pacific Rim the 'Anglo-Saxon Lake', a twist on Spate's 'Spanish Lake'. More than a decade later, however, the 'capitalist archipelago' that formed an Anglo-Saxon Lake with Japan at the conceptual centre looks far more like a prescient coda: one with China, and an entirely new kind of Chinese diaspora at its heart: no longer an Anglo-Saxon Lake at all but in some eyes an incipient Chinese Lake.[73]

In retrospect, the 1980s appears as a highly politicised era for historians of the Pacific. Alongside and linked to the 'Pacific Rim' idea, an 'Asia-Pacific' region was under diplomatic, economic, as well as intellectual construction, not least as an Asia-Pacific Economic Cooperation (APEC), a Canberra-initiated venture. At the same time, in another hemisphere, and for entirely different reasons, the Paris-based Institut du Pacifique declared the Pacific the new centre of the world (*nouveau centre du monde*).[74] The history of French engagement with the Pacific in particular is tortured and notorious, controversy that only continues with the exhibition of Oceanic art and artefacts at the Musée du quai Branly in Paris.[75] France had been testing nuclear weapons in the new centre of the world for several decades.[76] In response the (South) Pacific announced itself to be, if not free of France, then at least nuclear-free: the 1985 Treaty of Raratonga declared a South Pacific Nuclear Free Zone. New Zealand, in particular, set itself up in the international public sphere as the guardian of Pacific peace, against the nuclear-interested Goliaths, the USA and France. French nuclear testing, along with Soviet whaling, would spur the creation of Greenpeace, making the modern environmental movement a lasting – if unintended – consequence of this moment in global consciousness of the Pacific.[77]

It was also in the 1980s, with the economic ascent of Japan and the increasing economic vibrancy of the region, that pundits began to predict the advent of a new 'Pacific Century' – a future for the global economy centred particularly on the so-called Asia-Pacific and usually omitting Oceania. Any historian of the region can recall that the twenty-first century was not the first to be heralded as a 'Pacific' century. The same language of geopolitics had been common a hundred years before, beginning in Japan with Inagaki Manjirō's pronouncement in 1892 that the coming century would be the 'Pacific Age' (*Taiheiyō jidai*), in succession to the nineteenth century's Atlantic Age.[78] 'The fact is,' a German commentator writing from Hong Kong agreed in 1895, '*the fulcrum of the World's balance of power has shifted from the West to the East, from the Mediterranean to the Pacific*'.[79] It proved to be Japan that did most to shape a geopolitical Pacific over the first half of the twentieth century. Many in the English-speaking world claimed that Japan's defeat of Russia, and its rapid industrialisation and growing economy, signalled the rise of the 'Pacific Age'. 'The Pacific is the ocean of the future', proclaimed Australian journalist Frank Fox in 1912. Such predictions would be repeated throughout the twentieth century: in the internationalism of what is so often called the 'interwar' period (when Japan and China were in fact already at war), and in the Pacific War that created a truly 'world' war, as much as in the last third of the century.[80] 'The history of mankind is now entering the Pacific era', the Russian socialist Gregory Bienstock wrote in 1937: 'that is to say, it is within the Pacific region that the great historical events of the next hundred years will take place.'[81] Four years later, the Japanese philosopher Keiji Nishitani also saw the world passing into an emergent Pacific period, after its Mediterranean and Atlantic eras.[82]

The idea of the Pacific Century returned in the late 1960s and more continuously from the mid-1980s.[83] Japan's economic ascent in the decades after military defeat seemed to commentators around the world to have fulfilled such prophecies of a Pacific Century, albeit in unpredictable ways. Only with the stagnation of the Japanese economy in the late 1990s did this millennialist talk of a Pacific Century temporarily abate. When the US administration of President Barack Obama executed its so-called 'pivot' to the Pacific in 2011, such language returned once again in a new guise. 'The Asia–Pacific has become a key driver of global politics', wrote then US Secretary of State, Hillary Clinton, in November 2011, before heralding the advent of a new 'Pacific Century'. And President Obama echoed her sense of destiny when he told the Australian Parliament in the same month, 'Here we see the future'.[84] In light of these earlier visions, contemporary prophets like Clinton and Obama who foresee a new Pacific Century would do well to remember that the Pacific has had as many futures as it has pasts, not all of them reassuring or comfortable. As Robert Aldrich concludes his chapter, the 'fragmented rather than united hemisphere' revealed by the study of Pacific politics offers 'a corrective to simplistic ideas about the construction of a "new centre of the world" anchored in the US, China or another fulcrum'.[85]

\* \* \*

The Pacific clearly has a great future, but formed from what kind of past? To answer this question, *Pacific Histories: Ocean, Land, People* brings together, for the first time within a single volume, the full range of historians who study the Pacific, its peoples and the lands within and around it. Like Hauʻofa and Melville, they come from very different geographical positions, some from within and around the Pacific itself, others from further afield. The authors have not been asked to conform to any single vision of Pacific history nor have they converged on any agreed conception of their subject and its boundaries. Instead, they have offered their own perspectives on Pacific history, each chosen to capture most illuminatingly the subject at hand.

One division of labour does define their efforts. Four were asked to cover, between them, the whole sweep of human history in the Pacific. These opening essays periodise the Pacific from the first migrations to the future of the region as it looks from our own era. The remaining chapters survey various aspects of Pacific history across large swathes of time and space considered through major themes clustered into broad categories: 'Connections' (on the environment, migration and the economy), 'Knowledges' (on religion, law and science) and 'Identities' (on race, gender and politics). Each author of these thematic chapters was asked to answer – explicitly or implicitly – the questions,

'What light does a specifically *Pacific* perspective shed on this theme? And what light does *this* topic shed on Pacific history more broadly?'

The product, we hope, is a uniquely catholic collection that offers something greater than the sum of its individual parts. Taken together, the chapters comprise a set of mutually reinforcing Pacific histories, collected and plural, which reflect the diversity of the region and the multiplicity of approaches to it. The volume covers the whole Ocean, its northern and southern, western and eastern hemispheres, wherever possible. Several chapters focus on Oceania – those by Salesa, Thomas, Douglas and O'Brien in particular. These islands lie within Pacific history more definitively and exclusively than the littoral locations, which always have continental histories too: Japan is part of the Pacific, but it is also part of East Asia; Canton, as so many chapters here show, was the great Pacific port, but it was also always part of continental Chinese dynamics; and so on, for Russia, Chile, Canada, California and more. In this sense, Oceania is not equivalent to other Pacific sub-regions that are also explored in this book – the Asia-Pacific, the South-West Pacific, Australasia, the North-West, the China Sea; it has, we might say, a solely Pacific history. Other chapters, however, span the hemispheres, taking in the North and South, the islands and the littoral Pacific, to trace dynamically what Matt Matsuda calls 'an overlapping set of actors, transits and shifting boundaries'.[86]

The aim of *Pacific Histories* has been to interrogate, but not artificially to integrate, the histories of the insular Pacific and the littoral Pacific – the coasts of the Americas and the Asian and Australasian continents – and to show the shifts in their relations over time and space. Many of the chapters also relate the histories of islands and rimlands to the pasts of the Pacific conceived in terms of environmental history and the history of exploration and travel across the Ocean over the last forty millennia. In this sense, the volume maps a four-dimensional Pacific – insular and littoral, oceanic and maritime – and does so with an eye to the present but in the perspective of the *longue durée*. The outcome, all the contributors hope and expect, should be the reincorporation of the Pacific into the writing, and the re-writing, of world history today.

## Notes

1. Epeli Hau'ofa, 'Our Sea of Islands' (1993), in Hau'ofa, *We are the Ocean: Selected Works* (Honolulu, 2008), pp. 27–40.

2. Donald B. Freeman, *The Pacific* (London, 2010), p. 9.

3. Freeman, *The Pacific*, pp. 8–35.

4. Ryan Tucker Jones, 'The Environment', ch. 6 in this volume, p. 121; Henry F. Diaz and Vera Markgraf, eds., *El Niño: Historical and Paleoclimatic Aspects of the Southern Oscillation* (Cambridge, 1992).

5. O. H. K. Spate, '"South Sea" to "Pacific Ocean": A Note on Nomenclature', *Journal of Pacific History* 12 (1977), 205–11.

6. Damon Salesa, 'The Pacific in Indigenous Time', ch. 2 in this volume, p. 32; 'Dumont D'Urville's Divisions of Oceania: Fundamental Precincts or Arbitrary Constructs?', Special Issue, *Journal of Pacific History* 38, 2 (September 2003), 155–268; R. C. Green, 'Near and Remote Oceania – Disestablishing Melanesia in Culture History', in Andrew Pawley, ed., *Man and a Half: Essays in Pacific Anthropology and Ethnobiology in Honour of Ralph Bulmer* (Auckland, NZ, 1991), pp. 491–502.

7. Karl Haushofer, *Geopolitik des Pazifischen Ozeans* (1924), translation quoted in Alison Bashford, 'Karl Haushofer's *Geopolitics of the Pacific Ocean*', in Kate Fullagar, ed., *The Atlantic World in the Antipodes: Effects and Transformations since the Eighteenth Century* (Newcastle upon Tyne, 2012), p. 123.

8. D. H. Lawrence to John Middleton Murry (24 September 1923), in *The Letters of D. H. Lawrence*, gen. ed. James T. Boulton, 8 vols. (Cambridge 1979–2000), IV, p. 502; R. Gerard Ward, 'Earth's Empty Quarter? The Pacific Islands in a Pacific Century', *The Geographical Journal* 155 (1989), 235–46.

9. Akira Iriye, *Global and Transnational History: The Past, Present, and Future* (Basingstoke, 2013).

10. Fernand Braudel, *La Méditerranée et le monde méditerranéen à l'époque de Philippe II*, 2nd edn, 2 vols. (Paris, 1966); Peregrine Horden and Nicholas Purcell, *The Corrupting Sea: A Study of Mediterranean History* (Oxford, 2000).

11. Sugata Bose, *A Hundred Horizons: The Indian Ocean in the Age of Global Empire* (Cambridge, MA, 2006); see also Sunil Amrith, *Crossing the Bay of Bengal: The Furies of Nature and the Fortunes of Migrants* (Cambridge, MA, 2013).

12. For recent surveys, see Jack P. Greene and Philip Morgan, eds., *Atlantic History: A Critical Appraisal* (New York, 2009); Nicholas Canny and Philip Morgan, eds., *The Oxford Handbook of the Atlantic World, 1450–1850* (Oxford, 2011); Karen Ordahl Kupperman, *The Atlantic in World History* (New York, 2012).

13. Peregrine Horden and Nicholas Purcell, 'The Mediterranean and "the New Thalassology"', *American Historical Review* 111 (2006), 722–40.

14. Rainer F. Buschmann, 'The Pacific Ocean Basin to 1850', in Jerry H. Bentley, ed., *The Oxford Handbook of World History* (Oxford, 2011), p. 564.

15. Lauren Benton, 'No Longer Odd Region Out: Repositioning Latin America in World History', *Hispanic American Historical Review* 84

(2004), 427; Maxine Berg, 'Global History: Approaches and New Directions', in Berg, ed., *Writing the History of the Global: Challenges for the 21st Century* (Oxford, 2013), p. 6.

16. Iriye, 'A Pacific Century?', ch. 5 in this volume.

17. Teresia K. Teaiwa, 'On Analogies: Rethinking the Pacific in a Global Context', *The Contemporary Pacific* 18 (2006), 73; Damon Salesa, 'The World from Oceania', in Douglas Northrop, ed., *A Companion to World History* (Chichester, 2012), p. 391.

18. Margaret Jolly, 'Imagining Oceania: Indigenous and Foreign Representations of a Sea of Islands', *The Contemporary Pacific* 19 (2007), 508–45.

19. Martin W. Lewis, 'Dividing the Ocean Sea', *Geographical Review* 89 (1999), 188–214; Paul D'Arcy, 'Sea Worlds: Pacific and South-East Asian History Centred on the Philippines', in Rila Mukherjee, ed., *Oceans Connect: Reflections on Water Worlds across Time and Space* (New Delhi, 2013), pp. 20–35.

20. Greg Dening, 'History "in" the Pacific', *The Contemporary Pacific* 1 (1989), 134.

21. Matt K. Matsuda, '*AHR Forum*: The Pacific', *American Historical Review* 111 (2006), 759.

22. Bernard Bailyn, *Atlantic History: Concept and Contours* (Cambridge, MA, 2005), pp. 57–111; compare Gary Y. Okihiro, 'Toward a Pacific Civilization', *Japanese Journal of American Studies* 18 (2007), 73–85, and the essays in Fullagar, ed., *The Atlantic World in the Antipodes*.

23. James Cook, *A Voyage to the Pacific Ocean; Undertaken by Command of His Majesty ... in the Years 1776, 1777, 1778, 1779, and 1780*, 4 vols. (London, 1784), II, p. 192; Joyce E. Chaplin, 'The Pacific before Empire, *c.* 1500–1800', ch. 3 in this volume.

24. J. R. McNeill, 'Of Rats and Men: A Synoptic Environmental History of the Island Pacific', *Journal of World History* 5 (1994), 314; Alfred W. Crosby, *The Columbian Exchange: Biological and Cultural Consequences of 1492* (Westport, CT, 1972).

25. Peter Corris, *Passage, Port and Plantation: A History of Solomon Islands Labour Migration, 1870–1914* (Carlton, Vic., 1973); H. E. Maude, *Slavers in Paradise: The Peruvian Slave Trade in Polynesia, 1862–1864* (Stanford, 1981); Dorothy Shineberg, *The People Trade: Pacific Island Laborers and New Caledonia, 1865–1930* (Honolulu, 1999); Tracey Banivanua Mar, *Violence and Colonial Dialogue: The Australian–Pacific Indentured Labor Trade* (Honolulu, 2007).

26. James Belich, 'Race', ch. 12 in this volume.

27. Robert Aldrich, 'Politics', ch. 14 in this volume; Aldrich and John Connell, *The Last Colonies* (Cambridge, 1988).

28. Paul W. Mapp, 'Atlantic History from Imperial, Continental, and Pacific Perspectives', *William and Mary Quarterly* 3rd ser., 63 (2006), 718 (quoted), adding that, in the early modern period, 'it is easier to speak of histories in the Pacific than to talk about Pacific history';

compare Dennis O. Flynn and Arturo Giráldez, eds., *The Pacific World: Lands, Peoples and History of the Pacific, 1500–1900*, 17 vols. (Aldershot, 2001–9); Katrina Gulliver, 'Finding the Pacific World', *Journal of World History* 22 (2011), 83–100; Gregory T. Cushman, *Guano and the Opening of the Pacific World: A Global Ecological History* (Cambridge, 2013).

29. Damon Salesa, '"Travel Happy" Samoa: Colonialism, Samoan Migration, and a "Brown Pacific"', *New Zealand Journal of History* 37 (2003), 171–88; Gary Y. Okihiro, 'Afterword: Toward a Black Pacific', in Heike Raphael-Hernandez and Shannon Steen, eds., *AfroAsian Encounters: Culture, History, Politics* (New York, 2006), pp. 313–29; Gerald Horne, *The White Pacific: U.S. Imperialism and Black Slavery in the South Seas after the Civil War* (Honolulu, 2007); Keith Aoki, 'The Yellow Pacific: Transnational Identities, Diasporic Racialization, and Myth(s) of the "Asian Century"', *University of California, Davis, Law Review* 44 (2011), 897–953; David Armitage, 'Three Concepts of Atlantic History', in Armitage and Michael J. Braddick, eds., *The British Atlantic World, 1500–1800*, 2nd edn (Basingstoke, 2009), pp. 16–17.

30. Matt K. Matsuda, *Pacific Worlds: A History of Seas, Peoples, and Cultures* (Cambridge, 2012); David Igler, *The Great Ocean: Pacific Worlds from Captain Cook to the Gold Rush* (Oxford, 2013).

31. Hauʻofa, *We Are the Ocean*; Albert Wendt, 'Towards a New Oceania', *Mana Review: A South Pacific Journal of Language and Literature* 1 (1976), 49–60; I. Futa Helu, *Critical Essays: Cultural Perspectives from the South Seas* (Canberra, 1999).

32. Adam McKeown, 'Movement', ch. 7 in this volume, p. 143.

33. Lisa Ford, 'Law', ch. 10 in this volume, p. 216.

34. Salesa, 'The Pacific in Indigenous Time', p. 33.

35. Yoshio Masuda, *Taiheiyō: Hirakareta umi no rekishi* [*The Pacific: History of an Open Ocean*] (Tokyo, 2004); Dominique Barbe, *Histoire du Pacifique. Des origines à nos jours* (Paris, 2008); Freeman, *The Pacific*; Matsuda, *Pacific Worlds*.

36. Paul D'Arcy, *The People of the Sea: Environment, Identity and History in Oceania* (Honolulu, 2006); Walter A. McDougall, *Let the Sea Make a Noise…: A History of the North Pacific from Magellan to MacArthur* (New York, 1993); Ryan Tucker Jones, *Empire of Extinction: Russians and the Strange Beasts of the Sea in the North Pacific, 1709–1867* (Oxford, 2014); Igler, *The Great Ocean*.

37. Dan E. Clark, 'Manifest Destiny and the Pacific', *Pacific Historical Review* 1 (1932), 1.

38. Masthead, *Pacific Historical Review* 82 (2013).

39. For example, Laurie Maffly-Kipp, 'Eastward Ho! American Religion from the Perspective of the Pacific', in Thomas A. Tweed, ed., *Retelling United States Religious History* (Berkeley, 1997), pp. 121–48; Amy Kuʻuleialoha Stillman, 'Pacific-ing Asian American History',

*Journal of Asian American Studies* 7 (2004), 241–70; J. Kēhaulani Kauanui, 'Asian American Studies and the "Pacific Question"', in Kent A. Ono, ed., *Asian American Studies after Critical Mass* (Malden, MA, 2005), pp. 123–43; Bruce Cumings, *Dominion from Sea to Sea: Pacific Ascendancy and American Power* (New Haven, 2009); Kornel S. Chang, *Pacific Connections: The Making of the US–Canadian Borderlands* (Berkeley, 2012); Igler, *The Great Ocean*.

40. Damon Salesa, 'Afterword: Opposite Footers', in Fullagar, ed., *The Atlantic World in the Antipodes*, pp. 293–4, 299 n. 26.

41. J. W. Davidson, *The Study of Pacific History, An Inaugural Lecture Delivered at Canberra on 25 November 1954* (Canberra, 1955); Davidson, *Samoa mo Samoa: The Emergence of the Independent State of Western Samoa* (Melbourne, 1967); Doug Munro and Geoffrey Gray, '"We Haven't Abandoned the Project": The Founding of *The Journal of Pacific History*', *Journal of Pacific History* 48 (2013), 63–77.

42. Bernard Smith, *European Vision and the South Pacific, 1768–1850: A Study in the History of Art and Ideas* (Oxford, 1960); see also Smith, *Imagining the Pacific: In the Wake of the Cook Voyages* (New Haven, 1992).

43. O. H. K. Spate, *The Pacific Since Magellan*, I: *The Spanish Lake*; II: *Monopolists and Freebooters*; III: *Paradise Found and Lost* (London, 1979–88).

44. Greg Dening, *Islands and Beaches: Discourse on a Silent Land: Marquesas 1774–1880* (Carlton, Vic., 1980); compare Marshall Sahlins, *Moala: Culture and Nature on a Fijian Island* (Ann Arbor, 1962); Sahlins, *Islands of History* (Chicago, 1985).

45. http://uhpress.wordpress.com/books–in–series/pacific–islands–monograph–series/, accessed 31 January 2013.

46. Iriye, *Global and Transnational History*, p. 54.

47. For reflections on writing from different edges and centres, see Teresia K. Teaiwa, 'Lo(o)sing the Edge', *The Contemporary Pacific* 13 (2001), 343–57; Margaret Jolly, 'On the Edge? Deserts, Oceans, Islands', *The Contemporary Pacific* 13 (2001), 417–66.

48. Most recently and notably, Damon Salesa, *Racial Crossings: Race, Intermarriage, and the Victorian British Empire* (Oxford, 2011), based on an Oxford D.Phil. thesis written from British Colonial Office and Māori records.

49. James Belich, *Replenishing the Earth: The Settler Revolution and the Rise of the Anglo-World, 1783–1939* (Oxford, 2009); Tracey Banivanua Mar and Penelope Edmonds, eds., *Making Settler Colonial Space: Perspectives on Race, Place and Identity* (Basingstoke, 2010); Marilyn Lake, 'Colonial Australia and the Asia-Pacific Region', in Alison Bashford and Stuart Macintyre, eds., *The Cambridge History of Australia*, 2 vols. (Cambridge, 2013), I, pp. 535–59.

50. Alice A. Storey, et al., 'Radiocarbon and DNA Evidence for a Pre-Columbian Introduction of Polynesian Chickens to Chile', *Proceedings of the National Academy of Sciences of the United States of*

*America* 104, 25 (June 2007), 10335–9; Storey, et al., 'Pre-Columbian Chickens, Dates, Isotopes, and mtDNA', *Proceedings of the National Academy of Sciences of the United States of America* 105, 48 (December 2008), E99.

51. Bronwen Douglas, 'Religion', ch. 9 in this volume, p. 196.

52. Alan Frost, 'The Pacific Ocean: The Eighteenth Century's "New World"', *Studies on Voltaire and the Eighteenth Century* 152 (1976), 779–822.

53. C. A. Bayly, *The Birth of the Modern World, 1780–1914: Global Connections and Comparisons* (Oxford, 2004), pp. 100, 349–50, 437–8; Nicholas Thomas, 'The Age of Empire in the Pacific', ch. 4 in this volume.

54. John Gascoigne, *Joseph Banks and the English Enlightenment: Useful Knowledge and Polite Culture* (Cambridge, 1994); Rob Iliffe, 'Science and Voyages of Discovery', in Roy Porter, ed., *The Cambridge History of Science*, IV: *Eighteenth-Century Science* (Cambridge, 2003), pp. 618–45; Nicholas Thomas, *Discoveries: The Voyages of Captain Cook* (London, 2007).

55. For example, Margaret Sankey, 'Les premiers contacts: les Aborigènes de la Nouvelle–Hollande observés par les officiers et les savants de l'expédition Baudin', *Etudes sur le XVIII^e siècle* 38 (2010), 171–85; Anne Salmond, *The Trial of the Cannibal Dog: The Remarkable Story of Captain Cook's Encounters in the South Seas* (New Haven, 2003).

56. David A. Chappell, *Double Ghosts: Oceanian Voyagers on Euroamerican Ships* (Armonk, NY, 1997); David Turnbull, 'Cook and Tupaia: A Tale of Cartographic Méconnaissance?', in Margarette Lincoln, ed., *Science and Exploration in the Pacific: European Voyages to the Southern Oceans in the Eighteenth Century* (Woodbridge, 1998), pp. 117–32; Kate Fullagar, *The Savage Visit: New World People and Popular Imperial Culture in Britain, 1710–1795* (Berkeley, 2012).

57. McNeill, 'Of Rats and Men'; Jennifer Newell, *Trading Nature: Tahitians, Europeans, and Ecological Exchange* (Honolulu, 2010).

58. Patricia O'Brien, 'Gender', ch. 13 in this volume, p. 285; Margaret Jolly, 'Revisioning Gender and Sexuality on Cook's Voyages in the Pacific', in Robert Fleck and Adrienne L. Kaeppler, eds., *James Cook and the Exploration of the Pacific* (London, 2009), pp. 98–102.

59. H. E. Maude, 'Beachcombers and Castaways', *Journal of the Polynesian Society* 73 (1964), 254–93; Nicholas Thomas, *Islanders: The Pacific in the Age of Empire* (New Haven, 2010).

60. Classically in the works of Greg Dening: Dening, *Islands and Beaches*; Dening, *Beach Crossings: Voyaging across Times, Cultures and Self* (Carlton, Vic., 2004). For its extension to other spaces of encounter, see especially Chappell, *Double Ghosts*.

61. Roy MacLeod and Philip E. Rehbock, ed., *Darwin's Laboratory: Evolutionary Theory and Natural History in the Pacific* (Honolulu, 1994); Simon Schaffer, 'In Transit: European Cosmologies in the Pacific', in Fullagar, ed., *The Atlantic World in the Antipodes*, pp. 70–93; Sujit Sivasundaram, 'Science', ch. 11 in this volume.

62. For example, Ron Crocombe, *The Pacific Way: An Emerging Identity* (Suva, 1976); Stephanie Lawson, '"The Pacific Way" as Postcolonial Discourse: Towards a Reassessment', *Journal of Pacific History* 45 (2010), 297–314; Thomas Gladwin, *East Is a Big Bird: Navigation and Logic on Puluwat Atoll* (Cambridge, MA, 1970); David Turnbull, 'Pacific Navigation: An Alternative Scientific Tradition', in Turnbull, *Masons, Tricksters and Cartographers: Comparative Studies in the Sociology of Scientific and Indigenous Knowledge* (Amsterdam, 2000), pp. 131–60.

63. Dennis Flynn and Arturo Giráldez, *China and the Birth of Globalization in the 16th Century* (Farnham, 2010); Marshall Sahlins, 'Cosmologies of Capitalism: The Trans-Pacific Sector of "The World System"', *Proceedings of the British Academy* 74 (1989), 1–51.

64. C. C. Macknight, *The Voyage to Marege': Macassan Trepangers in Northern Australia* (Melbourne, 1976); Gerrit Knaap and Heather Sutherland, *Monsoon Traders: Ships, Skippers and Commodities in Eighteenth-century Makassar* (Leiden, 2004).

65. Ricardo Padrón, 'A Sea of Denial: The Early Modern Spanish Invention of the Pacific Rim', *Hispanic Review* 77 (2009), 1–27. Padrón, following the *Oxford English Dictionary*, dates the term 'Pacific rim' to 1926 (ibid., 3 n. 2), but it can be found almost thirty years earlier, for example, in William Elliot Griffis, *America in the East: A Glance at Our History, Prospects, Problems, and Duties in the Pacific Ocean* (New York, 1899), p. 205.

66. A. G. Hopkins, 'Introduction: Globalization – An Agenda for Historians', and C. A. Bayly, '"Archaic" and "Modern" Globalization in the Eurasian and African Arena, *c.* 1750–1850', in Hopkins, ed., *Globalization in World History* (London, 2002), pp. 1–10, 47–73; Charles H. Parker, *Global Interactions in the Early Modern Age, 1400–1800* (Cambridge, 2010).

67. McKeown, 'Movement', p. 150.

68. Karl Marx, *A Contribution to the Critique of Political Economy* (1859), trans. S. W. Ryazanskaya, ed. Maurice Dobb (London, 1971), pp. 22–3.

69. Mae Ngai, 'Western History and the Pacific World', *Western Historical Quarterly* 43 (2012), 282–8.

70. Thomas, 'The Pacific in the Age of Empire', p. 94.

71. For the broader economic context of these developments, see Kaoru Sugihara, 'The Economy since 1800', ch. 8 in this volume.

72. See Eric Jones, Lionel Frost and Colin White, *Coming Full Circle: An Economic History of the Pacific Rim* (Boulder, CO, 1993).

73. Bruce Cumings, 'Rimspeak; or, The Discourse of the "Pacific Rim"', in Arif Dirlik, ed., *What is in a Rim? Critical Perspectives on the Pacific Region Idea* (Lanham, MD, 1998), p. 59; Ron Crocombe, *Asia in the Pacific Islands: Replacing the West* (Suva, 2007).

74. Jean-Pierre Gomane, et al., eds., *Le Pacifique: 'nouveau centre du monde'* (Paris, 1983).

75. Margaret Jolly, 'Becoming a "New" Museum? Contesting Oceanic Visions at Musée du Quai Branly', *The Contemporary Pacific* 23 (2011), 108–39.

76. Bengt Danielsson and Marie-Thérèse Danielsson, *Poisoned Reign: French Nuclear Colonialism in the Pacific* (Ringwood, Vic., 1986).
77. Frank Zelko, 'Greenpeace and the Development of International Environmental Activism in the 1970s', in Ursula Lehmkuhl and Hermann Wellenreuther, eds., *Historians and Nature: Comparative Approaches to Environmental History* (Oxford, 2007), pp. 296–318.
78. Inagaki Manjirō, *Tōhōsaku* [*Eastern Policy*] (Tokyo, 1892), p. 1, quoted in Pekka Korhonen, 'The Pacific Age in World History', *Journal of World History* 7 (1996), 45.
79. E. J. Eitel, *Europe in China: The History of Hongkong from the Beginning to 1882* (London, 1895), p. iv (Eitel's emphasis).
80. Frank Fox, *Problems of the Pacific* (London, 1912), pp. 1–2, quoted in Korhonen, 'The Pacific Age in World History', 52; Tomoko Akami, *Internationalizing the Pacific: The United States, Japan and the Institute of Pacific Relations in War and Peace, 1919–45* (London, 2002).
81. Gregory Bienstock, *The Struggle for the Pacific* (London, 1937), 17.
82. Keiji Nishitani (1941), quoted in Chris Goto-Jones, 'The Kyoto School, the Cambridge School, and the History of Political Philosophy in Wartime Japan', *Positions: East Asia Cultures Critique* 17 (2009), 23.
83. Works such as William Irwin Thompson, *Pacific Shift* (San Francisco, 1985) and Frank Gibney, *Pacific Century: America and Asia in a Changing World* (New York, 1992), give a flavour of the fervour, at least in the United States.
84. Hillary Clinton, 'America's Pacific Century', *Foreign Policy* 189 (November 2011), 57; Barack Obama, 'Remarks by President Obama to the Australian Parliament' (17 November 2011): http://www.whitehouse.gov/the–press–office/2011/11/17/remarks– president–obama–australian–parliament, accessed 31 January 2013.
85. Robert Aldrich, 'Politics', p. 324.
86. Matt K. Matsuda, 'Afterword: Pacific Cross-currents', in this volume.

# Part I: Periodising the Pacific

# 2

# The Pacific in Indigenous Time

Damon Salesa

On 9 May 2011 Ratu Tevita Kapaiwai Lutunauga Uluilakeba Mara – otherwise known as Lieutenant-Colonel Tevita Mara – was collected from off the coast of Fiji by a Royal Tongan Navy patrol boat. Son of one of Fiji's most famous leaders, Ratu Sir Kamasese Mara, Tevita Mara had gone from being a key supporter of Fiji's military coup in 2006, to being charged with mutiny in 2011. In the context of Pacific Island international relations, the intervention of the Royal Tongan Navy was a startling development. The orders seem to have come essentially from the top, from the Tongan king, Siaosi Tupou V, himself. Asked why he would commit such an act of international intrigue, and risk escalation against what is a much larger and militarily more powerful nation, King George offered a simple answer: that Mara was his 'kinsman'. Few thought that a *good* explanation, but most Polynesians understood it as a valid one. Tongans could quickly place this in a longer history of Tongan engagement with Lau, an eastern part of Fiji or, more specifically, the history of Ma'afu, or through Mara's parents whether his famous father, or his equally prominent mother, who was related to the Tongan royal family. None of this needed much explanation for a Tongan or a Fijian, or even a Sāmoan, audience.

One cannot understand the intricacies of Sāmoan, Tongan and Fijian contemporary politics without a firm understandings of the great lineages of these different lands, such as Tui Lau, Tu'i Kanokupolu or Sā Malietoa. These and other lineages are not merely *alive* in the present, but actively shape it. Such lineages are mere tips to larger indigenous contours. Indigenous Pacific ways, histories, languages stand not in opposition to other great forces at work in the present – postcolonialism, development, globalisation, commercialisation – but are articulate with them, as well as with a deep and resonant past. Indigeneity, custom, tradition, culture, call it what we will (and mark the fine gradations amongst these terms),

31

the present resounds with the past, and as it is in this central part of the Pacific, so it echoes elsewhere. The 'rescue' of Mara is just one of many signs that in the Pacific we live, now, and for any imaginable future, in indigenous times.

The Pacific's 'indigenous times' are not just smaller sections of larger histories, but dimensions of their own. Such times and histories are entangled with other indigenous and foreign dimensions, but simply folding them into other narratives is to erase much of what is distinctive, and much that we might learn from them. Indigenous Pacific pasts are ancient, but what makes them truly exceptional is their diversity, and their oceanic nature. There are many times more languages spoken in the Pacific – more than a thousand – than in Europe or the Americas, and nowhere in the world have people made themselves at home, in the sea, in the way that Pacific Islanders have. This brief chapter is an attempt to capture some small part of this distinctiveness, and a small part of what is instructive about the Pacific's indigenous pasts.

The Pacific makes plain the contested and contingent nature of political, intellectual and geographical categories. Even amongst academic specialists the Pacific remains fundamentally shifting. New Zealand and even Australia are sometimes considered part of the Pacific, sometimes not. Archipelagoes which might otherwise appear to be 'in' the Pacific, are by convention usually excluded: Indonesia (excepting West Papua), the Philippines, the Aleutians or even Japan. And yet Timor Leste (East Timor) is an observer at the Pacific Island Forum. Various geographers and organisations carve up and sort this part of the world differently, using a range of labels such as Oceania, Asia-Pacific, the Pacific Basin, the South Pacific or South Seas (which commonly includes islands in the north) or the Pacific Islands. Of course, all the seas are connected, and there are no neat limits. But the struggle for putting the Pacific into discourse is partly decided by how it is defined. In this chapter the framing is of the Pacific, or Pacific Islands, which is most familiar to its present inhabitants (if still highly varied). This is the Pacific as an accumulation of the three 'nesias': Melanesia, Micronesia and Polynesia. Though these cultural-geographical categories are too blunt for many academic analyses, and flatten and distort the kalei-doscopic diversity they contain (especially Melanesia), they have retained a power, not least from ordinary use and an appropriation as usable identifications by the people in question.[1] People do in certain situations call themselves Micronesians, Polynesians or Melanesians, in effect recognising some deeper commonalities (though not often the ones that were originally referenced).

Certainly it is this 'indigenous Pacific' – Micronesia, Melanesia and Polynesia – that has been most neglected by, and troublesome to, scholars outside the region. Indeed, an emphasis on this vision of the Pacific exposes some of the grooves of global histories, means as many of the grand narratives struggle to narrate the indigenous Pacific in their accounts of world or global history.[2] The nearly universal absence of such a large presence from views that claim to be so broad prompted a telling reminder from one of the region's great scholars, about 'the other one third of the globe'.[3] Such a synoptic reminder of little appreciated indigenous pasts are useful here, too, as a beginning. The old excuses of a lack of general literature hold little water now, as there are a range of engaged Pacific history overviews, and some ambitious attempts to survey the multitudinous fields of ethnography and prehistory. A brief synopsis might be useful in order to frame other aspects of the indigenous past, and how one can engage with the plenitudes of indigenous societies.

### The horizons of indigenous time

Indigenous Pacific histories comprise an antiquity and diversity that stretches back, starting in New Guinea, 40–50,000 years. People first arrived in the Pacific when lower sea levels formed a single continent of New Guinea and Australia – 'Sahul'. These first Pacific Islanders were already amongst the world's great voyagers, having had to cross the waters from Eurasia. They were hardly less innovative on land: in New Guinea came great breakthroughs for humanity. A wide range of crops were domesticated, including one of humankind's most important – sugar cane – and many of the crops that have remained central to Pacific Islanders' culture and diets since: ti/si plant, (probably) breadfruit, several species of bananas and nuts and, most importantly, three major varieties of taro. The fertile plains of the New Guinea highlands were elevated and far distant from the sea, and yet were occupied at least 30,000 years ago. (The Highlands peoples were also hunters, of a range of now extinct marsupial megafauna.) There is evidence of irrigation at least 5,500, and perhaps as early as 9,000, years ago. In New Guinea, Pacific people were on the cutting edge of the great human revolution in agriculture, and were doing so as early as people anywhere in the world.

Yet in what is the major theme of Pacific history, Pacific peoples were voyaging earlier, and much further than anyone else. While some have suggested that the process of early settlement in Oceania could have been managed by drift voyagers, gambling away their lives, the likelihood is very low: repeated voyages of considerable distance (up to 100km) would have been required to make it to Sahul, and these distances were to grow exponentially. Though there are relatively few archaeological sites in 'Old Melanesia', these make clear that other, even more challenging voyages from Sahul were relatively soon completed: by 35,000 years ago New Ireland and New Britain were inhabited, and by 29,000 years ago so was Buka, in the northern Solomon Islands. Buka could not have been seen from elsewhere, and other evidence requires even more remote, and adventurous voyaging – to Manus, in particular. One author argues that this belt from the Bismarcks in northern New Guinea to the northern Solomons was a 'voyaging nursery', sheltered from storms, with predictable weather, and with mostly intervisible lands.[4]

Around 3,500–4,000 years ago the already diverse peoples of ancient Melanesia became even more so, as a new kind of cultural complex arrived. Particularly identified with a new kind of pottery, but associated with the widespread movement of objects and natural resources over hundreds of kilometres, much larger (always coastal) settlements, and the arrival of pigs, chickens and dogs. The peoples associated with these new developments have often been known as Lapita, for the location where pottery was first found. As DNA, linguistic and archaeological evidence suggests, these people were part of a larger movement of people from Taiwan south through the Philippines to Melanesia – 'Austronesians'. (Austronesian speakers were the most intrepid of all peoples: settling as far apart as Madagascar and Rapa Nui.) These peoples built lasting links with those already resident in Melanesia. Prehistorians debate (sometimes furiously) the precise nature of the relationship between these newcomers and residents, but that these relationships were critical there can be no doubt. Exchanges of technology, foodstuffs, inter-marriage and other combinations make this clear, and detail how the Lapita cultural complex was unique to the Pacific. By around 3,200 years ago the people associated with Lapita were engaged in long-distance voyaging and settlement, crossing out of the Solomon Islands which, for 30,000 years, had been the limit of human life, with the exception of the Australian continent. Around 3,100–2,900 years ago these bold voyagers had settled in Fiji: a voyage requiring an 850km open sea crossing.

The Lapita complex expanded relatively instantaneously. Shortly after Fiji's Lapita sites emerge, others could be found in Sāmoa,

Tonga and other nearby islands – all within two to three centuries around 3,100–2,800 years ago. This was the foundational period of a 'new' Pacific history, the moment and time that tied together the far and near parts of the western Pacific, and opened the way towards the full discovery and settlement of the northern, southern and eastern extent of the Great Ocean. In just a short period a kindred group of peoples had voyaged, settled and discovered lands over 4,000 kilometres apart, ranging over several millions of square kilometres of ocean. Out of the eastern sphere of this Lapita range, centred on Tonga, Sāmoa and Uvea, these people carved the foundations of what we would come to call Polynesia – Ancestral Polynesia, or to borrow into prehistory the relevant term from Polynesian histories, Hawaiki.[5]

What we now call Micronesia was settled in roughly this time frame. Probably there were two distinct movements of people into this massive region, with the oldest coming into Micronesia from the west, and perhaps having settled in the Marianas and Palau as early as 3,500 years ago. These peoples shared a common ancestry with those who made Lapita, but were from a different branch: likely coming from either the Philippines or possibly Taiwan. (The Chamorro and Palauan languages find their closest relatives not elsewhere in the Pacific, but in the Philippine-Sulawesi area.) A second movement of people, chiefly into central and eastern Micronesia, came as part of the Lapita complex to Micronesia's south. Material culture and language similarities suggest a connection with particular parts of the 'Lapita homeland', particularly the Bismarcks, Solomons and Vanuatu. The distances facing these voyagers are indeed vast, and the targets presented by their destinations were considerably smaller than the archipelagoes of Fiji, Sāmoa and Tonga. It is little wonder that it was in these parts great lines of navigators and canoe-builders descended into the present.

The wide and continuing distribution of objects throughout the Lapita sphere demonstrates ongoing networks or systems of exchange that are ancestral. Pottery, shells, oven stones, obsidian, religious objects, adzes, jewellery and other objects all found great distances from their point of origin attest to this. These new environments continued to throw up challenges: particularly in Micronesia, but also elsewhere, came the enormous challenge of making lives on atolls, which called for all kinds of social, agricultural and cultural innovation, and a deep embrace of the ocean as a place. Small size, lack of water, saltiness, little shelter from the sea, geological uniformity, scarcity of soil and exposure to storms and drought were a few of the many difficulties presented by atoll life. But with a palette of new techniques and approaches, and continued voyaging to integrate atolls and other islands with each other, these marginal spaces for human life became ones where Pacific Islanders could live sustainably, with relative comfort and abundance.

The discovery and settlement of the Pacific was to be the work of generations, but eventually all the habitable islands were found. The exact dating of the process will remain tentative, but the dramatic discovery of the furthest reaches of the Pacific, especially the eastern and southern reaches of Micronesia (for example, Kosrae, the Marshalls and the outliers), and the eastern parts of Polynesia (for example, the Cook and Society Islands, Marquesas and Tuamotus) – set the stage for discovering the distant corners of the inhabited Pacific (indeed, of the world), Hawai'i, Aotearoa/New Zealand, and Rapa Nui (Easter Island).

For Pacific Islanders, history did not begin with the arrival of foreigners, as most non-indigenous histories do. A focus on the unique achievement of Pacific civilisations, the discovery and settlement of its lands, has been the most potent answer to this presumption. But this process took millennia, and as the vibrant histories after settlement show, the capacity to adapt and innovate – to *change* – remained as characteristic of Pacific peoples as any other. The ongoing processes of change, kaleidoscopic in their range, are impossible to represent, but can be attested by the most dramatic remains in the region: monoliths from Palau to Rapa Nui, Tonga to Pohnpei; vast cultural works of terracing seen from New Zealand to Tahiti; irrigation networks and farms in the New Guinea highlands, enormous fishponds in Hawai'i; the majesty of the walled compounds and canal complexes of Nan Madol or Lelu; or the sacred sites of Pulemelei or Taputapuatea. Each of these was emblematic of ancient and changing pasts. They allow concise contexts for the later, and relatively brief, European and Asian presence in the Pacific.

The archipelagic and dispersed nature of Oceania meant that the arrival of Europeans after 1521 was locally dramatic, but regionally prolonged and haphazard. It would take over 400 years before all Pacific Islanders had discovered Europeans, with initial encounters still occurring in the New Guinea highlands in the 1930s. For most Pacific societies the arrival of these foreigners, their goods, ideas and technologies would prove profound. There would be no evenness to the unfolding of these histories, but there were some patterns: initial periods of European exploration were followed by the arrival of purposeful sojourners – traders, whalers, sealers, miners, missionaries – and then periods of informal and formal foreign claims to govern. In each place the time and nature would prove different, and the trajectory of colonialism would be specific. The histories of colonialism began relatively early: the first colony was Guam, from 1668, though most Pacific islands were subject to imperial and colonial claims only from the late 1800s (uniquely, the Kingdom of Tonga would stay formally independent). In each place colonialism was different, but nowhere was it benevolent, whatever its intent. The most damaging colonialisms, if one dared to so rank them, were probably those connected with land appropriation and/or large populations of settlers, or with nuclear testing, militarisation or mining (Micronesia, French Polynesia, New Caledonia, Hawai'i, New Caledonia, New Zealand, Fiji, Nauru, Banaba, Guam). Decolonisation, if it came, came to the region rapidly, beginning in 1962 with western Sāmoa. Many indigenous Pacific peoples are now minorities in their ancestral islands – in Hawai'i, New Zealand, Guam, for example. Others, such as New Caledonia, have not decolonised or, as in West Papua and much of the American Pacific, have limited sovereignty.

The looping of Europeans – and thus the Americas, Europe and Asia – back into Oceanian networks of exchange transformed the material, practices and ideas that circulated. Steel, literacy, glass, firearms, Christianity, crops (from onions to oranges), maritime technology, tools, timepieces, gunpowder, animals (from goats to cattle to horses), all came rapidly, to list only an obvious few. But probably the most critical imports from these voyagers were microscopic, as European and American voyagers brought a new range of diseases, including influenza, smallpox, leprosy, tuberculosis, measles, rubella and sexually transmitted diseases such as syphilis and gonorrhea. Amongst people and communities with no developed immunity the result was utterly disastrous. Population numbers are only estimates, but demographers of the Pacific have been unusually conservative in their estimates of 'pre-contact' populations (which also minimises the quantity of death resulting from foreign arrival).[6] Sāmoa's pre-European population, for instance, has been fixed at less than 40,000, or around 13 people per square kilometre, when archaeologists have shown historically intense settlement and agriculture that would seem to call for at least twice or thrice that population.[7] Historians have, prima facie, been suspicious of most large estimates by early European voyagers, which have been discarded in favour of massively lower ones: in Hawai'i, for instance, James Cook's estimate of around 400,000 people has been chopped by cautious demographers to around

100,000.[8] The latter figure is widely accepted but hotly contested, and seems absurdly low: but whatever the accepted estimate, the fall of the Hawaiian population to under 60,000 by the late 1800s signals devastation on an unfortunately familiar scale in the Pacific.

## Genealogies of time

As the diversity of the indigenous people of the Pacific suggests, there can be no single way of experiencing the present, and no unified way of representing the past. As Marshall Sahlins puts it, 'different cultural orders have their own modes of historical action, consciousness, and determination – their own historical practice': 'other times, other customs'.[9] Scholars have recently better appreciated that a deep awareness of a culture, of its ironies and complexities, is fundamental to rigorous and innovative history. Sāmoan scholar and leader Tuiatua Tupua Tamasese issued a powerful reminder in this regard, stressing the importance of language, names, honorifics, irony and allusion. In doing so he created an intersection between the lively and boisterous knowledge arenas of indigenous Sāmoan history – the *fono* (village councils), *malae* (village greens), *'āiga* (families), ceremonies and courts of Sāmoa – and the academy.[10] The controversy that ensued in Sāmoa would have instructed in just how seriously history is taken, were it not that all Sāmoans already know this.[11] In few places are Pacific Islanders *not* preoccupied with 'their own historical practice'. Albert Wendt, the Sāmoan novelist and historian, pointedly reminded that 'we are what we remember', and as his own disaffection from the history discipline demonstrated, it was not merely what we remember, but also *how* we remember, that matters.[12] 'Ōkusitino Māhina makes a similar point about a particular form of Tongan history, *Tala-ē-Fonua*.[13] The effort to reconstitute indigenous histories is bound to particular ways of knowing and representation, and attached to certain communities: it is a task far beyond any single author (and certainly beyond this one) and calls not just for discipline, but also for ethics. Fortunately, though, there are vibrant indigenous intellectual traditions, and much innovative academic work, that have taken up this task.

Since the rise of indigenous literacy, especially from the nineteenth century, earlier indigenous understandings of the past have been given new life and form, often knitted with traditional and oral forms. Though the majority of works about indigenous Pacific people have been collected and authored by non-indigenous scholars, these too have sustained indigenous histories, at least when collection was done critically and with due care as to provenance and context. But foreign authorship was not the rule: the Polynesian appropriation of literacy, for instance, produced some remarkable early works, not only in manuscript but even in monographic form. The works of David Malo, Mary Kawena Pukui, Apirana Ngata and Te Rangikaheke, for instance, remain as storehouses of ancient knowledge and offer powerful insights into earlier times. Such authors were forerunners and never singular: Pacific Islanders have not stopped writing since, and contemporary indigenous writers knowingly work in a written tradition that is itself old, as well as an oral one that stretches back millennia.

Writing about the past was only one of many dimensions of indigenous Pacific writing, but it has been key to most indigenous academic writing. Contemporary indigenous Pacific scholars have been particularly engaged with thinking about the interplay between foreign actors and native life and history. Much of this stems from the desire of most of these writers to work through what might be called the 'situatedness' of knowledge: as knowledge of the past is a dialogue engaged through the present, it is responsive to and shapes the politics of the present. Most indigenous historians engage with these thematics, and most have been suspicious of the apolitical claims of historians and other academics. But few amongst the relatively small set of indigenous Pacific Islanders have been attracted to the discipline of history: most write historically from other and interdisciplinary locations. In particular, the appeal of poetry and fiction to indigenous writers has been strong, and this is almost always historically engaged, and has been a primary and consistent source of intellectual sustenance and innovation.[14]

In predominant foreign discourses about the Pacific – especially travel, ethnography and official representations – two discursive themes about indigenous Pacific islanders have been particularly important. One narrates natives as belonging to a timeless ethnographic present, ancient primitive ways of life surviving to the present: as anachronistic survivals or people 'out of time'. Evident from Victorian social evolutionary tracts to contemporary tourism brochures, from the Discovery Channel to history textbooks, this is alive and well. The other approach has been to put natives entirely into the past, as people who *were* but who no longer exist: whose destruction might be lamented, but whose passing was unavoidable or perhaps even necessary. In this view there are no true natives left, and those who remain are somehow inauthentic. Sure enough, the claims that there are no such natives left (no 'full-blooded' ones, for instance, as often stated in Hawai'i or New Zealand), that they speak the wrong language or do putatively non-native things are easy enough to find. These two traditions seem to leave only a Hobson's choice: as Vicente Diaz puts it, some natives get to have culture, but no history, others get to have history, but no culture.[15] To properly explore any indigenous past such framings must be superseded: an ethical and full engagement with an indigenous past is through an indigenous present.

In those indigenous pasts, time itself long worked differently across indigenous societies, at least before the appropriation of European models of time. Before foreigners no Pacific Island society had an autonomous system of chronology – a way of stably indexing across years or other large measures of time. The oral nature of Pacific Island societies before the 1800s meant that measures, calendars, mathematics and other forms of enumerating time were necessarily different from those with literacy and other particular time technologies. But 'time' itself is stabilised through language and metaphors, it is cultural: oral cultures had their own metaphors and cultures of time, different ways of bringing order and sequence to the past. Many societies did so in ways that stretched into antiquity, but they stood apart from the ways of foreigners. Such differences need not be mistaken for absence, as they once frequently were by Europeans and Americans.

The hundreds of cultures of the Pacific each narrated and encultured 'time' differently. Many structured the past through a succession of ages or periods. These allowed narrations of the past to be grouped into significant collections of narratives and characters, or otherwise related bundles. They connected a sense of chronology or sequence with particular historical characters and activities. For the most part such conceptions of the past were culturally specific, shared across cultures mostly only when elements of history were shared or entangled. For example, in Pohnpei these eras were, in sequence, Mwehin Kawa (Building Time) or Mwehin Aramas (Time of Peopling), followed by the Mwehin Sau Deleur (Time of the Lord of Deleur), and Mwehin Nahnmwarki.[16] In Sāmoa there is a great division between Pouliuli (darkness/ignorance) and Mālamalama (light/understanding), and amongst New Zealand Māori there is a periodisation that began with Te Kore (nothingness or potentiality), followed by Te Po (Darkness), Te Ao Marama (The World of Light).

Such periods also frame other sequences, as in Polynesian oral literatures and traditions. Though the more than 30 Polynesian languages each organised the past differently, they are usually similar and related. Narratives begin in a cosmological age of creation and divinity, which accounts for the presentation of the world, the islands, and typically the people. This then merges into an age of culture heroes (or what Niel Gunson called 'national or tribal ancestors') which retains elements of the fabulous and cosmological, but establishes recognisable contours. This is succeeded by genealogical times, a past to which the present can be connected through the ancestors of the living. Gunson usefully breaks this period in two, into one that he considers a 'first genealogical period', and a second period where genealogies are firm and fixed, and through which chiefs can trace their lines 'without errors'.[17] Polynesian genealogies are not simple, however, and do not just go from parent to child, but typically encompass a range of familial relations. In Polynesia these genealogies are of variant lengths: above 20 or 30 generations is relatively common for great families, and many are much, much longer. Generational length fluctuated: some lives and periods of rule were short and others much longer (famously, Taufaʻahau, Tupou I of Tonga lived for nearly a century, and was Tuʻi Kanokupolu for half of that time). It is not just difficult, but unnecessary, to convert these time scales into western digital, calendrical ones.

Genealogy orients time towards ancestors and descendants, not to an external systematic or a disembodied calibration of time. Time was thus experienced and understood differently through different cultures of genealogy, and so with history and the past. Of course, this meant that time (especially the past and future) was not an absolute and stable quantity: all measures of past and future time are by necessity symbolic. And as the relevant symbolic systems must not only address the past, but integrate it with the present, all descriptions of time are sensitive to change, whether political, religious or cultural. Western calendars and measures of time have hardly stood unchanged themselves. And the great recent display of the political nature of time is itself from the Pacific: in 2011 the Sāmoan Prime Minister decided to lose a day (30 December) and move his nation (taking Tokelau with it) from one side of the dateline to the other – to be 'closer' to Australia and New Zealand.

Genealogies archive families and lineages. This is hardly surprising since families, lineages and localities, rather than states, framed most indigenous lives before 1880 or so. Genealogies rarely cohere as a pool of sources available for the reconstruction of customary academic or 'western' histories, because the subjects of indigenous genealogies have rarely been the subjects of historians. As one of the great indigenous Pacific historians, Queen Sālote Pilolevu Tupou III, has suggested, genealogy was the central element of a Tongan (and by implication, Polynesian) history.[18] Working with genealogies requires special knowledge and skills, as well as access, and was rarely the province of all. But it was not genetically inhibited: and amongst the indigenous elites and select few who have worked closely with genealogies are some foreigners. The most rewarding written histories working with indigenous genealogies have been those that have remade their own subject, recognising that genealogies themselves constitute histories, offering other ways of bringing order to the past which have particular valence for a certain culture or people. Genealogies are rarely straightforwardly secular: they are also highly allusive (and elusive), frequently esoteric or protected, and are political, often with real and present consequences, not least in present claims to lineage, property, office and chiefly titles. All this makes it intellectually difficult for any single scholar to deal, properly, with more than one culture's genealogies. The least successful and more troubling use of genealogies have often been driven by the desire to remake them as sources for straightforward westernised histories, which crassly 'decode' or convert them into other terms. In the Pacific this impulse has produced many inaccurate and misleading histories. In one of the most notorious examples different tribal genealogies were 'standardised' – cherry-picked to conform largely to the predilections of the author – and then coarse averages were applied to fix a speculative date that was then treated by the author, and others, as reliable.[19] Recent scholars, whether indigenous or non-indigenous, are far more thoughtful, critical and rigorous.

Genealogies, and other images of the past, can rarely be separated from the places in which Pacific peoples lived their lives. Such connections are evident in how people identify themselves: whether as *Tangata Whenua* in New Zealand, or '*Taotao Tano*' in Guam (both meaning People of the Land), or as *Na Kai Wai* in Fiji or *Re Matau* in Carolinian (both meaning People of the Sea). Where one's ancestors' bones rest (thus '*Oiwi* in Hawai'i), or where one's placenta is buried (the word for land and placenta are often the same in Polynesia) enshrine the connections between genealogy and place. From here the widely shared Polynesian concept of *wa*, or *va*, or *vaha'a*, key in understanding Polynesian concepts of time, is elaborative: the *vaha'a/va/wa* means not just time, but space (and often also relationships). The *va* is necessarily relational, implying not a static point of observation but a movement, or possible movement, between. There was no good equivalent in Polynesian languages for the term/concept 'time', and so in most contemporary Polynesian languages the word that now does duty is a transliteration of the English term, such as *taimi* in Tongan and Sāmoan.

So Polynesians have long lived with something like 'space-time', and it was understood to cross dimensions. Prior to Christianity, most Polynesians understood the ordinary space of human activity through contrast with *other* dimensions of human and spiritual activity: particularly the multiple heavens or *langi/lagi/rangi*. What in English is 'the world', or the earth, in Sāmoan is *lalolagi*, beneath the *lagi* (heavens). For Polynesians there were multiple *lagi*, and these were not disconnected, ethereal places, but ones that were, or had been, navigable under the right circumstances. The heavens had known histories and places and occupants. Divinity, consequently, was tied up with ideas of place, and of movement within these realms. This is to emphasise that for Polynesians, like many other indigenous Pacific people, places and time were not secular, but filled with the resonance of the spiritual and the divine. For most Polynesians, like most other Pacific people, the world is still pervaded with the divine, though now the origin of that divinity is more often Christian. The strictly secular time of academic history has consequently struggled to account for and express histories that were not, and are not, agnostic – which is to say most peoples, most of the time.

The historical nature of space-time also comes into focus because for many indigenous Pacific Islanders, including most of the Polynesian peoples, histories of great migrations and discoveries mean that the past is not just a time, but also a *place*. In eastern Polynesia the homeland and location of deep histories, of the cosmological and heroic ages laid out above, was to the west, in Hawaiki (or Avaiki or Savai'i). Roger Green and Patrick Kirch argue of Hawaiki: 'Beyond the shadow of a doubt, the Ancestral Polynesian homeland' was 'West Polynesia, i.e. the area bounded by Sāmoa, Uvea, Futuna and Tonga', between 3,000 and 1,800 years ago.[20] Such a claim draws on, and aligns with, a good deal of indigenous knowledge and scholarship. But in the societies that remained in West Polynesia, there are also narratives of a distant place of origin or action: Pulotu. Likewise, scholars have tried also to fix the location of Pulotu, with some arguing it refers to locations in the

Fijian archipelago, some pointing further afield. Not just genealogies of people, but genealogies of place tie Polynesia together.

## Native seas

Perhaps most revealing of indigenous genealogies of place is the genealogy of the Pacific Ocean. For although the peoples indigenous to the Pacific speak over a thousand languages and have at least as many cultures, they did not have a word for the Pacific until the past few centuries. This was because for indigenous Pacific people, until then, the Pacific was not a *place*. Oskar Spate argued that until the Europeans named and 'discovered' it, the Pacific Ocean did not exist.[21] He did not mean that the Islanders did not know where they were, but rather that, as geographers have realised, the human relationships of naming and activity are what turn the abstract, wordless encounters of experience into named, known, narrativised, *places*. Spate knew as well as any that this artefact, 'the Pacific Ocean', was a place that came to rest against, but not dislodge, multitudinous other indigenous places. These other places need to be recognised, avowed and explored. For although these indigenous maritime places never quite reached the full extent of what we now name the Pacific, many were enormous. Islanders created maritime places – what we might call 'native seas' – that often ranged over millions of square kilometres, places known and named, practiced and narrated.

Place is what people make of the territories and waters they inhabit. Place needs naming and narration, it does not exist prior to people making it. As Doreen Massey has put it, place is 'woven together out of ongoing stories, as a moment within power-geometries, as a particular constellation within the wider topographies of space, and as in process, as unfinished business'. If space is a 'simultaneity of stories-so-far, then places are collections of those stories', of intersections and non-meetings up.[22] Such insight helps steer towards the places in which people lived, and in which the multiplicities and differences of people's trajectories can be aired. These insights fit with the kind of usable category of 'native seas': for these can indeed by uncovered if approached as 'collections of those stories'. Inclusive enough to find some purchase in a variety of different indigenous traditions, 'native seas' are also sharp enough to maintain these distinctions.

The uniquely maritime environments of many indigenous Pacific societies were rendered in their sense of place. The advanced maritime technologies which made it possible to traverse the world's largest waters, and find small and difficult island targets, particularly of vessel design and navigation, are well known. The largest of the vessels of indigenous design and construction were indeed truly striking technologies: the *drua* (as it was known in Fijian) or *kalia* (Tongan) or *'alia* (Sāmoan), were large asymmetric double-hulled vessels, up to 100 feet in length, able to carry over 250 people on shorter voyages, and able to 'safely convey 100 persons and several tons of goods over 1,000 miles of ocean'.[23] Built by stitching large planks of wood together, without any need of iron, these were hardly 'canoes', as they have often been called, but large, powerful sailing vessels. Throughout the period of early European encounters these *kalia/drua* were often spotted at sea, along with other smaller vessels, in large and impressive fleets. Fleet sizes of upwards of 100, and in some cases over 200, capable of transporting thousands of people, were reported by Europeans. Not only large in size, but often distant from home, dozens of Tongan *kalia* were reported, for instance, taking the Tongan King/Tui Kanokupolu, along with hundreds and possibly thousands of people, to Sāmoa.

There was much more besides voyaging that showed the ways in which the waters were cultured, practiced, spaces. The capacity to make and sustain life on atolls is deeply instructive. So was the ability of some Islanders, such as the i-Kiribati, to discern and utilise 'seamarks' (or *betia* in Kiribati) – an oceanic equivalent of landmarks.[24] (The existence of these was long doubted by foreign mariners.) Another telling example was the highly sophisticated fishing and aquacultural knowledge of many Pacific Islanders. Marine biologists who have worked with Pacific indigenous fishing experts have discovered a depth of expertise, much of which is little known, or unknown, to the academy. One marine biologist who went looking for native expertise came across a Palauan master fisherman, Ngiraklang, in the mid-1970s. Amongst Ngiraklang's vast knowledge was his command of reef fish behaviour: 'he knew the lunar spawning cycles of several times as many species of fish as had been described in the scientific literature for the entire world'.[25] Indeed, two modern scientists mused that indigenous Pacific marine knowledge is 'of a stupefying richness, and at times of such precision that the corresponding poverty of our own conceptions makes inquiry very difficult'.[26]

In the Pacific it was, and is, rare for the meeting of land and water to translate into a simple boundary. Lagoons, harbours, reefs, estuaries, tidal flats, fishponds and hundreds of other waterscapes were places of indigenous practice. All over the Pacific one can find indigenous entities that criss-cross water, even vast waters, most obviously in the kind of archipelagic polities relatively common in the Pacific: whether Tokelau, Lau in Fiji, or Hawai'i or Ha'apai in Tonga. Other polities, such as the Aiga i le Tai (the Family in the Sea) in Sāmoa, assemble parcels of land and interest, which were held together across the water by stories and relationships. In a similarly revealing way the segmented land division of the *tapere* in Rarotonga, Mangaia, Aitutaki and Mauke – much like the *ahupua'a* in Hawai'i, or the *facl* in Kosrae – were divisions that were substantially based on water, and which followed a stream or water drainage from central mountain ridges not simply to the coast, but typically out into the sea, to particular points on the reef. These cultural acts, with countless others, educate as to how fully many island cultures lived in the sea.

Different 'native seas' were constituted differently – indeed, *had* to be constituted differently, as they entangled different cultures and peoples. Some of the larger, or more isolated, archipelagoes were 'native seas' in and of themselves. Aotearoa/New Zealand, with more land than the rest of Polynesia combined, occupied a vibrant and busy people for centuries, exploring, discovering, naming, building. This included a reorienting towards the place itself. Yet even though most of their exchanges were now across coastal waters, rather than deep seas, New Zealand Māori remained a people of the water. Acknowledging their water – whether a fresh water body, a river or sea – was and remains an integral part to establishing one's claim to place, and one's belonging to a people. This claim to ancestry, connection to a mountain, and to a body of water, is still recited in formal *whaikorero*. Likewise, in the ethnically diverse Fijian archipelago, particular groups of people were seen as uniquely maritime. At the time of early European encounters the people of Levuka and Butoni were famous as maritime people, 'who regard the sea as their home, and are known as "the inhabitants of the water"' – or Na Kai Wai.[27]

One of these 'native seas', in many ways the most striking, was centred in the north Pacific, in the waters surrounding Yap. Known as the *sawei*, it has been cast variously as an empire, a 'tribute network' and a trading zone. With Yap at its centre, it ran 300km to the west, and some 1,500km to the east, as far as Truk and including all of the Caroline Islands.[28] (This is roughly the distance from New York City to Omaha, Nebraska, or from Poland to England.) Emblematic of, and central to, the sawei were two kinds of money, *gau* or shell money, and the famous *fei*, stone money that took the form of wheels of aragonite stone, sometimes larger than two metres in diameter. As with all the 'native seas' described here, the *sawei* was an historical feature: constituted by social and cultural enactments, and cohered through narrations of distinctly Yapese, Palauan and Carolinian kinds, it was a process and always changing. The *sawei* went back over ten generations, and prehistorians reckon it even older, dating probably from the twelfth century, and certainly from the fourteenth century.

The extent of the *sawei*, knitting together a place that spanned so many islands over hundreds of thousands of square kilometres of sea, shows just how large some 'native seas' were. Other seas could nest inside them. There was the *katau* or *kachau*, for instance, another regional alliance that drew together Kosrae, Chuuk and Pohnpei. The *hu* drew together Elato, Satawal and Lamotrek. There were (and are) four 'distinct, but interconnected worlds' in this area – the three sets of high islands, Yap, Palau and the Marianas, and the atolls and coral islands between Yap and Chuuk, a shifting, multidimensional arena, where different places were made and remade, and which were highly situational.[29] In these parts of Micronesia this was apparent by the way some people named the individual bodies of water that connected different islands. In the case of Lamotrek atoll there were more than twenty 'seaways' integrating Lamotrek to surrounding islands. 'To the [Lamotrek] navigator the sea-lane is a known area', and the spatial ordering of the sea was manifest in the spatial ordering of the land on Lamotrek.[30]

Probably most famous of these maritime places or 'native seas' to outsiders was Massim, in eastern New Guinea. The centrepiece of Massim was the '*kula* ring' which included the Trobriand Islands and the D'Entrecasteaux Islands, and was the focus of some of the originary and most famous studies of modern anthropology by Bronisław Malinowski and Reo Fortune.[31] The focus of most of the many scholars who have studied the Massim has been the processes of exchange, the 'ceremonial' goods that were the lifeblood of the *kula*, but this exchange was only possible – or even conceivable – because the different peoples of Massim had jointly fashioned a place in which this exchange could occur. These people were surely, as Malinowski called them, *The Argonauts of the Western Pacific*.[32]

Melanesia is often neglected in accounts of the maritime qualities of Pacific peoples, but this is unjustified. Many Melanesians produced other 'native seas', maritime places, often no less impressive than Massim. Along the Sepik Coast, in northern New Guinea, were an extraordinarily diverse group of communities engaged in travel and exchange. The Siuai of Bougainville plied the waters between them and the islands of Alu and Fauro. The Vitiaz Strait between New Britain and Huon Peninsula in New Guinea, was another busy place, where the Siassi people, accomplished mariners and fishers, comprised a kind of merchant marine circulating and drawing together the diverse peoples of the Strait. (These kinds of intense relational arrangements are not only maritime, of course, as the *moka* and *te* of the Mt. Hagen area in the Highlands, show.) There were other 'native seas' in the Papuan Gulf, including the well-studied hiri which brought together the Motu and Elema, to the degree it even produced its own pidgin language; and another in and around Manus and the Admiralty Islands, a complex constellation of trade partnerships and market exchanges. Outside of New Guinea, in Santa Cruz, natives stitched together a place ranging from Vanikoro to the Duff and Reef Islands. Similar relationships were maintained in New Caledonia, between Mare, Lifu, the Isle of Pines and the Loyalties.

In Polynesia, most striking were two large 'native seas' – one often called the Moana-nui-a-Kiwa (or Moana-nui-a-Kiva) and the other sometimes known as Vaha Loa (or Vasa Loloa). The Moana-nui-a-Kiwa (Ocean of Kiwa), as it was called in the southern Cook Islands and Aotearoa/New Zealand, was an ocean named for a legendary ancestor and which surrounded these places and integrated them with neighbouring – though often extremely distant – archipelagoes. Like any ocean, it did not have definite limits, and for Cook Islands and New Zealand Māori encompassed an overlapping but different place. The Vasa Loloa (in Sāmoan) or Vaha Loa (Tongan) referred to the waters that surrounded the major groups of western Polynesia – Uvea, Futuna, Sāmoa, Tonga, Niuafoʻou, Niuatoputapu – and also included Fiji. The Vasa Loloa was pre-eminently 'a sea of stories', with each corner of the sea narrating the changing seascape that brought the different islands together.[33] The traditional histories of this sea are relatively well known, and are evident from the earliest cosmological histories, through the heroic age and remaining intensive throughout genealogical time.[34] Particularly important in the period before and immediately after European arrival was the role of Tongan mariners, who were most active in plying the waters of the Vasa, and indeed went beyond it.

The Vasa Loloa, a sea of stories, was the vast place in which so much western Polynesian history happened. As is true in the very different culture of Lamotrek, in the Vasa Loloa, the spatiality of the sea paralleled that on the land, and elsewhere: the Vasa inhered in the language, in songs, in tattooing and medicine, and was encapsulated in intergenerational names: of places, chiefly or orator's titles, even of villages. Important examples of these embodied genealogical connections include the Tongan lineage Tuʻi Kanokupolu (derived from the Tongan word for one of Sāmoa's main islands – Upolu/Kupolu), Sā Malietoa (derived from a famous utterance by defeated Tongan warriors), or the famous canoe-building people of Lemaki (in Fiji, but who descend from Manono in Sāmoa). Even small parts of a genealogy can be deeply revealing: in Queen Sālote's genealogies one can – just through a single person – draw multiple connections across the water. For example, Popuaʻuliuli was a daughter of Paleisāsā, a son of Tui Nayau of Lakeba in Fiji, and his wife Toafilimoeʻunga, daughter of Tuʻi Kanokupolu Mataeletuʻapiko.[35] These genealogies challenge the decomposition of indigenous histories into largely national forms, which although an artefact of only the past century or so, continues to trouble the comprehension of larger stories, as national ones became favoured over regional stories. Thankfully, a range of recent histories has sought to reconvene these larger narratives, whether according to indigenous or academic models.

'Native seas' sometimes nested in each other, or overlapped, and few were not connected to others. For most native seas there were more irregular and less storied relationships that tied distant seas each to another. These more distant ties often sat on boundaries of difference: between the Vasa Loloa and the Moana-Nui-a-Kiva, for instance, was the difference between western and eastern Polynesia. Between the *sawei* and those islands to the south was the difference between, in some sense, Micronesia and Polynesia. But for the most part these native seas had edges that were of place, not of the cosmos or universe. Knowledge of the other places outside of one's own 'native sea' was usual: the best-known example was the map drawn by the Raʻiatean navigator and priest, Tupaia, for James Cook. Tupaia's knowledge greatly exceeded his experience, and ranged far beyond the waters of eastern Polynesia, perhaps as far as Sāmoa. Similarly, in the Cook Islands Mangaians carry stories of settlement and connection from distant Tonga and Sāmoa. Taken as a collective, these native seas blanketed the inhabited Pacific, like a kaleidoscopic weave of maritime places, constantly being made and unmade, with Islanders holding all of it together with warp and weft-like voyages. It was a moving and changing map, like the ocean itself.

Native seas were often transformed by the arrival of foreigners and empires, but these were typically spurs to remake, rather than end, connections. After the Second World War Pacific Islanders began migrating even more intensely, mostly to former imperial centres on the edges of the Pacific – especially Australia, New Zealand, Hawai'i and the USA. The numbers that moved were proportionately very large, to the point where a majority of Polynesian nations now have larger descendant populations living outside their borders than within them, and this is also true of many parts of Micronesia. These Pacific 'transnations' criss-cross the region and beyond, making Pacific lives ordinarily expansive, if only occasionally visible via headlines about Sāmoan National Football League players or Fijian mercenaries in Iraq. The horizons of the native seas have continued to shift, though now connections are sustained less by watercraft than aircraft, and especially through other means such as social network websites, remittances, electronic media and the military.

For most people Pacific genealogies remain strong. That so many people now think of themselves, at least on occasion, as 'Pacific Islanders', marks not their appropriation to a foreign conception of where they live, but an indigenisation and repossession of the idea of the Pacific Ocean. This has become increasingly important as Pacific Islanders became increasingly transnational. For Pacific Islanders the claiming of the Pacific has mostly come in the past half-century: at the confluence of decolonisation, regionalisation and global capitalism to be sure, but more meaningfully through regional indigenous junctures that have produced new networks of exchange and solidarity – from the Pacific Games to the Pacific Arts Festival, from the University of the South Pacific (one of only two regional universities in the world) to the regional agencies such as (especially) the Pacific Islands Forum. Interlacing this are new identifications, customs and sensibilities, including the 'Pacific Way', much scrutinised and criticised, but also central to a crucial integrating discourse. This chimes with the 'sea of islands' of which Epeli Hau'ofa has so presciently written. Indigenous seaways and genealogies were always changing, but always connected here with there, and the present with the ancestors. So with the recent voyage of Tevita Mara, at once new and ancient: fetched by a Pacific class patrol boat built in Australia and given to Tonga so they might better patrol their Exclusive Economic Zone, he followed a seaway familiar to his ancestors, to find safe haven with his relatives, his *kāinga*.

## Notes

1. See 'Dumont D'Urville's Divisions of Oceania: Fundamental Precincts or Arbitrary Constructs?', Special Issue, *Journal of Pacific History* 38, 2 (September 2003), 155–268.

2. Damon Salesa, 'The World from Oceania', in Douglas Northrop, ed., *A Companion to World History* (Chichester, 2012), pp. 389–404.

3. Ben Finney, 'The Other One-Third of the Globe', *Journal of World History* 5 (1994), 273–97.

4. Geoffrey Irwin, *The Prehistoric Exploration and Colonisation of the Pacific* (Cambridge, 1992).

5. Patrick V. Kirch and Roger C. Green, *Hawaiki: Ancestral Polynesia: An Essay in Historical Anthropology* (Cambridge, 2001).

6. Patrick V. Kirch and Jean-Louis Rallu, eds., *The Growth and Collapse of Pacific Island Societies: Archaeological and Demographic Perspectives* (Honolulu, 2007), pp. 1–34, 203–56, 326–37.

7. R. C. Green and J. M. Davidson, *Archaeology in Western Sāmoa* (Auckland, 1974), pp. 281–2.

8. D. E. Stannard, *Before the Horror: The Population of Hawai'i on the Eve of Western Contact* (Honolulu, 1989).

9. Marshall Sahlins, *Islands of History* (Chicago, 1987), p. 34.

10. Tuiatua Tupua Tamasese Tupuola Efi, 'The Riddle in Samoan History', *Journal of Pacific History* 29 (1994), 66–79.

11. On the controversy see the chapters by Asofou So'o and Damon Salesa in Tamasa'ilau Suaalii-Sauni, I'uogafa Tuagalu, Tofilau Nina Kirifi-Alai and Naomi Fuamatu, eds., *Su'esu'e Manogi – In Search of Fragrance: Tui Atua Tupua Tamasese Ta'isi and the Samoan Indigenous Reference* (Apia, 2008).

12. Albert Wendt, 'Novelists and Historians and the Art of Remembering', in Antony Hooper, et al., eds., *Class and Culture in the South Pacific* (Suva, 1987), pp. 78–92; Damon Salesa, 'Cowboys in the House of Polynesia', *The Contemporary Pacific* 22 (2010), 330–48.

13. 'Ōkusitino Māhina, 'The Poetics of Tongan Traditional History, Tala-ē-fonua: An Ecology-Centred Concept of Culture and History', *Journal of Pacific History* 28 (1993), 109–21.

14. A short list would include with Albert Wendt, Epeli Hau'ofa, Grace Molisa, Vincent Eri and Konai Helu-Thaman.

15. 'Sacred Vessels: Navigating Tradition and Identity in Micronesia', produced by Christine T. Delisle and Vicente Diaz (Hagåtña, 1997).

16. D. L. Hanlon, *Upon a Stone Altar: A History of the Island of Pohnpei to 1890* (Honolulu, 1988), pp. 13–25.

17. Niel Gunson, 'Great Families of Polynesia: Inter Island Links and Marriage Patterns', *Journal of Pacific History* 32 (1997), 140–50; E. K. McKinzie, *Hawaiian Genealogies: Extracted from Hawaiian Language Newspapers*, ed. Ishmael W. Stagner, II, 2 vols. (Honolulu, 1983), I, p. 1, quoted in ibid.

18. Elizabeth Bott with the assistance of Tavi, *Tongan Society at the Time of Captain Cook's Visits: Discussions with Her Majesty Queen Sālote Tupou* (Wellington, NZ, 1982).
19. D. R. Simmons, *The Great New Zealand Myth: A Study of the Discovery and Origin Traditions of the Maori* (Wellington, NZ, 1976).
20. Kirch and Green, *Hawaiki: Ancestral Polynesia*, p. 100.
21. O. H. K. Spate, *The Spanish Lake* (London, 1979), p. 1.
22. Doreen B. Massey, *For Space* (London, 2005), p. 131.
23. Thomas Williams, *Fiji and the Fijians* (London, 1858), p. 76.
24. Arthur Francis Grimble, *Tungaru Traditions* (Honolulu, 1989), pp. 48–51.
25. R. E. Johannes, *Words of the Lagoon: Fishing and Marine Lore in the Palau District of Micronesia* (Berkeley, 1981), p. 7.
26. P. Ottino and Y. Plessis, 'Les classifications Ouest Paumotu de quelques poissons scaridés et labridés', in J. M. C. Thomas and L. Bemot, eds., *Langues et techniques, nature et société* (Paris, 1972), pp. 361–71, and W. A. Gosline and V. E. Brock, *Handbook of Hawaiian Fishes* (Honolulu, 1960), both cited in Johannes, *Words of the Lagoon*, p. viii.
27. Williams, *Fiji and the Fijians*, p. 93.
28. M. L. Berg, 'Yapese Politics, Yapese Money and the Sawei Tribute Network Before World War I', *Journal of Pacific History* 27 (1992), 150–64.
29. Paul D'Arcy, 'Connected by the Sea: Towards a Regional History of the Western Caroline Islands', *Journal of Pacific History* 36 (2001), 163–82.
30. William H. Alkire, *Lamotrek Atoll and Inter-island Socioeconomic Ties* (Urbana, 1965), pp. 124–5.
31. Both Reo Fortune and Bronisław Malinowski did their research here.
32. Bronisław Malinowski, *The Argonauts of the Western Pacific* (London, 1922).
33. This is the subject of chapter 1 of my *Empire Trouble: Sāmoans and the Greatest Powers in the World* (Auckland, NZ, forthcoming).
34. Niel Gunson, 'The Tonga–Sāmoa Connection 1777–1845', *Journal of Pacific History* 25 (1990), 176–87; Judith Huntsman, ed., *Tonga and Sāmoa: Images of Gender and Polity* (Christchurch, NZ, 1995).
35. Ko e Tohi 'a 'Ene 'Afio ko Kuini Salote Tupou, 'Ngaahi Fetu'utakianga Kehe', p. 9: Rev. Dr. Sione Latukefu, 'Collected Tongan Papers 1884–1965', Pacific Manuscript Bureau, College of Asia and the Pacific, Australian National University, Microfilm 11.

# 3

# The Pacific before Empire, c.1500–1800

Joyce E. Chaplin

Bound for China from Peru, a European ship threads the Strait of Magellan and enters the 'South Sea'. Adrift on the ocean, the mariners are desperate to find land; one-third of them have scurvy. They are overjoyed to come across Bensalem, an island inhabited by a people who – amazingly – are Christian, fluent in multiple European languages and adept in every form of natural science, which they perfect in 'Salomon's House', a learned society plus laboratory. This pointedly named 'New Atlantis' of the Pacific Ocean offers so much more than anything Europeans had discovered in the Atlantic. Bensalem is a part of the world entirely unknown to the western travellers and yet, somehow, perfectly prepared for them. Most of the elements of Francis Bacon's utopian fantasy, *The New Atlantis* (1627), were too good to be true.[1] No one ever discovered Bensalem. And yet Bacon captured quite well European mariners' hapless state while drifting on the Pacific Ocean, as well as their related desire for natural knowledge. Within the worlds of the Pacific, Europeans were frequently reduced to mere (scorbutic) bodies rather than being the (embodied) vessels of civic identity and functions that elsewhere carried empire outward from Europe. The Pacific was different, and it is the interface between natural conditions and human ambitions that shows why.

It would be difficult, looking at the literatures on European expansion into other parts of the world, not to come away with some sense of European empires as successful, by a variety of measures, but the Pacific is another story. What does European *non*-imperialism look like? The history of the Pacific, from Balboa to Bligh (roughly 1513 to 1808), is our best answer. It would have been unremarkable, as little as ten years ago, to present European 'discovery' of the Pacific as a chapter in a story of some kind of incremental progress.

The progress might have been conceived as either positive or negative, but, either way, it would have moved relentlessly forward to an
imperial apotheosis. That form of analysis may still help scholars to
describe and criticise European imperialism elsewhere, but it has
little merit within and around the Pacific.[2]

There was no comparable incremental process in the Pacific
because European entry into this part of the world constituted almost
three centuries of overwhelmingly passive and decidedly inconclusive events. The passivity is apparent in the way that Europeans were
dependent on local peoples for their knowledge of the Pacific, beginning with the Indians who guided Vasco Núñez de Balboa over the
isthmus that separated the Atlantic from an ocean entirely new to
him and to other Europeans. More often than not, however,
Europeans were unable to learn anything from indigenous populations because they had no contact with them. Their encounters with
Micronesia were unsustained; for over two centuries, they failed to
locate members of one of the world's most skilled maritime populations, Polynesia.[3] Not until the late 1760s would Samuel Wallis and
Louis-Antoine de Bougainville make independent landings at Tahiti,
the beginning of a long-deferred encounter. Moreover, Europeans
found themselves barred from nations on the Asian side of the
Pacific, and they failed to maintain consistent contact with other
large landmasses, including Australia and New Zealand. Even as
Europeans were creating political empires elsewhere, they were
unable to do so within much of the Pacific over the seventeenth and
much of the eighteenth century, meaning all areas from the western
edge of the Americas to the Philippines, from Patagonia to China.
William Bligh's faltering career in the South Seas, where he barely
survived mutiny at sea and insurrection on land, is prime evidence of
the weakness of Europeans' sociopolitical control within the Pacific,
even over each other.

Their lack of impact, autonomy and knowledge allows us to see
Europeans not only as civic beings who (sometimes) achieved things
for the nations or trading groups whom they represented, but also as
natural entities, as physical bodies whose presence in and around the
Pacific measured and had consequences for the natural world. Even
in this way, however, Europeans did not set off early natural disasters
of the proportion seen in the Atlantic world, where European
settlers, often within a generation, had extirpated native plants and
animals in order to embed their preferred, Old World replacements.
The time lag mattered. By the point that similar shifts began to affect
parts of the Pacific, in the eighteenth century, Europeans knew what

they were doing. This is significant, because it reveals the extent to which Europeans realised that, in places where they could not colonise, domesticated plants and animals were their shock troops of invasion. Meanwhile, Europeans began to regard the Pacific as an unique platform for science. They never discovered Salomon's House, but tried to create their own versions of it, convinced that scientific activity would demonstrate a different kind of imperium, one built to fit over the physical world, even (or perhaps especially) in the absence of settled empire.

Although the 'discovery' of America, and its unfolding on European world maps, has drawn a great deal of scholarly attention, the subsequent unveiling of the Pacific Ocean was in fact even more astonishing to Europeans. Since the classical period, Europeans had generated reports and legends of lands (including Atlantis) that lay to their west, and they knew some things about the 'Asia' located to their east, but there was no comparable information stream about whatever might be beyond the Atlantic, or even if there was any beyond, anything substantial between the Atlantic and Asia. The globally distinct parts of humanity had generated bases of knowledge about their local oceans, but these did not coalesce into a common geography. Although Asian, Melanesian and Polynesian seafarers were proficient in navigating the waters of what would later be called the Indian and Pacific Oceans, their expertise was for a long time unknown to outsiders. Europeans were aware only of local seas (especially the Mediterranean) and of the greater ocean that bounded the western coasts of Europe and Africa, not yet consistently labelled the 'Atlantic'.[4]

Gradually, European travellers converged on an ocean that could not be encompassed by these older designations. They did so primarily by exploiting the maritime knowledge that other people possessed, gaining natural knowledge by following global societies. On his two-year journey to India, between 1497 and 1499, for instance, the Portuguese mariner Vasco da Gama had acquired a pilot in Malindi, in what is now Kenya, who guided him into the Indian Ocean. From 1500 onwards, the Portuguese grew adept at extracting still further information about the Indian Ocean from Asian maps and Asian individuals. As they moved eastwards, the Portuguese also gleaned knowledge of the waters that ran toward China and Japan.[5]

Europeans did not understand, however, how these bodies of water might coincide with the Atlantic Ocean, which was being explored from the other direction. Christopher Columbus thought that the Atlantic and Indian Oceans might simply merge somewhere or other, and insisted that, by crossing the Atlantic, he had bridged the only divide between Europe and Asia. But the zones he claimed for Spain (which promptly sent soldiers and settlers to them) did not resemble any part of the Asia known to Europeans. Was it really possible that his discoveries were mere leagues away from India, the Spice Islands, China or Japan? If they were distinct from those places, were they separated from Asia (and therefore from Europe) not only by land, but perhaps by an additional sea?

An extra ocean seemed a plausible explanation. Martin Waldseemüller, in his *Universalis cosmographia secundum Ptholomaei traditionem et Americi Vespucii aliorumque lustrationes* ('The Universal Cosmography according to the Tradition of Ptolemy and the Discoveries of Amerigo Vespucci and Others'), published in 1507, bounded the western side of the Atlantic with a vestigial America and indicated another ocean on its far side. This was not entirely unprecedented. As Waldseemüller's title admitted, he followed earlier accounts and charts that had planted a new continent and ocean on the world map. Balboa confirmed the body of water in 1513 when, with the assistance of Indian guides, he trekked over the Isthmus of Panama and spotted open sea. He named it the 'South Sea', deferring to opinion that it must be water that lay to the south of China and Japan, which were presumed to bulge out so far that they were not very distant from America (or from westbound travellers from Europe).[6]

Not everyone was convinced. Among the notable doubters was Ferdinand Magellan, who thought that the Spice Islands (part of the Malaku Peninsula) that the Portuguese had reached from India must be even closer to the new world that the Spanish Monarchy had claimed. Magellan convinced Charles V of Spain to bankroll a westbound expedition, meant to go around the Americas and into what he called the Sinus Magnus, a narrow gulf that he expected would lead towards China. Magellan did find a way through South America, via the strait that would thereafter bear his name. He had by that point recruited (possibly voluntarily) a Brazilian man and had kidnapped two Fuegian men. Two of these Indians survived passage through the Strait of Magellan, but they died, as many of Magellan's own men did, as he drifted for weeks on an ocean he had assumed did not exist. He and his men named it 'Pacific' for its absence of storms (Figure 3.1). It is incredible that, as he kept sailing north and west, Magellan did not encounter a single populated place within the Pacific Ocean. Surviving narratives document an attempt to stop at two small uninhabited islands, with waters too deep to anchor. Without any guidance from other human beings, the three surviving ships (of an original five) wandered onwards until they reached

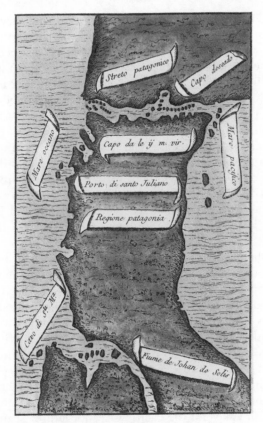

*Figure 3.1*   The Pacific 'discovered' and named.
*Source:* Map from Antonio Pigafetta, 'Journal of Magellan's Voyage', *c.*1525.

Guam. Magellan paid the price in high mortality to scurvy, and his weakened fleet kept dwindling, all the way back to Spain.[7]

The Pacific's constant, fatal erosion of European mariners and their ships would remain the general pattern for European reconnaissance of the ocean until the second half of the eighteenth century. The South Sea's various points of entry might as well have been embellished with the warning: abandon hope, all ye who enter here. It is commonplace to note that the ocean was dangerous because it was so large. But this was only part of the problem for European mariners. The other – and less commonly noted – difficulty was that the ocean was inconveniently far from Europe; ships and crew were already worn and weary by the time they entered the Pacific, and *then* had to fight their way through the world's largest body of water. After Magellan's experience, mariners hugged any available Pacific shoreline. European sailors tended to do that anyway, wherever they were, and they may have assumed that the Pacific, like the Atlantic and Indian oceans, had only open water at its centre. Their caution guaranteed that people on the cornucopia of populated islands within the Pacific Ocean were spared their meddling attention. It took two centuries for Europeans to establish themselves on scattered and tentative footholds around the Pacific Rim. The results there were imperial – just about. Watch how it happens, in the slowest of slow motion.[8]

In the earliest years, Spain, the first European claimant to the Pacific, strategically claims the ocean's edges, at places designed to maximise profit. Spanish decisions reflect a general European fixation on Asia. Trade with India and China is regarded as the biggest prize of European expansion; the Dutch, Spanish and Portuguese outposts in Indonesia and the Philippines represent, for that reason, the greatest achievements. Unexpected bounty comes from silver mines in the Andes. Spanish silver fleets that cross from South America to the Philippines (with the silver then going into Asia) are the most important European connection across the Pacific. Once it has footholds in the Philippines and South and Central America, Spain closes them to outsiders. Only Catholics are permitted entry, and then only when authorised. Linking up Spain's far-flung Pacific outposts is serious work, and constitutes the overwhelming majority of all trans-Pacific traffic done by the newcomers. Only well-equipped and officially sanctioned galleons typically make the long run from the Philippines to Acapulco, and only infrequently. The term 'Spanish Lake', for the Pacific Ocean, captures Spain's sense of seaborne proprietorship, though the designation also reflects ignorance that other people lived on islands and landmasses within the Pacific, as well as denial of the ocean's massively un-lakelike extent.[9]

European attempts to expand outwards from the edges of the Pacific begin, however, to reveal the ocean's true contours. Travelling eastwards from their colonies in Indonesia and the Philippines, Portuguese, Spanish and Dutch mariners make the first known contact with New Guinea. In 1526–7, the Portuguese explorer Jorge de Menezes sails to the largest island within New Guinea, which someone in his expedition names Papua, using a Malay word to describe the crinkled texture of Melanesian hair. A Spaniard, Yñigo Ortiz de Retez, adds the name New Guinea in 1545, because he thinks its people resemble those in West Africa, which Europeans call Guinea. (Note that both names show an intellectual reliance on what Europeans know of worlds *outside* the Pacific.) The Spanish settle in Formosa (later Taiwan) from 1626 to 1642, and in the Marianas beginning in the 1660s, but they do not establish a settlement in New

Guinea and the Dutch take over their post in Taiwan. They have their hands full, as it is. In the first hundred years of Spanish colonisation of the Philippines, there are over a dozen indigenous rebellions. In Guam, Chamorro natives plot in 1684 to kill all Jesuit missionaries and Spanish officials. The Spanish may be proud, glittering conquistadors in the Americas, but they cling by ragged fingernails to their Pacific outposts.[10]

One solution would be to amass greater military force within the Pacific. This is hard. The colonising powers are often preoccupied with war elsewhere, or else stymied by the consequences of imperial overreach within the Atlantic and Asia. The English are notoriously slow to establish colonies in North America and the Caribbean, and are so inconsequential within the Near East and Asia that they are often taken captive or simply enslaved. Invasion of the North American continent is difficult for everyone, as the Pueblo Revolt of 1680 demonstrates to the Spanish and as resistance from the Iroquois Confederation makes clear to the Dutch, English and French. On the other side of the Pacific, within greater Asia, Europeans are unable to establish a presence within China, Japan or Korea, and are barely able to do so in India. Within this wider geopolitical context, greater financial and military commitment to the Pacific costs too much.

Above all, the Pacific Ocean's distance from Europe, and then its implacable immensity, mean that conveying a fleet of battleships into the Pacific is nigh impossible. (It would not be done successfully until the nineteenth century.) The Spanish learn this the hard way, with the expedition of Garcia Jofre de Loaiasa, who departs Spain in 1524 with four ships and a crew of 450. After many accidents and delays, a mere 28 survivors eventually return to Europe; the Spanish will thereafter do trans-Pacific sailings only if they do not have to go to or from Spain, as well. Subsequent war fleets meet with similar disaster. When George Anson sets out in 1740 to harass the Spanish enemy in the Pacific, he sails with six ships and 1,939 men, far too many to manoeuvre into and across the Pacific without scurvy eating away the ship-bound humanity. Only one ship and 145 men make it back, even though the Britons see almost no enemy action. The Spanish do not kill them – their imperial and global overreach is quite disastrous enough.[11]

Francis Bacon's scurvy-struck travellers knew what they were doing – the whole trick of navigating the Pacific is to find other humans and use what they produce, whether they want to give it up or not. At first, the easiest targets in this regard are the Spanish outposts around the Pacific. Predation on Spanish colonies, and on the ships that connect them, constitute an important secondary opportunity for English and Dutch mariners. Plunder of the precious and the essential (silver, but also food) is Francis Drake's strategy in the 1570s, which Thomas Cavendish will imitate in the 1580s and Joris Spilbergen in the 1610s. As well as lifting goods from Spanish settlements and ships, these Pacific marauders kidnap people for information about navigation – where to go next, and how to get there. They take just about anyone for this purpose, including Europeans, but also Indians, enslaved people of African ancestry, and Asians. But they do not take the peoples within the Pacific, for the simple reason that encounters with them remain rare. Hugging the coastlines, especially those known to have Europeanised landscapes and economies, remains the popular option.[12]

The search for Terra Australis is the big exception. Some think this southern continent is necessary to create a planetary balance with the known bodies of land in the northern hemisphere. Many maps, from the sixteenth to the eighteenth centuries, spread a hypothetical landmass within the southern ocean, beneath the two known southernmost continental points, Cape Horn and the Cape of Good Hope. Dutch landings on Australia give the most promising hints of a southern continent. Even in this case, the Dutch proceed from the Indian Ocean world, namely their colonies in the Indonesian archipelago. Having sailed from there, and gone past New Guinea, Willem Janszoon makes what is the first recorded European contact with Australia (in Queensland) in 1606. But fatal encounters with Aboriginal men in what Janszoon calls Nieu-Zeeland (New Holland) discourage any lengthy stay. Dirk Hartog makes the next recorded Australian landing, in 1616, though this was on the coast that faced the Indian Ocean, and therefore less of an event in 'Pacific' history. Unawareness of the place's size, and inability to fix one name upon it, both signify just how faltering is knowledge of one of the largest inhabited landmasses within the Pacific world.

Other Pacific islands continue to be added to printed maps. In the 1640s, the busy Abel Tasman makes the first documented stops at Van Diemen's Land (later Tasmania), New Zealand and Fiji. The islands of Juan Fernández off Chile become a routine stopping point for non-Catholic mariners who need to get food or fresh water while avoiding Spaniards. Discovery of the 'Incantadas', islands so elusive they seem enchanted (later called Galapagos), is likewise haphazard. In 1684, John Cook explores those islands, duly named for members of the British ruling establishment, though the names do not stick. And unlike Juan Fernández, the Incantadas are not a favoured stopping point. They are, of course, notoriously rocky and unproductive, though the same is not true of Easter Island, which Jacob Roggeveen names on a brief stop in 1722, but which is rarely visited for over a century. Finally, Samuel Wallis and Louis-Antoine de Bougainville independently fall across Tahiti in, respectively, 1767 and 1768. This is the start of a long, eventful, if ultimately troubled encounter between westerners and Polynesians.

While making the belated reconnaissance of the intra-Pacific islands that Magellan and others had kept missing for nearly 250 years, European explorers of the late eighteenth century also manage to locate some larger landmasses towards the bottom of the South Pacific. Cook, on his first voyage into the Pacific (1768–71), circumnavigates both of New Zealand's main islands, verifying they are distinct both from each other and from Australia. He does the same for New Guinea, confirming its status as a distinct island, and he gets close enough to Antarctica to encourage further speculation that a southern continent must exist, though it must be composed mostly of ice and populated only by penguins. After Cook's death in Hawai'i in 1779 (on his third voyage into the Pacific, 1776–9), one of his subordinates, George Vancouver, continues the work of charting the coastlines of the Pacific, culminating with a survey of the Pacific Northwest, the last inhabited continental coast to be put onto the world map. Many places remain to be explored (notably Antarctica), but western geographical knowledge of the greater Pacific seems – at last – to exist in a working rough draft.

★ ★ ★

Empire did not smoothly follow, however. To be sure, many plans to establish civil settlements throughout the Pacific were drawn up – but few were enacted. Settled European outposts around the Pacific remained sparse, and any European presence on the newly described islands and archipelagoes within the ocean was discontinuous. For good reason, several scholars of the early European presence in the Pacific have described the mariners, travelers and even settlers as 'beachcombers' or even 'ghosts'.[13]

In the absence of settled posts, which would have had formal political (and military) representation from their originating nation, European authorities instead delegated the capacity to deliberate legal and political affairs to naval officers, sometimes even to captains of merchant vessels. Well into the nineteenth century, American trading ventures into the Pacific were undertaken by private initiative; the first vessels to go into the Pacific Northwest were funded by Boston merchants, for example, although they bore official letters from Congress, by which the United States outsourced the risk and effort.

In similar fashion, American whalers, Russian fur traders and French explorers represented their various nations, remotely and haphazardly, with captains of vessels given considerable autonomy as to how they would behave toward others.

Simply using rather than replacing naval or merchant marine command made some sense, given that European ships had been the exclusive agents of foreign authority within the Pacific Ocean basin for so long. Why not begin there, with a modified, if not reformed version of military command at sea? At first, European governments began to regulate how naval commanders treated any people they might encounter en route; later, they extended this somewhat reformed behaviour as the new standard for governing individuals on ships as well as settlers ashore.

The first reform was to stop kidnapping pilots. In the absence of navigational information, and as a continuing sign of the terribly slow accumulation of knowledge about the Pacific, captives kept being taken during the early eighteenth century – even when mariners were navigating stretches of water that had been known to Europeans since the sixteenth century. Putting geographical knowledge on paper, back in Europe, was in this case not definitive; the Pacific may have been acquiring known dimensions and land features on maps and globes within Europe, but that did not invariably translate to the ocean's knowability among mariners who navigated it.

The practice of kidnapping pilots ceased, not because of greater knowledge of the Pacific, but as European mariners began to make decisions, informed by their ruling powers, about which populations were not to be harrassed in this way. At first, Europeans stopped taking other Europeans. They also switched to hiring rather than kidnapping Asians, probably to avoid annoying ruling powers with which they might want to trade. By the early 1700s, mariners became wary about taking native Americans. Their new stance implied another larger geopolitical context. In the years leading up to the Seven Years' War, Europeans had become aware that effective diplomacy with native Americans was the key to their imperial ambitions. The Indians themselves knew this and, as a recent generation of historians of North America have shown, the search for alliances among various European and native American groups was a persistent and important feature of warfare and trade throughout the eighteenth century.[14]

The trends also reflected the global geopolitics of empire, in which a variety of people who had once been forced onto ships were now given more careful consideration. Englishmen had long been impressed into naval service in times of war, for example, while French convicts had served as galley slaves in the Mediterranean.

African captives, transported from the interior of the continent, were transferred to European ships to be sold as slaves in the Americas. Prisoners of war taken in naval battles were kept to be ransomed. When these practices had been unquestioned, the taking of captives within the Pacific to serve as unwilling pilots seemed unobjectionable – at least to the captors. But as naval impressment and the Atlantic slave trade began to be questioned, and after France abolished galley slavery in 1748, it began to be less acceptable to take people aboard ships against their will, particularly if it might impair, rather than enhance, imperial goals. A variety of people would be reduced to unfree statuses within the Pacific – prisoners of war, slaves, convicts, and indentured labourers among them – and some would be used to yield information. But not aboard ships, where captivity and knowledge were uncoupled.[15]

However reformed, naval command was a poor model for imperial government in the Pacific. In quick succession, two Royal Navy men came to grief over their inflexible determination to keep order within Pacific contexts. Although fans of James Cook point out that his early career showed he had a gift for command, measured and reasonable, even they must concede that his patience and judgement shrank during his final two Pacific voyages. He was anxious lest his men seem to challenge his authority, and furious whenever native people did so. His newfound capacity to whip, mutilate or otherwise punish individuals who took ship's property was especially dangerous in eroding any welcome for his ships. After evading an attempt on his life in Tonga, his luck ran out in Hawai'i, where in 1779 he pursued some local men who had appropriated a ship's boat, and was killed by them.[16]

One of Cook's officers, William Bligh, was convinced that his commander could have been saved by responsible action on the part of the men who had accompanied him to the fatal Hawai'ian beach. Because they were tired of Cook's disciplinarianism, they were complicit in his death. From this episode, Bligh may have decided that more discipline, not less, was necessary. His command of HMAV *Bounty* (1787–9), during which his short-tempered perfectionism concluded in the famous mutiny led by Fletcher Christian, was proof of that. Bligh later extended his exacting sense of authority to dry land. While acting as governor of New South Wales, the British colony in what was not yet called Australia, his attempted reforms from 1806 onwards alienated many leading civilians as well as the soldiers who were competitors for control in the colony. Bligh was arrested in 1808 and kept prisoner for a year until he at last agreed to leave New South Wales. A trial of his chief antagonist led to that man's conviction, in effect a legal exoneration of Bligh, and a statement that British authority in the Pacific must radiate outwards from the homeland through its constituted officials – clear in theory, though not yet in practice.[17]

Still less did Europeans manage firmly to claim other parts of the Pacific. California is a good case in point. Any well-schooled child in the Golden State can recite the sequence of national flags that once flew over the territory now contained in the state: Spain, England, Russia and Mexico, which were then succeeded by ensigns featuring the stars or bears of various independent English-speaking republics, and only in 1850 by the Stars and Stripes of the United States, which created a still restive border between Mexican Baja California and the US 'alta' California. At no point did California's native inhabitants have reason to accept any of these fluttering claims to their territories, which only adds to the sense of conflicted and decidedly underdetermined destiny for this part of the Pacific Rim. The status of the different islands within the ocean was likewise indeterminate. France would not secure claims to Tahiti, let alone the rest of 'French Polynesia', until well into the nineteenth century; British command of Australia could not be considered as definitive until 1863, when the Northern Territory was annexed to South Australia.

And whatever the consolidation of western European empires over the interior parts of the Pacific, it was immediately contested by emerging, westernised powers that resided closer to that ocean. The United States and Russia were the first to do so, both of them entering the fur trade in the Pacific Northwest, with Russia setting up permanent posts from Unalaska to California. In parallel, the United States made commercial and later political interventions in Hawai'i, which effectively blocked British pretensions to the islands. The Japanese later would demonstrate their desire for sea routes and footholds within its eastern ocean, no longer a barrier between themselves and the rest of the world, but a way to claim the world on their own terms. Even in these cases, the Pacific claims were belated. Alaska and Hawai'i would not be admitted to the United States until 1959.[18]

★ ★ ★

If we must conclude that empire was built in the Pacific belatedly and brokenly, this is not to say that nothing happened between 1513 and 1808. Rather, stripped of civic consequence, puzzled by the seascapes and landscapes they encountered, reduced to bare bodies that steadily lost teeth to scurvy, Europeans who ventured into the Pacific learned to think of that part of the globe as the realm of nature, a place of material forces that might someday be decoded by science. To be sure, they knew that nature existed everywhere. Likewise, Europeans were active in pursuing science elsewhere, within Europe itself and in a variety of colonised settings. But if there is a historically unusual proportion between culture and nature, it occurred in the Pacific before empire, where European attempts to control and comprehend the natural world did not operate within a stable sociopolitical foundation for science.[19]

If dominion over people and sovereignty over territory were slow and difficult for Europeans to achieve, transformation of the Pacific's natural worlds proceeded without formal empire. Credit must be given to the historian who has done the most to analyse this scenario, Alfred W. Crosby, whose seminal *The Columbian Exchange: Biological and Cultural Consequences of 1492* (1972) presented the natural world as an essential part of empire, not just a passive backdrop to it. Colonisation represented flows not only of human beings, but also of the many other natural entities that could be connected to them, from tiny microbes to large ruminants. The traffic went both ways, with potatoes going to Europe as sugar went to the Americas. And yet because Europeans carried with them contagious diseases to which Americans had no resistance, the exchange was always uneven, with well-fed European populations sending people to places depopulated by epidemics. Even more pertinent to Pacific History was Crosby's *Ecological Imperialism: The Biological Expansion of Europe, 900–1900* (1986), which used examples from Pacific islands and from Australia to show how natural worlds were transformed almost as soon as Europeans arrived in them.[20]

As early as the late sixteenth century, commentators noted how Spanish settlements had significantly altered the Pacific coasts of its empire. In South America, where corn had once grown, and llamas had grazed, wheat and cattle signified Iberian inhabitation; garlic and onions forever transformed American cooking, just as tomatoes and potatoes were doing in Europe. Although settlers prized European crops as signifiers of European heritage and social status, that did not prevent the Spaniards from transplanting several American products to their settlements in the Philippines, including chilies, tomatoes and corn. So readily did some of these non-human invaders adapt to new environments that they went wild. They did so almost as quickly as they arrived, so, as early as the end of the seventeenth century, for example, herds of feral horses were described as swarming along the coast of Chile.[21]

From these observations, it seems, Europeans may have begun to regard their domesticates as obliging shock troops. Certainly, the mariners who made their way into the Pacific from the Atlantic Ocean, via Cape Horn or the Strait of Magellan, were grateful for the untended European provisions they found on uninhabited islands. The best examples of this were the small islands of Juan Fernández, off present-day Chile. The islands' discoverer, Fernández himself, is blamed for the first introduction of four goats in 1540, though several subsequent visitors probably restocked that primal herd and made other additions. By the late seventeenth century, the islands were overrun by goats, rats and cats. As Fernández had expected, the goats were handy for passers-by in search of food. That was certainly true for Alexander Selkirk, one prototype for Robinson Crusoe, who was stranded on one of the islands and resorted to the goats for food, clothing and sexual relief. Visitors to Juan Fernández, including Selkirk's rescuers (who enjoyed their host's goat stew), noted that the cats, which were preoccupied with decimating the islands' bird populations, had done little to get rid of the almost equally damaging rats.[22]

Juan Fernández was only one of a series of islands where Europeans were learning that their activities, including the introduction of new species, as well as felling of timber, could have dire consequences. As Richard Grove has demonstrated, islands were the first physical environments where observers witnessed actual extinctions, as with the dodo of Mauritius, which had vanished probably around 1662. This new consciousness about the frailty of islands as natural arenas was in contrast to the prevailing sense that continents, let alone oceans, were vast, replenishing and unchangeable. In these larger places, the disappearance of native animals was often assumed to be the result of their migration. On islands, that comforting thought was hard to sustain. But its corollary, that islands could be easily transformed for human convenience, seems to have provided an alternative form of comfort.[23]

For that reason, John Byron's Pacific-bound expedition (1764–6) was tasked with creating a series of useful, stepping-stone-like outposts into and over the Pacific waters that were still assumed to be uninhabited. At the Falklands, which the British had claimed (not least because it was a stopping point before entry into the Strait of Magellan), the surgeon of Byron's relief vessel, the *Tamar*, 'made a pretty little Garden near the Watering Place which we surrounded with a Fence of Turf, for the benefit of those that may come next'.

The surgeon did the same at Tinian, for the same reason. Those efforts were meant to replicate the usefulness of the Juan Fernández Islands – just as well, given that the Spanish had garrisoned the islands precisely to prevent them from being used by non-Spaniards. The idea of convenient stepping stones across the ocean would mean that many more goats, and so on, were scattered into Pacific islands.[24]

This was the case even after Europeans began to integrate inhabited Polynesia into their geography. Although western travellers welcomed, and exploited, the hospitality of the humans on these islands, they assumed that the tropical sites could be much more intensively cultivated using iron tools, domesticated animals and crops adapted to warm and moist climates. Samuel Wallis had fruit stones and garden seeds planted on Tahiti, and he gave away pairs of fowls to breed and a cat 'big with kitten'. He regretted he had no pregnant goat to bestow on the island (his billy goat had died at sea). Bougainville, who adored the 'beautiful disorder which it was never in the power of art to imitate' on Tahiti, nevertheless had a garden sown with European vegetables and gave his island contacts sets of breeding ducks and turkeys. Sometimes, the Polynesians welcomed these gifts. The animals, in particular, resembled the manufactured goods that indicated access to – and sometimes alliance with – European visitors, and also offered new sources of food. One of Tahiti's leading women had, by the time of Bligh's first extended visit to the island, a favourite cat she had received from Cook. At that point, it is possible that introduced European pigs, which outweighed their Polynesian cousins, had shouldered them out of some coastal parts of Tahiti.[25]

These processes would continue onwards (with swine or other European animals), to be repeated on many other islands, sometimes to the detriment of native flora and fauna. It is, of course, the case that this was a historical repetition – Pacific islands had already gone through a phase of settlement, including the introduction of domestic animals, thousands of years earlier. But the European presence brought a more intensified use of land, for the moment on the edges of islands, later more deeply into their interiors. And the eventual arrival of settled agriculture and domestic animals in Australia would represent an unprecedented transformation of that part of the Pacific.[26]

Contagious disease was an invader with more directly deadly consequences, in this case entirely unprecedented. In some ways, the bundle of Old World contagions were worse killers in the Pacific than in the Atlantic worlds. In the latter, at the least, syphilis had been known, even as smallpox, especially, was a terrible scourge. But in no part of the Pacific (except perhaps part of the coasts of the Americas) did the inhabitants have resistance to either. In the first two decades of contact, venereal diseases, tuberculosis and other contagions became endemic on Tahiti, whose population was estimated to have declined from 200,000 in 1772 to only 30,000 by the time of Bligh's visit with the *Bounty*. The first epidemic in Australia, possibly of smallpox, among the Aboriginal inhabitants around Port Jackson (Sydney) in 1789, is a usually forgotten and yet critical event in that historically famous year, representing, as it did, the arrival of rapidly transmitted contagious diseases in the South Pacific. Here again, the Europeans were not innocent of what they were doing. Although there had been some initial confusion, in the sixteenth- and seventeenth-century Americas, as to the source of the epidemics, by the late eighteenth century in the Pacific, knowledge was dawning that the comparable episodes were not indigenous events, but had been caused by the outsiders. The British and the French indignantly blamed each other for the introduction of sexually transmitted diseases to Tahiti. They might have conceded that the shared rivalry between their nations had carried the scourge there, along with the pigs and the cats.[27]

Western science was another export, and one that also emphasised Europeans' assumption that the Pacific was a distinctive natural space, and they themselves distinctive investigators into it. During the eighteenth century, science became a notable part of imperial expeditions. Between 1698 and 1700 Edmond Halley charted magnetic variation in the Atlantic Ocean; and in the 1730s Pierre Louis Maupertuis and Charles Marie de La Condamine carried out important geodetic expeditions. But the most formalised and ambitious of such efforts were projected for Pacific voyages, particularly to observe a pair of transits of Venus across the Sun, a once-in-a-lifetime opportunity for European astronomers to calculate the distance between the Sun and the Earth. Europe offered only limited visibility of the events, and multiple sites of data collection were in any case necessary. Colonised parts of the world were well suited for this, including the borders of the Pacific, as in Spanish California, but the lack of empire within the Pacific Ocean was a serious problem. The necessary equipment and experts would have to be shipped out. And so it was done, a great experiment in floating science. Bougainville set out in 1766 with plans to make observations of Venus. Commanding the *Endeavour* on his first Pacific voyage, Cook did the same, with an even more complex array of scientific instruments and naturalists to be unpacked and set up at what would be called 'Point Venus' on Tahiti, the nearest approximation of Salomon's House to exist before the modern period.[28]

It is significant that members of these and similar expeditions thought that some Pacific Islanders might be partners in scientific work, rather than unwilling providers of navigational advice. By the 1760s, with the path-breaking voyages into the middle of the Pacific, European voyagers had announced that they would offer no violence to anyone they met, and would not carry away anyone against his or her will. Whether this was universally honoured is impossible to verify. But it is true that the only Pacific Islanders who are known to have sailed away with Europeans had done so voluntarily. Philip Carteret pointedly renamed a Melanesian volunteer 'Joseph Freewill'. At Tahiti, Bougainville recruited a Tahitian man named Ahu-turu; James Cook took the Ra'iatean man named Mai. The most celebrated of informants was the Ra'iatean man named Tupaia, whom Cook recruited on Tahiti, along with his servant, a boy named Taiata. As a priest-navigator, Tupaia was especially prized for his information about the islands around Tahiti. A map printed in 1778, based on a prototype on which Cook and Tupaia had collaborated, was given the title, 'A Chart representing the Isles of the South Sea … collected from the Accounts of Tupaya' (Figure 3.2).[29]

It has been a signal effort in the history of science, in the past decade, to emphasise these non-European contributions to western science, in order, not least, to document the extent to which the science was, in some fundamental ways, not entirely western. Certainly, the contributions of the peoples of the greater Pacific to cartographic knowledge upholds this position while also underscoring how Europeans, without fixed imperial sites and colonial populations within the Pacific, needed and welcomed any help. Assessing Étienne Marchand's expedition into the Pacific, Claret Fleurieu urged 'all the nations which share the empire of the OCEAN' to share information about the seas. He criticised the United States and Spain for not allowing the publication of narratives for their recent voyages into the Pacific; the Spanish narratives were consigned to 'the dusty archives of some chancery', lost to the 'maritime coalition' of seafaring nations. For the most part, he meant western nations. But when he praised Tupaia's contributions to knowledge, Fleurieu suggested that the empire of the ocean might, somehow, include everyone within the Pacific. He predicted that Hawai'i would become the *'caravansary'* of the Pacific, a well-intentioned comparison between those islands and the polyglot, multi-ethnic caravan routes of the Near East.[30]

It would be difficult to demonstrate, however, that the peoples of the Pacific benefited from the science to which they made contributions. Indeed, it could be said that their efforts were often counterproductive to their own interests. Putting their part of the

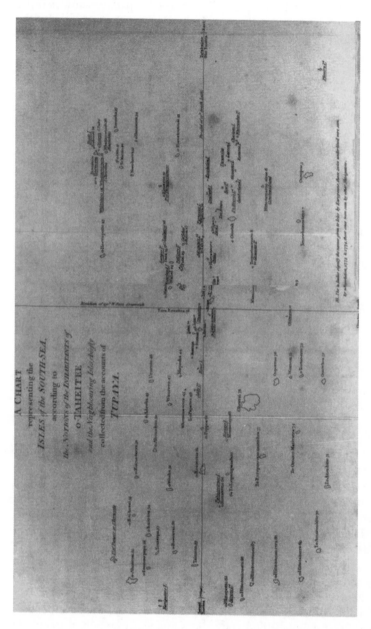

*Figure 3.2* Indigenous knowledge of the Pacific mapped.

*Source:* 'A Chart representing the Isles of the South Seas Collected from the Accounts of Tupaya', in Johann Reinhold Forster, *Observations Made during a Voyage round the World* (London, 1778).

world on the map made it easier for subsequent visitors to get to them; informing the visitors of the glories of their natural worlds created incentive for Europeans to return and exploit those resources, a process that would bring more greenery-chewing goats, more syphilis and smallpox, more extraction of labour, and more displacement from ancestral homelands.

In the end, the most telling and lasting of European actions taken across the Pacific could in fact be described as imperial, although it was something that was invisibly inscribed over the natural world. This was the placement of a 180th meridian, the line that would demarcate one global day from the next. 'The Circumnavigator's Paradox', as it had been known since the return of the Magellan expedition in 1522, showed that the globe may have shared a single solar day, but not all at the same time. Somewhere, a day ended and another began; at that point, a traveller gained or lost a day. But where was that point? Because they thought that Europe was the centre of the world, Europeans assumed that the critical temporal break must exist opposite to them, meaning somewhere in the Pacific. Each European nation put the Prime Meridian through its own capital, with the 180th at its globally opposite point. Pious mariners, who found themselves in different parts of the Pacific, were often befuddled or angered by the outcome: complete disagreement over what day Christians (or Muslims) ought to attend weekly religious services proved a significant challenge to the presumed universality of these religions.[31]

In practice, western mariners of all nations would eventually adopt the line of longitude through Greenwich, England, as their Prime Meridian, because they had, since 1767, relied on the annual publication of the Greenwich-based *Nautical Almanac*. Accordingly, the present-day location of the International Date Line (IDL), 180 degrees away from Greenwich, is based on long-standing maritime custom, even as it has never been adjudicated by any international body. (Several international congresses would in the nineteenth century debate other possible solutions, without resolution.) A highly imperialist vision of global time was in this way instantiated over the planet, with a key demarcation run straight through the Pacific Ocean, though this was quite definitely a part of empire 'acquired in a fit of absence of mind', because it was never formally done – custom gave it authority. It preceded any territorial pretensions within the Pacific, imperium over the planet if not over people. (Later, it was adjusted to empire, made zig-zag, in order to keep different imperial archipelagoes on the same clock.) In this way, Europeans' imagining of the Pacific space as blank, as the zone where one day became another, was a legacy of their ignorance at what actually existed within it.[32]

None of the residents of islands through which the IDL passes would have appreciated their being described as living at the back of beyond, where time ended, rather than where it began. Continuing adjustment of the IDL's zigs and zags (as recently happened in Sāmoa), and occasional postcolonial suggestions that it be swapped with the line through Greenwich, in order to give Europeans a sense of how it feels to live at the back of beyond, show the lasting problem of early European comprehension of the Pacific before empire: as a natural world without civil meanings. Indeed, the political consequences of imperialism may be fleeting, compared to the natural damage that European expansion caused within the Pacific basin. Filipinos managed to get the Spanish out of their islands in 1898, for example, but rats still infest the Juan Fernández islands. For the natural world, there is no postcolonial condition. The history of the Pacific before empire is not unique in its collision between nature and culture. But the starkness of the contrast within that context may help us to see how this is the shared human condition everywhere.

## Notes

1. Francis Bacon, *The New Atlantis* (1627), in Bacon, *The Major Works*, ed. Brian Vickers (Oxford, 2002), pp. 457–89.
2. Robert N. Proctor, 'Agnotology: A Missing Term to Describe the Cultural Production of Ignorance (and Its Study)', in Proctor and Londa Schiebinger, eds., *Agnotology: The Making and Unmaking of Ignorance* (Stanford, 2008), pp. 1–36.
3. See Damon Salesa, 'The Pacific in Indigenous Time', ch. 2 in this volume.
4. Felipe Fernández-Armesto, *Pathfinders: A Global History of Exploration* (New York, 2006), pp. 1–152.
5. Ibid., pp. 153–242; Sanjay Subrahmanyam, *The Career and Legend of Vasco da Gama* (Cambridge, 1997).
6. Martin Waldseemüller, *The Naming of America: Martin Waldseemüller's 1507 World Map and the Cosmographiae introductio*, trans. John W. Hessler (London, 2008).
7. Antonio Pigafetta, *Magellan's Voyage: A Narrative Account of the First Circumnavigation*, trans. and ed. R. A. Skelton (New York, 1969).
8. Jonathan Lamb, *Preserving the Self in the South Seas, 1680–1840* (Chicago, 2001); Joyce E. Chaplin, 'Earthsickness: Circumnavigation and the Terrestrial Human Body, 1520–1800', *Bulletin of the History of Medicine* 86 (2012), 515–42.

9. O. H. K. Spate, *The Spanish Lake* (London, 1979).

10. Stephanie Mawson, 'Disobedience and Control in the Early Modern Pacific: Labour Disputes on the Margins of the Spanish Empire', paper given at Fourth University of Sydney International History Graduate Intensive, July 2012.

11. Joyce E. Chaplin, *Round about the Earth: Circumnavigation from Magellan to Orbit* (New York, 2012), pp. 38–9, 106–7.

12. Chaplin, *Round about the Earth*, pp. 32–3, 51–2, 80, 91–2.

13. Greg Dening, *Islands and Beaches: Discourse on a Silent Land: Marquesas, 1774–1880* (Carlton, Vic., 1980); David A. Chappell, *Double Ghosts: Oceanian Voyagers on Euroamerican Ships* (Armonk, NY, 1997).

14. Chaplin, *Round about the Earth*, pp. 99, 101, 113.

15. Cf. Anne Salmond, 'Kidnapped: Tuki and Huri's Involuntary Visit to Norfolk Island in 1793', in Robin Fisher and Hugh Johnston, eds., *From Maps to Metaphors: The Pacific World of George Vancouver* (Vancouver, BC, 1993), pp. 191–226.

16. Anne Salmond, *The Trial of the Cannibal Dog: The Remarkable Story of Captain Cook's Encounters in the South Seas* (New Haven, 2003).

17. Greg Dening, *Mr. Bligh's Bad Language: Passion, Power, and Theatre on the Bounty* (Cambridge, 1992); Anne Salmond, *Bligh: William Bligh in the South Seas* (Berkeley, 2011).

18. On the 'unevenness' of colonial histories, see Nicholas Thomas, 'The Age of Empire in the Pacific', ch. 4 in this volume, p. 76.

19. Compare Sujit Sivasundaram, 'Science', ch. 11 in this volume.

20. Alfred W. Crosby, *The Columbian Exchange: Biological and Cultural Consequences of 1492* (Westport, CT, 1972); Crosby, *Ecological Imperialism: The Biological Expansion of Europe, 900–1900* (Cambridge, 1986).

21. Crosby, *The Columbian Exchange*, pp. 64–121.

22. Chaplin, *Round about the Earth*, p. 98.

23. Richard H. Grove, *Green Imperialism: Colonial Expansion, Tropical Island Edens, and the Origins of Environmentalism, 1600–1860* (Cambridge, 1995), pp. 1–308.

24. John Byron, *Byron's Journal of His Circumnavigation, 1764–1766*, ed. Robert E. Gallagher (Cambridge, 1964), pp. 60, 122.

25. Salmond, *Bligh*, pp. 145, 161; *An Account of the Voyages Undertaken by the Order of His Present Majesty for Making Discoveries in the Southern Hemisphere*, ed. John Hawkesworth, 3 vols. (London, 1773), I, pp. 469, 476, 488; Louis-Antoine de Bougainville, *A Voyage round the World*, trans. John Reinhold Forster (London, 1772), pp. 231, 244.

26. J. R. McNeill, 'Of Rats and Men: A Synoptic Environmental History of the Island Pacific', *Journal of World History* 5 (1994), 299–349; Jennifer Newell, *Trading Nature: Tahitians, Europeans, and Ecological Exchange* (Honolulu, 2010); and Ryan Tucker Jones, 'The Environment', ch. 6 in this volume.

27. Salmond, *Bligh*, p. 195; Crosby, *Ecological Imperialism*, pp. 196–216, 232–4, 309–11.

28. Harry Woolf, *The Transits of Venus: A Study of Eighteenth-Century Science* (London, 1959).
29. Glyndwr Williams, 'Tupaia: Polynesian Warrior, Navigator, High Priest— and Artist', in Felicity A. Nussbaum, ed., *The Global Eighteenth Century* (Baltimore, 2003), pp. 38–51; Chaplin, *Round about the Earth*, pp. 128–9.
30. Simon Schaffer, Lissa Roberts, Kapil Raj and James Delbourgo, eds., *The Brokered World: Go-betweens and Global Intelligence, 1770–1820* (Sagamore Beach, MA, 2009); C. P. Claret Fleurieu, *A Voyage round the World, Performed by … Étienne Marchand*, 2 vols. (London, 1801), I, pp. xcix, cxi, 155–7, 162, 171, II, p. 8.
31. Ian R. Bartky, *One Time Fits All: The Campaigns for Global Uniformity* (Stanford, 2007), pp. 1–4.
32. Bartky, *One Time Fits All*, pp. 21–120.

# 4

# The Age of Empire in the Pacific

## Nicholas Thomas

If you spend any time at all in the Marquesas Islands, and ask locals where something or someone is, you soon become familiar with directional terms that, you realise, govern life in the islands. You will be told that a person is *'i tai*, towards the shore or sea, or *'i uta*, inland, up the valley, towards the mountain, and you find that almost everywhere you go involves movement seawards, or landwards. Life, places and social relationships are distributed one way or the other, on this axis. In these same islands, a historian or anthropologist might begin by assuming that islands amounted to, or corresponded with, social units. Any one island, you might suppose, would be, or would have been, divided into tribes, yet the populations of these tribes together surely constituted some unity, relative to the peoples of other islands. Obvious this might be, it would also have been false of collectivities in the historic period. The peoples of valleys did constitute social groupings; in larger valleys there were several such groups; but they commonly shared an ancestry with people on another island, while being strangers to, perhaps enemies of, the peoples of the valleys that neighboured their own. Everywhere in Oceania, geography and political affiliation was lived and social in these senses rather than merely natural: witness the contrast between saltwater and bush people commonly encountered in island Melanesia, for example.[1] Geography cannot, in other words, be read off the map; it must be understood through prisms of local practice, the mode of inhabiting the environment, the places that gift-giving linked.

These observations are tangential to the larger purpose of this chapter, which is to attempt a concise survey of what empire was, and was not, in the Pacific over the long nineteenth century. I focus on the Pacific Islands rather than on the rims of the adjacent continents, or linked regions such as insular Southeast Asia, in order to try to present a coherent overview of a succession of key engagements in this region, beginning with exploration and turning to commerce, evangelism, indentured labour and the establishment of formal colonial administration. At the outset it should be added that although the latter came after the former, these forms of imperial engagements carried on in parallel: exploration did not stop when trade or evangelism began, nor was missionary work done and dusted before the labour trade was inaugurated. To the contrary, it is vital to the story that these projects more or less overlapped, and were in tension.

The tangent with which I began is essential to the argument, however, because the vantage point of this chapter, and the book as a whole – which considers large processes over the *longue durée*, with periodisation in mind – risks embracing a naturalism or physicalism in its characterisation of the geographical region that is its subject, and within which these historical processes evolved. In Oceania, 'the fifth part of the world',[2] it is too easy to envisage intrusions having consequences like ripples across a pond, or like tsunami, to adapt the figure more appropriate to the scale of the Pacific. And it is natural to speak of a 'wave' of missionisation or colonisation; this was the metaphor thematised in Kerry Howe's *Where the Waves Fall* (1984), which remains one of the stronger surveys of Pacific history of the last thirty or so years.[3]

My point is simply that even the most broad-brush of surveys needs to be situated within a human and social sense of Oceania's geography, of the paths and passages that have connected localities and islands. This makes a difference to how historic process is understood, since what came from elsewhere always entered into and became articulated with local geographies, even as it distorted or overrode them. This is crucial inasmuch as it underpins the fundamental characteristic of the Pacific's colonial histories: their unevenness. In one sense, the transformations that took place were the same, right across the Pacific: barter on the beach was succeeded by extractive commerce, ancestral religions were displaced almost everywhere by colonial Christianity, lands were appropriated, and varying proportions of the population drawn into wage labour. But these developments played out in different ways in different archipelagoes and within different, if proximate communities. If empire's reach into the Pacific appears extraordinary from a global perspective, its grasp within the region was often partial and insecure.[4] The London Missionary Society (LMS) did, for example, bring about an astonishing colonisation of consciousness among communities right across the ocean. But scholars are increasingly aware that whatever religious conversion amounted to, it looked and it looks different, from the inside out.[5]

At the time scholars of my generation were trained in Pacific History, the notion of the 'fatal impact' was routinely cited as the myth that it was our task to expose and replace.[6] 'Revisionists' have since been subjected to revision in turn, not once but several times (in the context of debate about the labour trade, for example),[7] but the fatal impact has not quite gone away, not only because variations upon imperial nostalgia remain compelling for popular western imaginaries, but also because no succinct rubric emerged that captured any succeeding paradigm. A history is not, of course, a marketing project: it should not need a slogan or strapline, but the elusiveness or awkwardness of any catchy characterisation may signal that those who struggle to interpret and narrate Pacific histories have some way to go.

## Exploration

Pacific intellectuals such as the late Epeli Hau'ofa have been understandably irritated by the preoccupation with Captain James Cook among the western public and among western historians.[8] Certainly, Cook has been treated as a superstar to an absurd extent, and as a result has arguably been misunderstood by both worshippers and detractors. Yet, if an effort to map the age of empire in the Pacific, and the creativity of Islanders in that context, has little interest in the cult of Cook's personality, it must try to come to grips with the very varied ramifications of Cook's three expeditions. The previous chapter reviews the longer history of exploration in the Pacific,[9] but the six voyages undertaken by Wallis, Byron, Cook and Vancouver in the period from the 1760s to the early 1790s, together with those of their French and Spanish contemporaries, transformed the character and pace of European engagement in the Pacific, in a manner that was to have far-reaching consequences and that, in many respects, shaped the patterns of contact and colonisation over the succeeding half-century.

In particular, Cook's voyages were different from any that came before, not because they were exploratory rather than commercial or military – there had been more or less purely investigative expeditions before. Cook's were different because the investigative role was embraced with unprecedented energy – these were peculiarly extended and sustained missions, that simply went to many more places, and dedicated more extended effort, than any predecessor had, to the investigation of parts of the world until then unknown or only partially known to Europeans. Nor anyway were the ventures limited to narrowly navigational or geographical inquiries; they were embedded in a wide-ranging, genuinely curious natural history.

Coasts actually were traced systematically, lands and islands were visited and studied, resources were observed, and plants and animals collected, in astonishing quantities. Most importantly, this inquisitiveness extended to people, to their manners and customs, to their institutions, and to their knowledge.[10]

Some degree of interaction with locals, therefore some gathering of knowledge about them, was unavoidable in a practical sense, because ships needed food, firewood and fresh water, and it was easier to obtain whatever could be had through negotiation and trade rather than through violence and seizure. But both official instructions and the mariners' inclinations prompted not only commerce but also social engagement, to whatever extent Islanders would welcome or suffer. Both the voyagers themselves, and British propaganda of the time, made these meetings out to be benevolent. Though some Islanders trenchantly resisted initial landings, in the Society Islands and Hawai'i, among other places, they mostly soon discovered an interest in engagement that converged fortuitously with that of the Europeans. They made the most of their visitors, gifts were exchanged, meals and physical intimacies were shared, ceremonies were performed, while people were sketched, wordlists were compiled, arts and manufactures were collected, again in astonishing quantities. Though many of the artefacts collected during Cook's voyages were lost during or after the voyages, and many disappeared into private collections, never to be convincingly provenanced to Cook again, over 2,500 objects are distributed among museum collections in Europe, North America, Australasia, southern Africa and Russia – their dispersal an index in itself of the reach of the natural history that the voyages generated. What might be called 'reverse collections' of iron, fabric, mirrors, books and many other things were acquired by Islanders, the most prestigious pieces, such as a portrait of Cook, being monopolised by pre-eminent political and ritual leaders, the rest distributed through customary networks of reciprocity.

During the first expedition, some four months were spent at Tahiti in order to prepare for and perform the astronomical observations that were ostensibly the voyage's aim. If the necessity was scientific rather than social, the upshot was a far longer period of interaction and observation than any European since Álvaro de Mendaña in the late sixteenth and early seventeenth centuries had had anywhere in the Pacific beforehand – Bougainville, for instance, had spent only nine days at the island. The visit was followed by a complete circuit of both the North and South islands of New

Zealand, involving a good deal of contact with Māori at a number of points around the coasts. Though the Spanish who visited, and settled missionaries, on Tahiti's eastern peninsula, would be there for longer, Cook's voyages acquired almost immediate fame, and the publications arising from them were enormously influential for European understandings of Oceania for decades afterwards. It was the second voyage, especially, that featured a genuinely unprecedented series of meetings with Islanders: islands such as the Marquesas that had not been visited since 1595 were called at, and a considerable amount of time spent in Vanuatu and New Caledonia as well as in various parts of Polynesia. Again, encounter was not an aim in itself. Cook was dedicating the southern summers to the search for a continent, but his cruises through the frigid Antarctic waters could not be sustained through the colder months, during which his ships returned to the tropics for refreshment, and as it were incidentally, further exploration.

An obvious consequence of these many visits and contacts was a new level of western knowledge concerning the Pacific. A few of the mariners acquired something approaching fluency in Tahitian, many others acquired some competence in Tongan and Māori among other Polynesian languages. None of the Europeans were equipped, either linguistically or methodologically, to study matters such as religious belief, in anything like the systematic fashion of the twentieth-century ethnographer. But with respect to what could be observed or asked about straightforwardly, their accounts were good as far as they went. Subsistence activities, crafts, forms of body decoration and the conduct of rites were all carefully described; political relationships were among the matters that tended to be more roughly translated. But the question of whether the emerging European knowledge of the Pacific was accurate or otherwise is less important than the fact that it did emerge. It created a published literature. Voyagers who followed thought they knew what sorts of people were to be found, in Tahiti or Tonga; they thought they knew what kinds of resources they might traffic in, and what trade would be wanted in return. They thought they knew which islands they would run a risk in visiting, and at which they might count on hospitality.

Equally obviously, Islanders began to know Europeans. Certain Islanders, such as the Tahitian high chief, Tu, became intimate with particular Europeans such as Cook and, myths of benevolence aside, Tu among a number of others appear to have counted Cook as a true ally, and maybe even a friend. More generally, Islanders came to know the effect of European weapons, and their own desires for certain

European goods, particularly iron, and manufactured cloth – which they treated, not as a novelty, but as a form of their own barkcloth, which had always had not only quotidian but refined forms, associated with prestige, sanctity and sovereignty. Introduced fabrics, for as long as they remained rare, were assimilated to that special class.[11]

A good deal more could be said about various aspects of this emerging mutual knowledge. But, interesting as this two-sided process is, it was not all that was going on. Cook's voyages also enabled Islanders to get to know each other. 'Omai' (Mai) has become an iconic figure for having been the first Polynesian to visit Britain. Yet what was equally or more important about his biography, and that of Mahine, who joined the *Resolution* during its South Seas cruise of 1774, was their observation of many parts of the islands, of places and peoples well beyond the range of customary voyaging. He encountered Rapa Nui, the Marquesas, New Caledonia and New Zealand; some people from those places garnered through his person and his conversation, some knowledge of Tahiti, among other places. Social and cultural affinities were discovered or rediscovered, comparisons were made, those who visited, those who were visited, and those who stayed at home but eventually heard these travellers' tales all began to acquire a knowledge of their own region different to any that they had had before. These meetings created a cross-cultural knowledge similar in scope to the comparative understanding of manners and customs acquired by Johann Reinhold Forster and other such naturalists. This indigenous knowledge in a sense anticipated the encompassing Oceanic imagining that Epeli Hau'ofa would articulate so affirmatively in the 1990s, 'the ocean in us'.[12]

## Commerce

Of the various ramifications of Cook's voyages, two are particularly salient. First, various seamen who collected furs during the cruise along the far northwestern American coast were able to sell them to Chinese markets when, fortuitously from their perspective, the *Resolution* and *Discovery* called at Macau on the way back to Europe, after Cook's death and the final foray into Arctic waters. Though the 'fur trade' had already been inaugurated by Russians who had undertaken comparatively short voyages from Kamchatka, earlier in the eighteenth century, this commerce gained new trans-Pacific momentum as Cook's former men launched their own voyages soon afterwards.[13] Secondly and notoriously, it was upon Sir Joseph Banks's recommendation that Botany Bay was selected as an appropriate site for a British penal colony, the upshot being the First Fleet of 1788 and the Sydney settlement. Early on, the shortages of food motivated voyages to Tahiti to obtain pork;[14] as the colony grew, it became a base for extractive and trading voyages, to New Zealand for timber and for seals. From the 1790s the involvement of ships from New England mounted and later the whaling enterprise in the Pacific got under way. The 1790s thus marked a sea change in the intensity of contact. Whereas visits to most archipelagoes prior to that decade had been occasional and widely separated, the best-known ports on islands such as Tahiti and Oahu were now being visited by several vessels a year, very soon by several dozen.

The scope for resource extraction from the Pacific Islands began to excite Europeans during the first years of the nineteenth century. A beachcomber named Oliver Slater, who had earlier spent time in Canton and knew of the value of sandalwood in the Chinese markets, recognised the wood in Fiji, and probably specifically along the coasts of the second-largest island of Vanua Levu. He was able to secure backing for a voyage from Sydney, and Philip Gidley King, then governor of New South Wales, was troubled that Americans appeared to gaining control of south Pacific commerce, and therefore supported at least two semi-official trading voyages by ships based in the colony in 1807–8. Although violence between Fijians and traders was chronic, and Fijians scrambled to control the new resources that traders introduced, causing an escalation of local warfare, the wood was extensively exploited for over a decade, but largely cut out by 1816. Some timber was found towards the end of this period in the Marquesas, but stands on those relatively smaller islands were limited, and by 1817 little was left. In Hawai'i a sandalwood trade was carried on from 1816 to the mid-1820s. The focus of this commerce then shifted to Vanuatu and, subsequently, New Caledonia. Across all of these regions, considerable numbers of Islanders were involved in the trade, often as entrepreneurs rather than merely as labourers or suppliers. It is characteristic of the emerging cosmopolitanism of the Pacific in this period that one of the first voyages to southern Vanuatu, mounted by Captain Samuel Henry, the son of a missionary, took a Tongan labour force to the island, and this was quickly followed by a larger, Hawaiian-led enterprise, with two ships, one commanded by Boki, Kamehameha's Governor of Oahu. In early 1830, there were four ships off the island, which brought working parties of 113 Tongans, 130 Rotumans, 179 Hawaiians and over 100 Rotumans, and 200 Rotumans respectively. The Hawaiians approached the venture as one of conquest rather than trade, but the party was ravaged by disease (presumably by malaria, to which they had had no exposure) and the adventure was soon abandoned. If individual voyages were certainly high-risk enterprises, the values of cargoes were high – Shineberg estimated that Pacific sandalwood was worth at least £40 per ton – and on the Islanders' side, considerable volumes of trade goods were introduced into local communities in the context of this interaction.[15]

Around the time sandalwood was first extracted, traders became aware too that *bêche-de-mer* (sea cucumbers or trepang, *Holothurioidea*), which were not used as food in the islands, was regarded as a delicacy in China, and were to be found in considerable numbers in the extensive and shallow lagoons of various Pacific islands, including again Vanua Levu.[16] Agreements were made with local chiefs to procure, gut and cure *bêche-de-mer*; the operations required shore stations and hence protracted contacts between traders and Islanders. Some beachcombers became less hangers-on, on the fringes of indigenous communities, and more the agents of European merchants. Ships and shore stations themselves required supplies of food and firewood, access to fresh water, and men sought sexual services from Islander women. In some cases these were readily offered, in others neither were individuals disposed to provide physical intimacy, nor did communities see a sexual traffic as desirable or advantageous. Though the demographic histories of the islands of the Pacific are varied for many reasons, the fact that sexual exchanges started earlier, and took place far more extensively in eastern Polynesia than elsewhere must have had an impact on the relative incidence of sexually transmitted disease, upon relative rates of depopulation, and the resilience or otherwise of local institutions such as chiefly hierarchies, which over the longer term exhibited much greater continuity in western than eastern Polynesia.[17]

While sandalwood and *bêche-de-mer* are the textbook commodities of early Pacific trade, it is important to recall that cross-cultural exchange had many other dimensions. Natural specimens and artefacts were gathered in very considerable numbers and, as early as the 1830s, certain art forms such as Tahitian barkcloth (the making of which had lapsed, since imported fabrics were preferred) had essentially been sold out. Elsewhere, Islanders began to make artefacts for sale, at least occasionally, during the first half of the nineteenth century; forms such as model canoes, earlier made as children's toys, acquired a new life as souvenirs. Later, it appears to have been primarily missionaries who organised what were in effect craft workshops, encouraging the regular production of handicrafts for sale. Though the extent to which missions should engage in trade was controversial, and those who aspired to do so tended to be relatively unsuccessful, missions in due course created demand, particularly for imported cloth, and also encouraged church members to produce exportable commodities such as arrowroot, sold to benefit missions.

From the 1790s to around 1820, the archipelagoes of the Hawaiian and Society Islands could be seen as the crucibles of change across Oceania: they were the places most intensively visited, and also those that provided the launch sites for endeavours elsewhere. Contacts were typically far less frequent in much of Melanesia until the 1830s and subsequently, and more isolated islands such as Niue and Rapa Nui were seldom called at as late as the 1850s. But generally there were a host of consequences: ad hoc barter gave way to more regular trade, which was managed or monopolised to some degree by prominent chiefs and brokers; firearms were introduced, altering and often intensifying the pattern of local conflict; larger numbers of local men and some women worked as crew and thus travelled to Australasian, east Asian, New England and European home ports, as well as many ports of call in-between, a good many either returned or resettled on other Pacific islands, creating the beginnings of what would become in due course multicultural beach communities. On virtually every Pacific island, some kind of milieu would emerge, in some cases limited to a few individuals and households, in others a considerably bigger port community, consisting of such Islander travellers-turned-immigrants, beachcombers of European, Asian or Afro-American descent, white traders, and local partners and mixed families. These populations emerged and they became brokers for other sorts of contacts, and they represented significant expressions of colonial society, decades ahead of formal colonial ventures.

These ramifications were refracted across local forms of sociality with much resulting local variation. However, it was broadly the case that substantial new resources became available to local political players. Iron, fabrics and clothes, guns and ammunition, shell valuables, indigenous artefacts from other islands and communities, printed books and images, scissors and knives and many other imports all possessed, to varying degrees, high initial rarity values, and considerable longer-term use and prestige value in many communities. These dynamics acquired local intensity in particular cases, where traders were seeking, for example, localised stands such as sandalwood, meaning a succession of repeat visits to particular harbours and communities, and the channelling of substantial trade goods to particular chiefs and brokers in those localities. Given that what was traded in, in the case of the Fijian sandalwood trade, did not consist of trinkets of whatever sort, but rather the whale teeth (*tabua*) that locally represented the supreme exchange valuables, that could prospectively be gifted to secure political alliances and military support, the upshot was a period of competitive escalation. Groups that had already been rivalrous stepped up the level of ambition and conflict; their projects ranged more widely; the stakes were higher; fighting became more frequent and destructive. Chiefs, frequently misrecognised as kings by early visitors, made every effort to secure the pre-eminence they had been erroneously assumed to possess. While their campaigns were more or less successful in some cases (the ascendancy of the Pōmares and Kamehameha in the Society and Hawaiian islands respectively) in others what missionaries referred to as 'civil war', again assuming a form of political unity that was an aspiration of some parties rather than a pre-existing order, continued to break out and resurface for decades (in Tonga and Fiji, for example).

## Conversion

The less direct ramifications of Cook's voyages included the impact on the evangelical movement within Britain. Although missionary activity had a much longer history, involving not least the participation of the Catholic Church in the Iberian colonisation of central and southern America, the evangelical missionary effort, which was essentially a movement of dissenters that lacked backing on the part of the state or the navy, gained particular vigour in the 1790s and in succeeding decades. William Carey, one of the founders of the Baptist Missionary Society, was among those upon whom the published narratives and printed images from Cook's voyages had a profound effect. The empirical quality of these accounts and their graphic representations of human sacrifice and rumours of cannibalism gave the heathen societies that everyone knew existed beyond Europe a vivid reality and an immediacy that fired the imaginations of those who conceived of their religious commitments in activist terms. Relatively few – a tiny few – were actually interested in severing connections with kin and with home in order to dedicate their lives to missionary work. But a movement to sponsor those few was enthusiastically embraced by much wider communities, who would avidly consume missionary propaganda for decades to come.[18]

The Missionary Society, later known as the London Missionary Society, would become the most important agent of Protestant activity in the Pacific. Its initial plan was highly ambitious. Though focussed on Tahiti, it was anticipated that a Tahitian mission would be just one of a number of stations that would in due course take the word of God right across the islands of Oceania (Figure 4.1). Palau, well known to the European public as a result of George Keate's bestselling and sentimental *Account of the Pelew Islands* (1788, much reprinted and translated), was among the island groups considered appropriate for the settlement of missionary parties. Though neither the initial voyage nor any subsequent LMS expedition did in fact deposit missionaries there, a group were left in Tonga, and one man, William Pascoe Crook, elected to see what he could achieve alone at Tahuata in the Marquesas, after his prospective companion was too terrified by a night onshore to contemplate remaining there. Crook struggled to survive, let alone proselytise, and was fortunate to obtain passage back to England a couple of years later. Several of the group in Tonga were caught up in warfare and killed, the survivors departing on the first ship to pass by.[19] Even for the larger party on Tahiti, the initial years were extremely difficult for the missionaries, marked by a lack of security and an absence of 'progress' in their terms. They failed to gain a secure status within indigenous polities, or proximate

*Figure 4.1* 'The cession of the district of Matavai in the island of Otaheite to Captain James Wilson for the use of the missionaries' [179–?], painted by Robert Smirke; engraved by Francesco Bartolozzi.

to indigenous leaders, in part because they were unprepared to fight or to act as brokers in a trade for the guns and ammunition which by this time were the key imports that local powers sought. Whereas beachcombers, and notably Hawaiian beachcombers, made themselves indispensable to Pōmare partly because they did offer some military advantage, and thus entered the chief's inner circle, both ordinary people and leaders were ambivalent about the evangelicals, who might indeed facilitate access to other goods that Islanders sought, such as fabrics, but were also bothersome: their interventionist intentions and their wish to disrupt and displace customary ritual were recognised and initially considered ridiculous, where they were not actively resented.[20]

The reasons why Pacific populations did in due course embrace Christianity – and the actual meaning of the deceptively simple concept of 'conversion' – have been very extensively debated, as have the same issues in Africa and elsewhere. It may be obvious, but it is important to emphasise that there were various reasons for change across the Pacific. Christianity arrived in communities at different times, not merely in a chronological sense but relative to other developments that altered the context and apparent content of what the missionaries offered. In Tahiti, the evangelists arrived nearly thirty years after Cook, Bougainville and de Boenechea; the intervening period was marked not only by the growth of commerce, but also by the painfully deleterious impact of a succession of diseases, which Islanders saw European visitors as having brought. They therefore quite understandably perceived Europe as a source of harm, of mortal illness. In the Cook Islands, to take just one other example, the missionaries who arrived in the 1820s had been preceded by far fewer Europeans and by little exposure to introduced disease. Whereas the LMS in Tahiti were not the bringers of iron or of other prestigious items – they were just another odd set of Europeans – Cook Islanders in contrast identified them more closely with iron, novel valuables, hugely impressive ships and so forth. Elsewhere, in the Austral Islands in the early 1820s and later in many other places, 'conversion' was a local initiative, responsive to stories of transformation elsewhere, a step taken in the absence of any engagement with white missionaries.

Why, given the unpropitious circumstances, did the Tahitians turn towards Christianity? In reflecting upon this question it is important to recall that there was nothing unprecedented about a transfer of ritual affiliation. It is well known from Society Islands traditions that the cult of the god 'Oro, centred upon the great marae of Taputapuatea in Raiatea, had been embraced more widely throughout the Society

Islands at a late date, in the mid-eighteenth century. Particular cults were seen to bring and offer different forms of power and sanctity. Christianity did entail a positive draw – it had a close association with literacy which was considered a potent practice by Islanders and one that many embraced in advance of formal affiliation with the church – but it also surely gained ground in part through sheer attrition over an extraordinarily difficult period. By 1810, Tahitians particularly, and Society Islanders in general, had suffered four decades of malaise and depopulation. In a culture in which gods were propitiated and loved for their efficacy, a failure of morale can only have eroded support for customary priests and for the ancestral ritual regime (which had, in any case, always entailed some tensions between what the folklorist Teuira Henry referred to as 'family', 'national' and 'international' marae, the last category embracing ritual precincts such as Taputapuatea, which were acknowledged across the archipelago, rather than merely by Raiateans).[21] In other words, while the propensity of recent scholarship has been to affirm continuities in local culture, it is important to make distinctions between certain underlying values and assumptions, which no doubt have been more resilient, and commitments to particular cults, which individuals and communities have been prepared to surrender. There is a risk that an uncritical theoretical commitment to the paradigm of indigenous agency and cultural resilience has obscured the extent to which religious beliefs suffered fatigue and indeed failure among various populations at various times.

The second and third decades of the nineteenth century were critical for the LMS. By 1815 a Christian party among the Tahitian chiefs was in the ascendancy and some level of adherence to Christianity was becoming general among the population. The mission's ambitions were renewed by John Williams who arrived from England in 1818. He fully exploited what could be seen as the secret weapon of the evangelical missions. The sheer numbers of British missionaries were always small – amounting to just a few hundred over the period up to the 1860s, and that number included a good many who defected, died of illness, or otherwise abandoned the mission after just a few years. In other words the enterprise was simply never supported by a critical mass, by numbers sufficient to sustain effective engagement with more than a handful of local communities. Unless, that is, indigenous missionaries, mostly referred to as 'native teachers', were recruited and empowered to carry out the work. Their role would be vigorously debated; the 1828 polemic of the Russian explorer Otto von Kotzebue accused the LMS of pious bigotry and of stifling native societies. The critique incorporated a distorted account of the military successes of the Pōmares, but struck at the heart of the venture by ridiculing a project of civilisation that relied upon the efforts of 'half-savages' themselves supposedly educated by sailors-turned-preachers (the missionaries were typically of artisanal backgrounds, and benefitted only from basic seminary education, but in fact virtually none were maritime men); it was an absurdity he implied to imagine that natives might convert or civilise themselves.[22]

The missionaries themselves argued about the strengths and weaknesses of Islander workers but there is no doubt that the wider reach of the enterprise came to be entirely reliant upon them. John Williams devised what was in effect a method, that involved visiting 'heathen' islands, endeavouring to make an impression with his own presence, his ship and with trade goods, and leaving Islander missionaries or teachers with the people, whom he would revisit periodically. These Islanders also, of course, facilitated contact in the first place by acting as translators and through their understandings of local social protocols and strategies, particularly within Polynesia, where cultural affinities were sufficient to make them effective brokers. The experiences, and, in the mission's terms, the effectiveness of Islander teachers varied, but they brought about at least formal adherence to Christianity on many islands far more swiftly than the British missionaries had in their initial Tahitian campaign. 'Progress' was far more tentative in island Melanesia, where Polynesians were seen as scarcely less foreign than the whites, but the numbers of teachers and their staying power brought about, eventually, the conversions the missions sought.

The LMS was was joined by many other missionary agencies, some of which were perceived as brethren, others as unscrupulous competitors. The Methodists inaugurated work in Tonga and Fiji in the 1830s and much later extended their activities to New Britain and other areas within Melanesia. The Melanesian Mission, an arm of the Anglican Church, traces its activities back to Bishop Selwyn's 1848 cruise on the *Dido*; John Coleridge Patteson gave it greater momentum from the mid-1850s; like the LMS it relied upon local teachers, but worked by removing them from their communities to a mission school, to be repatriated upon completion of their training. The American Board of Commissioners for Foreign Missions was active in Hawai'i and subsequently in Micronesia and parts of the Marquesas; the latter regions were evangelised primarily by Hawaiians, with limited success, though today most Marquesan Protestants are descended from mixed Marquesan–Hawaiian families.

Catholics attempted to establish themselves in Hawai'i from 1827; the Congregation of the Sacred Hearts of Jesus and Mary was active also in the Marquesas and Tahiti; the Marists worked in Tonga and Fiji and later in New Caledonia and elsewhere in Melanesia. The fact that the bulk of the Marquesan population ended up adopting Catholicism reflects in part a similar dynamic to that of early Tahiti – depopulation and social and cultural loss in these islands was appalling, as Greg Dening made evident in his elegiac *Islands and Beaches* (1980).[23] The sheer failure of morale over time diminished locals' resistance to the efforts of the Catholic fathers, and enhanced the appeal of the basic welfare in health and education that the mission stations offered. Yet Marquesans certainly also preferred the Catholics to the LMS because of the latter's associations with Tahiti and Pōmare. Joining the Protestants would have entailed acquiescence in Tahitian hegemony, which the Catholic affiliation appeared independent of. In many other parts of the Pacific, Islanders would join missions or breakaway churches as a project of social and political autonomy. This is a dynamic that continues up to the present. Whereas Fijians in the early twentieth century who were disaffected with or marginalised by a chiefly Methodist hegemony turned to Catholicism or Seventh-day Adventism they have more recently joined new churches such as the Assemblies of God and various other Pentecostal congregations, indeed they commonly create congregations themselves, some of which, such as the Christian Fellowship Church in the Western Solomons, have become well-established.

## Labour

In the southwestern Pacific, Islanders began to work for Europeans from the first years of the nineteenth century. The traders who sought *bêche-de-mer* and sandalwood neither had the sea cucumbers gathered, nor the wood cut, by their own crews. In Fiji, early in the nineteenth century, the captain of a trading ship, or an agent such as William Lockerby, dealt with a chief and it was the chief who was paid, in trade goods rather than cash. The common men who did the actual work were not entering into any sort of labour contract with the white man themselves, they were simply performing work on a collective basis for their chief, as they might at other times have laboured to build a canoe, fortify a village, or gather garden food or fish for a feast. The work they did was no doubt hard but it was short-term and irregular, and it was reciprocated with chiefly largesse. Those who worked would have been offered a feast, as those who work for chiefs, or on communal or church projects, still are in villages across Fiji today.

Traders such as New England men like John Eagleston and Benjamin Vanderford, who visited and revisited Fiji through the 1830s, and spoke the language, certainly had an impact, but it was an impact commensurate with the fact that they came and went. Their presence was intermittent, and in many ways Fijian societies and economies carried on as they had. Those who could do so capitalised on new foreign trade, chiefly ambitions were enhanced, and conflict accelerated, but the conception of work, and the place of work in the life of a Fijian man or woman, cannot have been changed profoundly.

James Paddon, who established himself on Aneityum in southern Vanuatu in January 1844, was among those responsible for the creation of a new set of relations. From Vanuatu, he sent loads of sandalwood to China, recruited settlers, provisioned whalers and other sandalwood ships, and set up further stations, on the Isle of Pines and elsewhere. Other entrepreneurs, notably Robert Towns, a Sydney settler and capitalist, quickly entered the field, and by the mid-1850s there were a number of rival trading bases in various parts of Vanuatu, the Loyalties and New Caledonia. The establishment of the French colony in New Caledonia meant greater potential profits, and Paddon was quick to respond, obtaining official contracts to provide supplies for Noumea, and subsequently working as an immigration agent, encouraging white settlement from the Australian colonies.

What this led to was the recruitment of Islander labour. Both Paddon and various itinerant traders called at Tanna to pick up workers, typically woodcutting parties of twenty or so men. While Hawaiians, Tahitians and others had long been maritime workers, men from southern Vanuatu, the Loyalties and the Isle of Pines made themselves available to an increasing degree as ships' crew. It became common for smaller trading vessels to be crewed largely by Islanders, who might be supervised by just two or three white officers. At the same time, Islanders became involved in these new, shore-based trading operations, not only as labourers, but as go-betweens, agents and managers. In the early 1860s, Paddon's sometime employee, then trader-colonist in his own right, Andrew Henry, worked with one Toriki Rangi, 'a Polynesian of unknown origin' resident on Erramanga.[24]

The labour trade gained momentum as colonial settlements in Fiji, Sāmoa and New Caledonia expanded, and the sugar economy in Queensland developed. The demand for workers escalated and what would become a violent and controversial business got under way. It was widely understood that unscrupulous recruiters routinely kidnapped men and women from various parts of Vanuatu and the Solomon Islands, and there were indeed proven cases of abduction. Islanders who considered themselves wronged attacked boats and killed traders, while traders were not infrequently guilty of pre-emptive violence or unauthorised punitive raids. Yet recruitment and migration came to involve tens of thousands of Melanesians and the great majority of those were more-or-less willing recruits, younger men who had much to gain from travel, and the status that their experience, and the goods that they brought back, in due course earned them (Figure 4.2). The upshot was not only the experience of an onerous plantation regime and the ports and towns of Queensland among other colonies, it was the formation of new communities among workers from many islands, the formation of a pidgin language and much else that they shared.[25]

After the federation of the Australian colonies in 1901, the White Australia Policy resulted in the end of recruiting and the deportation of the thousands of Islanders who had, by this time, established viable communities up and down the Queensland coast. Though conces-sions were made, over 7,000 Islanders were repatriated between 1904

*Figure 4.2* J. W. Lindt, 'Recruiting, Pangkumu, Mallicolo [Malakula]', albumen print, *c.*1890

and 1908 and only 1,654 permitted to remain, with official exemptions. Most of those forced to return had been away for a decade or longer. They had absorbed experiences and understandings remote from those of kin at home. Some would not be welcome, some would not choose to rejoin their communities. Many had affiliated themselves with missions that had been established specifically to work among the Queensland 'Kanakas'. On returning they often claimed or appropriated lands distinct from those of their communities of origin and established new Christian settlements. Repatriation took a much deeper understanding of colonial society back to the islands than that possessed by Islanders in situ, who had responded in some cases to missionaries but otherwise had only dealt occasionally with men off boats. In manifold ways, which cannot now be fully reconstructed, cosmopolitan experience was diffused among communities, and it changed them. The Solomon Islands had become a British protectorate in 1893, efforts had been made to pacify the head-hunting peoples of New Georgia in 1897–8, and in the years that followed a colonial administration was gradually put in place. The islands of Vanuatu became the Anglo-French condominium of the New Hebrides from 1906 onwards. Over the decades that followed, indeed until independence in 1978 and 1980 respectively, Islanders in both colonies would struggle against the diverse oppressions of their rulers. To no small degree, they had been equipped to do so by the experience of the labour trade, by the great window it had opened onto the workings of world economies and the inequalities that energised them.

A distinct angle on the legacies of the labour trade is provided by an unconventional source, at first sight an object of no relevance to labour migration. A figure of a man, from the village Sakavas on the island of Malo in north Vanuatu, among a small number of objects representing what are called 'les arts premiers' in the Louvre is strikingly painted blue, never a customary colour in the arts of Melanesia, but a scarce and prestigious import. Reckitts Blue, a bleach invented in Hull in the mid-nineteenth century, was mentioned regularly by labour traders among the goods such as mirrors and scissors that had to be distributed among the kin of prospective recruits during often tense and hurried exchanges, before a young man or woman would be allowed away, to enter a boat.[26] In the islands it was employed, not as a laundry product but a paint, on the 'Blue Man' in the Louvre and on many other similar sculptures. For all the upheaval and violence of the time, these works do not just represent a local art tradition. They were innovations and bold ones on the part of individuals seeking to create new things and enhance their status in local terms. They were expressions of a knowing engagement, a capacity, against all the odds, to balance the rapacious demands of an international economy against a group's interest in celebrating ancestors, a capacity to celebrate them in what was a fresh and splendid way.[27]

## Sovereignty

The final dimension of empire's formation in the Pacific that this chapter considers is the formal assumption of sovereignty over island communities. In hindsight, this may appear to possess historical inevitability. At the beginning of the nineteenth century the British had taken possession of New South Wales, and the Spanish had been long established in Guam but no other islands were colonised in this sense. By 1900 the bulk of the Pacific archipelagoes and islands came under some form of colonial sovereignty, though this was yet to be implemented in the islands that now form the nation of Vanuatu, which became the Anglo-French condominium of the New Hebrides in 1906, and Tonga retained formal independence while being closely associated with the British Empire and later with the Commonwealth. Yet this seeming inevitability has a farcical underside. Most territories were claimed more than once, some by explorers of different nationalities in rapid succession, through declarations that often were not even officially noticed at home, let alone repudiated. In other cases, colonial adventures that were violently prosecuted, like David Porter's in the Marquesas, swiftly fell apart and were soon forgotten generally, if long resented by the local populations that were immediately affected.[28]

The chronology of the formation of Pacific protectorates, territories and colonies cannot be explored in detail here, but it is worth signalling that some, notably New South Wales and New Caledonia, were established as convict settlements, in 1788 and 1853 respectively. In due course both attracted considerable numbers of free settlers and they evolved into settler colonies, based around ranching on appropriated tribal lands, and on mining and other extractive activities. Many settlers in New Caledonia were in fact from one or other of the Australian colonies, and the territory's development in the late nineteenth century had an Australian character, obscured historically by the fact of its French administration. In other cases treaties and formal governance followed growing settlement, substantially by those of British descent, in the cases of New Zealand (1840) and Fiji (1874). In Hawai'i too American annexation followed the large-scale appropriation of Hawaiian lands by planters, many of them descended from

New England missionaries. Military intervention succeeded, but did not put an end to, sophisticated Hawaiian efforts to use the legislature among other channels to protect such native rights as had not already been largely negated.[29]

France's Pacific engagement was interrupted by the Napoleonic Wars. By the time of Dumont d'Urville's voyages in the 1820s and 30s there was a sense that the chance to secure Pacific colonies that might provide some counterweight to those of Britain was receding. Dumont D'Urville had hoped to raise the flag in both Western Australia and New Zealand, only to come just too late, though a French establishment at Akaroa on the South Island was established in 1838 and sustained until purchased by the New Zealand Company in 1849. The annexation of the Marquesas, the Society Islands and other archipelagoes that in due course became the territory of French Polynesia was in effect a last-ditch effort to give France a strategic presence in Oceania. Other island groups were grabbed during a scramble associated with imperialism's most vigorous decades, the 1880s and 1890s: Germany claimed Sāmoa, northern New Guinea and parts of Micronesia; the British assumed control over the Solomon Islands and Papua; and the Dutch had claimed west New Guinea, later known as Irian Jaya and now as West Papua, from 1828 but had exercised minimal actual control until very much later. These acquisitions were varied in their meanings and effects but were typically incomplete. The borders or shadings shown on maps belied the existences of indigenous communities and worlds that would in many instances be shaped by Islanders' own values for generations to come.

I return finally to that question of the much-disowned 'fatal impact' thesis, and the seeming incapacity of historians since to come up with any comparably succinct characterisation of what empire has meant in the Pacific. An unserious suggestion might propose that if there is no apt concept or rubric for this great region's entangled histories, one could turn to a notorious object of cross-cultural traffic in the Pacific – the tattoo. The widespread belief that modern tattooing in the West and elsewhere originated in the encounter between Cook's sailors and the Polynesians is not quite correct, but it is true that the adoption by maritime men and beachcombers of this form of body art was formative, for its presence in modern culture.[30] This trajectory thus represents a cross-current, a fatal impact of the Pacific upon Europe. But my point is rather that the transformation of the Pacific is like the tattoo. We all know that tattoos are at once permanent and skin deep. What we don't know is whether 'skin deep' means merely superficial, or in fact profound.

## Notes

1. Nicholas Thomas, *Marquesan Societies: Inequality and Political Transformation in Eastern Polynesia* (Oxford, 1990); Joel Bonnemaison, *The Tree and the Canoe: History and Ethnogeography of Tanna* (Honolulu, 1994).

2. The terminology of nineteenth-century geography, for example. J. L. Domeny de Rienzi, *Océanie, ou la cinquième partie du monde*, 3 vols (Paris, 1836–7).

3. Kerry Howe, *Where the Waves Fall: A New South Seas History from the First Settlement to Colonial Rule* (Sydney, 1984).

4. Compare Joyce E. Chaplin, 'The Pacific before Empire, *c.*1500–1800', ch. 3 in this volume.

5. Compare Bronwen Douglas, 'Religion', ch. 9 in this volume.

6. Alan Moorehead, *The Fatal Impact: An Account of the Invasion of the South Pacific, 1767–1840* (London, 1966).

7. Tracey Banivanua-Mar, *Violence and Colonial Dialogue: The Australian-Pacific Indentured Labor Trade* (Honolulu, 2007).

8. Epeli Hau'ofa, 'Our Sea of Islands' (1993), in Hau'ofa, *We are the Ocean: Selected Works* (Honolulu, 2008), pp. 27–40.

9. Chaplin, 'The Pacific before Empire'.

10. Johann Reinhold Forster, *Observations Made During A Voyage Round the World,* ed. Nicholas Thomas, Harriet Guest and Michael Dettelbach (Honolulu, 1996).

11. Anne Salmond, *Aphrodite's Island: The European Discovery of Tahiti* (Auckland, NZ, 2009).

12. Epeli Hau'ofa, 'The Ocean in Us' (1997), in Hau'ofa, *We are the Ocean*, pp. 41–59.

13. O. H. K. Spate, *Paradise Found and Lost* (London, 1988), pp. 173–6; Patrick V. Kirch and Marshall Sahlins, *Anahulu: The Anthropology of History in the Kingdom of Hawai'i* (Chicago, 1992).

14. H. E. Maude, 'The Tahitian Pork Trade: 1800–1830', in Maude, *Of Islands and Men: Studies in Pacific History* (Melbourne, 1968), pp. 178–232.

15. Nicholas Thomas, *Islanders: The Pacific in the Age of Empire* (New Haven, 2010); Dorothy Shineberg, *They Came for Sandalwood: A Study of the Sandalwood Trade in the South-West Pacific, 1830–1865* (Melbourne, 1968).

16. R. Gerard Ward, 'The Pacific *Bêche-De-Mer* Trade with Special Reference to Fiji', in Ward, ed., *Man in the Pacific Islands* (Oxford, 1972), pp. 91–123.

17. Patrick V. Kirch and Jean-Louis Rallu, eds., *The Growth and Collapse of Pacific Islands Societies: Archaeological and Demographic Perspectives* (Honolulu, 2007).

18. Thomas, *Islanders*; Niel Gunson, *Messengers of Grace: Evangelical Missionaries in the South Seas, 1797–1860* (Melbourne, 1978).

19. George Keate, *An Account of the Pelew Islands*, ed. Karen L. Nero, Nicholas Thomas and Jennifer Newell (London, 2002); Niel Gunson, 'The Coming of Foreigners', in Noel Rutherford, ed., *Friendly Islands: A History of Tonga* (Melbourne, 1977), pp. 90–113.

20. John Davies, *The History of the Tahitian Mission, 1799–1830*, ed. C. W. Newbury (Cambridge, 1961).
21. Teuira Henry, *Ancient Tahiti* (Honolulu, 1928).
22. Thomas, *Islanders*, pp. 106–8.
23. Greg Dening, *Islands and Beaches: Discourse on a Silent Land: Marquesas, 1774–1880* (Carlton, Vic., 1980).
24. Shineberg, *They Came for Sandalwood*, pp. 134–5.
25. Peter Corris, *Passage, Port and Plantation: A History of Solomon Islands Labour Migration* (Melbourne, 1973); Roger M. Keesing, 'Plantation Networks, Plantation Culture: The Hidden Side of Colonial Melanesia', *Journal de la Société des Océanistes* 82 (1986), 163–70.
26. For example, William T. Wawn, *The South Sea Islanders and the Queensland Labour Trade* (1893), ed. Peter Corris (Canberra, 1973), p. 9.
27. Peter Brunt, Nicholas Thomas, Sean Mallon, Lissant Bolton, Deidre Brown, Damian Skinner and Susanne Küchler, *Art in Oceania: A New History* (London, 2012), p. 189.
28. Dening, *Islands and Beaches*; Thomas, *Islanders*, pp. 60–73.
29. Pökä Laenui, 'The Overthrow of the Hawaiian Monarchy', in Donald Denoon, Stewart Firth, Jocelyn Linnekin, Malama Meleisea and Karen Nero, eds., *The Cambridge History of the Pacific Islanders* (Cambridge, 1997), pp. 232–7.
30. Nicholas Thomas, Anna Cole and Bronwen Douglas, eds., *Tattoo: Bodies, Art and Exchange in the Pacific and the West* (London, 2005).

# 5

# A Pacific Century?

## Akira Iriye

There are three ways of periodising Pacific (or any region's) history: national, international and transnational. The national way is to deal with each country of the wider Pacific (including East Asia and Southeast Asia) in terms of its own development. Pacific history would then amount to the sum of all national or local histories. But such nation-centric history would belie the very idea of regional history, such as Pacific history, so we may disregard this approach. Of the remaining two, the international approach is the one that is most frequently used to periodise the history of the world and of its regions. That approach has been supplemented, and at times superseded, by a transnational perspective, and this chapter will pay greater attention to it than the more familiar international history framework.

International history is a record of relations among nations, but in the historiographical literature this has tended to be seen in terms of what the 'great powers' do to each other, thus amounting to the chronicling of geopolitical vicissitudes. 'The rise and fall of the great powers', 'the road to war', 'the diplomacy of imperialism', and similar titles of books on international history exemplify the key roles played by the powerful countries in shaping, or destroying, a regional, even global, order. An 'international system' is conceptualised as constituting the 'world order' that is maintained by the great powers. Periodisation, then, is a task of determining which powers rose and fell, and what sort of 'order' or 'system' existed regionally or globally at a given moment in time.

It is easy to examine Pacific history in the twentieth century in such a framework. The century began in the middle of the age of the great European empires in Asia and the Pacific, which were now joined by the United States and Japan. Imperialism was thus a key feature of international history at that time. What William Langer described in his monumental study, *The Diplomacy of Imperialism* (1935), is still valid today.[1] But the book covered the period 1890 to 1902, whereas the story of imperialist diplomacy in the Pacific really got under way from around 1902. The United States had emerged as a colonial power by then, having annexed Hawai'i, established control over a portion of Sāmoa, acquired the Philippines from Spain, and suppressed the Filipino uprising. Simultaneously, Japan was also emerging as an imperialist, having taken Taiwan from China in the wake of the Sino-Japanese War of 1894–5. The United States, Japan and the European imperialist powers all undertook military action in China during the Boxer uprising of 1899–1900 and turned the Qing empire into a 'semi-colony'. The imperialists then fell upon one another, seeking to augment their respective spheres of influence. The year 1902 was of pivotal importance in this regard as Japan and Britain concluded an alliance that year, which emboldened the Japanese to take on the Russian empire and to establish control over the Korean peninsula. Russia and Japan fought in Manchuria during 1904–5, and as a result Russia retreated temporarily from East Asia and turned its attention to the Middle East, and its ambitions in the Ottoman empire contributed to the coming of a major war in Europe. That war gave an opportunity to Japan to entrench its power further on the Asian continent and to expel Germany from its Pacific possessions. In the meantime, Japan and the United States grew as naval rivals in the Pacific, a situation that was temporarily alleviated by the naval disarmament agreements among the United States, Britain and Japan in 1921 and 1930, but conflict flared up again when Japan began its aggressive war against China in 1931. Full-scale war between the Asian neighbours started in 1937; four years later this was transformed into a war across the Pacific Ocean as Japan attacked US and European territories and possessions in the region, both in order to prevent the United States, Britain and the Netherlands from coming to the aid of China, and also to acquire the rich resources of Southeast Asia, most of which were in European hands. It was as if the history of the Pacific was perpetually that of wars through most of the first half of the twentieth century.

Then, after Japan's defeat in 1945, a semblance of regional order prevailed, one that is usually referred to as the 'Cold War in Asia'. The global confrontation between the United States and the Soviet Union took the form, in the Pacific, of what is sometimes called the 'Yalta system', after the Yalta Conference of 1945, according to which the United States, China and the Soviet Union would be the major powers to maintain the post-war status quo in the region. But there was to be no status quo, as the decolonisation of Korea and Vietnam triggered civil strife in these countries, into which the United States was drawn to restabilise regional order. China also experienced a civil war, but here

US intervention took the form of establishing a military alliance with Taiwan, which separated itself from the mainland. Japan, gaining independence after 1952, also tied itself to Taiwan. The Cold War in Asia thus pitted the pan-Pacific alliance of Canada, the United States, Australia, New Zealand, the Philippines, Taiwan, South Vietnam, Thailand, South Korea and Japan against the Sino-Soviet bloc that included North Korea and North Vietnam. This situation changed drastically in the 1970s, when the United States withdrew from Vietnam (which was now unified) and also normalised its relationship with the People's Republic of China. In the meantime, China and the Soviet Union became antagonistic towards one another, as did China and Vietnam. Thus, during the 1970s and 1980s the Cold War in the Pacific (if such a term is to be used) assumed a very different character from what had preceded it. By the late 1980s, however, as the Cold War came to an end in Europe, in the Pacific region, too, a 'pacific' era began for the first time in nearly a century. Or so it seemed.

Such, in crude outline, is the international history of the Pacific in the twentieth century as seen through the vicissitudes of geopolitics. All in all, this was a volatile, conflict-ridden region through most of the period, giving us a straightforward chronology on the basis of geopolitical developments. It would not be difficult to periodise this history. One could go, as most history books do, from the turn of the century to the First World War and characterise it as a period of struggle for mastery among the imperialist powers, and then periodise the 'interwar years' of the 1920s, followed by the Asian-Pacific War of 1931–45. The second half of the century can be considered broadly as part of the global Cold War, lasting till 1990, although this long period could be subdivided into the 'high' Cold War from 1945 to 1970 and then the relaxation of tensions during the 1970s and the 1980s. In the European context some historians have written of the 'second Cold War' from the late 1970s to the middle of the 1980s, a view that does not make much sense in view of the abrupt ending of the bipolar system in the late 1980s. In any event, it is an easy task to fit the history of the wider Pacific region into such a geopolitically defined chronology.

Nor is it surprising that in such a chronology, the role of the United States is almost always emphasised, for the nation was involved in most of the military conflicts in the Pacific during the century. Historians thus continue to write Pacific history with a strong focus on US foreign policy and military strategy. Bruce Cumings's *Dominion from Sea to Sea* (2009) is a good example of this approach, as is Michael Hunt and Steven Levine's *Arc of Empire* (2012).[2] Both of these books portray the Pacific as having been an arena for the steady expansion of American power. Similarly, in the volume edited by Tsuyoshi Hasegawa, *The Cold War in Asia* (2011), the contributors all assume that there was an Asian Cold War as a story within the larger Cold War history in which the United States played the key role.[3] That all such distinguished scholars continue to conceptualise Pacific history in the twentieth century in terms of geopolitical vicissitudes and link them to the rise of US power may make it difficult to consider other ways of understanding that history.

Of course, simply because so many books have been written on the wars in the wider Pacific, or because many seek to understand the history of the region within a framework of the rise of an American empire, it does not follow that we should belittle their contribution to knowledge. The chronicle of wars in the Pacific is, of course, extremely important in many respects, especially in terms of historical memory, a subject to which I shall return. Nor should one deal casually with the tragic consequences of the mass slaughters, the uncivilised treatment of combatants and non-combatants, the wholesale destruction of cities, the use of poisonous agents against humans, nuclear tests that destroy the natural habitat, and many other consequences of war and the preparations for war. But we should also be aware of the limits of what we may term geopolitical determinism in understanding the past.

To begin with, do we allow wars to periodise the twentieth century? Which wars? Here, the overwhelming bulk of history books tend to adopt a Euro-centric (or Atlantic-centric) chronology and to fit events elsewhere into that scheme. In the widely accepted chronology, the twentieth century is schematised in terms first of 'the road to 1914', which is followed by the Great War, the 'interwar years', the Second World War, the Cold War and the post-Cold War period. Pacific history is simply fitted into such a chronology, which makes it simply a Pacific chapter of European or western history. We see this, for instance, when considering the Cold War. Historians, including myself, have written about 'the Cold War in Asia', but such a perception gives the impression that the Cold War, which had its origins elsewhere, somehow came to embrace Asia. How it did so, and what came about as a result are interesting questions, but not as fundamental as the question of whether there indeed was a Cold War in Asia. China, after all, was no mere carbon copy of the Soviet Union, and, besides, Asia and the Pacific were never divided neatly for any extended period of time into two camps as occurred in Europe. One could argue that the Cold War, even if we grant that it did come to the Pacific, was a far less significant development then than the projects of de-colonisation and nation-building in all parts of the region. The inhabitants of the countries that went through these dramas comprised the bulk of humanity in the Pacific and indeed of the whole world.

It should be noted in this context that the vast ocean contains numerous islands that used to be governed as colonies of the great powers but that have achieved their independence in the second half of the twentieth century. A periodisation that focused on wars would assign only passive roles to those islands and their inhabitants. The German islands in the Pacific briefly became battlegrounds between German and British (mostly Australian) as well as Japanese forces during the First World War, and during the Second World War, often called the Pacific War in its Asian dimension, US and Japanese forces fought for control over Midway, Guam and many islands in the western Pacific as well as off the coast of Indonesia and the Philippines. The 'island-hopping' campaign ultimately won the war for the United States. During the Cold War, some Pacific islands and their surrounding waters became testing grounds for nuclear weapons. In all of these military developments, the fate of the vast ocean continued to be determined by the policies and strategies of the great powers. To give the many islands their due in a reconceptualised Pacific history, one would have to get away from a chronology that privileges geopolitics and consider the fates of the people who inhabit the ocean. How can this be done? How can we take note of the islands as well as the larger countries of East and Southeast Asia in order to establish a meaningful chronology of Pacific history? Certainly not within the usual framework adopted for either national history or conventional international history.

Transnational history offers one solution. In contrast to international history, it pays primary attention to non-national entities, non-state actors, and cross-border themes.[4] By non-national entities are meant races, religions and even civilisations that define their own existences apart from nations. Non-state actors exist within nations, or across nations, but they are distinct from states. The best examples of such actors are non-governmental organisations and private business enterprises. These organisations have their own agendas and often challenge governmental authority. Then there is a whole array of cross-border themes and phenomena that are subjects of transnational history, ranging from economic, social and cultural globalisation to migrations, human rights, diseases and natural disasters, the spread of (and the efforts to prevent) drug abuses, terrorism, environmental degradation, advances in scientific and medical research, cultural and educational exchanges (including the development of shared memories), tourism and world sporting events. Of course, all of these and other transnational themes can be examined within the framework of international history. Nations have participated in various conferences and signed international agreements for the promotion of human rights, the protection of refugees, and similar reasons. But non-governmental organisations have played active roles in these conferences as well as providing for their own programmes and activities outside the state apparatus. Non-national identities such as religions and ethnic groups have been of critical importance in the promotion of an interdependent world community. These phenomena can only be understood if put in the context of transnational history.

In considering a vast region such as the Pacific, the transnational approach seems particularly helpful because this immense space consists of countries and people of divergent races, religions and civilisations. The international history perspective usually pays scant attention to these non-national existences, but that would result in a serious distortion of this region's past and present. To take an example, in contemporary discussions it is customary to view China as a military and economic power, whether actual or potential. But China is a civilisation before anything else, so the future of the Pacific would hinge on how various civilisations, as well as the region's diverse populations, may accommodate themselves to develop a community of interdependence and interpenetration, not just on balance of power, economic competition and other geopolitical considerations. What follows is an illustration of how this history would look if we paid attention to transnational themes and developments. I shall choose for consideration a few transnational themes as examples that may help periodise the history of the Pacific region in the twentieth century: economic globalisation (including labour migrations), human rights, cultural internationalism and historical memory. These phenomena played roles that were just as crucial in the making of the twentieth-century Pacific as the stories of international rivalries, wars and empires. In contrast to the latter themes, the former set of phenomena may be considered regional aspects of global transnational history. Because international dramas tend to be stressed in most accounts of Pacific history, it is as well to recognise that, put in the context of transnational developments, the region's history may be seen to have depicted different dramas and pointed to alternative possibilities.

Of all the transnational themes, arguably the most important would be economic globalisation, namely the movement of capital, goods, technology, people and markets throughout the world.

Historians usually date the acceleration of such globalising trends from the middle of the nineteenth century, but how global was globalisation at that time? Much of the phenomenon was limited to Europe and North America until the second half of the twentieth century, and the Pacific region initially did not partake of the globalising trends to any significant degree. Although visions of trans-Pacific trade had excited generations of Americans in the nineteenth century, it was only in the first decade of the twentieth century that telegraphic cables were laid between the west coast of the United States and Japan, and between that of Canada and Australia and New Zealand.[5] Even so, intra-Pacific economic transactions continued to pale in significance in comparison with intra-European and Atlantic trade and investment activities until towards the end of the twentieth century. As statistical data provided in Kaoru Sugihara's chapter demonstrate, the Pacific Rim countries minus the United States and Canada accounted for less than 15 per cent of the world's total trade in 1900.[6] While the entire region's trade comprised roughly a quarter of the world's total in 1900, the United States accounted for more than half of this, and the bulk of it consisted of transactions with the countries of Europe and Latin America. Neither Japan nor China played a major role in world trade at this time, and virtually all Asian countries were net importers of goods and relied on foreign borrowing and investment to pay for their trade deficits. As for the circulation of labour, a key aspect of economic globalisation, it was virtually non-existent between Asian countries and North America or the Antipodes. As McKeown's chapter shows, most intra-Pacific migrations consisted of Chinese moving into Southeast Asia, more an Asian than a Pacific phenomenon. There was nothing like the trans-Atlantic movements of people. Thousands of Japanese settled in Taiwan, Korea and Manchuria, but the scale of such movement was a fraction of global migrations.[7]

After the war of 1914–18 devastated European countries, the United States took over the leading position as an exporter of capital and goods, and there were moderate increases in trans-Pacific trade and investment, but no change in migration statistics. With Britain, the world's major trading nation as well as the principal supplier of capital, having had to focus on the military conflict in Europe, the United States emerged as the lynchpin of international economic activities. That included the Pacific region, where there was an expansion in US trade with, and investment in, Japan and its colonies, while at the same time Japan, which also became a net exporter of goods and capital, contributed to enhancing the share of the region in global trade and investment. Even so, as Sugihara shows, during the 1920s the Pacific Ocean, East Asia and Southeast Asia in combination (but excluding the United States and the British Commonwealth) accounted for no more than a few percentage points of the world's commercial transactions.[8] (Total Japanese trade in 1928, for instance, amounted to less than US$2 billion, or less than 6 per cent of the world total of over US$33 billion dollars.) Globalisation was very slow to reach this region, in part because the European colonies remained predominantly agricultural and the prices for farm products remained stagnant during the post-war years, and also because China, the largest potential market for foreign goods and capital, was politically unstable, the country being divided at the time into various areas, each under the control of a warlord or a political faction. While the United States and Europe steadily reglobalised their economic affairs, that is, restored the international system of economic interchanges, the Pacific region played a relatively small part in the story. It goes without saying that there was no change in the white countries' immigration policy so that there was no trans-Pacific movement of Asians to the United States, Canada, Australia or New Zealand. Although, as McKeown notes in his chapter, small numbers of Chinese and Japanese migrated to Brazil in the 1920s, the region as a whole continued to reflect the 'global colour line'.[9] Such an arrangement was inherently against globalisation.

Even the limited scale of economic globalisation shrank drastically after 1929, and economic historians speak of the 'turn to autarchy' during the 1930s and beyond.[10] We may speak of the age of deglobalisation to refer to the decades of the 1930s and the 1940s. It is interesting to observe, however, that compared to the Atlantic region, the Pacific area suffered less economically during the Depression. US trade with Japan, for instance, not only did not shrink, as did the trade with the European countries, but it actually expanded in the second half of the 1930s. (Japanese exports to the United States increased from 506 million yen in 1930 to 569 million yen in 1940, while imports from the latter shot up from 443 million yen to 1,241 million yen in the same period.)[11] Much of this, to be sure, was due to Japan's military expansion on the continent of Asia. Japanese purchases of arms such as tanks and aircraft from the United States increased steadily, until the trade was restricted and ultimately embargoed by Washington. In the sphere of investment, too, there were joint US and Japanese projects in Manchuria, both actual and potential.[12] China, which had a silver-monetised economy and did not suffer as seriously from the global economic crisis as the capitalist, industrialised countries whose currencies were based on the gold-exchange standard, began taking its first steps toward industrialisation, and its per capita income actually increased before the beginning of a large-scale war between China and Japan. In the meantime, US investment in the oilfields of the Dutch East Indies and rubber plantations in Malaya grew steadily. It was precisely because of the growing economic ties between the United States and these countries that Japan was adamant about establishing its 'new order' in East Asia, in order to control the resources and markets of Asia and to deny them to the United States and Europe. (In 1940, the Japanese military estimated that of roughly ten million tons of oil being produced in Southeast Asia – the petroleum resource that they were determined to possess – the Dutch East Indies accounted for roughly 80 per cent, and Burma and British Borneo the remainder.)[13] The Pacific War was, at this level, a conflict over natural resources in the region. The US government, however, also saw the clash as involving the future of globalisation, insisting that Japan accept an open door policy throughout the Pacific region. Once Japan gave up its autarchic scheme for Asian–Pacific economic hegemony, the United States would invite it, as well as all other countries, to join a reglobalised world economy. The Bretton Woods mechanism, combined with the new United Nations, envisaged a Pacific that would be economically integrated into the world economy.

Even the US visions of reglobalisation, however, did not include the globalisation of labour or the unrestricted migration of people. Although there were some both in the United States during the 1930s who promoted immigration revision so as to establish a solid basis of US–Japan relations, neither the US government nor American society was open to the idea of globalisation of labour.[14] Even the number of immigrants into the United States drastically diminished during the 1930s. In contrast, there was a vast expansion of Japanese emigration to the Asian continent, but this was mostly undertaken as an instrument for Japan's control over China. The fact remains that the migration of people was never part of the initial phase of the reglobalisation in the Pacific. If we were to focus on the transnational theme of migrations, therefore, we would have to say that the Pacific region played no significant role. Dirk Hoerder's monumental history of global migrations through ten centuries devotes little space to this region, except for a brief (three pages in a 700-page book) reference to 'racism and exclusion', and quite understandably so.[15]

Considerations of immigration restriction lead us to the subject of human rights. To the extent that human rights has emerged as a key theme in transnational history, the history of human rights in the Pacific region, too, will need to be put in that context.[16] Here, obviously, the situation was rather dismal during the first half of the twentieth century. Racism is, of course, inherently against the principle of universal human rights, and it was manifest in the extreme hostility on the part of Europeans towards people of coloured and mixed races, in particular Euro-Asians, at the turn of the century. But this was only one instance of the denial of human rights in the region. Imperialism, by definition, denies the rights of indigenous people, and the wider Pacific area exemplified the phenomenon. An Australian administrator of Melanesia that was occupied by Dominion forces during the First World War remarked in 1918, 'The natives as a race are most indolent, and their ideas seldom extend beyond eating, sleeping, smoking, and an occasional "sing-sing" dance.'[17] Even as the victorious powers conferred on transferring the former German colonies to a mandate system to be set up under the League of Nations, this sort of race prejudice remained. Wilsonian internationalism, it may be said, did not mean an embrace of the transnational principle of race equality. Internationalism, in other words, did not lead to transnationalism. Even after Japan officially accepted post-war internationalism as a framework for its foreign policy, it continued to violate the rights of Koreans who remained under Japanese jurisdiction. Japan's policy of cultural assimilation deprived Koreans of their right even to adopt their traditional names or to speak their own language at school. In the history of race prejudice, the early twentieth century may have been a particularly ugly moment in that it manifested itself both domestically and transnationally. It may be said that globalisation at the time was a very partial phenomenon not only geographically but also anthropologically.

But racism and colonialism were not the only instances of denial of human rights during the first half of the twentieth century. By the standards of the United Nations' definition of human rights that were adopted in the 1960s, the records of most Asian countries were poor. Such principles as freedom of speech, democratic government, equal employment opportunities, the universal right to education, gender equality, the right of the physically and mentally disabled to live in dignity – these were conspicuous by their absence in the Pacific region, except for the United States, Canada, Australia and New Zealand where at least some of these rights, in particular democracy and free speech, were honoured. Even there, however, we should recall that until after the First World War, only in New Zealand and Australia did women have the right to vote. It would be too easy to attribute such a sorry situation to the 'backwardness' of Asian countries, whether because of their tradition of 'Oriental despotism', the absence of western-style individualism or economic underdevelopment. They were obviously not as 'modernised' as western nations, but modernisation is not synonymous with human rights. The 'traditional' societies of Persia, India and elsewhere produced their own visions of human unity, which is a necessary foundation of the concept of human rights that are not drastically different from the avowal of personal integrity and dignity to be encountered in Christianity, Judaism, Confucianism and other religions.[18] In other words, to the extent that human rights were being extensively violated throughout the world, and specifically in the Pacific, that may have had less to do with traditional ideologies than with the growing awareness of the gap between those ideologies and the reality. The ideologies were present in the Pacific as well as elsewhere, but the realities did not match them.

What the above brief sketch suggests is that, in terms of economic globalisation, migrations and human rights, the Pacific region was only superficially transformed during the first decades of the twentieth century. Whether or not there was military conflict or relative quiet throughout the region, the Pacific did not change drastically in economic and social affairs, in contrast to some other parts of the globe. In one area, however, we may note developments there that paralleled those elsewhere. This is the cultural sphere, where what we may term cultural internationalism began to take on particular significance in Pacific history during the first decades of the century.

Cultural internationalism refers to transnational exchanges of ideas, artistic productions and ways of life so as to enhance a sense of interconnectedness and interdependence among all people.[19] For this reason, 'cultural transnationalism' would be a more appropriate term than 'cultural internationalism' for these activities. In any event, it may be promoted through professional conferences, educational exchange programmes, exhibitions at museums, musical performances, sporting events and the like. Usually put in the framework of cultural westernisation, the phenomenon has by no means been entirely unidirectional. Pan-Pacific cultural internationalism entailed intellectual, educational and artistic crossings in all directions. These phenomena may sometimes be promoted by governments as part of their foreign and domestic policies, but private individuals and organisations also play vital roles, creating their own universes that are not interchangeable with the world defined by inter-state relations. The familiar story of the penetration of Asian countries by

American and Canadian missionaries and educators would have to be supplemented by the activities by Japanese Buddhist missionaries in China or Korean Christian missionaries all across the Pacific. Various social reform movements, ranging from alcoholic prohibition to birth control, were promoted not just by Americans and other westerners but also by Chinese, Japanese and Koreans. They, as well as those from Southeast Asia, frequently participated in international conferences as well as sporting events such as the Olympics. Asian artworks were a familiar sight in American museums, just as western paintings and sculptures were to be found in Asian museums. One impulse behind all such activities was the promotion of cross-cultural communication and understanding, which the proponents of cultural internationalism believed was a necessary foundation of peace among nations. Some went further and believed that a culturally interconnected world would be able to function with its own momentum and follow its own agendas. If so, it would define its unique global order, just as military power and economic transactions might construct their world systems.

If the Pacific region saw a series of military conflicts during the first half of the twentieth century, and if, during this period, there was little evidence of economic globalisation or the promotion of human rights, in the cultural sphere some important developments could be observed. This became particularly clear in the 1930s, the decade of war and of global economic crisis. In the history of cultural internationalism, the 1930s are notable because cross-cultural activities never disappeared and may even be said to have intensified. Student exchange programmes between East Asia and the United States continued unabated despite the Depression and may even have intensified through various programmes sponsored by various organisations, most notably the Institute of Pacific Relations. It became quite active during the 1930s and promoted trans-Pacific student conferences as well as symposia attended by journalists, business people and others.[20] The League of Nations' committee on intellectual cooperation, as well as its national branches all over the Pacific, continued their activities so that, as late as 1938, Chinese and Japanese scholars were meeting to discuss subjects of their common concern.[21] A pan-Pacific conference on education, organised jointly by the University of Hawai'i and Yale University, was held in Honolulu in 1936, bringing together educators from the United States, Mexico, China, India, Australia, New Zealand, New Guinea, the Gilbert Islands, Sāmoa and Papua, as well as from Japan, Britain, France and the Netherlands. Likewise, the World Federation of

Education Associations, established in 1923, continued to meet during the 1930s. It is interesting that while its biannual meetings were held in Europe or the United States until 1935, the 1937 gathering was convened in Tokyo and that the 1939 meeting was to take place in Rio de Janeiro, although this latter did not materialise because of the European war.[22] The Tokyo conference opened nearly a month after the start of the Chinese–Japanese war, triggered by the Japanese army's assault on Beijing, and brought together nearly nine hundred educators from all over the world, the majority of whom were women – a remarkable phenomenon at that time. The participants came from both North and South America, the West Indies, Europe, Asia and the Pacific, and Africa. These gatherings were among the numerous cultural exchanges taking place in all parts of the Pacific. It is well to recall that the United States government's Good Neighbor policy included student and educational exchanges with countries of South America. In sport, the 1932 and 1936 Olympics, the former held in Los Angeles and the latter in Berlin, established global connections,[23] as did American baseball players' visits to Japan during the 1930s.[24] In the meantime, Hollywood movies continued to connect moviegoers all over the world, including the Pacific, but we should also note that there was an influx of Japanese films into China. That this was not all wartime propaganda but that there were often close exchanges and cooperation by Chinese and Japanese film makers has been well documented.[25] Until Pearl Harbor, Chinese theatres offered a choice of Chinese, Japanese and Hollywood movies. It may be said that in the history of cultural internationalism in the Pacific, the 1930s were particularly important and indicated that in this one area the Pacific region may even have been ahead of other parts of the world.

To periodise Pacific history, then, the transnational perspective would offer a different perspective from the traditional international chronology. The 1930s, usually understood in the framework of Japan's war against China that led to the conflict in the Pacific, could, in transnational history, be seen as a rather fertile decade in educational and cultural interactions. Of course, these interactions did not prevent war, but the legacy of cultural internationalism was to survive the war and would feed directly into post-war transnational history. In this story, all countries in the Pacific took part.

The Pacific War, 1941–5, did mark a major turning point in the international history of the Pacific region, but what were the war's transnational implications? In the history of economic globalisation, the war was not a significant landmark. The state of deglobalisation continued more or less into the 1950s. It was in the 1960s that Japan rejoined the global economy by slowly but steadily removing exchange restrictions and launching a huge export drive, emerging by the end of the decade as a top economic presence in the region. With the United States, Canada and other countries likewise expanding their trade, the role of the Pacific in world commerce expanded significantly for the first time in modern history. As detailed in Kaoru Sugihara's chapter, the volume of world trade expanded spectacularly in the last decades of the twentieth century, and the share of the Pacific countries (including the United States in the east and China in the west) increased steadily, exceeding 50 per cent by the turn of the new century.[26] Trans-Pacific trade, namely exchanges among the countries in the region, expanded accordingly. By 1990, the incomes of all the Pacific countries (exclusive of Central and South America) combined were approaching $11 trillion, more than the combined total income of the European nations.[27] In short, the wider Pacific had become an integral part of the history of economic globalisation.

This is an important story, and the chronology of Pacific history should probably stress that theme as well as, or even more than, the Vietnam War and other aspects of the lingering Cold War – even if we grant that there was a Cold War in Asia. The 1960s through the 1980s, in other words, were a significant milestone in modern Pacific history. Whereas the period through the early 1960s was character-ised by slow, even stagnant trans-Pacific economic development, the years after the 1960s saw rapid growth, which became phenomenal after the early 1980s when the People's Republic of China adopted an open system of international economic transactions. Very rapidly, China joined other Pacific countries in those transactions, providing labour, capital and markets for the whole world, but particularly for the United States, Canada, Australia and Japan. It is unsurprising, under the circumstances, that by the early twenty-first century the value of intra-Pacific trade would come to exceed that between the region and other parts of the globe.

What of the history of human rights in the Pacific region in the second half of the twentieth century? Quite obviously, the story is not as straightforward as it is in respect of economic transformation. Insofar as immigration restrictions are concerned, there occurred a sea change during the 1960s and the subsequent decades as the United States, Canada and Australia modified or abolished race-based immi-gration policies so that in these countries the number of Asian visitors and residents grew rapidly. Most notably, the proportion of the American population originating in Asia and the Pacific grew from a mere 0.2 per cent in 1950 to 0.7 per cent in 1970 and 2.6 per cent in 1990. These figures suggest the steady opening of the United States to people from the wider Pacific. (In 1990, there were as many immigrants from Sāmoa and Guam as there had been those from China in 1950. Of 1,766,000 refugees admitted to the United States from 1961 to 1990, nearly one half came from the Pacific region.)[28] Quite clearly, in terms of the globalisation of labour and less restricted immigration policies on the part of the United States and other 'white' countries, the 1960s and the 1970s mark a significant turning point. These decades would have to be given greater significance than the 1940s or the 1950s if we were to periodise Pacific history in transnational terms and not in geopolitically determined ways.

During the 1970s human rights came to be seen in terms of the freedom and dignity of each person as a human being, not as a citizen or a member of a race, religion or civilisation.[29] Would such an interpretation be applicable to the wider Pacific region? This definition of human rights as the dignity of the individual and respect for each person regardless of his or her background would be hard to apply to the majority of the four billion or more people living in this region at the end of the twentieth century. From time to time, there did arise movements for democratisation. One thinks of the student demonstrations in China in 1989, which were preceded by the political transformation of South Korea and the democratisation of the Philippines. The near coincidence of these developments suggests that they were not just separate national political episodes but constituted a transnational phenomenon, much like '1968' across Europe.[30] The dignity of the individual was one of the goals of all these movements, and there did grow awareness that personal freedom was a universal principle that transcended political boundaries. Unfortunately, such promising beginnings in human rights development in the Pacific region were frequently frustrated by the power of the state, as happened in China in the wake of the Tiananmen uprising, or by inter-ethnic rivalries that became serious in Southeast Asia. It should be added, however, that the number of non-governmental organisations grew in all Pacific countries toward the end of the century. These organisations are in a sense intermediaries between state and society. Few of them are totally independent of the state, but in most instances they are formed for the purpose of carrying out tasks that the state would not, including the promotion of human rights. The fact that non-governmental organisations expanded globally and regionally during and after the 1970s to an unprecedented degree indicates that human rights were making some headway even in politically oppressive countries like China. It seems significant that the Disabled Peoples' International, an NGO dedicating itself to the human rights of disabled persons, was founded in Singapore in 1981 with an initial membership of 67 countries. And in 1991 the UN's Economic and Social Commission for Asia and the Pacific, meeting in Beijing, adopted a ten-year plan for regional cooperation to help the disabled, calling the years 1993–2002 'the decade for the disabled in Asia and the Pacific'. These landmarks are rarely mentioned in studies of human rights history but clearly belong in Pacific transnational history as a major turning point in recognition of the rights of the physically and intellectually disabled.[31] It must be recognised, however, that few countries in the wide Pacific region have done enough to promote the human rights of the physically and intellectually handicapped persons.

In the meantime, cultural internationalism continued to grow in the Pacific region in the last decades of the twentieth century. It was boosted, in particular, by the opening of China to foreign influences. From the 1980s onwards, students and researchers from the People's Republic began visiting other countries, and soon their total number – including even middle-school pupils – would come to number 500,000. Most of the exchange students and scholars went to study in other parts of the Pacific, although a significant number went to Europe. A large number of them stayed and worked in the host countries, contributing to the diversification of academic scenes everywhere. Likewise, it became commonplace for Chinese musicians to perform abroad, for people in other countries to visit China – and later Vietnam – and for both to enjoy each other's food products. There was no diminution in the number and extent of cultural exchange programmes elsewhere in the Pacific, so that at the end of the twentieth century it could be said that the wider Pacific had become culturally interconnected. A consequence of such interconnection could be diversification and even hybridisation of culture across the wide region.

Hybridity is a notion that anthropologists, sociologists and even some historians have begun to use to refer to the coming together and blending of people of diverse backgrounds, in the process reproducing themselves as a mixture, not definable in terms of autonomous categories. Hybridisation is a process that has been going on through human history, and it may be said that the process accelerated in the twentieth century, especially towards its end because of the increasing mobility of people as well as the goods, ideas and lifestyles they bring. Innovations in information and communication technology accelerated the tendency towards the sharing of experiences, whether actual or 'virtual'. In such circumstances, nothing remains 'pure', if there ever was such a thing as a 'pure', homogeneous race, nation or civilisation. Because the Pacific is more diverse than other regions of the world in the make-up of its people, there are considerable chances of its becoming a more and more hybridised region. That may mean that nations in the Pacific, like those elsewhere, will become less and less distinguishable in terms of the people who inhabit them. Whether national identities and nationalistic assertiveness would become mitigated as a consequence remains to be seen.

A century ago, at the beginning of the twentieth century, dreamers like Kang Yuwei in China and Paul Otlet in Belgium visualised a world in which all nations and people would become united and live in peace. Gustav Hervé, the French journalist, wrote in 1910, 'The nineteenth century was a century of nationalism. The twentieth century will be a century of internationalism.' He was hopeful that modern civilisation had reached a stage where nations would prefer to cooperate with one another, eventually even organising 'a united states of the world', rather than persisting in their antagonistic relations.[32] His optimism proved premature, but one may note that Hervé's vision of nationalistic antagonisms eventually giving way to internationalism was unrealistic so long as national units remained as the key autonomous existences in the world. Nations would have to be transformed, becoming more hybridised, before there could be an international community – or, rather, a transnational world. And a transnational world will come to pass only when nations have lost some of their distinctions and become interchangeable in the composition of their inhabitants and their ways of life and thought. Is the Pacific region on the road to such transformation? That would appear to be one of the interesting questions facing the twenty-first century.

In this connection, the question of memory, both individual and collective, becomes of paramount importance. As the Pacific region steadily transforms itself, whether or not it will come to form a community, not just a sum of the countries and their people that happen to share geographical proximity, will hinge on the level of shared memory in all areas. Historians have noted that the development of 'a community of shared memory' in post-war Europe has been a prerequisite for the construction of the European Union.[33] Quite obviously, there is at present no 'community of shared memory' in the Pacific region. The best-known examples come from conflicting memories of the Second World War in China, Japan and Korea. Neither the Chinese nor the Koreans would accept the view presented by those in Japan who commemorate the memory of the war as having been waged for Asia's liberation from the West. Chinese and Korean memories of modern history reflect their national humiliations – going back to the Opium War in the case of China, to the Japanese colonisation in the case of Korea – and neither is easy to reconcile with Japan's view of its recent history. Transnationally-minded scholars and teachers have come together from these countries in search of a shared understanding of the past, but there is nothing comparable to the record in Europe where French and Germans, or Germans and Poles have been far more successful in reconciling their memories of the Second World War. They have been writing joint textbooks for a long time so that students in France and Germany, for instance, learn their shared history. Despite some sporadic attempts, nothing comparable exists among China, Korea and Japan.

But not just between China and Japan, or between Korea and Japan, but in many other pairs of countries in the Pacific region, it has been extremely difficult to develop any sense of shared memory. For instance, Indonesians' memories of the Second World War are at variance with those held by segments of the Japanese population that emphasise their country's role in assisting Indonesia's independence from the Netherlands. Although officially sanctioned memories have varied from the period of Sukarno's presidency to Suharto's and then to more democratic governments in the recent years, the overwhelming majority of the Indonesians remember the war, whether personally or vicariously, in connection with the brutal occupation of the country by Japanese military forces. If the war ultimately helped liberate Indonesia from Dutch rule, the Japanese occupation during the war was relevant only insofar as it made the people more determined than ever to struggle for their freedom.[34] Between Americans and Filipinos, there persists a similar contrast in the two countries' perceptions of their war, as there has been for a long time between Americans and Mexicans about the war of the 1840s. The bicentennial commemoration of the War of 1812 revealed that Canadians and Americans have contrasting perspectives on that war across the border along Lake Ontario. Between two geopolitical allies of sixty years, the United States and Japan, the seemingly unbridgeable gap has persisted in the ways in which the atomic bombings of 1945 are understood and explained, to such an extent that a planned exhibit of the *Enola Gay* at the Smithsonian's Air and Space Museum in 1995 that was initially designed to present both countries' perspectives never materialised. In the end it became a US-centric presentation, and Martin Harwit, the director of the Museum, had to quit in distress.[35]

These examples reveal that forces of nationalism remain strong, over-shadowing more global, transnational tendencies. In such circumstances, it will take a long time before a Pacific community on the basis of shared memory will develop. The twentieth century was a century in which two chronologies, one determined by geopolitics and the other by trans-nationalism, competed. This still remains the case at the beginning of the twenty-first century. On one hand, the outpouring of sympathy and support for the Japanese victims of the 2011 earthquake and tsunami revealed the depth of transnational empathy and heroic efforts by non-governmental organisations of all countries to offer humanitarian aid. On the other, territorial disputes between China and Japan, as well as among China, Vietnam and Indonesia reveal the tenacity of nationalistic emotions. There is much concern over the growing power of China, a geopolitical phenomenon, but there is equally notable support for human rights in China, notably freedom of the press. Perhaps transna-tionalism would prevail if something like the Trans-Pacific Partnership, a scheme that has been vigorously promoted in Washington, Wellington, Lima and several other capitals, should materialise. But its success would depend on whether these and other countries in the region took steps to turn it into a community of shared memory. That may be the most important, and the most difficult, task facing the Pacific countries today. Will they be able to establish Pacific history on the same footing as Atlantic history or European history? How can this be done? History education would play a critical role, not just the teaching and studying of one's own country's development but also informing students about wider regions and the whole world. Would this ever be realisable? The competing ways in which world history is still understood and taught in China, Germany and the United States are not very encouraging in that each country has its own set of ideas to bring to the subject.[36] But if Europe is successfully developing a community of shared memory, there is no reason why the Pacific may not someday do likewise. For that to happen, we would have to develop a conception of the Pacific as a community, as a region of transnational people, including transna-tional teachers and students ready to transcend the particular and embrace the universal.

## Notes

1. William Langer, *The Diplomacy of Imperialism, 1890–1902* (New York, 1935).
2. Bruce Cumings, *Dominion from Sea to Sea: Pacific Ascendancy and American Power* (New Haven, 2009); Michael H. Hunt and Steven I. Levine, *Arc of*

*Empire: America's Wars in Asia from the Philippines to Vietnam* (Chapel Hill, 2012).

3. Tsuyoshi Hasegawa, ed., *The Cold War in Asia, 1945–1991* (Stanford, 2011).

4. Akira Iriye, *Global and Transnational History: The Past, Present and Future* (Basingstoke, 2013).

5. Roland Wenzlhuemer, *Connecting the Nineteenth-century World: The Telegraph and Globalisation* (Cambridge, 2013).

6. Kaoru Sugihara, 'The Economy since 1800', ch. 8 in this volume.

7. Adam McKeown, 'Movement', ch. 7 in this volume. On the restriction of Asian immigration into the United States, Australia and other 'white' countries, see, among other works, Akira Iriye, *Pacific Estrangement: Japanese and American Expansion, 1897–1911* (Cambridge, MA, 1972); Adam M. McKeown, *Melancholy Order: Asian Migration and the Globalization of Borders* (New York, 2008).

8. Sugihara, 'The Economy since 1800', pp. 174–8.

9. McKeown, 'Movement', p. 159; Marilyn Lake and Henry Reynolds, *Drawing the Global Colour Line: White Men's Countries and the International Challenge of Racial Equality* (Cambridge, 2008).

10. Jeffry A. Frieden, *Global Capitalism: Its Fall and Rise in the Twentieth Century* (New York, 2006), chapter 9.

11. Kokuseisha, ed., *Nihon no 100 nen* [*One Hundred Years of Japan*] (Tokyo, 1991), p. 337.

12. Haruo Iguchi, *Unfinished Business: Ayukawa Gisuke and US–Japan Relations, 1937–1953* (Cambridge, MA, 2003).

13. Miwa Munehiro, *Taiheiyō sensō to sekiyu* [*The Pacific War and Oil*] (Tokyo, 2006), p. 135.

14. Izumi Hirobe, *Japanese Pride, American Prejudice: Modifying the Exlusion Clause of the 1924 Immigration Act* (Palo Alto, 2001).

15. Dirk Hoerder, *Cultures in Contact: World Migrations in the Second Millennium* (Durham, NC, 2002), pp. 401–3.

16. Akira Iriye, Petra Goedde and William I. Hitchcock, eds., *The Human Rights Revolution: An International History* (Oxford, 2012).

17. Quoted in Hermann Joseph Hiery, *The Neglected War: The German South Pacific and the Influence of World War I* (Honolulu, 1995), p. 186.

18. Hamid Dabashi, *The World of Persian Literary Humanism* (Cambridge, MA, 2012).

19. See Akira Iriye, *Cultural Internationalism and World Order* (Baltimore, 1997).

20. Tomoko Akami, *Internationalizing the Pacific: The United States, Japan and the Institute of Pacific Relations in War and Peace, 1919–45* (London, 2002).

21. Iriye, *Cultural Internationalism and World Order*, p. 106.

22. Gotō Ken'ichi, *Kokusaishugi no keifu* [*The Development of Internationalism*] (Tokyo, 2005), pp. 131–62.

23. Barbara Keys, *Globalizing Sport: National Rivalry and International Community in the 1930s* (Cambridge, MA, 2006).

24. Sayuri Guthrie-Shimizu, *Transpacific Field of Dreams: How Baseball Linked the United States and Japan in Peace and War* (Chapel Hill, 2012).

25. Yan Ni, *Senji Nitt-Chū eiga kōshōshi* [*The Cinematic Relationship between Japan and China during the War*] (Tokyo, 2010).
26. Sugihara, 'The Economy since 1800', p. 184.
27. Sakamoto Masahiro, ed., *Zusetsu 20 seiki no sekai* [The Twentieth-Century World in Graphs] (Tokyo, 1992), pp. 218–19.
28. Jean Heffer, *The United States and the Pacific: History of a Frontier* (Notre Dame, 2002), pp. 352, 402.
29. Samuel Moyn, *The Last Utopia: Human Rights in History* (Cambridge, MA, 2010).
30. Jeremi Suri, *Power and Protest: Global Revolution and the Rise of Détente* (Cambridge, MA, 2003).
31. See Henry Ninomiya Akiie, *Ajia no shōgaisha to kokusai ngo* [*The Disabled in Asia and International Non-governmental Organisations*] (Tokyo, 1999).
32. Quoted in Akira Iriye, 'The Internationalization of History', *American Historical Review* 94 (1989), 6.
33. Martin Conway and Kiral Klaus Patel, eds., *Europeanization in the Twentieth Century: Historical Approaches* (London, 2010).
34. Gotō Ken'ichi, *Tōnan Ajia kara mita kingendai Nihon* [*Modern and Contemporary Japan as Seen from Southeast Asia*] (Tokyo, 2012), pp. 337ff.
35. Martin Harwit, *An Exhibit Denied: Lobbying the History of Enola Gay* (New York, 1996).
36. Dominic Sachsenmeier, *Global Perspectives on Global History: Theories and Approaches in a Connected World* (Cambridge, 2011).

# Part II: Connections

# 6

# The Environment

Ryan Tucker Jones

On 27 January 1700, the usual small waves on the coast of Nakaminato, Japan began building unexpectedly. Residents, long accustomed to the signs of tsunami, fled from the seacoast. This time, the waves soon slackened. Villagers recorded the event in their local history books, wondered at the provenance of waves with no nearby earthquake, and thought little more of it. One day earlier, along the coast from present-day California to British Columbia, on the other side of the Pacific, the earth had shaken violently and gigantic waves more than 30 feet tall rushed upon the panic-stricken people. Oral histories told of the death of thousands.[1] More than three hundred years later, on 11 March 2011, inhabitants of the same Japanese villages woke to the ground shaking beneath them before massive walls of water smashed into their houses. All around the Pacific Ocean, from Alaska to Hawai'i to Chile to Australia, people quickly received tsunami alerts, both from buoys placed in the ocean itself and from the satellites positioned above the globe (see Figure 6.1). Residents of the eastern Pacific knew of the waves heading their way hours before arrival. One man, part native Yurok, was swept to sea when he came to the mouth of the Klamath River in Northern California hoping to observe the incoming waves. His body later washed ashore more than 300 miles to the north.[2]

In the twentieth century, large tsunami waves have surged across the breadth of the Pacific at least twice per decade, devastating and connecting human settlements in Russia, California, Japan, Chile, Alaska, Hawai'i, Sāmoa and elsewhere. The earthquake in Chile in 1960, which measured 8.8 on the Richter Scale (the largest of the century) sent 25-foot waves surging into Japanese towns over 10,000 miles away from their point of origin.[3] Tsunamis are a useful example and metaphor for the environmental history of the Pacific Ocean, pointing as they do to the connective force that the ocean itself has projected on humans over long distances. As a force felt on every side of the Pacific, tsunamis also demonstrate the importance that energy

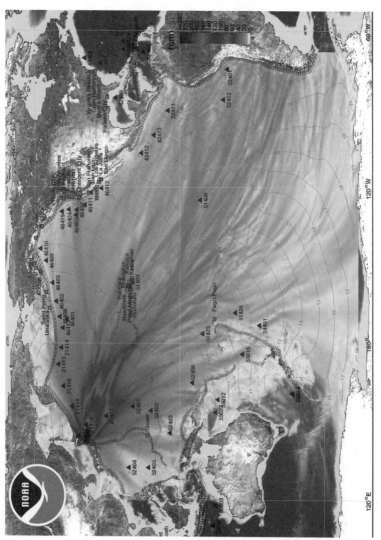

*Figure 6.1* Map of waves generated by the March 2011 Japan tsunami

*Figure 6.2*   Monument to Victims of 1964 Tsunami, Laupāhoehoe, Hawaiʻi

transfers – in the form of living organisms and moving matter – have played in the ocean's history. The environmental history of the Pacific over the past 500 years can be conceived of as a series of changing energy flows within this space – sometimes generated within the Pacific, sometimes generated outside of it, but always rearranging life there. Only humans, whales and the El Niño/La Niña (ENSO) climate pattern have been able to compete with tsunamis in transferring energy throughout such a large Pacific area.[4] The waves of the Pacific Ocean have also been a powerful mental construct for imagining connections between people separated by vast distances. To stand at one of the locations where tsunamis have concentrated Pacific energy, such as the north shore of Hawaiʻi (see Figure 6.2), the harbour at Valdez, Alaska, or Fukushima, Japan, is to feel straight, powerful lines of energy connecting distant shores and humans.

This chapter examines the history of the Pacific Ocean with a focus on the marine environment, revealing three distinct flows of energy. Before 1741, humans spread throughout the Pacific in search of the opportunities presented by unequal energy distributions. In the process they made a start at homogenising local environments above and below the equator. Between 1741 and 1880, colonial powers colluded with indigenous peoples to mine the Pacific's abundant energy sources, in turn reducing the numbers of large organisms and encouraging the success of smaller, less energy-needy creatures. After 1880, an era of intense energy infusion followed with the advent of modern warfare, tourism and economic development. These forces are still under way and have once again shifted Pacific energy flows, mostly impacting nearshore ecosystems. A focus on oceanic energy flows reveals an increasingly connected world, reshaped several times in strikingly similar ways throughout the Pacific – on foggy Kodiak fishing grounds, the coral reefs of Rarotonga, and anywhere else humans have encountered the Pacific's watery space. Tragically, it was these very physical and mental connections which brought death in 2011 to the Klamath River man, whose European and native American ancestors had done so much to link together the many sides of the Pacific. He never would have ventured to the ocean's shore if he had not known the waves were coming.

## Circulations

The nearly continuous volcanic 'Ring of Fire' surrounding the Pacific Ocean has suggested a unified space since at least the nineteenth century. These active, volcanic landmasses and islands contribute to an ocean rich in nutrients, and thus energy usable to living creatures.[5] The Pacific's energy is not evenly spread though. Just as a few locations generated most of the tsunami waves radiating through the basin, so many of the plant and animal species that dispersed throughout the ocean came from two evolutionary hot spots – the tropical Indo-South Pacific and the cold North Pacific.[6] Easterly flowing currents have distributed marine species from Indonesia throughout the Solomon Islands and Near Oceania, but long open-ocean passages have left Remote Oceania relatively bereft of fish variety and dependent upon human migration to receive mammals. The North Pacific sees both a large number of species, but, due to its primary productivity, also a massing of energy in higher trophic level species such as whales. These places of rich speciation are matched or exceeded in marine biomass by several corners of the ocean, including numerous marginal seas. Upwelling, which supports abundant fish populations, occurs along the eastern boundary, especially off the coasts of Ecuador, Chile and California. Warmer, cyclonic currents bathe the Japanese and Australian coastlines, with correspondingly smaller marine biomasses (though not necessarily less biodiversity).[7] Exceptions occur off the island of Hokkaido and in the Russian Far East, where the Oyashio and Kurile counter-currents provide the nutrients for large animal populations.[8]

None of these patterns are stable, as seasonal, decadal and even longer and more unpredictable oscillations shift energy. ENSO, in particular, makes the Pacific a uniquely coherent oceanic space, with heat moving thousands of miles between Chile and Australia in mere months. Extreme cases, such as the 1998 El Niño event, bleached corals from New Guinea to Cabo San Lucas. As in other oceans, Pacific trade winds blow steadily in the low latitudes. This was crucial for European navigators, who saw in the Pacific a recognisable navigational pattern, and early Polynesian voyagers also took advantage of the relatively weak easterlies of the southern hemisphere to make remarkable progress towards (or to) South America. Strong tropical storms, termed typhoons, commonly gather in the equatorial Pacific after the summer solstice, and spin westwards to collide with landmasses from Queensland to Japan. Much further north, the Aleutian Low spews out frequent, soaking cyclones towards Alaska and Canada throughout the winter. Although there are rarely clear demarcations between oceans, the Pacific terminates at a zone of sharply differentiated currents around 35°S, after which begin the permanently raging winds of the Antarctic.[9]

Pacific animals inhabited and created their own Pacific worlds. The Laysan albatross nests on several small equatorial islands, but ranges throughout the entirety of the Pacific Ocean in search of squids, fish and other prey. The birds have an intimate knowledge of the ocean's most productive locations, concentrating much of their feeding over submerged seamounts midway between the Hawaiian and Aleutian Islands and the rich mixing of Antarctic and Pacific waters.[10] Other seabirds literally remake the Pacific environment, depositing the ocean's nutrients in the form of faeces on eastern Pacific islands. Fused with coral limestone, bird waste created mountains of guano that provided nesting locations and later, an energy-rich fertiliser that would attract humans.[11] Other animals – especially other predators such as whales, seals, sharks and salmon – used the Pacific's geographical and seasonal energy differentials to craft migratory strategies, allowing them to reproduce in places of low biomass (usually equatorial) and to feed in more abundant locations (usually in high latitudes). Consuming, dying and being preyed upon, migratory animals redistributed energy throughout the ocean, a role Pacific humans also played.

Pacific humans have long followed and reshaped these energy flows, especially as they migrated out of agricultural homelands and on to islands. Research on Kinmen Island, near Taiwan, shows more than a millennium of wildly fluctuating human population and total biomass, as Chinese settlers exploited, abandoned, re-inhabited and re-thought their low-energy homeland. By the 1600s they had adapted architecture and beliefs that attempted to blunt the howling sandstorms that had replaced pre-contact forests.[12] Austronesians, as they colonised much of Oceania, brought similar transformations to previously uninhabited oceanic islands. With a suite of coevolved domesticates and a preference for settled agriculture, these Polynesians-in-the-making helped eliminate hundreds of endemic species, including about half of all Hawaiian bird species. Species introduction, forest clearance and heavy use of nearshore environments reshaped Hawai'i and other islands to more closely resemble the heavily cultivated Southeast Asian islands whence Oceanians originated.[13] Often the chain of ecological change in Pacific environments was complex, interwoven with the ocean and other species' lives. For example, seabirds were the crucial fertilisers of the otherwise low-energy landscape of Rapa Nui (Easter Island). When humans killed too many of the birds, agriculture faltered and depopulation followed.[14]

In the North Pacific the story was somewhat different, due in part to the difficulty of practicing agriculture. The seafaring Eskimo peoples who colonised much of the region significantly reduced other large animal populations, and probably caused the local extinction of Steller's sea cow.[15] The Aleuts living on Sanak Island, on the other hand, established a less volatile relationship with their abundant ecosystem. After an initial period of overharvesting of marine mammals and intertidal invertebrates, human predation played a stabilising role on the ecosystem, and little long-term change in their prey species' populations can be seen until Aleuts themselves were removed in the 1940s.[16] Despite such differences, prehistorical human demographic trends show an astounding similarity from Tahiti to Alaska, explained probably by a common orientation to the ocean and a shared vulnerability to changes in sea temperature and nutrient flow.[17] These same circum-Pacific factors could also encourage divergent trends. With the onset of the Little Ice Age (*c.*1300 CE), Oceanian voyaging ceased (or diminished), probably due to lower sea levels and decreased oceanic productivity.[18] In the North Pacific, increased energy due to a strong Aleutian Low storm system fostered a stronger oceanic orientation, and growing trade and warfare linked a wide area from Siberia to the Northwest Coast.[19]

By the sixteenth century, an axis stretching from China to Sumatra had become the centre of Pacific ecological exchange. There, Chinese demand for the products of forest and sea drove rapid environmental change. The hunt for dyewood, civet cats, *bêche-de-mer*, tortoiseshell and other items of consumption and decoration further directed local communities throughout the Southwest Pacific towards the ocean and linked them with distant, agricultural civilisations. After initially harvesting off Hainan and Japan, from the fifteenth to eighteenth centuries Chinese ships scoured the convoluted shorelines from the Philippines to Maluku to Sumatra, sometimes collecting the remnants of sealife for years before returning to China. Harvesting marine life could mobilise entire local communities, as men, women, and children caught animals like sea slugs by hand.[20] Such ease of capture and insatiable demand when intersecting with ecosystems high in endemism could mean swift decline. As early as the eighteenth century hawksbill turtles were extinct around the Togian Islands.[21] A counterexample to increasing pressure on non-humans is found on the island of Okinawa, which fell under Japanese control in 1609. In line with the developing policy of isolation (*sakoku*), its overseas trade withered. Sugar cane production – and thus deforestation – proceeded at a much slower rate for the next several centuries, while afforestation and soil conservation efforts were stepped up. Still, devastating trifectas of earthquake, tsunami and typhoon twice struck the islands (in 1664 and 1709), killing thousands of Okinawans and demonstrating that no state's policies could completely keep out the Pacific world.[22]

Pacific people had various ways of understanding and regulating their changing relationships with the ocean. Throughout Oceania, periodic *tabu* restrictions put moratoria on the harvest of some species (often to reserve them for aristocratic feasts). Nearly half of Tongan gods were fish, and each possessed a mythological history and place of origin. Milkfish, for example, were said to have come from Sāmoa and therefore were guests that should be treated with respect. Knowledge of these histories and associations was crucial for fishing success and determined which members of the species a fisherman would target.[23] Aleuts explained sea-otters' humanlike behaviour through the creatures' origins as a pair of incestuous lovers.[24] Other humans made explicit compacts with fellow predators, as the Palawans did with crocodiles in order to prevent attacks.[25] Even today, Papua New Guineans reserve shark fishing for special, high-ranking members of society who possess the ability to call sharks in to shore.

Hawaiians possessed perhaps the best-known articulation of humans' relationship with the surrounding sea. They believed that spirit-ancestors, called *'aumakua*, would choose to enter specific sharks in order to aid descendants. These sharks would help drive fish into nets or provide guidance to lost seafarers.[26] Thus, Hawaiians,

Aleuts and others described the ways in which human and animal worlds overlapped and resembled each other, tracing multiple species' interconnected circulations around a Pacific world. Pacific stories also described the limits of human habitation. The Humalgüeño Indians of Cedros Island attributed their lack of contact over the treacherous currents separating them from Baja California to a demon that made it a sin to even look in that direction. This tale held a fearsome truth – when Spanish Jesuits convinced the Humalgüeños to leave the island and accept baptism in 1732, a shark grabbed the group's shaman 'and carried him away between its teeth, with the onlookers on the beach unable to do anything'.[27]

The entrance of Iberians, Dutch, and English beginning in the fifteenth century did little to reroute human circulations, but did impact trans-Pacific biological exchanges. Seafaring people throughout the region had exchanged sweet potatoes, originally obtained from Peru, but they had not spread to the Philippines until the Spanish brought them sometime after 1571.[28] From the Philippines this nutritious tuber entered existing Asian maritime circuits, becoming established in Okinawa in 1606 and in Japan slightly later. The Japanese merchant who imported it to Satsuma about 1665 was later worshiped as the 'Master of the Chinese Potato'.[29] The sweet potato then began a return voyage eastwards across the Pacific, becoming established with the Mexican name of *camote* throughout Micronesia. Many other plants, important and trivial, crossed the Pacific on European ships. Spanish mercantilists attempted to transplant several profitable Asian spices to the Philippines and Mexico, but it was often informal, decisively Pacific circuits that connected these separate botanical worlds.[30] For example, in the late sixteenth century Filipino sailors spread coconut groves through Western Mexico and Panama, finding a source of familiarity in the scattered trees which, like them, had managed to survive the long float across the Eastern Pacific.[31] Even as Spanish Pacific links declined after the eighteenth century, their botanical circuits continued to function. Don Francisco de Paula Marin, a Spaniard in King Kamehameha's Hawaiian court, travelled the Pacific from Palau to Nootka Sound and planted seeds from every corner of the world – coffee, papaya and prickly pear were notable – in his Pearl Harbor garden. Despite the alien nature of his global cache of crops, Marin was careful to offer a selection to the Hawaiian gods at the beginning of every Makahiki festival.[32]

The impact of this Magellanic Exchange did not rival that of the Columbian Exchange, where Old World weeds, animals and – most importantly – disease, caused rapid demographic change and shepherded European colonisation. Some evidence showing declines of up to two-thirds of the population in the Philippines, Guam and Spice Islands has emerged, and epidemic disease would later hit the North Pacific hard, but in much of the Pacific, colonial populations were small, distances vast and fewer Old World animals were unknown.[33] At places like Tahiti, European introductions of novel plants and animals were often foiled by Tahitian indifference or competition by indigenous species (though guava was an aggressive if tasty exception throughout the Pacific). Additionally, some Pacific peoples, with flexible cosmologies, easily appropriated exotics, as was the case with the Aboriginal 'cat dreaming' of Northern Australia.[34] Thus, the effect of human and biological circulations before 1750 was primarily one of Pacific homogenisation, as Spanish galleons, Chinese merchants and Filipino sailors completed the work of Oceanians in fulfilling the coconut, sweet potato and prickly pear's Pacific destinies.

In the nineteenth century, Pacific colonists turned increasingly to more deliberate methods of homogenising the vast region. Founded in 1861, Australia's Victoria Acclimatisation Society brought alpacas, llamas and other 'useful and beautiful productions of nature' to the continent.[35] Another example was the successful introduction of North American salmon to various South Pacific rivers. Between 1875 and 1907 supporters of New Zealand acclimatisation efforts released millions of juvenile salmon into South Island rivers, where the fish have since established permanent runs.[36] Though in Chile successful introduction took longer, by the 1980s coho and chinook salmon had colonised many Pacific-facing rivers. Previously, only the warm equatorial waters had prevented this colonial fish's expansion into the ideal salmon habitat of the fast-flowing, cold rivers of New Zealand and Chile, fronting rich marine ecosystems of frequent upwelling. Salmon today are increasingly a Pacific species, as the wild Atlantic variety has been eliminated from much of its former range.[37] Thus, energy transfers in the Pacific over the last 500 years have in some cases made the ocean resemble the rest of the world, and in other ways taken on a more definite and expansive biogeographical identity. Meanwhile, peoples in the Pacific and from outside had begun remaking the ocean in another way, by extracting many of its largest inhabitants.

## Energy extraction

In 1741, the shipwrecked, starving men of Vitus Bering's Russian voyage of exploration – a cosmopolitan mixture of Siberian natives,

Russians and other Europeans who had just sighted Alaska – killed their first Steller's sea cow, a gigantic thirty-foot-long species of manatee. Though the energy expenditure was enormous, the reward was even greater; the first sea cow fed the thirty men for three months. Steller's sea cow had provided food, but in the eighteenth and nineteenth centuries nutrition would be the least important reason for killing the Pacific's animals. Along the shores and islands between the Kurile Islands and Vancouver Island, Russian traders soon organised the export of sea-otter, fur-seal and sea-lion skins to Europe and – mostly – to China. Sea cows became collateral victims, used to fuel the hunters who were after more oil- and fur-rich species. There were not many of the slow-moving behemoths anyway, and the last was probably killed in 1768.

The killing of the sea cow and the fur rush that followed it would be typical of a new era in several ways. From the 1750s through the 1910s, the Pacific was transformed into the world's larder, for it held massed energy in the form of whales, seals and fish on a greater scale than any other ocean (save the then inaccessible Antarctic). Though still oriented towards the Chinese market, the removal of Pacific energy increased in scale and involved ever more cosmopolitan coalitions of people. It required both the strengthening of European-style property rights on land and the removal of any restraints in the ocean. Focused increasingly on areas remote from large human populations, the era of extraction created a Pacific more extensively and less intensively inhabited, one poorer in large creatures and richer in smaller, opportunistic organisms.[38] The Pacific hunt coincided with the last years of the Little Ice Age, when the North Pacific experienced an unprecedented abundance of large marine mammals. Its conclusion also matched the onset of warmer weather after 1880, which likely helped to reduce animal numbers. In the South Pacific, on the other hand, the modern warm period has seen the return of a more productive sea, blunting the effects of the era of extraction.

After Cook's third voyage, which visited the small Russian establishments in 1778, English, French and American fur traders came to the North Pacific in search of sea otters and fur seals. Many of these fur bearers had been hunted by Kamchadals, Aleuts, Tlingits and Haida before European arrival, and these people continued to do most of the killing as they entered into wider Pacific relationships, sometimes for profit, sometimes against the threat of kidnap and worse. Aleuts, in particular, became great travellers in pursuit of marine mammals, using their superbly crafted kayaks and finely honed hunting eyes to spread their homelands' ecologies – with reduced marine mammal numbers – between Baja California and the southern Kurile Islands, the heartland of North Pacific energy abundance. This native hunt peaked around the 1820s and continued through the middle of the twentieth century. Unsurprisingly, the scraping of the sea provoked resistance. Tlingits and others furiously defended long-held rights to specific parts of the ocean, seeing few advantages to incorporation into a Pacific open to all. As Russians departed the eastern Pacific in the 1860s, Canadian, Japanese, American and Indian fur- and seal-seekers increasingly pressed into remote Alaskan and Siberian inlets, proudly defiant of any state attempts at conservation.

There were fewer coalitions of lethal hunter and European merchants in the South Pacific, but nor were there huge numbers of fur-bearing animals. Tasmania and the Bass Strait Islands provided exceptions; there in the early nineteenth century abducted or hired Aboriginal women would pose as seals, swimming unnoticed right up to the creatures before dispatching them.[39] Some sealing also took place in New Zealand, with miserable crews of British, French and Māori hunters left to do bloody work. In Queensland, Australia, after 1850, European settlers began killing green turtles and dugong, a smaller, more plentiful relative of Steller's sea cow.[40] South of the line, however, humans mostly set their sights lower, on the *bêche-de-mer*. While sea otters warmed Chinese bodies, the slugs when smoked fueled Chinese libidos. The *bêche-de-mer* trade had been important in the Pacific for centuries, but as they had in the North Pacific, Europeans expanded the scope and scale of biomass extraction, beginning in Fiji in the 1830s, and spreading throughout Micronesia and Melanesia.[41] Tropical waters, lower in nutrients, supported smaller (and thus more numerous) animals, which were harder to extinguish entirely. Not so sandalwood, the aromatic bark harvested in unsustainable quantities in a series of rushes from Fiji (*c.*1800) to the Solomon Islands, shipped to China, and still difficult to find throughout its former range.[42]

One extractive enterprise that spanned both hemispheres was whaling. In general, the pursuit spread northwards through the Pacific, beginning in the 1790s off the coasts of Chile and Peru, moving to New Zealand and Fiji that same decade, to Japanese, Hawaiian and equatorial seas in the 1820s, the Kodiak grounds off Alaska in the 1840s, the sheltered grey whale breeding lagoons of Baja California in the 1850s, and, finally, to the Sea of Okhotsk and the Bering Sea in the 1860s. Whaling was the ultimate cosmopolitan enterprise, employing Americans, Swedes, Inuit, Māori, Hawaiians, Fijians and countless other Pacific peoples. The men who killed leviathan not only harvested increasingly remote stretches of the sea, but visited their appetites upon out-of-the way islands, such as Juan Fernández off the Chilean coast, where provisions were found in the form of transplanted Eurasian animals such as pigs.[43] Because whales, more than any other Pacific creature with the exception of humans, ranged and migrated throughout the entire basin, their pursuit knit the ocean together like no other. Voyages touching Chile, Honolulu, Sāmoa, Japan and Kamchatka – spilling out deserters and removing whales at all points – were not uncommon, and they reproduced the geography of tsunami energy. Debate continues about the hunt's impact on Pacific whale numbers, with sperm and humpback whales probably faring better than grey, right and bowhead whales, species that had nearly met the sea cow's fate by the early twentieth century.

At times Pacific harvests could be breathtaking in their savage suddenness and thoroughness. In the early 1900s, Japanese fowlers alighted on a series of Central Pacific islands in search of albatross feathers to feed the global hat market for the long-lived (and slowly reproducing) birds. As a shocked visitor to Midway Atoll wrote in 1902, 'Everywhere ... great heaps, waist high, of dead albatrosses were found. Thousands upon thousands ... had been killed with clubs ... the carcasses thrown in heaps to rot.' Two years later, the Japanese left devastated Midway, landed on Lisiansky Island, and killed a further 284,000 birds. Even after the American government proclaimed the islands a bird sanctuary, poaching continued through the 1930s.[44] Further north, in the waters off Kamchatka, it was the Japanese, Americans and Canadians who evaded Russian conservation efforts and destroyed sea otters, fur seals and whales. A Pacific focused on exporting living energy that mostly concentrated in the remaining uninhabited places was a space that defied state control, and for that reason remained cosmopolitan and interconnected.

It is not simple to reconstruct the social consequences of the era of energy extraction. *Bêche-de-mer* harvesting in Oceania seems to have increased the power of local chiefs, as the benefits of controlling labour increased dramatically. On the Northwest Coast it is thought that the wealth received in exchange for pelts allowed a flourishing of traditional culture, manifested, for example, in a boom in totem pole construction.[45] On St Lawrence Island near the Bering Strait, on the other hand, American whalers who killed walruses so decimated this crucial food resource that thousands of Inupiat starved to death in the 1880s.[46] More typical may be the recent experience of the inhabitants of Ontong Java, a small island in the Solomon Islands, where the *bêche-de-mer* boom and bust of the early 2000s saw dramatic increases in both cash income and the levels of social inequality.[47] Animal communities also restructured in this era, with smaller organisms inhabiting lower trophic levels thriving as their predators were removed. Abalones and sea urchins exploded along the western United States and Mexico with the decline of sea otters, and fish everywhere found more abundant food as their competitors were turned into furs and oil.[48] These smaller organisms were less mobile, however, and thus could not link the Pacific world in the way that their migratory predators could; the era of energy extraction contained within it the seeds of its own demise.

The origins and the end of the age of energy extraction came together on the Farallon Islands, today uninhabited, wave-battered sentinels visible on a clear day from San Francisco. These islands may have played host to occasional Yurok visitors from thousands of miles to the north before European arrival – mysterious artefacts hint at such. What is certain is that by 1806 Russians were depositing groups of up to 100 Alaska and California natives there to harvest sea lions and murres. Every autumn these same factors drew great white sharks from around the Pacific. This Pacific blend of people lived in rough rock and earthen huts and cooked their food on fires stoked by sea-lion bones. Sea lion genitals were later ground up and sold to the Chinese market in San Francisco, an Eastern Pacific extension of older South Asian circuits. In 1896 the California Academy of Sciences prohibited further capture of bird eggs, whose numbers had been cut by 82 per cent. Today, while humans have only a fleeting presence on the Farallons, the sharks have returned. However, all life around the Farallons faces new environmental conditions in the form of sunken nuclear waste, deposited there after the Second World War, harbinger of a new Pacific era.[49]

Humans have not stopped extracting energy from the Pacific. Today, its commercial fisheries are the largest in the world, shark populations are crashing as a result of horrifyingly wasteful and cruel finning, and dynamite fishing spreading throughout Southeast Asia holds the threat of permanent marine extinctions. However, with the global replacement of animal fats by fossil fuels, energy flows in the Pacific began to reverse from around the 1880s. Like the first outgoing rush of water that tempts many into harvesting the exposed creatures of the ocean but heralds an imminent tsunami, the era of energy extraction would be followed by something in many ways more powerful.

## Energy infusion

The Japanese, drawn into the Pacific after decades of isolation to harvest birds, marine mammals and phosphate, soon discovered a need to invest more energy into the development of these industries, especially when their nation was granted trust control over the Marianas, Carolines and Marshall Islands in the aftermath of the First World War. Turning the Marianas into 'one vast cane plantation', the Japanese also came to appreciate the beauty of the islands and started to pursue some reforestation measures and fish conservation.[50] As war approached in the 1930s, the Japanese sensed the new strategic importance air travel had given remote Pacific islands, and constructed airfields using conscripted indigenous and Korean labour. Cutting down palm trees and dynamiting coral, Japan's forceful re-entry into the Pacific brought to a head the defining environmental story of the modern Pacific – massive energy infusions in the form of war, development, tourism and global warming.[51] The effects on the environment were also typical of this new era when landside developments impacted the ocean, especially the nearshore, taking an especially great toll on coral reefs (which flourish in low-energy environments) and reversing the focus on the ocean itself. While much of the rest of the world busied itself extracting the remains of long-dead sea creatures pressed into fossil fuels, the Pacific's living biomass received that energy back.

Second World War combat in the Pacific shattered forests, beaches and reefs with an unprecedented onslaught of steel, concrete and human bodies. Allied forces arrived in Micronesia in 1945 to scenes of devastation. On Ulithi Atoll, the lagoon was 'strewn with wreckage' and most of the trees had been cut down during the period of occupation. Americans would leave their own trail of discarded military equipment from the Aleutian Islands to Guam, rusting heaps that still poison streams and bays. However, immediate wartime damage was often quickly recouped. American inspectors noted that, already by 1946 on Chuuk the jungles had 'taken over during the year that has elapsed since the Japanese surrender'. [52] In fact, war in some ways temporarily reduced the environmental pressures brought by high-modern economies, as the Japanese fishing and whaling fleets went dormant during the conflict. The momentum created by wartime mobilisation was recaptured though, and by the 1950s the Japanese had rebuilt the fleet and were fishing above historical levels.[53] In Micronesia, Americans soon rebuilt beyond the level of prewar infrastructure, mainly by tearing out live coral in order to build airstrips and roads.[54] Over the past seven decades, Chuuk lagoon has seen the spectrum of the Pacific War's environmental entanglements – on its floor still sit 52 Japanese wrecks (out of approximately 7,000 remaining Second World War vessels on the Pacific seabed), slowly leaking oil. At the same time, these wrecks have become biodiversity hot spots that draw dive tourists, serving as artificial reefs supplanting the living versions increasingly on the retreat.[55]

Other massive, one-time insertions of energy into Pacific ecosystems also had less enduring effects than lower-energy additions of the infrastructure required to support war and economic development.[56] For example, the 1989 Exxon Valdez oil spill in Prince William Sound, Alaska – still the largest in Pacific history – killed thousands of animals, but left few discernible traces in the ecosystem ten years later.[57] The greatest human release of energy in the first half of the twentieth century occurred during the Hiroshima and Nagasaki atomic bombings, but their environmental effects were also surprisingly minimal. Plant and animal life seemed largely unaffected over the long run. Similarly, nuclear testing on Bikini, Enewetok and Moruroa, while causing real human health problems and pulverising reefs, left longer impacts in the form of increasingly urbanised, commercialised, import-dependent Pacific societies. By the 1980s the small Micronesian Island of Kwajalein, which received missiles and US army personnel from across the ocean, was the most urbanised spot in the Pacific.[58] Warfare also hastened biological exchanges throughout the ocean, with the explosion of bird-devouring brown tree snakes transported to Guam on US military vessels the most famous example.

Such massive growth of military and state power stunned potential opposition in the Pacific. Critics of California oil pollution fell silent after the 1930s, Oregonians dammed their salmon rivers to provide the energy necessary for frantic ship construction, while Koreans and Panamanians had little choice but to accept US military bases. Plans to remake the environment often outran rational bounds. San Francisco's wartime Reber Plan would have created two land crossings through the bay, permanently dividing California's largest estuarine ecosystem.[59] Northwards, the USA used Second World War technology such as sonar to develop a new Alaskan crabbing industry by the 1950s, while evacuations of Aleuts during the war opened Attu and Amchitka Islands to military control and nuclear testing.[60] On Oahu, through a massive influx of sewage the Kaneohe Marine Corps Air Station ruined the reefs, poisoned the fish, and created permanent algae blooms in what had been Hawai'i's largest lagoon. As elsewhere, some species benefitted from the added nutrients, including exotic imports like the Chesapeake oyster and

Philippine mangroves.[61] Reef destruction throughout the Pacific enhanced the ocean's impact on the land, as storm energy encountered fewer buffers, slamming already vulnerable places such as the Philippines.

From an environmental perspective, the arrival of modern warfare and the explosion of modern tourism in the Pacific look almost identical. Linked to the advent of air travel, both phenomena encouraged the rampant growth of extremely long-lasting physical infrastructure, the radical reshaping of local topography, intensive use of otherwise lightly peopled habitats, and the further ecological and cultural integration of the Pacific. Often warfare and tourism overlapped. In the 1940s American servicemen stationed in Cairns, Australia, took regular 'field trips' to the nearby Great Barrier Reef, returning to base with huge numbers of corals hacked off. The creation of Honolulu as a major military outpost initiated mass tourism to the most diverse ecosystem in the United States. Elsewhere, the parallel intensification of agriculture through fertiliser (often supported by developmental aid) and the build-up of tourist and military complexes restructured Pacific ecologies. From Rarotonga to Queensland, as nutrients entered the sea and killed fish, crown of thorns starfish populations exploded and ravaged coral reefs.[62] Tourism was also tied directly to resource extraction. In 2004 China struck a deal with the Cook Islands to add it to the coveted 'approved destination status' for Chinese tourists in exchange for a stake in fishing within the nation's Exclusive Economic Zone.[63]

The impetus for tourist and military development did not come solely from the circum-Pacific powers, but often came from within indigenous Pacific populations. When, in the 1990s, Maui's tourist board proposed lengthening the island's airport, which had the potential to destroy important bird habitat, a native Hawaiian man lent the infrastructure supporters his family's *'aumakua*, the owl

*Figure 6.3* 'Protect and Defend (Don't Dredge My Home)'. Highway mural near the US Naval Base on Guam protesting Pacific military developments.

(*pueo*), as a logo for the project.[64] The Maui Pueo Coalition then backed the successful plan, which led to a dramatic increase in tourists from around the Pacific Rim in the 2000s. Similarly, although Guamanians lost control of their land through tourist development and saw their reefs dredged to support US naval expansion on the island, they largely welcomed the move of an American air base from Okinawa because of the massive economic stimulus it represented (Figure 6.3).[65] One of the major logistics suppliers of the American navy there is the Alutiiq Corporation, the native corporation of Alaska's Kodiak Islanders. Thus, those seen largely as environmental victims of the era of energy extraction have at times helped to coordinate a new era of development in the Pacific.[66]

In a less direct manner, but perhaps of even longer-term import, the Pacific has also become the world's largest receptacle of heat energy in the form of carbon dioxide captured from industrial emissions around the world. Increased acidification threatens the Great Barrier Reef, while at the same time higher sea temperatures offer coral polyps opportunities further from the equator. Superheated El Niños have become more frequent, and – amazingly – may be tied to an increase in tsunami frequency.[67] Just as animals have redistributed, Pacific humans are beginning to change their habitation as sea levels rise, though some particularly vulnerable South Pacific Islanders believe that the Christian god will intervene before crisis is reached.

Pacific pollution in many forms has had the ironic side effect of drawing together humans from different sides of the ocean. Since the mid-twentieth century material evidence of distant consumers has washed up on Pacific beaches every day. In the 1950s, radioactive walruses sometimes showed up on Alaskan shores, eerie evidence of secret Soviet Pacific activities.[68] Additionally, the use of the Pacific as a nuclear testing and dumping ground galvanised new environmentalist organisations. Greenpeace, formed in Vancouver in 1971, focused on the twin Pacific issues of extraction and energy dumping, launching its defining campaigns against Soviet whaling off California and nuclear testing in French Polynesia and the Aleutian Islands. These causes found adherents from New Zealand to Baja California.[69] Efforts to undo the results of energy extraction have thus far been more successful than stemming the tide of development; whales have rebounded, while tourist growth and military buildup continues.

Such circum-Pacific environmental developments fostered Pacific identities. In 1960, in the northern Alaskan town of Point Hope, Tikarmiut Eskimos challenged the American Energy Commission's plans to test out a 'peaceful' atomic bomb nearby. One participant recalled that the group finally succeeded in halting tests because,

> The Atomic Energy Commission was dealing with people who had been in the Pacific theaters of war in World War II. People who had traveled down to California, Hawai'i. Many of the people who were in the National Guard were familiar with nuclear effects of the bombs dropped on Hiroshima and Nagasaki.[70]

While atomic fear may have been a global issue in the second half of the twentieth century, for those living in Alaska it was profoundly a Pacific issue, and their resistance to nuclear testing resulted from the specifically Pacific experiences gained in an era of energy bombardment. A hallmark of modern Pacific environmentalism is an insistence that solutions to environmental problems do not lie within any state's territorial boundaries. The North Pacific Fur Seal Convention of 1911 and the South Pacific Forum's Fisheries Agency have validated the environmental resonance of the Pacific as a category. While the ocean in its entirety may fail on current management grounds, after 1965 the Soviet Union, Chile, Japan and the United States merged their tsunami early-warning systems in recognition of the pan-Pacific force such waves represented.[71]

In the last 500 years, tsunamis have not been the only transporters of Pacific energy. Humans have joined waves, whales and ENSO as significant, Pacific-wide ecological agents (in the process blunting whales' connective power and perhaps strengthening that of El Niño). Today's ocean has been reshaped by circum-Pacific exchanges, massive energy extraction and the even more massive energy infusion of the last century. The Pacific in the twenty-first century looks both more like the other world's oceans, and in such cases as its growing monopoly on salmon, more uniquely Pacific. Still, one would do well not to forget tsunamis – the 2011 event devastated Japanese salmon aquaculture, spilled nuclear radiation into the sea and transferred previously isolated sea creatures to the Oregon coast.[72] In its mixture of powerful human and natural energy, the tsunami encompassed the Pacific and its history.

## Notes

1. Brian Atwater, *The Orphan Tsunami of 1700: Japanese Clues to a Parent Earthquake in North America*, http://pubs.usgs.gov/pp/pp1707/pp1707.pdf.

2. 'Tsunami Victim Remains Wash Ashore', http://www.koinlocal6. com/news/local/story/Tsunami-victim-remains-wash-ashore-near-Fort/S2ii-Y--j0WNKCAEV0tzcA.cspx.

3. Walter Dudley and Min Lee, *Tsunami!*, 2nd edn. (Honolulu, 1998), p. 165.

4. J. R. McNeill, 'The Nascent Field of Pacific Environmental History', in McNeill, ed., *Environmental History in the Pacific World* (Aldershot, 2001), p. xix.

5. McNeill, 'The Nascent Field', p. xvi.

6. P. H. Barber, 'The Challenge of Understanding the Coral Triangle Biodiversity Hotspot', *Biogeography* 36 (2009), 1845; C. R. Harrington, 'The Evolution of Arctic Marine Mammals', *Ecological Applications* 18 (2008), 23–40.

7. Moshe Rapaport, ed., *The Pacific Islands: Environment and Society* (Honolulu, 1999).

8. George L. Hunt, Jr. and Phyllis J. Stabeno, 'Oceanography and Ecology of the Aleutian Archipelago: Spatial and Temporal Variation', *Fisheries Oceanography* 14, Suppl. 1 (2005), 292–306; Alan Longhurst, *Ecological Geography of the Sea* (Burlington, MA, 2007).

9. Donald Freeman, *The Pacific* (London, 2010), ch. 1; Longhurst, *Ecological Geography of the Sea*, ch. 12.

10. Carl Safina, *The Eye of the Albatross: Visions of Hope and Survival* (New York, 2002).

11. Gregory Rosenthal, 'Life and Labor in a Seabird Colony: Hawaiian Guano Workers, 1857–70', *Environmental History* 17 (2012), 744–82.

12. Huei-Min Tsai, 'Island Biocultural Assemblages – the Case of Kinmen Island', *Geographiska Annaler: Series B, Human Geography* 85 (2003), 209–18.

13. Patrich V. Kirch, 'Hawaii as a Model System for Human Ecodynamics', *American Anthropologist* 109 (2007), 8–26.

14. D. W. Steadman, 'Extinction of Polynesian Birds: Reciprocal Impacts of Birds and People', in Patrick V. Kirch and T. L. Hunt, eds., *Historical Ecology in the Pacific Islands: Prehistoric Environmental and Landscape Change* (New Haven, 1997), pp. 51–79.

15. David Yesner, 'Effects of Prehistoric Human Exploitation on Aleutian Sea Mammal Populations', *Arctic Anthropology* 25 (1988), 28–43.

16. Herbert D. G. Maschner, et al., 'Biocomplexity of Sanak Island', *Pacific Science* 63 (2009), 673–709.

17. Patrick D. Nunn, *Climate, Environment and Society in the Pacific during the Last Millennium* (Amsterdam, 2008).

18. Patrick V. Kirch and Jennifer Kahn, 'Advances in Polynesian Prehistory', *Journal of Archaeological Research* 15 (2007), 191–238.

19. Herbert Maschner and James W. Jordan, 'Catastrophic Events and Punctuated Culture Change: The Southern Bering Sea and North Pacific in a Dynamic Global System', in Dimitra Papagianni, Robert Layton and Herbert Maschner, eds., *Time and Change: Archaeological and Anthropological Perspectives on the Long Term in Hunter-Gatherer Societies* (Oxford, 2008), pp. 95–113.

20. Kathleen Schwerdtner Mañez and Sebastian C. A. Ferse, 'The History of Makassan Trepang Fishing and Trade', *PlosOne* 5, 6 (2010), 1: e11346. doi:10.1371/journal.pone.0011346.

21. Heather Sutherland, 'A Sino-Indonesian Commodity Chain: The Trade in Tortoiseshell in the Late Seventeenth and Eighteenth Centuries', in Eric Tagliacozzo and Wen-chin Chan, eds., *Chinese Circulations: Capital, Commodities and Networks in Southeast Asia* (Durham, NC, 2011), pp. 180–7.

22. George H. Kerr, *Okinawa: The History of an Island People* (Rutland, VT, 1957), pp. 198–207.

23. Marie-Claire Bataille-Benguigui, 'The Fish of Tonga: Prey or Social Partners?', *Journal of the Polynesian Society* 97 (1988), 185–98.

24. Waldemar Jochelson, comp., *Unangam Uniikangis Ama Tunuzangis: Aleut Tales and Narratives*, ed. Knut Bergsland and Moses L. Dirks (Fairbanks, AK, 1990), p. 707.

25. Ian van der Ploeg, Merlijn van Weerd and Gerard A. Persoon, 'A Cultural History of Crocodiles in the Philippines: Towards a New Peace Pact?', *Environment and History* 17 (2011), 232.

26. Martha Warren Beckwith, 'Hawaiian Shark Aamakua', *American Anthropologist* 19 (1917), 503–17.

27. Matthew Des Lauriers and Claudia García Des Lauriers, 'The Humalgüeños of Isla Cedros, Baja California, as Described in Father Miguel Venegas' 1739 Manuscript *Obras Californianas*', *Journal of California and Great Basin Anthropology* 26 (2006), 135, 138, 139. The Jesuit chronicler remarked with callous indifference, 'in truth, if someone had to die before receiving baptism, it should have been him, since he deserved it anyway': ibid., 139.

28. Chris Ballard, Paula Brown, R. Michael Bourke and Tracy Harwood, eds., *The Sweet Potato in Oceania: A Reappraisal* (Sydney, 2005).

29. Kerr, *Okinawa*, p. 184.

30. Paula de Vos, 'The Science of Spices: Empiricism and Economic Botany in the Early Spanish Empire', *Journal of World History* 17 (2006), 416–18.

31. Henry J. Bruman, 'Early Coconut Culture in Western Mexico', *The Hispanic American Historical Review* 25 (1945), 212–23.

32. Kenneth M. Nagata, 'Early Plant Introductions in Hawai'i', *The Hawaiian Journal of History* 19 (1985), 44.

33. Linda Newsom, *Conquest and Pestilence in the Early Spanish Philippines* (Honolulu, 2009), pp. 19, 20; Robert Boyd, *Coming Spirit of Pestilence: Introduced Infectious Diseases and Population Decline among Northwest Coast Indians, 1774–1874* (Seattle, 1999); Robert Rogers, *Destiny's Landfall: A History of Guam* (Honolulu, 1995).

34. Jennifer Newell, *Trading Nature: Tahitians, Europeans and Ecological Exchange* (Honolulu, 2010); David Trigger, 'Indigeneity, Ferality, and What "Belongs" in the Australian Bush: Aboriginal Responses to "Introduced" Animals and Plants in a Settler-Descendant Society', *Journal of the Royal Anthropological Institute* 14 (2008), 628–46.

35. Quotation from Thomas Dunlap, *Nature and the English Diaspora: Environment and History in the United States, Canada, Australia, and New Zealand* (Cambridge, 1999), p. 57.

36. Cristián Correa and Mart R. Gross, 'Chinook Salmon Invade Southern South America', *Biological Invasions* 10 (2008), 615–39.

37. Robert M. McDowall, 'The Origins of New Zealand's Chinook Salmon, *Oncorhynchus Tshawytscha*', *Marine Fisheries Review* 56 (1994), 1–7.

38. David Igler, *The Great Ocean: Pacific Worlds from Captain Cook to the Gold Rush* (Oxford, 2013).

39. Lyndall Ryan, *The Aboriginal Tasmanians* (Vancouver, BC, 1981).

40. Elaine Brown, *Cooloola Coast: Noosa to Fraser Island: The Aboriginal and Settler Histories of a Unique Environment* (St Lucia, Qld., 2000), pp. 170–1.

41. R. Gerard Ward, 'The Pacific Bêche-de-Mer Trade with Special Reference to Fiji', in Ward, ed., *Man in the Pacific Islands: Essays on Geographical Change in the Pacific Islands* (Oxford, 1972), pp. 91–123.

42. Dorothy Shineberg, *They Came for Sandalwood: A Study of the Sandalwood Trade in the South-West Pacific, 1830–1865* (Melbourne, 1967).

43. Daniel Francis, *The Great Chase: A History of World Whaling* (New York, 1991).

44. Safina, *The Eye of the Albatross*, pp. 150–2.

45. Robin Fisher, *Contact and Conflict: Indian–European Relations in British Columbia, 1774–1890* (Vancouver, BC, 1992).

46. John Bockstoce, *Whales, Ice, and Men: The History of Whaling in the Western Arctic* (Seattle, 1986).

47. Andreas Egelund Christensen, 'Marine Gold and Atoll Livelihoods: The Rise and Fall of the *Bêche-de-Mer* Trade on Ontong Java, Solomon Islands', *Natural Resources Forum* 35 (2011), 9–20.

48. James Estes, et al., eds, *Whales, Whaling, and Ocean Ecosystems* (Berkeley, 2006).

49. Peter White, *The Farallon Islands: Sentinels of the Golden Gate* (San Francisco, CA, 1995).

50. David C. Purcell, Jr., 'The Economics of Exploitation: The Japanese in the Mariana, Caroline and Marshall Islands, 1915–1940', *The Journal of Pacific History* 11 (1976), 202, 205.

51. Mark Peattie, *Nan'yō: The Rise and Fall of the Japanese in Micronesia* (Honolulu, 1992), p. 253.

52. Report of the Inspection of the Caroline Islands by the U.S. Pacific Fleet, August–October 1946, pp. 10, 34, RG 126, Records of the Office of Territories, San Francisco National Archives.

53. William M. Tsutsui, 'Landscapes in the Dark Valley: Toward an Environmental History of Wartime Japan', *Environmental History* 8 (2003), 294–311.

54. Stewart Firth, 'The War in the Pacific', in Donald Denoon, Stewart Firth, Jocelyn Linnekin, Malama Meleisea and Karen Nero, eds., *The Cambridge History of the Pacific Islanders* (Cambridge, 1997), p. 313.

55. Ulrike Guerlin, Barbara Egger, and Vidha Penalva, *Underwater Cultural Heritage in Oceania* (Paris, 2010), p. 18, http://unesdoc.unesco.org/images/0018/001887/188770e.pdf.
56. Judith A. Bennett, *Natives and Exotics: World War II and the Environment in the Southern Pacific* (Honolulu, 2009), p. 201.
57. Jeff Wheelwright, *Degrees of Disaster: Prince William Sound: How Nature Reels and Rebounds* (New Haven, 1994).
58. Mark D. Merlin and Ricardo M. González, 'Environmental Impacts of Nuclear Testing in Remote Oceania, 1946–1996', in J. R. McNeill and Corinna R. Unger, eds., *Environmental Histories of the Cold War* (Cambridge, 2010), pp. 167–202; Stewart Firth, *Nuclear Playground* (Sydney, 1987), p. 66.
59. Roger W. Lotchin, 'The City and the Sword: San Francisco and the Rise of the Metropolitan-Military Complex, 1919–1941', *Journal of American History* 65 (1979), 1012.
60. Mansell Blackford, *Pathways to the Present: US Development and its Consequences in the Pacific* (Honolulu, 2007), pp. 7, 107.
61. John Cullihey, *Islands in a Far Sea: Nature and Man in Hawaii* (San Francisco, 1988), pp. 116–18.
62. J. E. Randall, 'Chemical Pollution in the Sea and the Crown-of-Thorns Starfish (*Acanthaster planci*)', *Biotropica* 4 (1972), 132–44.
63. Tamara Renee Shie, 'Rising Chinese Influence in the South Pacific: Beijing's Island Fever', *Asian Survey* 47 (2007), 311.
64. Mansell G. Blackford, 'Business, Government, Tourism, and the Environment: Maui in the 1980s and 1990s', *Business and Economic History* 27 (1998), 209.
65. Frank Quimby, 'Fortress Guahan', *Journal of Pacific History* 6 (2011), 368.
66. United States Senate Committee on Homeland Security and Governmental Affairs, *New Information about Contracting Preferences for Alaska Native Corporations (Part II)*, 15 July 2009.
67. J. E. N. Veron, *A Reef in Time: The Great Barrier Reef from Beginning to End* (Cambridge, MA, 2008); César N. Caviedes, *El Niño in History: Storming through the Ages* (Gainesville, 2001).
68. Paul Josephson, *Red Atom: Russia's Nuclear Power Program from Stalin to Today* (Pittsburgh, 2005), pp. 135, 144.
69. Rex Weyler, *Greenpeace: How a Group of Ecologists, Journalists, and Visionaries Changed the World* (Vancouver, BC, 2004).
70. Dan O'Neill, *The Firecracker Boys* (New York, 1994), pp. 125, 221.
71. Dudley and Lee, *Tsunami!*, p. 319.
72. 'Autumn Salmon Season Opens in Tsunami-hit Minami-Sanriku', *The Asahi Shimbun* (27 September 2011); 'Tsunami Dock Cleared from Agate Beach, Cleanup Continues', *The Oregonian* (5 August 2012).

# 7

# Movement

## Adam McKeown

Historians often depict large bodies of water as contact zones, areas where different peoples and societies have interacted and developed common institutions.[1] The Pacific Ocean, however, has largely resisted this kind of framing. The vast distances and great diversity of peoples have foiled most attempts to imagine a coherent Pacific World.[2] At best, we have diverse histories of portions of the Pacific, such as the Pacific Rim, the Pacific Islands, the Asia Pacific or the American Pacific. Each of these Pacifics does frame a certain contact zone. But those spaces are each only a part of what could legitimately be considered the Pacific, and they are rarely conceived in ways that have significant interaction with each other.

The massive geography of the Pacific is not the only reason that it is usually treated more as a zone of fragmentation than as one of interaction. Perceptions of unity and diversity across the Pacific are as deeply grounded in the creation of social distinctions, cultural imaginaries and political boundaries as in the geographical challenge of crossing such distances. Improved communication technologies can help to overcome geographical boundaries. But technology is always deployed within particular social and historical contexts. Sometimes communication technologies were important tools for the expansion of political and cultural ambitions. At other times, social borders and cultures of difference blocked the effects of technology. New communication technologies could even be used to enforce these cultural borders and make them into very concrete obstacles against interaction.

By following the movement of peoples and goods around the Pacific, we can trace some of these shifting social geographies over time. We can see when different Pacific worlds expanded and contracted and how they related to each other. We will also find that following the movement of peoples and goods frequently brings us beyond the borders of the Pacific. At certain times, some parts of the

Pacific have been more significant as hubs for movement and interaction beyond the Pacific than within the Pacific.

A few major Pacific zones of interaction appear repeatedly throughout history. The Austronesian-speaking Pacific has connected the maritime world from Hawai'i and Easter Island all the way to Madagascar in the Indian Ocean. The eastern branch of this language group has long defined a distinct Island Pacific made up of Melanesia, Micronesia and Polynesia, a Pacific world that has had relatively infrequent contact with the outside world until the past two centuries. The western Austronesian branch of Malay speakers has, by contrast, played an important role in the creation of an integrated, multi-ethnic Southwest Pacific/maritime Southeast Asian world. This has long been a hub of global interaction and an important interface between the maritime and littoral societies, but could just as easily be conceived as part of an Indian Ocean or Eurasian world than as part of the Pacific. As we move around the Pacific coasts, we find many other rimland societies that have had even less consistent interactions with the maritime Pacific. Many of these, such as China, Japan, the Moche Empire in Peru, the Spanish Empire and the United States have been anchors of economic and political power in the Pacific. But their interactions with each other and the rest of the Pacific have been sporadic. Tracing the ebb and flow of trans-Pacific relations between these rimland states is yet another way to map out Pacific zones of interaction. And as we extend our gaze, we will find that other places, such as Australia, the Russian Pacific and the ships and men involved in whaling and the early China trade, often cross, relocate or fall in the cracks between these bigger categorisations of island, rimland, regional and trans-Pacific spaces.

Whether all of these fragments can be tied together as 'Pacific History' is still an open question. But the Pacific does frame a space in which to think about the possible relationships between these different zones. And following the movement of goods and people will also remind us of the extent to which the ebbs and flows of Pacific history have been connected to the outside world and the broader processes of global interaction.

## Rimland settlement and the Austronesian Pacific

The Pacific rimlands and islands of Southeast Asia were settled long before the majority of islands. The first migrations of Homo sapiens out of Africa about 60,000 years ago travelled along the northern coast of the Indian Ocean. By 50,000 BCE, people had settled throughout the area from what is now mainland Southeast Asia to New Guinea and Australia, beginning the long association of this region to the Indian Ocean. Many of these migrants probably moved along the coastline living off ocean resources and travelling with basic maritime technologies. Sea levels were generally lower than contemporary levels, and much of the region between Southeast Asia and Australia was above water, although some significant deep-water voyages were still necessary to get to Australia. Humans spread to the northern tip of coastal Asia by at least 40,000 years ago. The dates for movement into the Americas are still disputed. The first waves may have crossed over as long as 40,000 years ago or as recently as 15,000 years ago. But it is clear that humans reached the southern tip of the Americas no later than 12,000 years ago.

The original rimland settlements grew in quite isolated circumstances. Indeed, Aboriginal Australians are the most genetically isolated human group in the world. Powerful states such as China, Japan, the Maya, and Chavin and Moche in coastal Peru emerged but had little, if any contact with each other. As late as the nineteenth century, the descendants of original settlers were still predominant populations in the Americas, Australia and highland New Guinea (where this is still the case). Isolated pockets of these aboriginal settlers also remained in other parts of Asia, but most had been pushed out or had intermingled with later waves of migrants. Among the most notable of those later migrants were the Austronesian speakers, who were the first to penetrate significantly beyond the rimlands to the interior of the Pacific. They also came to dominate many of the coastal areas and islands of the southwestern Pacific and reestablished connections with the Indian Ocean.

The movement of Austronesian speakers across the islands of the Pacific is one of the great human migrations of the past 5,000 years, helping to shape the linguistic and cultural map of the contemporary world. Like the contemporaneous movements of Bantu, Sino-Tibetan and Indo-European speakers, it was associated with the spread of powerful technologies. For Austronesian speakers, these included domesticated rice, terrace agriculture, pottery, stilt houses, domesticated pigs, dogs, chickens and tattoos. But the Austronesian speakers were the only group before the sixteenth century to move primarily by sea, using advanced navigational technologies and outrigger canoes. It was also the only migration of this period that included the extensive discovery and colonisation of unsettled lands. In the other migrations, the movement of language, culture and technologies was not always accompanied by a significant movement of people. But the spread of Austronesian languages was clearly accompanied by people and genes. Even when Austronesians moved into already settled lands, genetic analysis provides evidence for a significant mixing with with local populations.

The Austronesian languages probably emerged near the Yangtze Delta or further south in China. Some speakers may have moved north-wards, but the most important migrations moved away from the main-land, reaching Taiwan as early as 4000 BCE.[3] After further migration into the Philippines, Borneo and Java by 2000 BCE, Austronesian speakers divided into two main groups: Malay speakers who spread into Southeast Asia and the Indian Ocean; and Eastern Malayo-Polynesian speakers who spread throughout the islands of the Pacific. Malay speak-ers became the mainstays of a densely integrated maritime Southeast Asian region that also became a hub of extensive global connections. Malayan sailors travelled as far as East Africa and Madagascar during the first millennium CE, probably pioneering deep-water voyaging along the monsoon winds in the Indian Ocean. The current languages of Madagascar are branches of Austronesian, and the gene pool is nearly half Malay in origin. [4] At this same time, Southeast Asia also grew into a nexus for merchants and missionaries from across East Asia, the Indian Ocean, Arabia and, eventually, Europe.

The second branch of Austronesian speakers that spread across the Pacific had its origins in the Lapita culture that began around 1500 BCE in what are now called the Solomon Islands, just east of New Guinea. This culture emerged as a mix of Austronesian immigrants and pre-existing residents (the linguistic and genetic descendants of whom can be found in highland New Guinea). Over the next 2,500 years, Austronesian speakers used their seagoing skills to spread to nearly all of the islands of the Pacific. One branch moved into what is now Micronesia. Another branch of what came to be known as Polynesian speakers spread into the farthest reaches of the Pacific. By about 1200 CE they had arrived in New Zealand, Hawai'i and Easter Island, some of the last unsettled frontiers in the world. Evidence such as the spread of sweet potatoes from South America throughout the Pacific and common DNA between chickens in Colombia and the south Pacific suggests that Polynesian voyagers may even have reached South America.

After settlement, Micronesians and Polynesians continued to maintain contact across an integrated Pacific space. Anthropologists who have worked with contemporary native navigators, charted the winds and currents of the Pacific, and launched experimental expedi-tions are convinced that long-distance voyaging was intentional, and that the voyages could be repeated. Founding a new settlement was a way for an explorer – whether a junior member of a chiefly lineage or a group acting communally – to show valour and bravery, establishing new chiefdoms of their own. The outrigger canoes were equipped with sails and enough space for shelters, small animals, seeds, water and other supplies for extended voyages. After the main island groups were settled, inter-island voyaging and communication probably continued until after 1600 CE. Genetic testing on rats has produced estimates of regular contact between Tahiti and Hawai'i until at least the sixteenth century, and Dutch voyagers drew pictures of long-distance outrigger canoes in the 1610s.[5]

Despite these extensive connections, the Polynesian Pacific remained largely isolated from the surrounding rimlands and Southeast Asia. There is some evidence of contact between Micronesia and Southeast Asia, with the spread of lateen sails such as those used in the Indian Ocean into Micronesia.[6] However, by and large, the Polynesian Pacific was a self-contained world, very different from the rise of Southeast Asia as an important global corridor. Nonetheless, the decline of Polynesian voyaging by the mid-seventeenth century corresponds with a decline of indigenous shipping in Southeast Asia.[7] Both declines may be linked to climactic shifts in the mid-seventeenth century, which was also the context for a general decline in the global economy. More specifically, the end of Polynesian voyaging may also be linked to increased island population. Fewer resources could be spared to provision extensive overseas voyages, and ambitious young men turned their attention to struggles over local resources and politics. European explorers in the late eighteenth century found many of the islands embroiled in civil war.

## Pacific integration, 1760–1840

Starting in the sixteenth century – but not really gaining steam until the late eighteenth century – Europeans began to create new links across the Pacific that integrated the rimlands more closely with each other and with the Island Pacific. The Spanish were the first to do so with their establishment of Manila in 1570 as the western end of a regular trans-Pacific galleon trade between Mexico and the Philippines. Thousands of Chinese settled in Manila to manage the last leg of the trade to China. Many of the ships were built by Asians in Manila. The crews also included Chinese, Filipinos and Japanese, some of whom settled in Mexico. The Japanese even built their own ship with the help of Spanish shipbuilders in 1614, to carry a diplomatic delegation to Mexico, and from there on to Rome.

The galleon route is of significance not only as the first regular trans-Pacific route, but also as the last link in establishing trade routes that encircled the globe. The silver that flowed out of Mexico to China was an important part of a globally integrated silver market that linked the economies of the world. The silks, ceramics and furniture from Asia that flowed back to Mexico also played an important role in establishing global tastes in luxury goods.[8] But the galleons only had a limited effect on reconfiguring the Pacific. The Spanish engaged in little exploration beyond the main galleon route, and kept secret any knowledge they did gain. Commercial interests invested in the galleon trade also protected their trade against competition from outsiders. The galleons became a thin thread linking two nodes across the Pacific, isolated by secretive politics and monopolistic interests until they stopped sailing after 1815.[9]

A more significant transformation of the Pacific as a geographical and social space happened after the 1760s, with increased European and American voyaging. Many of the initial voyages were the famed voyages of exploration made by German, French, Russian and (especially) British explorers. They were driven by scientific curiosity, imperial ambition and the search for goods to trade with China. They charted and mapped the Pacific Ocean as a basin, as a distinct body of water surrounded by land and dotted with islands. This laid the groundwork for later European territorial claims, colonisation and settlement in the Pacific that expanded significantly in the middle decades of the nineteenth century.

This imagined Pacific was also given substance through the impetus of an increasingly voracious China trade. Across Southeast and East Asia, a resurgent Chinese junk trade reinvigorated the region after a decline in native and European shipping in the late seventeenth century. Tribute missions to China – as much about trade as about politics – also peaked in the late eighteenth century.[10] Europeans and Americans helped expand this trade into the Pacific and across the globe. Explorers and traders scoured the islands and rimlands for products such as furs, sandalwood, tortoise shells, pearls, bird's nests and sea slugs to sell in China. New routes were established throughout the islands and along the Pacific coasts of the Americas. After the independence of the United States, traders from New England increasingly appeared in the ports of China, Southeast Asia and Polynesia, reinvigorating the flows of silver (from Mexican mines) into the region and incorporating the Pacific into networks of trade that were global in scale.

The links created by traders were augmented by whalers, who were perhaps most responsible for the early, ground-up integration of the Pacific. The British ship *Emilia* was the first European ship to catch a whale in the Pacific, off the coast of Chile in 1789. In the next half-century, as they chased their prey to all corners of the ocean, the whalers made even the most abstract, empty oceanic spaces on the map into regions of human activity. Flourishing ports were established to service the whalers in distant places around the Pacific such as Honolulu and Papeete. Whalers also made some of the earliest contacts with isolated islands throughout the Pacific, and with local Japanese lords. The crews of whaling and trading ships were themselves heterodox groups of Pacific Islanders, Europeans and rimlanders who brought the peoples of the region together on board these small ships. Many would subsequently desert to become beachcombers and respected members of local island societies.

## Integration and stagnation, 1850–1914

The first boom in Pacific integration slowed after the 1820s. The US–China trade declined after the 1810s, partly as a result of the decreased availability of quality silver coins after Mexican independence (Figure 7.1). Some of the mainstays of the Pacific–China trade

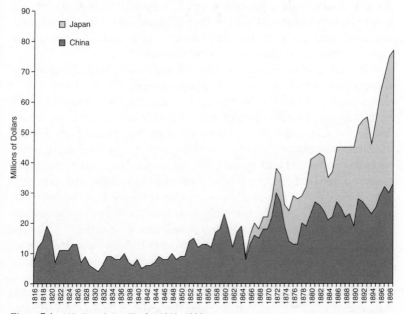

*Figure 7.1* US–East Asian Trade, 1813–1899

Sources: Susan Carter, et al., eds., *Historical Statistics of the United States: Earliest Times to the Present*, 5 vols. (New York, 2006), V, pp. 534–6, 540–2; Shü-lun Pan, *The Trade of the United States with China* (New York, 1924), p. 15.

such as fur and sandalwood were overharvested by the 1840s, and
Chinese shipping was gradually replaced in the southwestern Pacific
by larger square-rigged European vessels that diverted growing
portions of the China trade to India and Europe. Whaling also began
a long decline after the 1830s as petroleum products began to
supplant whale oil.

Pacific mobility entered a new period of growth during the two
decades after 1850. Indeed, the 1850s were perhaps the apex of Pacific
integration, as the last remains of the whaling and old China trades
were now augmented by the rapidly growing trans-Pacific movement
that connected the expanding rimland economies in South America,
Southeast Asia, Australia and, in particular, North America. The most
immediate impetus was the gold rushes in North America and
Australia, which attracted large numbers of immigrants who produced
and consumed goods that moved across the Pacific in increasingly
large quantities. But these were just part of a larger global boom in
trade and mobility. In the Pacific, this boom also took the form of
expanding plantations and mines, which included cotton and sugar
plantations in Cuba and Peru; guano (for fertiliser), copper and silver
mines in Chile and Peru; sugar, rice and mining throughout Southeast
Asia, and sugar and especially copra (coconut flesh used for oil and
soap) plantations throughout the Pacific islands. All of these industries
attracted (and coerced) migrant labour and produced products for
export across the Pacific and around the world.

This integration began to stagnate after the 1870s. Planters and
miners continued to search out new frontiers. But there was a
slowing of regional – and especially trans-Pacific – movement. In
part, this was the effect of a global economic downturn between the
1870s and the early 1890s. However, this was also a period when
cultural boundaries between Asians and Europeans were more
intensely imagined and enforced as migration laws and extraterritoriality. The Pacific became less a zone of interaction and more of a
border between a 'civilised' West and 'uncivilised' East. In-between,
the island Pacific was increasingly seen as a 'barbarian' no-man's land
subject to colonial annexation and plantation 'development'. The rise
of Japan after the 1870s, and especially after the 1890s, mitigated this
stagnation to some extent. Its trade with the United States grew
slowly but steadily, and its general economic development challenged
binaries between the uncivilised East and civilised West. It gradually
became a nexus for East Asian trade. But even as Japan reinvigorated
the integration of the Pacific, it also helped consolidate a space of
regional interactions in East Asia and the division of the Pacific into

competing spheres of influence between the United States and Japan.

## Migration

The gold rushes brought millions of immigrants into California and Australia. Nearly a quarter of the mining population in each region was Chinese, as roughly 900,000 Chinese migrated across the Pacific to Australia and the Americas from the 1850s to the 1870s. This amounted to a quarter of all Chinese emigration during this period – and as much as 40 per cent in the 1850s during the gold rush heyday. The majority of this migration was financed and organised by Chinese themselves, although over a quarter were indentured migrants to Cuba and Peru.

Many of the early migrants travelled on sailing ships. But by the 1850s steamer routes were already established within East and Southeast Asia, from Asia to Europe and from Panama to San Francisco. The first trans-Pacific steamer travelled from San Francisco to Sydney in 1853. Regular routes were established across the Pacific by the 1860s, with the most successful being the British-run Panama, New Zealand and Australia Royal Mail, and the American-run Pacific Mail Steamship Company from San Francisco to Japan and China. Chinese were the main passengers on the long-distance runs from China to the Americas and Southeast Asia. They also made up the majority of the crew members on all of the routes.[11] The rise of coastal and trans-Pacific steam routes did much to integrate the Pacific rimlands. Travel within the Island Pacific was also made easier with the establishment of steamer lines. But the trans-Pacific voyagers increasingly bypassed the island Pacific, except for major ports such as Honolulu. And, unlike with sailing ships, islanders were rarely hired as crew on the steamers.[12] This contributed to a growing separation between the rimlands and the island Pacific, even as movement itself was on the increase.

Trans-Pacific migration peaked in the 1870s, however, and remained stagnant for the next century as the Pacific became more of a barrier than a channel for human mobility. Overall Chinese emigration increased massively after the 1870s, but this was largely confined to Asia. Chinese emigration to Southeast Asia increased twentyfold by the 1920s (Figure 7.2), and over 30 million Chinese travelled to Manchuria after the 1880s.[13] In contrast, Chinese migration to Australia and the Americas remained steady, dropping to less than 5 per cent of all emigrants. After the 1890s, the rise of Japanese emigration took up some of the slack. About half of approximately

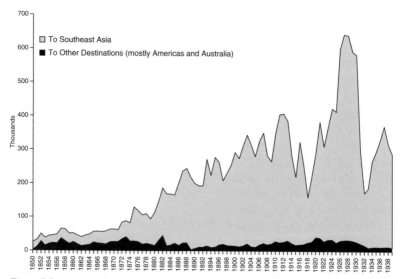

*Figure 7.2*   Chinese Emigration, 1850–1939

*Source*: Adam McKeown, 'Chinese Emigration in Global Context, 1850–1940', *Journal of Global History* 5 (2010), 120–4.

one million Japanese emigrants went to the Americas and Hawai'i, with the other half moving to Japanese colonies in Korea, Taiwan and Manchuria.[14] But overall Japanese emigration never came close to the scale of Chinese emigration, and the half million Chinese who went to the Americas were just a drop in the bucket of total emigration.

Reasons for the decline in Asian migration are not hard to find. The indenture trade to Peru and Cuba was stopped in 1874 after widespread accusations and evidence of abuse. More importantly, white miners on the gold mining frontiers strongly resented the concurrent inflows of Chinese miners, and repeatedly passed discriminatory laws against them. These culminated in the 1880s in anti-Chinese immigration restrictions in the Australian colonies and New Zealand (1881), the United States (1882), Hawai'i (1883), British Columbia (1884) and Canada as a whole (1885). These polities watched and learned from the successes and difficulties of laws enacted around the Pacific and continued to reform their own laws over the next three decades. The techniques and principles were eventually extended to other Asian groups, and were especially successful at nipping in the bud an incipient Indian migration to North America and Australia in the first decade of the twentieth century.[15]

This confluence of exclusion laws was not accidental. Anti-Chinese ideas had circulated widely around the Pacific since the 1850s. White miners in California, Australia and Canada read each other's newspapers and anti-Chinese pamphlets, and forged a common vocabulary of 'Yellow Peril', and of the filthy, uncivilised, degraded Chinese. Extensive international media coverage of the abuses of Chinese indenture was appropriated as yet more evidence of the degraded nature of Chinese who were unable to defend or even know their own best interests, and victimised by unscrupulous brokers and greedy capitalists who imported them to undermine the wages and dignity of honest labour. American congressmen even wielded the reports of Hong Kong officials about indenture in Congress as proof that Chinese were not genuine migrants but only 'in the bond thralls of the contractor – his coolie slaves'.[16] Such characterisations helped justify that abrogation of treaties that guaranteed 'free migration' from China, in order to enact unilateral exclusion laws. In fact, less than 3 per cent of Chinese were ever indentured to Europeans. But the image of indenture and of Asian migrants as being fundamentally different from European migrants has dominated understandings of Asian migration to this day. The translation of these racist beliefs into concrete immigration laws made the imagined differences into reality. They excluded Asians from wide circulation around the Pacific, helping entrench the different sectors of the Asian, American and Island Pacific.

Japan maintained an ambivalent status in this division. By the 1890s, its economic success and power was the basis for many successful claims to be treated as one of the 'civilised' countries, and many Japanese intellectuals called for Japan to 'Quit Asia'. But acceptance as a Western nation was never complete. This was especially clear with regard to issues surrounding migration. After Chinese exclusion was successfully implemented, popular movements in white settler nations also demanded the exclusion of Japanese as equally undesirable Asian immigrants. The governments were reluctant to enact such laws because of strong diplomatic protests from an increasingly powerful Japanese government. They instead reached compromises, such as laws which were non-discriminatory on the surface but contained language tests or other provisions that could be selectively enforced against Asians. In The United States and Canada the solution was a 'Gentleman's Agreement' in 1907 in which Japan agreed to restrict its own emigration to those countries. At the same time, however, Japanese freely restricted the migration of Chinese into the interior of Japan.

Migrations from the Pacific islands were relatively small in comparison to the massive flows of Chinese and European immigrants to
the goldfields. But as a proportion of their home populations, they
were some of the largest emigrations in history. As opportunities to
work on sailing ships declined, Islanders, especially from Melanesia,
were increasingly recruited to work in the emerging Pacific plantation economy after the 1860s, often in deceptive and coercive
manners known as 'blackbirding'. The once-independent island
states that had been important sites for the provisioning of whalers
and China traders were becoming increasingly subject to the
demands of planter minorities and were outright annexed into colonial empires. European and (after the First World War) Japanese
power increasingly penetrated the interior of the Pacific, but in the
process transformed the islands into an increasingly backwards
no-man's land of undeveloped and isolated 'savages' between the
American and Asian rimlands.

## Trade

The promises of trans-Pacific trade that had emerged in the 1850s
also failed to attain their potential after the 1870s, although regional
trade within East Asia and to countries outside of the Pacific
continued to expand. The trade between the United States and
China stagnated after 1873 (Figures 7.1 and 7.3). To some extent
this reflected the overall slow growth of Chinese trade during the
global economic downturn in the 1870s. But even during the
upturn in the 1890s, the US trade remained a relatively insignifi-
cant proportion of the overall Chinese trade, hovering between 5
and 10 per cent of the total between the 1860s and the First World
War. Most of the growth of Chinese trade after 1885 was to the
result of increased trade within Asia (of which Japan accounted for
one-third) and with European countries other than Britain.
Chinese trade grew stronger both regionally and globally, but not
across the Pacific.

A similar story unfolded on the Pacific coast of the Americas.
North American trade with Asia and Australia grew rapidly in the
1860s and 1870s, but failed to live up to that potential in subsequent
years. In the first years of the gold rush, prices for goods and labour
in California were so high that laundry was famously sent from San
Francisco to Hong Kong to be washed. By the end of the 1850s,
California had begun shipping wheat, quicksilver, hides, lumber, oats,
beans, potatoes and wool across the Pacific to Asia and the Australian

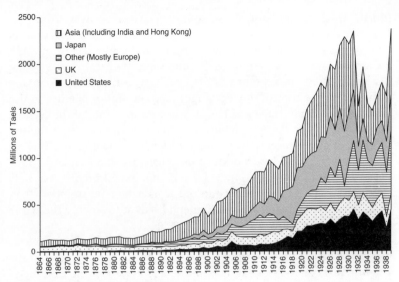

*Figure 7.3*  Chinese Trade, 1864–1939

*Sources*: Hsiao Liang-lin, *China's Foreign Trade Statistics, 1864–1949* (Cambridge, MA, 1974). Most of the trade through Hong Kong passed to and from East Asia and India, although a small portion (not reflected in this chart) also went to Britain. See A. J. H. Latham, 'The Reconstruction of Hong Kong Nineteenth-Century Trade Statistics: The Emergence of Asian Dynamism', in Sally Miller, A. J. H. Latham and Dennis Flynn, eds., *Studies in the Economic History of the Pacific Rim* (London, 1998), pp. 155–71.

colonies. By the 1870s, however, the great majority of West Coast products went to the East Coast and Europe. Milled flour was one of the most successful of California's exports to China, where much of it was purchased by European residents in the treaty ports. But even this declined after the 1880s as China developed its own methods of milling. After the 1870s, the most successful exports to Asia were silver from mines in Mexico and Nevada, kerosene and Singer sewing machines, but Asia rarely amounted to more than 5 per cent of total US trade before the 1910s. This orientation towards Europe was even stronger for Latin America. The transcontinental railway and various transport services established across the Central American isthmus served more to bring the West Coast of the Americas to the Atlantic than to integrate Asia with the Americas.[17]

The relative stagnation of trans-Pacific trade after the 1870s is more difficult to explain than the decline of migration. The growing ethos of civilisational difference that blocked Asian migration had something to do with it. The exclusion of Asians from

North America and Australia encouraged a turning away from Asia as a source of trade, despite continuing fantasies of the China market and the persistent interest of businessmen and diplomats promoting an 'open door' policy after 1899. The same political rhetoric that depicted Asian immigrants as an unfair threat to local jobs and economies because of lower wages and cunning practices, also depicted the Asian trade as a threat. For example, one of the 'yellow peril' fears of the late nineteenth century was the idea that the use of cheaper silver money in China and Japan (the latter until 1897) undercut prices and livelihoods of producers in gold standard countries. Winston Churchill's uncle Lord Randolph Churchill concisely synthesised the racial and economic fears when he quipped that, 'The yellow man using the white metal holds at his mercy the white man using the yellow metal.'[18]

Civilisational differences also meant the establishment of extra-territorial jurisdictions within East Asia. Imposed on China after the Opium Wars of 1839–42 and 1856–60, and as part of the first international treaties with Japan in the 1860s, extraterritoriality was meant to facilitate trade by establishing spaces of property and other legal rights that were amenable to Europeans. But the results in terms of increased trade may have been the exact opposite. Because foreigners could not be subject to local law, both China and Japan were allowed to restrict the movement of foreigners into the interior beyond the areas of extraterritorial jurisdiction. This restriction limited the access of global markets into East Asia, at the same time as it restricted the ability of Chinese and Japanese businesses to take a robust role in the trade of extraterritorial ports. Both British and American trade stagnated under this regime, providing opportunities for competitors.[19]

The growth of Japan as a regional power both shows the limit to this explanation and also provides a supplemental explanation in the effects of its increased hegemony over Pacific trade. Japanese economy and trade grew rapidly after the 1860s despite extraterritoriality. It quickly became nearly as important a trading partner for the United States as China (Figure 7.1). But US trade only amounted to 10 per cent of all Japanese trade before the 1890s, and well over half of Japanese trade was directed outside the Pacific to Europe. Japanese trade really began to boom in the 1890s when extraterritoriality was being enforced more lightly than in China, and especially after 1899, when extraterritoriality was abolished. For the next three decades, Japanese trade expanded in equal measure across the Pacific, within Asia and globally (Figure 7.4).

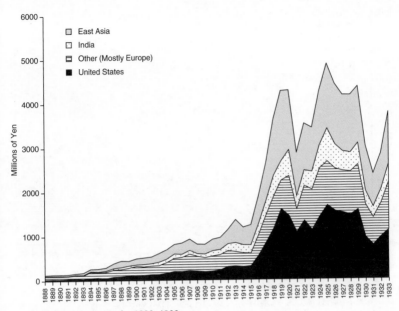

*Figure 7.4*  Japanese Trade, 1883–1933
Source: *The Oriental Economist, Foreign Trade of Japan* (Tokyo, 1935).

The increasing importance of Japan in shaping Pacific flows can be seen more strongly in shipping than in the area of trade. Using substantial government subsidies (which was rarely the case for US and British shipping other than mail contracts) from 1875 onwards the Japanese established regular steamship lines to Shanghai, outcompeting both the Pacific Mail and the British Peninsular and Oriental Line. Nippen Yushen Kaisha established its first line out of East Asia to Bombay in 1893, and extended services to the Pacific Coast, Australia and Europe by 1896. Several Japanese companies established trans-Pacific lines over the next 15 years, including the only line that ran direct from Asia down the Pacific coast of Latin America, which was opened by Toyo Kisen Kaisha in 1905. Japanese shipping soon came to dominate the Asia-to-India trade, and competed intensely with American and Canadian shippers on the trans-Pacific trade – a competition in which the United States was severely hampered by the 1915 Seamen's Act which prohibited American shipping companies from hiring less expensive Chinese labour.[20] By the 1920s, Japanese tonnage accounted for two-thirds of all shipping in Japanese ports and one-third in Chinese ports (Figures 7.5 and 7.6). The rise of Japan

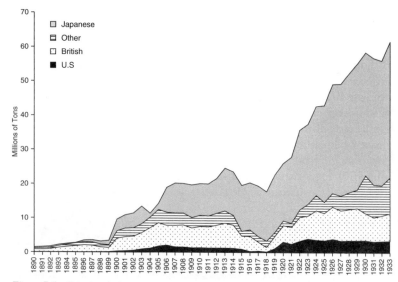

*Figure 7.5*  Shipping in Japanese ports, 1890–1933

*Source*: *The Oriental Economist*, *Foreign Trade of Japan* (Tokyo, 1935), pp. 440–7.

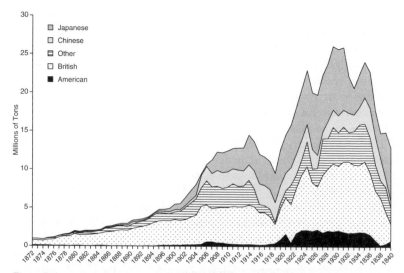

*Figure 7.6*  Shipping in Chinese ports, 1872–1940

*Source*: Hsiao Liang-lin, *China's Foreign Trade Statistics, 1864–1949* (Cambridge, MA, 1974).

simultaneously helped consolidate regional East Asian interactions and revivify trans-Pacific connections.

## Tensions and flows, 1914–present

Borders and flows both grew stronger over the twentieth century, alternately working against and reinforcing each other. Most of the borders remained grounded in imaginations of the Pacific as a border between East and West. In the course of the twentieth century, this manifested itself first as the competition between Japan and the United States to control spheres of interest during the first half of the century, and then in the Cold War conflicts of the second half of the century. Flows of goods and peoples also reached new peaks and troughs. The movement of goods and peoples in East and Southeast Asia and of goods across the Pacific reached unprecedented rates in the 1920s. They declined in mid-century, replaced by the massive mobilisation of resources and people associated with war. By the end of the century, however, flows of both goods and peoples in all directions resumed dramatically.[21] Regional differences still remain but the Pacific is becoming increasingly integrated once again, recovering the trends of the mid-nineteenth century.

By the 1920s, the Pacific had become an important centre of globalisation. The 1920s are often depicted as a period of decline in globalisation compared to the pre-war years. But this is only plausible from the perspective of the Atlantic (if even there). In the Pacific, the movement of goods and people reached new heights. The regional Asian flows and connections beyond the Pacific continued to grow into the 1920s. Chinese migration, for example, reached new peaks of over 600,000 a year into Southeast Asia and over 1.1 million a year into Manchuria. Even trans-Pacific migration reached new heights, with large numbers of Japanese migrating to Brazil and more than 20,000 Chinese a year migrating to the Americas in the early 1920s, and around 2,000 a year to Australia. These were the highest rates of trans-Pacific migration since the 1870s, although still only a trickle compared to Southeast Asia.

Trade in the Western Pacific and beyond the Pacific also continued to grow in the 1920s (Figures 7.3 and 7.4). In particular, Southeast Asian products such as tapioca, rice and rubber became increasingly important in world markets. But the rejuvenation of the trans-Pacific trade was the most significant development of this period. Much of this growth was stimulated by the rise of Japan, but changes in US trade also played an important role. US trade in the Pacific had grown modestly since 1900. But the opening of the Panama Canal in 1914 and the decline of European trade in the Pacific during the First World War created new opportunities for the resumption of trans-Pacific trade. By the 1920s, the US proportion of the China trade had doubled to 16 per cent compared to before the war, and its proportion of the Japan trade had grown by half to 30 per cent. Southeast Asian products like rubber were also increasingly important for the United States, and the overall importance of Asia to the US trade doubled after the war to 11 per cent of total US trade. The increased importance of the United States and Japan could be seen in the number of foreign firms in China (Figure 7.7). In 1887 both Japan and the United States had about 25 firms based in China. However, by 1931, the United States had established 559 firms and Japan a whopping 7,249 firms. No other country expanded its interests so rapidly.

Even as the flows increased, the Pacific was increasingly divided politically between American and Japanese spheres of interest. By the 1870s, the Pacific had become an important theatre for the 'New

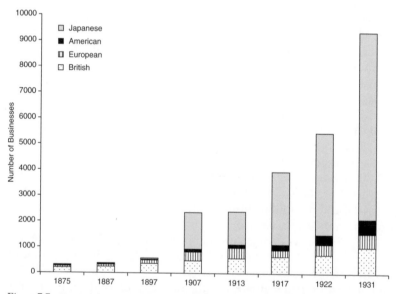

*Figure* 7.7   Foreign firms in China, 1875–1931

*Source*: Peter Schran, 'The Minor Significance of Commercial Relations between the United States and China, 1850–1931', in Ernest May and John Fairbank, eds., *America's China Trade in Historical Perspective: The Chinese and American Performance* (Cambridge, MA, 1986), p. 225.

Imperialism' with Japan and multiple European countries annexing territories, consolidating power over existing colonies and forcing concessions from independent nations in China, Southeast Asia and the Pacific Islands. After the turn of the century, Japan and the United States grew increasingly aggressive in their claims while the European nations began to dig their heels into the existing possessions. Japan annexed Taiwan in 1895, placed Korea under a protectorate 1905 and became increasingly aggressive in search of concessions from China. The United States annexed Hawai'i, the Philippines and Guam in 1898, and took control of American Sāmoa in 1899. Struggles over Japanese immigration to North America in 1906 had both sides talking about sending the warships for a tour of the Pacific: the US 'Great White Fleet' did so, as part of its 1907–8 circumnavigation. Politicians on both sides increasingly perceived the Pacific as a geopolitical space of conquest, colonisation and competition. Over the next two decades, politicians in Japan spoke the need for a Japanese-led Asian empire or other Japanese-led federations such as the East-Asian Co-Prosperity Sphere, while Americans looked to the Pacific as an expansion of the Manifest Destiny that had led them across the North American continent. In this rhetoric, the oceanic Pacific was largely emptied of people, polities and societies. Instead, it was imagined as a network of coaling stations, frontiers of unexploited resources, space for colonial settlement and a geopolitical chessboard. Many people thought that war between the two powers was inevitable.

At the same time, many people – especially academics and merchants engaged in the ever-expanding trans-Pacific trade – spoke of bridging the Pacific and finding common values and interests. Such discussions were rarely framed as a recovery of the intensive interactions of the mid-nineteenth century. Instead, they started from the assumption of timeless differences of race, culture and commercial development that only now were being overcome for the first time in history by improved communication technologies and enlightened elites. The culture of difference that had been cultivated in the late nineteenth century had erased the memory of the earlier century of interactions, and reinterpreted modern borders as the legacy of timeless distinctions between East and West.

Such efforts at bridging failed most notably in the realm of migration. Australia – with the covert support of the United States – vocally opposed the Japanese attempt to insert a racial equality clause into the League of Nations covenant for fear that it would be required to modify its anti-Asian immigration laws. The United States then unilaterally strengthened anti-Japanese immigration laws in 1924. For many Japanese this was proof that any compromise with western racism was impossible, and that conflict was inevitable. At the same time, the Treaty of Versailles recognised Japanese power in the region by handing German concessions in China and Germany's Pacific Islands north of the equator over to Japan as mandate territories (those south of the Equator were given to Australia and New Zealand).

The political manoeuvring hardened into military conflict by the late 1930s. The Pacific theatre of the Second World War, fought largely between Japan and the USA, gave way after 1945 to a series of wars followed by a series of anti-colonial struggles against the Dutch, French and British in Southeast Asia. These overlapped with a series of wars between Communist and anti-Communist forces first in China (1946–9), then Korea (1950–3), throughout mainland Southeast Asia until the late 1970s, and in Central America and Peru until the 1980s. In all of latter conflicts except Peru, the United States played a major role, with Japan now as a non-military ally.

From the perspective of labour migration and trade, this period of war from the late 1930s to 1970s was a nadir of Pacific integration. This decline started as early as 1930, with the Great Depression which hit Japan and the USA very hard (although Asian trade and migration did not decline as much as in the Atlantic). After the Second World War, Cold War security fears and postcolonial nationalism both promoted rigid migration controls and high tariffs. Interaction was seen as a threat to security and development. The rise of jet travel, massive shipping and improved telecommunications was not enough to overcome these barriers.

From another perspective, however, this period can be seen as a pinnacle of interaction. Massive amounts of American resources and soldiers were moved across Asia, first in the war against Japan, then to anti-Communist wars in Korea and Vietnam. American military bases, advisors and aid were also deployed throughout the Pacific, including China before 1949, Japan, Indonesia, Thailand, Central America and numerous Pacific islands. Military expansion helped entrench American political power throughout the Pacific, and produced numerous marriages, children and refugees that helped restart Asian migration to North America as early as the 1950s. The US military occupation of Japan also promoted the growth of strong bilateral trade after the 1950s, which became one of the more significant mid-century flows. The wars also stimulated regional economic networks, and played an important role in the development of successful economies in South Korea, Taiwan, Hong Kong, Singapore, Malaysia and Thailand.

The resurgence of East Asian economies and the loosening of immigration and trade laws in North America and Australia helped to spur trans-Pacific movement in the 1970s. Container ships, jet travel and the opening of China in 1979 helped flows of goods and money reach unprecedented levels by the 1980s. Trans-Pacific movement between China and the United States has grown especially rapidly. The Americas and Australia have become favoured destinations for East Asian and Pacific emigrants, who now come from a variety of countries in addition to China. Chinese emigration has not recovered the per capita rates of the 1920s, but Chinese are nonetheless one of the major immigrant groups in North America and Australia. Mirroring patterns of the previous century, regional trade and migration in East and Southeast Asia have also grown since the 1980s alongside the resurgence of trans-Pacific connections.[22]

The Pacific has become a major zone of global interaction once again. But the integration is still uneven. The bulk of Pacific interaction now concentrates on the rimlands, especially the great anchors of the USA, China and Japan. The island Pacific is deeply impacted by this growth, with extensive emigration and economies that are dependent on the rimlands. But because of their small populations and resources, they still remain marginal to the rimland economies and modern communication routes except as tourist destinations. Latin America still interacts only modestly with the Pacific world. The regional integration of Southeast Asia is resurgent after a period of political fragmentation in the middle of the twentieth century, spurred by ASEAN and other regional political and trade alliances. But it is no longer the crucial node of global interaction that it once was. Instead, major cities like Hong Kong, Los Angeles, Seoul, Shanghai, Singapore and Tokyo are the new archipelago that integrate the Pacific and connect it with the outside world.

## Notes

1. Jerry Bentley, 'Sea and Ocean Basins as Frameworks of Historical Analysis', *Geographical Review* 89 (1999), 215–24.
2. Arif Dirlik, ed., *What Is In a Rim: Critical Perspectives on the Pacific Region Idea*, 2nd edn (Lanham, MD, 1998); O. H. K. Spate, 'The Pacific as Artefact', in Niel Gunson, ed., *The Changing Pacific: Essays in Honour of H. E. Maude* (Melbourne, 1978), pp. 32–45.
3. Andres Abalahin, '"Sino-Pacifica": Conceptualizing Greater Southeast Asia as a Sub-Arena of World History', *Journal of World History* 22 (2011), 659–92.

4. Peter Bellwood, *Prehistory of the Indo-Malaysian Archipelago* (Honolulu, 1997); Bellwood, James Fox and Darrell Tyron, eds., *The Austronesians: Historical and Comparative Perspectives* (Canberra, 2006).
5. Peter Bellwood, *Man's Conquest of the Pacific: The Prehistory of Southeast Asia and Oceania* (Oxford, 1979); Andrew Pawley, 'Prehistoric Migration and Colonisation Processes in Oceania: A View from Historical Linguistics and Archaeology', in Jan Lucassen, Leo Lucassen and Patrick Manning, eds., *Migration History in World History: Multidisciplinary Approaches* (Leiden, 2010), pp. 77–112.
6. Paul D'Arcy, 'No Empty Ocean: Trade and Interaction across the Pacific Ocean to the Middle of the Eighteenth Century', in Sally Miller, A. J. H. Latham and Dennis Flynn, eds., *Studies in the Economic History of the Pacific Rim* (London, 1998), p. 29.
7. Pierre-Yves Manguin, 'The Vanishing *Jong*: Insular Southeast Asian Fleets in Trade and War (Fifteenth to Seventeenth Centuries)', in Anthony Reid, ed., *Southeast Asia in the Early Modern Era: Trade, Power and Belief* (Ithaca, NY, 1993), pp. 197–213.
8. Luke Clossey, 'Merchants, Migrants, Missionaries and Globalisation in the Early Modern Pacific', *Journal of Global History* 1 (2006), 41–58; Dennis Flynn and Arturo Giráldez, '"Born with a Silver Spoon": The Origin of World Trade in 1571', *Journal of World History* 6 (1995), 201–21; Benito Lagarda, Jr., 'Two and a Half Centuries of the Galleon Trade', *Philippine Studies* 3 (1955), 345–72.
9. Donald Brand, 'Geographical Exploration by the Spaniards', in Herman Friis, ed., *The Pacific Basin: A History of its Geographical Exploration* (New York, 1967), pp. 109–44.
10. Leonard Blussé, 'Chinese Century: The Eighteenth Century in the China Sea Region', *Archipel* 58 (1999), 107–30; Anthony Reid, 'Flows and Seepages in the Long-term Chinese Interaction with Southeast Asia', in Reid, ed., *Sojourners and Settlers: Histories of Southeast Asia and the Chinese: In Honour of Jennifer Cushman* (St Leonards, NSW, 1996), pp. 15–50.
11. Robert J. Chandler and Stephen J. Potash, *Gold, Silk, Pioneers & Mail: The Story of the Pacific Mail Steamship Company* (San Francisco, 2007); John Niven, *The American President Lines and Its Forebears: From Paddlewheelers to Containerships* (Newark, DE, 1987); E. Mowbray Tate, *Trans-Pacific Steam: The Story of Steam Navigation from the Pacific Coast of North America to the Far East and the Antipodes, 1867–1941* (New York, 1986).
12. Frances Steel, *Oceania under Steam: Sea Transport and the Cultures of Colonialism, c. 1870–1914* (Manchester, 2011).
13. Thomas Gottschang and Diana Lary, *Swallows and Settlers: The Great Migration from North China to Manchuria* (Ann Arbor, 2000).
14. Alan Takeo Moriyama, *Imingaisha: Japanese Emigration Companies and Hawai'i, 1894–1908* (Honolulu, 1985), pp. 154–5.
15. Adam McKeown, *Melancholy Order: Asian Migration and the Globalisation of Borders* (New York, 2008).
16. *Chew Heong* v. *United States*, 112 US, 536, 568.

17. Thomas Cox, 'The Passage to India Revisited: Asian Trade and The Development of the Far West, 1850–1900', in J. A. Carroll, ed., *Reflections of Western Historians* (Phoenix, 1967), pp. 85–103; Daniel Meissner, 'Bridging the Pacific: California and the China Flour Trade', *California History* 76 (1997/98), 82–93; David St. Clair, 'California and Nevada Minerals in the Pacific Rim 1850–1900', in A. J. H. Latham and Heita Kawakatsu, eds, *Asia-Pacific Dynamism 1550–2000* (London, 2000), pp. 216–41.

18. Quoted in Jeffrey Frieden, *Global Capitalism: Its Fall and Rise in the Twentieth Century* (New York, 2006), p. 114.

19. Eiichi Motono, *Conflict and Cooperation in Sino-British Business, 1860–1911: The Impact of the Pro-British Commercial Network in Shanghai* (New York, 2000); Mary Wright, *The Last Stand of Chinese Conservatism: The T'ung-Chih Restoration, 1862–1874* (Stanford, 1957), pp. 232–8.

20. Tomohei Chida and Peter, Davies, *The Japanese Shipping and Shipbuilding Industries: A History of their Modern Growth* (London, 1990); Keiichiro Nakagawa, 'Japanese Shipping in the Nineteenth and Twentieth Centuries: Strategy and Organisation', in Tsunehiko Yui and Nakagawa, eds., *Business History of Shipping: Strategy and Structure* (Tokyo, 1985), pp. 1–33; William Wray, *Mitsubishi and the N.Y.K., 1870–1914: Business Strategy in the Japanese Shipping Industry* (Cambridge, MA, 1984).

21. Kaoru Sugihara, 'The Economy since 1800', ch. 8 in this volume.

22. Peter Petri, 'Is East Asia Becoming More Interdependent?' *Journal of Asian Economics* 17 (2006), 381–94; Richard Pomfret, *Regionalism in East Asia: Why Has It Flourished since 2000 and How Far Will It Go?* (Singapore, 2011).

# 8

# The Economy since 1800

## Kaoru Sugihara

This chapter traces the evolution of economic integration in the Pacific region since 1800. Treating the economies of both sides of the Pacific as a single analytical unit is a relatively recent idea. In the late 1960s, Japan, Australia and the Association of Southeast Asian Nations (ASEAN) countries had various ideas for regional integration on the western side of the Pacific (through liberalisation measures such as the reduction of tariffs and non-tariff barriers, and of barriers to capital flows), which had direct bearings on the economic integration of the entire Pacific region. By the mid-1980s there was a widespread notion (on various statistical and conceptual grounds) that the Pacific trade had become larger in volume than the Atlantic trade, and East Asia had become the centre of world economic growth. By the 1990s, the Pacific Rim (or basin) had emerged as the key category which captured the notion of the region as the driving force of the world economy, with several concrete expressions such as the establishment of Asia-Pacific Economic Cooperation (APEC). The contesting categories at that time were the model of the United States as the single hegemon and the notion of the tripartite engines of growth (United States, EC/EU and Japan).

The Rim idea appealed to those who saw the potentiality of the dynamic fusion, not just between the rich industrial economies but also among the diverse economies across the Pacific Rim, including Asia's emerging economies and resource-rich countries (formerly the 'regions of recent settlement') such as Canada, Australia and New Zealand. Behind the Rim idea was the notion that vast ecological and cultural diversities on both sides and all latitudes of the Pacific could be the greatest resource for global development, if properly connected and sensibly governed. In the context of *economic* integration, larger Rim economies dominated the discussion and policy dialogues, and their impact on the rest of the region, including the Pacific Islands and the Pacific side of Latin America, has not been discussed as fully as they perhaps deserved. Nevertheless, economic integration and the growth of the Pacific Rim economy and trade fundamentally altered the character of the Pacific region as a whole.

For the last twenty years Asian economic growth has continued, led by China and supported by other East, Southeast and South Asian countries. The policy tool for integration changed from multilateral to bilateral, and then back to multilateral negotiations to some extent (in the form of the Trans-Pacific Strategic Economic Partnership Agreement), while China replaced Japan as the main economic actor in East Asia. At the same time, many observers have come to regard the twin importance of US-led globalisation and Asia-led economic growth, and hence the economic integration of these economies, as essential to the smooth running of the world economy even more clearly than twenty years ago. Thus the key ingredients that led to the identification of the Pacific as the driving force of the world economy remain intact to this day.

In this chapter I seek to establish a narrative on the origins and development of this process of economic integration, in the same way that Sidney Pollard attempted to account for European economic integration.[1] It is a historical reconstruction based on reading key economic statistics, and does not rely on deep intellectual foundations comparable either to national history narratives or even regional histories such as the histories of East Asia or Latin America. Put in other words, there has been no recognised political, cultural or environmental context that had anticipated or prepared the economic integration of this magnitude at the time when it occurred. This chapter aims to locate the most recent, industrialisation-driven narrative in the longer and more environmentally and culturally rooted history of the region.

## 1800–1930

In 1820, East Asia was the most populous region along the Pacific Rim, with a population of 427 million people.[2] The Americas and Australasia had 23 million, while Southeast Asia had 34 million. China (with 381 million) was a vast empire, her landmass stretching thousands of miles away from the sea, but the majority of her population lived in the littoral region or areas easily accessible from there.[3] Because the difference in the standard of living between European settlers and Asians at this time was relatively small, the size of the economy largely reflected the size of the population. Thus one cannot dispute the centrality of East Asia in the economies of the Pacific Rim. Of the 29 countries along the Pacific Rim, 15 countries or colonies in the Americas and Australasia (summed up in 1 to 9 of Table 8.1)

Table 8.1  Maddison Estimates of GDP: Pacific Rim Countries, 1820–2008

| | 1820 | | 1870 | | 1913 | | 1928 | | 1950 | | 1980 | | 2008 | |
|---|---|---|---|---|---|---|---|---|---|---|---|---|---|---|
| 1 Canada | 738 | (0.2) | 6,407 | (1.7) | 34,916 | (3.4) | 52,269 | (3.5) | 102,164 | (4.3) | 397,814 | (4.3) | 839,199 | (2.9) |
| 2 United States | 12,548 | (4.2) | 98,374 | (26.1) | 517,383 | (49.8) | 794,700 | (53.0) | 1,455,916 | (61.4) | 4,230,558 | (45.7) | 9,485,136 | (33.0) |
| 3 Mexico | 5,000 | (1.7) | 6,214 | (1.6) | 25,921 | (2.5) | 30,846 | (2.1) | 67,368 | (2.8) | 431,983 | (4.7) | 877,312 | (3.1) |
| 4 The Pacific Caribbean and Ecuador | 0 | (0.0) | 0 | (0.0) | 0 | (0.0) | 7,450 | (0.5) | 22,422 | (0.9) | 104,394 | (1.1) | 219,235 | (0.8) |
| 5 Colombia | n.a. | | n.a. | | 6,420 | (0.6) | 11,357 | (0.8) | 24,955 | (1.1) | 113,375 | (1.2) | 284,921 | (1.0) |
| 6 Peru | n.a. | | n.a. | | 4,434 | (0.4) | 9,319 | (0.6) | 17,613 | (0.7) | 73,727 | (0.8) | 157,224 | (0.5) |
| 7 Chile | 535 | (0.2) | 2,509 | (0.7) | 10,252 | (1.0) | 13,798 | (0.9) | 22,352 | (0.9) | 63,017 | (0.7) | 216,948 | (0.8) |
| 8 New Zealand | 40 | (0.0) | 902 | (0.2) | 5,781 | (0.6) | 7,475 | (0.5) | 16,136 | (0.7) | 39,141 | (0.4) | 77,840 | (0.3) |
| 9 Australia | 173 | (0.1) | 5,810 | (1.5) | 24,861 | (2.4) | 34,368 | (2.3) | 61,274 | (2.6) | 210,642 | (2.3) | 531,503 | (1.8) |
| 10 Japan | 20,739 | (7.0) | 25,393 | (6.7) | 71,653 | (6.9) | 124,246 | (8.3) | 160,966 | (6.8) | 1,568,457 | (16.9) | 2,904,141 | (10.1) |
| 11 Korea | 8,244 | (2.8) | 8,616 | (2.3) | 13,463 | (1.3) | 16,105 | (1.1) | 25,887 | (1.1) | 205,467 | (2.2) | 974,216 | (3.4) |
| 12 China | 228,600 | (77.2) | 189,740 | (50.3) | 241,431 | (23.2) | 274,090 | (18.3) | 244,985 | (10.3) | 1,041,142 | (11.2) | 8,908,894 | (31.0) |
| 13 Taiwan | 1,100 | (0.4) | 1,290 | (0.3) | 2,545 | (0.2) | 4,762 | (0.3) | 6,828 | (0.3) | 93,563 | (1.0) | 479,645 | (1.7) |
| 14 Hong Kong | 12 | (0.0) | 84 | (0.0) | 623 | (0.1) | 961 | (0.1) | 4,962 | (0.2) | 53,177 | (0.6) | 222,516 | (0.8) |
| 15 Philippines | 1,271 | (0.4) | 3,159 | (0.8) | 9,272 | (0.9) | 17,458 | (1.2) | 22,616 | (1.0) | 121,012 | (1.3) | 281,120 | (1.0) |
| 16 Vietnam | 3,453 | (1.2) | 5,321 | (1.4) | 14,062 | (1.4) | 15,656 | (1.0) | 19,992 | (0.8) | 49,261 | (0.5) | 302,276 | (1.1) |

| | | | | | | | | | | | | | |
|---|---|---|---|---|---|---|---|---|---|---|---|---|---|
| 17 | Thailand | 2,659 | (0.9) | 3,511 | (0.9) | 7,304 | (0.7) | 9,568 | (0.6) | 16,375 | (0.7) | 120,116 | (1.3) | 573,073 | (2.0) |
| 18 | Malaysia | 173 | (0.1) | 530 | (0.1) | 2,776 | (0.3) | 5,865 | (0.4) | 10,032 | (0.4) | 50,333 | (0.5) | 260,126 | (0.9) |
| 19 | Singapore | 3 | (0.0) | 57 | (0.0) | 413 | (0.0) | 498 | (0.0) | 2,268 | (0.1) | 21,865 | (0.2) | 129,521 | (0.5) |
| 20 | Indonesia | 10,970 | (3.7) | 18,929 | (5.0) | 45,152 | (4.3) | 68,099 | (4.5) | 66,358 | (2.8) | 275,805 | (3.0) | 1,007,750 | (3.5) |
| 1–9 Total | | 19,034 | (6.4) | 120,216 | (31.9) | 629,968 | (60.7) | 961,582 | (64.2) | 1,790,200 | (75.5) | 5,664,651 | (61.1) | 12,689,318 | (44.2) |
| 10–20 Total | | 277,224 | (93.6) | 256,630 | (68.1) | 408,694 | (39.3) | 537,308 | (35.8) | 581,269 | (24.5) | 3,600,198 | (38.9) | 16,043,278 | (55.8) |
| 29 countries Total | | 296,258 | (100.0) | 376,846 | (100.0) | 1,038,662 | (100.0) | 1,498,891 | (100.0) | 2,371,469 | (100.0) | 9,264,849 | (100.0) | 28,732,596 | (100.0) |
| World Total (share of 29 countries) | | 693,502 | (42.7) | 1,109,684 | (34.0) | 2,733,190 | (38.0) | 3,696,156 | (40.6) | 5,335,860 | (44.4) | 20,029,995 | (46.3) | 50,973,935 | (56.4) |

*Sources and Notes:*

Angus Maddison, 'Statistics on World Population, GDP and Per Capita GDP, 1–2008 AD (Horizontal file)' http://www.ggdc.net/maddison/ (made available in 2009), unless otherwise stated.

Indonesia includes Timor until 1999. Korea includes both South and North.

The Pacific Caribbean refers to Costa Rica, El Salvador, Guatemala, Honduras, Nicaragua and Panama.

Singapore 1928: Estimated assuming that per capita GDP grew proportionately to 'Malaysia' from 1913.

China and Thailand 1928: Figures for 1929 were used.

Hong Kong: 1928: Estimated assuming that per capita GDP grew proportionately to Singapore from 1913.

Vietnam: Includes Cambodia and Laos from 1950. Figure for 1928 was estimated assuming that per capita GDP remained the same as 1913, and population grew: at 11 per cent, that is at the same speed as countries of a similar make-up.

1928 World Total: Figure for 1929 was used. This figure was taken from Angus Maddison, *Monitoring the World Economy, 1820–1992* (Paris, 1995). p. 227.

accounted for 6 per cent of GDP, while 14 in East and Southeast Asia (10 to 20 of the same table) contributed 94 per cent. If we take 60 per cent of China's GDP as the portion produced in the littoral, East and Southeast Asia still produced 91 per cent. Littoral China alone produced 67 per cent of the GDP of the Pacific Rim.[4]

This state of concentration of people and economic activities in East Asia dramatically changed during the next century (see Table 8.1). By 1928 the Americas and Australasia accounted for some 64 per cent of GDP. The standard of living in North America and Australasia was among the highest in the world, with per capita GDP often higher than that in Western Europe and nine times higher than recorded in China. The share of East and Southeast Asia in the Rim declined to 36 per cent, or, excluding 40 per cent of China's non-littoral GDP, to 31 per cent. Admittedly, most of this wealth, especially in North America, came from the eastern and central parts of the continent connected more closely to the Atlantic, so these percentages are gross exaggerations of the economic activities of the eastern side of the Pacific Rim. However, even if we exclude most (90 per cent) of North America's GDP,[5] the share of the Americas and Australasia would still amount to 32 per cent (excluding non-littoral China from the total). This reflects the fact that the western coast of North America, as well as the Pacific side of Latin America and Australasia, became increasingly populated by the end of the nineteenth century, and the economic activities along the entire Pacific Rim became more evenly spread and diversified. In summary, there was a significant shift in economic gravity, from East Asia, led by China, to the regions of recent settlement including the Pacific side of the US economy, between these two benchmark years.

Does this result imply the growth of modern economic connections across the Pacific, or is it no more than a statistical aggregation of economic growth in different parts of the Rim? I propose to divide the discussion into four topics: the role of silver, the volume of commodity trade, exports of primary products and the US demand for them, and intra-Asian trade and Japan's industrialisation. I shall argue that, while all of these features expanded with signs towards integration, two of the forces, namely US demand and Japan-centred industrialisation-driven trade, remained relatively independent from each other. In terms of the linkages along the Pacific Rim, the growth of the Atlantic side of the US economy played a vital role in the growth of the Pacific trade, by offering the Rim countries export opportunities, while East Asian development was largely driven by its connections with Western Europe. The growth of an integrated trading network across the Pacific Rim was rather limited during this period.

*The role of silver*

As can be seen in the influx of Spanish silver from the new continent to China via Manila in the sixteenth and seventeenth centuries, Pacific trade has at times played an important role in the development of the world economy.[6] Latin American silver remained the main medium of exchange for economies on both sides of the Pacific well into the nineteenth century, partly because the Manila galleon trade continued, and partly because silver remained the global currency. By the early nineteenth century, however, with the independence of Latin American countries, there was a deterioration of the quality of silver coins (the silver content was reduced deliberately), which created problems in monetary circulation in East Asia. As China's internal trade, as well as intra-Asian trade, was largely dependent on American silver for its transactions, this resulted in a transoceanic shock, which destabilised both Asian trade and the Chinese polity.[7]

Meanwhile, as Karl Marx famously noted, the Pacific region also contributed to the transformation of the world economy through the discovery of gold in California and Australia.[8] Between 1845 and 1848 more than 1.2 million square miles of the west coast of North America (including California) were added to the territories of the United States. The United States quickly exploited the economic opportunities created by the discoveries of gold.[9] This was followed by another discovery of gold mines in Australia in 1851, and both contributed to the growth of world gold production, which came to meet the European demand, eventually preparing the move towards the international gold standard. It is important that Pacific trade remained silver-currency-based, as Europe began to move towards gold especially from the 1870s. After the middle of the nineteenth century Mexico began to produce reliable silver coins. When Japan opened herself to foreign trade, the domestic bimetallic ratio, which had diverged from the international ratio as a result of the seclusion policy, was quickly adjusted, and the value of the currency came to be linked with Mexican silver. Together with China and a large part of Southeast Asia, the western side of the Pacific remained as a silver-using area for most of the nineteenth century.

Thus in 1868 most countries on both sides of the Pacific were on the silver (or bimetallic) standard, and went through a long period of the depreciation of the value of their currencies, along with the depreciation of the value of silver against gold from the 1870s to the 1890s. This had a profound impact on the relative position of the Pacific in the world economy, which was to be dominated by the Atlantic economy based on the gold standard. By 1908 most Pacific countries converged to the gold standard, except for China and Hong Kong (and some Caribbean countries).[10]

Even so, China remained on the silver standard well into the 1930s, in spite of repeated suggestions by western experts to adopt gold. Japan, on the other hand, adopted the gold standard in 1897. But, while importing capital from London, Japan kept the exchange rate low, in order to compete with silver-using Asian countries in the regional market for manufactured goods. Even in 1931, Japan's abandonment of the gold standard after the Great Depression severely devalued the yen, partly in order to compete with China. To the extent that the Chinese market mattered, the tendency for the exchange rate to respond to the movement of silver prices continued even after silver circulation was largely withdrawn from the rest of the Rim.

*The volume of commodity trade*

Before 1880 the volume of trans-Pacific commodity trade was small. Frequently cited world trade statistics tend to give the impression that nineteenth-century world trade was dominated by Europe, because European trade has been better recorded and studied. Rostow's estimates show that, while Europe's share was 77 per cent in 1800 and 74 per cent in 1840, the shares of North America and Latin America in world trade were 5 and 7 per cent respectively in 1800 and 7 and 8 per cent in 1840. Most of the trade was likely to be conducted on the Atlantic side, and the trade of Pacific Asia and Australasia was unrecorded.[11] A more detailed study for 1840 suggests that the share of the Pacific Rim countries in world export trade was 19 per cent, although, if we deduct 90 per cent of North America's trade as belonging to the Atlantic, this figure is reduced to 10 per cent. Still, we can confirm that in 1840 there were over $1 million of exports from 11 countries.[12] This list was extended to nine more countries or regions by 1900, and Pacific trade came to grow slightly faster than world trade (see Table 8.2). I have argued that the figures for 1840 could be increased, by considering junk trade as well as long-distance trade within China. This might bring the Rim's share in world trade to around 25 per cent, or 17 per cent excluding 90 per cent of North America.[13] My observations are confined to intra-Asian trade. An upward revision is also feasible with regard to trans-Pacific trade.

Even so, the overall picture is that most Pacific countries traded more heavily with Europe (and other regions outside the Pacific) than within the Pacific region. The more regionally oriented trade patterns were to be found in Asia, but even here the main impetus to open Asian ports to foreign trade came from ideological and

*Table 8.2*   Exports from Pacific Countries, 1840–1900

| | | \$ million | | | | | | |
|---|---|---|---|---|---|---|---|---|
| | | **1840** | | **1860** | | **1880** | | **1900** |
| 1 | Canada | 15.6 | (6.9) | 36.2 | (5.3) | 68.9 | (4.7) | 148.0 | (6.0) |
| 2 | United States | 111.7 | (49.4) | 316.2 | (46.3) | 823.9 | (56.2) | 1,370.8 | (56.0) |
| 3 | Mexico | n.a. | (0.0) | n.a. | (0.0) | 29.7 | (2.0) | 74.6 | (3.0) |
| 4 | Colombia | 1.2 | (0.5) | 11.8 | (1.7) | 22.4 | (1.5) | 10.5 | (0.4) |
| 5 | Ecuador | 0.9 | (0.4) | 2.1 | (0.3) | 3.7 | (0.3) | 7.7 | (0.3) |
| 6 | Peru | 1.9 | (0.8) | 24.9 | (3.6) | 20.0 | (1.4) | 21.9 | (0.9) |
| 7 | Chile | 7.0 | (3.1) | 25.5 | (3.7) | 51.6 | (3.5) | 60.7 | (2.5) |
| 8 | New Zealand | n.a. | (0.0) | 2.8 | (0.4) | 24.4 | (1.7) | 57.2 | (2.3) |
| 9 | Australia | 7.0 | (3.1) | 76.4 | (11.2) | 113.0 | (7.7) | 153.2 | (6.3) |
| 10 | Japan | n.a. | (0.0) | 3.8 | (0.6) | 25.4 | (1.7) | 101.8 | (4.2) |
| 11 | Korea | n.a. | (0.0) | n.a. | (0.0) | n.a. | (0.0) | 4.7 | (0.2) |
| 12 | China | 37.7 | (16.7) | 78.0 | (11.4) | 106.2 | (7.3) | 117.5 | (4.8) |
| 13 | Philippines | 4.5 | (2.0) | 9.7 | (1.4) | 21.1 | (1.4) | 23.0 | (0.9) |
| 14 | French Indochina | n.a. | (0.0) | n.a. | (0.0) | 9.7 | (0.7) | 30.0 | (1.2) |
| 15 | Siam | n.a. | (0.0) | 6.5 | (1.0) | 8.7 | (0.6) | 15.2 | (0.6) |
| 16 | Sarawak | n.a. | (0.0) | n.a. | (0.0) | n.a. | (0.0) | 4.4 | (0.2) |
| 17 | Staraits Settlements | 8.0 | (3.5) | 32.0 | (4.7) | 63.0 | (4.3) | 116.4 | (4.8) |
| 18 | Dutch East Indies | 30.5 | (13.5) | 57.0 | (8.3) | 68.7 | (4.7) | 103.7 | (4.2) |
| 19 | Fiji | n.a. | (0.0) | n.a. | (0.0) | n.a. | (0.0) | 3.0 | (0.1) |
| 20 | Hawaii | n.a. | (0.0) | n.a. | (0.0) | 4.4 | (0.3) | 22.6 | (0.9) |
| | 20 countries Total | 226.0 | (100.0) | 682.9 | (100.0) | 1,464.8 | (100.0) | 2,446.9 | (100.0) |
| | World Total | 1,195.5 | *(18.9)* | 3,194.8 | *(21.4)* | 6,480.5 | *(22.6)* | 9,769.7 | *(25.0)* |

*Source and Notes:*
John R. Hanson, II, *Trade in Transition* (New York, 1980), pp. 139–41.
Below are countries not in Hanson's table, but picked up by Charles C. Stover, 'Tropical Exports', in
W. Arthur Lewis, ed., *Tropical Development, 1880–1913: Studies in Economic Progress* (London, 1970), pp. 47–9.

| | 1883 | 1899 |
|---|---|---|
| El Salvador | 5.9 | 3.7 |
| Honduras | 0.8 | 2.7 |
| Costa Rica | 2.1 | 4.9 |
| Venezuela | 19.7 | 15 |
| North Borneo | 0.5 | 2 |
| Papua | 0.1 | 0.3 |
| New Caledonia | 0.6 | 2.1 |
| French Polynesia | 0.7 | 0.8 |

institutional changes in Britain and Western Europe from mercantilism to free trade, and the imposition primarily by European, as well as American, powers, of the principle of free trade on Asian countries. China, Siam, Japan and Korea opened their ports to foreign trade, in the form of the treaty port system under the 'unequal treaties', while much of Southeast Asia became colonies of western powers. In Southeast Asia, the Anglo–Dutch Treaty of 1824 marked the establishment of a free trade order, which prepared the intra-Asian context in which Hong Kong was established in 1845. Thus the system of 'forced free trade' emerged, linking treaty and colonial ports across East and Southeast Asia. The Asian Pacific Rim in the period from 1800 to 1930, which contributed to the growth of the regional dimension of the Pacific trade, was substantially a free trade area under the dominance of western political and military powers.

*Exports of primary products and US demand*

Between 1820 and 1870, China's internal political and environmental disruptions pulled down the growth of GDP of the Rim countries. Between 1870 and 1913, the new government in Japan led the process of industrialisation, and other economies also grew steadily. This trend continued into the interwar period, with major contributions to the growth of GDP from the United States and, to a lesser extent, Japan (see Table 8.1). By 1928 the United States, though predominantly driven by the Atlantic connections, and Japan, though much smaller in size than China but enjoying more rapid growth, emerged as the two major trading nations of the Pacific.

Figure 8.1 shows the main trading routes along the Pacific Rim countries in 1928. At this point many Rim countries exported their primary products or semi-manufactured goods (such as raw silk) to the United States, which constituted the mainstay of trans-Pacific trade. Thus the US demand for primary products was the driving force behind Pacific trade. Industrialisation and urbanisation, as well as the rise in the standard of living and increase in consumption, induced the demand for both food and drink and raw materials.

Chinese and Japanese trade with the United States was among the first regular and sustained trans-Pacific traffic, consisting primarily of exports of tea and raw silk. The famously fast 'tea clippers', which dominated the trans-Pacific traffic, were replaced by steamships only in the late nineteenth century.[14] The first transport and communication revolution, in the form of the introduction of steamships, railways and telegraphs, enabled different regions of the Pacific to connect with one another. The opening of the Panama Canal in 1914 linked the Pacific to the Atlantic, making the trans-Pacific route more attractive to the trade between Asia and the eastern side of the United States.

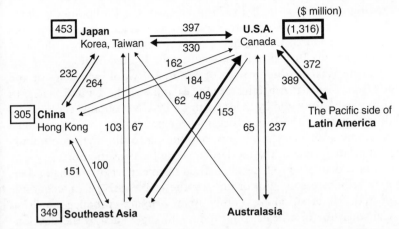

*Figure 8.1*   Pacific Rim Trade, 1928

*Sources and Notes*: League of Nations, *Network of World Trade* (Geneva, 1942), Annex III. For Japan–Korea–Taiwan (Formosa) trade, Kaoru Sugihara, *Ajia-kan Boeki no Keisei to Kozo* [Patterns and Development of Intra-Asian Trade] (Kyoto, 1996), p.114. Figures in boxes indicate the value of trade within the region (e.g. trade between Japan and Korea). A large proportion of trade between the U.S.A. and Canada was land- or Atlantic-based, and only 11 per cent of U.S. exports and 12 per cent of U.S. imports went through the customs of the Pacific coast (United States, Bureau of the Census, *Historical Statistics of the United States, Colonial Times to 1970* (Washington, DC, 1975), pp. 884, 896). The total volume of world trade was $33,547 million. Arrows were shown for trade of more than 25 million 'old' US dollars only.

Equally important were exports of tropical produce, most important of which were those from Southeast Asia to the United States. At this time a number of primary producers emerged across the Pacific Rim and Ocean. Early exports included many tropical foods and beverages: coffee from the Dutch East Indies and the Caribbean, sugar from the Dutch East Indies, the Philippines and the Pacific Islands, and cocoa from Ecuador. Some of the migration, for example Indian migration to the Caribbean and Fiji, and Chinese and Japanese migration to Hawai'i, may be interpreted as a spin-off of this export growth. Other food and beverages were exported from both temperate and tropical zones: tea from China, the Dutch East Indies and Japan, tobacco leaf from the United States, China and the Dutch East Indies, and rice from French Indochina and Siam. They also included raw materials for industrial and agricultural use: raw cotton from the United States (largely to Japan), nitrate from Chile, timber from the Dutch East Indies and Canada, hemp from the Philippines, rubber and tin from the Dutch East Indies and Malaya, fertilisers from Peru and Chile, and copper from Chile and Mexico.

Only a small portion of this was part of the Pacific trade, as large plantations and mines were often products of European investment and shipping routes were directed towards Europe. By the 1920s, however, a large quantity of rubber was exported from Malaya to the United States via the Pacific, some of which was handled by Japanese trading companies. In 1928, 75 per cent of the Philippines exports, 42 per cent of British Malaya's exports and much more than 13 per cent of the Dutch East Indies' exports (there was a large volume of re-exports via British Malaya) went to the United States.[15]

There was also the growth of exports of wool, wheat, meat and fur from Canada, Australia, New Zealand and the United States. In summary: stimulated by the growth of the US economy, ecologically diverse parts of the Pacific became integrated into the international economy as primary producers, responding to the rhythm of industrial production and the modern appetite for consumption.

Some primary producers benefited from exports more than others for various reasons. According to the staple theory of economic growth, internationally competitive primary produce, such as Canadian fur or wheat, could induce linkages such as the development of processing industry and the construction of railways, as well as providing purchasing power to primary producers, which would stimulate the demand for necessities in the local population.[16] By and large, the regions of recent settlement benefited from the former type of linkage effects, both forward and backward.

On the other hand, the tropics with a large population benefited from the latter final demand linkage. For example, the high price of rubber offered in the international market induced a relatively high wage for plantation workers in Malaya, who purchased their food and clothing locally or through regional trade. In this way long-distance trade was linked to the growth of local and regional trade in Southeast Asia. In contrast to the Philippines, which were tied strongly to the US economy after the 1880s, most Southeast Asian countries were heavily engaged in local and regional trade, often conducted by overseas Chinese merchants, in addition to (largely colonial) long-distance trade.

Other regions less committed to trade were also affected by the growth of trans-Pacific and regional trade, as their network of communication penetrated into the entire region. A large part of the Pacific side of the Caribbean and South America did not exploit land and other resources, due partly to difficult geographical access and other ecological conditions, but also to the institutions which reinforced them.[17]

*The growth of intra-Asian trade and Japan's industrialisation*

Along with the trans-Pacific trade induced largely by US demand, there was another development, shown in Figure 8.1, that was crucial at the regional level. This is the growth of intra-Asian trade driven largely by Japan's labour-intensive industrialisation. Japan's comparative advantage lay in the supply of cheap labour of good quality, and it seemed sensible to specialise in labour-intensive manufacturing in order to become the first industrial nation in Asia. Thus, while Japan imported modern machinery and capital from the West, and earned foreign exchange by exporting tea and raw silk there, it also imported raw cotton, first from China, then from India, and eventually the United States, and exported cotton yarn to China, and gradually cotton cloth, apparel and other sundries all over Asia. The Japanese strategy was essentially to make itself competitive in the production of labour-intensive goods, by maximising the use of low-cost (and good-quality) labour and by minimising the use of capital, which was scarce. Cheap manufactured goods were in demand among the ordinary people in Asia, and Japan was able to capture a large share of the Asian market for modern consumer goods. Thus the Japanese path of development was quite different from the path followed by the United States, which was characteristically capital- and resource-intensive.

It was this emerging Asian international economy, following the labour-intensive path, into which China was integrated. China initially imported Japanese machine-made yarn, and Chinese hand-weavers used it to expand domestic demand. This was followed by the growth of the modern cotton textile industry, again using imported Japanese textile machinery. The Japanese cotton textile industry in turn upgraded the quality of its products to meet low-wage competition from China. In this way East Asia went through labour-intensive industrialisation on a regional scale. Throughout the pre-war period, Japan, China, Southeast Asia and India traded relatively freely and benefited from the gains from international trade. Even in the 1930s, the share of intra-Asian trade in world trade grew larger, due mostly to the growth of yen-bloc trade.

Yet, the US-demand-driven trans-Pacific trade and Japanese-industrialisation-driven regional trade were not directly integrated into a unified force. The rise of the Atlantic economy from the latter half of the nineteenth century, and the establishment of the Suez–Malacca Straits route as the main sea lane following the opening of the Suez Canal in 1867, brought about a large increase of Atlantic and East–West trade, and hence the relative decline in the Pacific trade. At the close of the nineteenth century, with the emergence of London as the international financial market, which was compounded by the rise of Hamburg and Rotterdam as centres of international shipping, the centre of organisation of world trade was located overwhelmingly in Western Europe. Shippers engaged in the export of Japanese raw silk to the United States perceived their business as a 'side route' affair. Major trade fluctuations came mostly from the Suez route, which was the 'trunk route' of world trade. Meanwhile, US trade policy was inclined towards protectionism, and Asian migration to the region of recent settlement came to be subjected to severe restrictions. The gap in per capita GDP between the regions of recent settlement and the rest of the Pacific Rim countries widened. As late as the 1920s the Pacific economy was developing in the shadow of the Atlantic.

## 1930–1980

Three economic and political shocks determined the changes in Pacific Rim trade during the next half-century: the Great Depression originating in the Wall Street Crash of September 1929, the Asia-Pacific War beginning with the Manchurian Incident of 1931, which led to the outbreak of the Sino-Japanese War in 1937 and the opening of the Pacific theatre of the Second World War in 1941, and the establishment of the Cold War regime with the withdrawal of mainland China and many East and Southeast Asian countries from the 'free world' and the free trade regime. The first two shocks resulted in severe disruptions of the Pacific trade, while the third split Asia into two blocs, disconnecting many countries from the Pacific trade. Nevertheless, as the United States came to exercise an unparalleled militaristic, political and economic hegemony across the Pacific, the Asian side of the Rim, including Japan, South Korea, Taiwan, Hong Kong, Malaya-Singapore and later other ASEAN countries, went through a sustained period of economic growth. It was a US-centred phase of Pacific economic integration, under which per capita GDP of East and Southeast Asian Rim countries, led by Japan, rose at a speed faster than the world had ever seen.

An equally important change was that East Asia was now exporting manufactured goods to the United States, as much as it was importing high technology and managerial know-how from that country. Not only did the US–Japan economic relations become much more equal in nature, the entire Pacific trade also became more industrialisation-driven, as developmental states in East and Southeast Asia became progressively involved in a complex system of international division of labour in modern manufacturing. By 1980 the Pacific economy was substantially an autonomous force in the world economy, capable of generating its own dynamism.

## The impact of the Great Depression and the Second World War

The Great Depression since 1929 marked the beginning of the powerful, though destructive, American impact on the economies of East Asia. The Europe-centred network of world trade collapsed, and tariff and currency blocs were set up to protect national and imperial economic interests. Britain left the gold standard in 1931, and by 1933 the US dollar converged to sterling rather than to gold. The international gold standard was replaced by the dual key currency (sterling-dollar) regime.

An important but unintended consequence of the Great Depression was China's abandonment of the silver standard and the establishment of an effective central government which could regulate the relationship between the domestic economy and the international economy. The Nationalist government pursued an economic policy to proceed with labour-intensive industrialisation, and linked the value of Chinese currency to sterling (hence to dollar) in 1935. The state became responsive to macroeconomic signals of modern capitalism, including external shocks, for the first time.

Faced with intensified competition from China, Japan was determined to proceed with heavy and chemical industrialisation in the same period. Yet the expansion of the yen bloc increased, rather than reduced, Japan's dependence on the imports of raw materials, especially from the United States and the British formal and informal empire in the Pacific Rim. As the Chinese adopted the strategy of the protracted war, Japan needed increasing amounts of raw materials and energy resources from outside the yen bloc, in order to sustain its war efforts. Its failure suggested that there was little chance that autarky, such as the Japan-centred project envisaged in the name of the 'Greater East Asia Co-prosperity Sphere', would succeed in the region.

These two shocks left East Asia with a greater awareness of the region's position in the world economy. Together with war destruction in Europe, it prepared the emergence of the post-war order, with US hegemony on the one hand, and the emergence of the Soviet-led communist bloc on the other.

## The Cold War regime and the rise of East Asia

During the late 1940s and the 1950s most Asian countries achieved independence and began implementing their own programmes of industrialisation. However, these efforts were invariably affected by the coming of the Cold War. The pre-war pattern of intra-Asian trade was replaced by a rather strict division between the US-led regime of free trade, and other countries either under the influence of the Soviet-led communist bloc or following the non-aligned movement led by Nehru and Sukarno. The latter groups substantially withdrew from world trade. Only a small number of countries along the Pacific Rim remained fully integrated into the international economy.

Japanese 'high-speed growth' during the 1950s and the 1960s was the first successful response to this new international order. Following her defeat in the Second World War, the Japanese government was determined to pursue a programme of full economic modernisation, primarily through the expansion of its domestic market. But the problem of resource constraints (mentioned above as a background to Japan's aggression in the 1930s) remained a critical bottleneck. It was the Cold War that changed the American attitude towards Japan's economic future. By the late 1940s Japan was regarded as a country whose economic strength should be deployed to protect and further the 'free world' in East Asia. Accordingly, she was allowed to pursue the systematic introduction of capital-intensive heavy industries. Although heavy industrialisation was attempted in the 1930s and, in some ways, accelerated during the period of the wartime controlled economy, it was at this point that the character of Japanese growth shifted from labour-intensive industrialisation to the fusion of the two paths: the East Asian labour-intensive path and the western capital-intensive one, and its experiment began to assume global significance.

While the United States specialised in resource- and capital-intensive industries (such as military, space, aircraft and much of the petrochemical sectors), it was happy to help East Asia enlarge its industrial structure from light industries (such as cotton textiles) to the non-military and relatively labour-intensive segments of heavy industries. These included shipbuilding, cars and consumer electronics. A number of newly industrialising economies (NIEs) and ASEAN countries (the four leading members of which were the Philippines, Indonesia, Thailand and Malaysia) were under politically repressive authoritarian regimes, which were nonetheless committed to economic growth, and were able to get political and military support from the United States. The Cold War regime in turn was implicitly supported by East Asian growth, as it demonstrated the best side of capitalism. In this sense, the Cold War regime and East Asian growth were two sides of the same coin.

As the Cold War turned to a period of 'long peace', military demand flattened, while the mass consumer goods market in which East Asia specialised expanded, and the region's industrial exports to the United States, as well as intra-Asian trade, rapidly increased. Both US–Europe trade and intra-European trade grew steadily but slowly. Europe, gradually recovering from war, managed to create a politically charged European Economic Community, with a rather protectionist stance against the rest of the world. With decolonisation, the sterling area gradually disintegrated, but those newly independent countries not directly connected to the Asia-Pacific were slow to feel intense competition, and failed to exploit the potential gains from international trade. The Soviet-centred communist-bloc trade also failed to generate the dynamics of technological advance in labour-intensive industries and new consumer demand. Thus, the growth of post-war trade was led by the United States and driven by the high-speed growth of Japan and other East Asian countries.

From the perspective of Pacific economic integration, it was important that the United States became a major exporter of manufactured goods to the Rim countries. Until the 1940s the most important commodity export was raw cotton. By 1980 by far the largest proportion of exports was machinery. Industrial linkages became the new, and the more powerful, binding element of the Pacific economy.

Figure 8.2 shows that by 1980 the main trade routes, which had been active in 1928, were re-established, with the exception of

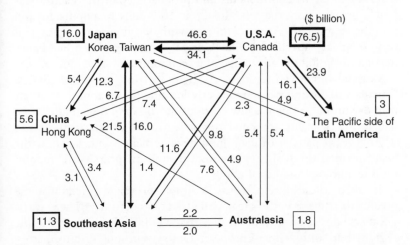

*Figure 8.2*  Pacific Rim Trade, 1980

*Sources and Notes*: IMF, *Direction of Trade Statistics Yearbook 1987* (Washington, DC, 1988). For Taiwan, Department of Finance, Government of Taiwan, *Returns of the Trade of Taiwan for Forty Years*. For figures in boxes, see Notes for Figure 8.1. 17 per cent of U.S. exports and 14 per cent of U.S. imports went through the customs of the Pacific coast in 1970 (United States, Bureau of the Census, *Historical Statistics of the United States, Colonial Times to 1970* (Washington, DC, 1975), pp. 884, 896), and these figures were probably larger in 1980. The total volume of world trade was US$1,915 billion. Arrows were shown for trade of more than US$1 billion only.

mainland China. In the figure shown, China and Hong Kong are grouped together. It is telling that in 1980 Hong Kong traded more than mainland China. The latter's withdrawal was fairly complete, leaving the Rim with a large blank spot. Integration remained shallow in this respect.

## *The second transport revolution and cross-cultural fusion*

The most immediate force that united the economies along the Pacific Rim in this period was the 'second' transport revolution, involving the introduction of large tankers, the upgrading of port and related facilities, road and railway connections and the containerisation of key industrial goods transport.[18] Suddenly, the largest ocean on earth began to provide the greatest opportunities for trade, as the reduction of transportation costs connected countries with great ecological and cultural diversities, as well as differences in capital and labour intensity.

How should we explain the explosion of trade growth in the Pacific? Ricardo (and later Hecksher–Ohlin) argued for the 'gains from international trade', according to which, if two countries with different factor endowments or productivity begin trading, both would be better off than in the case of no trade. This was the basis on which the rise of the Atlantic economy can be explained. But the diversity of factor endowments and productivity in the Pacific was much greater. On the one hand, it had densely populated and resource-poor East Asian countries with varying wage rates and technological capabilities. The United States, on the other hand, needed to exploit the advantage of its economies of scale in resource- and capital-intensive industries. At the same time, the United States, Canada and Australasia were eagerly looking for customers for their primary products (such as raw cotton and iron ore), now that Europe had lost its capacity for rapid import growth. Within East Asia, a 'flying geese pattern of economic development', with Japan at the head, formed the basis of the rapid growth of intra-Asian trade of high technology industrial goods.

In all of these developments, a simple principle ruled: that the greater the diversity, the greater the trade opportunity. There was a good case for 'open regionalism', with lower tariff barriers within the region, but, unlike the European Union, without discriminatory measures against countries outside the region. While economic nationalism often qualified and delayed the process, especially in trade in agricultural products, Asian countries enjoyed the presence of Hong Kong, and to a lesser extent Singapore, as free ports. Most growth economies of East and Southeast Asia traded heavily via these ports, especially with the United States and among the growth economies of East and Southeast Asia. As long as the region's growth rates remained the fastest in the world, it was believed that the region would have the most to gain from trade. Open regionalism was thus adopted as the guiding principle for the formation of APEC.

Furthermore, there occurred a much more comprehensive technological and cultural fusion between different civilisations than the world had ever seen. Already in the 1960s, East Asia had made a significant contribution to the emergence of the mass consumer market in the United States. For example, the East Asian textile complex, made up of Japanese man-made fibre manufacturers, Taiwanese weavers, Hong Kong finishers and Japanese general trading companies, was competing well in the lower end of the American market of clothing and apparel. During the 1980s and 1990s technological fusion became a two-way process. Not only did Japan absorb a wide range of American technology and culture and produce internationally competitive cars and consumer electronics, the American manufacturers responded in turn to the Japanese challenge by adopting some Japanese production methods. In other words, convergence, as well as specialisation through trade, occurred. Under such circumstances, international competition for finding the best input mix became fierce, and Pacific economies became used to constant change and rapid growth.

The Asian market of mass consumer goods has also seen an unprecedented degree of fusion of consumer tastes. Part of the dynamism of the American mass consumer market during the 1950s and the 1960s came from the fact that a variety of European cultures and tastes were freely blended to form a new mass consumer culture. In East and Southeast Asia in the 1980s and the 1990s, a much wider range of cultures and tastes came to be actively blended, to create diverse patterns of food, clothing and housing. Furthermore, with the rapid rise of per capita income, routine household expenditure began to include a variety of consumer electronics, cars and computers. While this meant a greater demand for relatively culture-neutral goods (including intermediate goods), much of it coming from the machinery industry, this did not necessarily result in the 'universalisation' of consumer tastes. For example, a piece of simple computer software in a local language (but the size of the Chinese population could make it a potentially huge market) might need a design matching the 'feel' of Chinese characters and culture. It was usually those East Asian entrepreneurs who inherited the skills of translating local cultural codes into economic values that could respond to these needs. Meanwhile, with technology flowing from the United States, western merchants could secure a fair share of the long-distance trade relating to it. The point is that if two or more different civilisations develop slightly different types of mass consumer markets based on different languages and cultures while at the same time a strong tendency for technological and cultural convergence is at work, business opportunities are greater than in the monocultural situation. Here too the principle that the greater the diversity, the greater the trade opportunity, ruled.

## 1980–2010

A major structural change in the world economy occurred in the early 1970s. The United States began to lose her dominant position, leading to the change from the fixed exchange rate system, in which world trade was anchored by the dollar as the key currency, to the regime of floating exchange rates, to allow for the more flexible adjustments to changing economic strengths of each country (the rapid revaluation of yen is one such example). At the same time, the first oil crises in 1973–74 signalled the rise of commodity prices, which affected the relationship between producers and consumers of primary products and energy. Nevertheless, the economies of Japan, the NIEs, and then-recently-formed ASEAN countries performed relatively well.

Such a success was an important background to the change in Chinese policy in the late 1970s, which vastly enlarged the population and market of the Pacific economy. In turn, economic forces based on East Asia's industrial strength, rather than the Cold War regime, began to affect the region's international relations. With the collapse of the Soviet Union in 1991, the United States began to reduce its commitment to military industry and developed a strong will for financial supremacy. The 'Wall Street–Treasury Complex' offered a new complementarity between the American financial interests and East Asia's industrialisation, adding to the old (military/ non-military) division of labour, and provided the basis for the continued growth of trade.[19]

In 1950 the 29 countries shown in Table 8.1 took up 25 per cent of world GDP, by 1980 39 per cent and by 2008 56 per cent. As pointed out above, these figures are exaggerations, as they include non-littoral China and non-Pacific North America. Even so, the figure for 2008 unmistakably suggests the centrality of the Pacific in the world economy in both scale and the speed of growth. In particular, intra-Asian trade became the growth core of world trade.

Comparison between Figure 8.2 and Figure 8.3 shows the huge impact of the reentry of China. By 2010 the share of ten Asian countries (China, Japan, NIEs and ASEAN 4) in world export trade had reached 28 per cent, 74 per cent of which was intra-Asian trade.[20]

Today, the Pacific economy is often associated with *Asia*-Pacific, as the degree of economic integration among the Asian countries became deepest in the region. Of course, East and Southeast Asia has never been successfully integrated politically or institutionally on their own initiatives, and the economic diversity within Asia remains great. Twenty-one APEC member countries, which are variously linked to this growth core, only loosely monitor the stability of Asia's international order.[21] East and Southeast Asia also depends increasingly on imports of natural resources from outside the region for its growth, as well as on imports of technology from the United States. But, compared to thirty years ago, the combined weight of the western side of the Pacific has clearly increased. The process of Pacific economic integration shifted from the US-centred phase to the more Asia-focused phase of US-led globalisation and Asia-led economic growth.

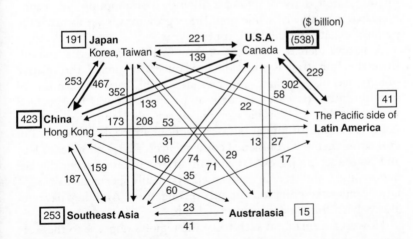

*Figure 8.3* Pacific Rim Trade, 2010

*Source and Notes*: IMF, *Direction of Trade Statistics Yearbook 2011* (Washington, DC, 2012). For figure in boxes, see Notes for Figure 8.1. The proportion of trade going through the customs of the Pacific coast in 2010 was probably larger than in 1980. See a different set of data on state exports in Cornelia J. Strawser, Sohair M. Abu-Aish and Linz Audain, eds., *Foreign Trade of the United States, including State and Metro Area Export Data*, 2nd edn (Lanham, MD, 2001). The total volume of world trade was US$15,319 billion. Arrows were shown for trade of more than US$10 billion only.

*Industrialisation and environmental sustainability*

How should we assess the evolution of industrialisation-driven integration along the Pacific Rim in the long run? I maintain that the
increase of population and the rise in the standard of living over the
last two centuries are major achievements, to which integration
contributed greatly. But the process was accompanied by a range of
negative consequences. One major concern is the environmental
consequences of industrialisation. As soon as industrialisation-driven
trade began, the exploitation of natural resources, construction of
ports, roads and railways, and deterioration of urban living conditions had serious consequences on the environment, as well as on
local populations.

If we define environmental sustainability as a state where the path
of economic development is consistent with the logic of nature, the
Pacific region had been arguably governed by forces of the geosphere
(smooth energy and material flows are maintained in accordance
with the circulation mechanism of the earth) and the biosphere (the
eco-system and food chains function by incorporating human interventions rather than vice versa), until industrialisation-driven trade
arrived. Even in the populated parts of East Asia humans depended
for their food on their land and labour, and for their heat energy on
(mainly forest-derived) biomass. Energy consumption per capita
increased very slowly, while population growth was yet to reach the
point of exhausting the land frontier.

A massive increase of the use of fossil fuels (especially coal and oil)
since the Industrial Revolution fundamentally altered the relative
importance of geosphere and biosphere. The basic mechanism of
sustaining the local environment and population was broken, and
was replaced by an invisible web of contacts through trade and technological and institutional transfers without a recognised method of
evaluating their environmental consequences. The economies of East
and Southeast Asia grew faster than anywhere else during the last
half-century, and were accompanied by equally spectacular deforestation, industrial pollution and urban congestion. And they have not
always been fully and swiftly attended to.

However, arguably at such costs, the region's response to the scarcity of resources resulted in their more efficient use. The labour-
intensive path, which this region followed, is historically associated
with resource- and energy-saving technology. The energy intensity
of Japan and more recently of other East Asian countries, measured
in terms of primary energy consumption per GDP, has been lower

than the countries following the capital- and resource-intensive path, especially the United States. Put more simply, East Asia used biomass energy for household use during the period of industrialisation much more than western countries did, and, largely because of the shortage of resources, resource- and energy-saving technology developed more fully there than in the West. In the more recent period, intensified intra-Pacific economic competition contributed to the global diffusion of resource- and energy-saving technology, and the two paths, capital-intensive and labour-intensive, began to converge towards the resource- and energy-saving one. The energy intensity of China, which was exceptionally high before 1980, also fell significantly by 2010.

### Integration and oceanic path dependency

On the other hand, the impact of economic integration on the Pacific Ocean and Islands was conditioned by a remarkably thinly populated and environmentally powerful oceanic space. On the one hand, the linguistic and cultural path dependency in the Pacific Islands goes back thousands of years and remains alive today.[22] The Islanders have sustained a certain sense of lineage, time and space, in spite of repeated and increasingly powerful external shocks, and this is deeply related to the dependence of their livelihood on sea and the distance it creates. At the same time, the ocean is connected by the movements of currents, birds and fish, as well as by the geospheric transmission of energy resulting in earthquakes and tsunami, in a more dynamic way than any other ocean on earth.[23] It is an environmentally integrated space.

Thus the impact on the Islanders of industrialisation-driven trade and the growth of exports of primary products have been more variable, if not always less intense, than on the inhabitants along the Rim. Their export trade was small relative to that of the Rim countries (compare Table 8.3 with Table 8.1). Even so, the volume of combined exports probably increased more rapidly than world exports between 1928 and 2010. (Note that some of the 2010 figures do not include exports to the United States mainland.) The United States-led demand for primary products, combined with European, American and Japanese rule, brought the establishment of plantations, mines and fisheries, while Japanese interventions before and during the Second World War created violent disruptions. This was followed by the post-war establishment of American military bases and the more recent growth of Japanese, American and other Asian

*Table 8.3*   Exports from the Pacific Islands, 1928–2010

| | | ($ million) | | |
|---|---|---|---|---|
| | | 1928 | 1980 | 2010 |
| Micronesia | Guam | 0* | 61* | [30] |
| | Japanese Pacific Islands | 2 | n.a. | n.a. |
| | Nauru | 1 | 125 | 50 |
| | Kiribati | 1** | 3 | 30 |
| Melanesia | Papua New Guinea | 6*** | 1,133 | 9,888 |
| | Solomon Islands | 1 | 73 | 439 |
| | Vanuatu | 2**** | 36 | 230 |
| | New Caledonia | 7 | 411 | 1,520 |
| | Fiji | 7 | 358 | 1,262 |
| Polynesia | Tuvalu | n.a. | 1 | 0.0 |
| | Samoa | | 17***** | 135 |
| | American Samoa | 0* | 127* | [100] |
| | Tonga | 1 | 8 | 13 |
| | Cook and Niue Islands | 1 | | |
| | French Polynesia | | 39 | 330 |
| | Total | 29 | 2,392 | 14,027 |
| | Hawai'i | 119* | 932****** | [684]******* |
| | World total in $ billion | 33.55 | 1,915 | 15,319 |

*Sources and Notes:*

Figures for 1928 are from League of Nations, *Network of World Trade* (Geneva, 1942), Annex III, unless otherwise stated.

Figures for 1980 and 2010 are from IMF, *Direction of Trade Statistics Yearbook 1987* and *2012* (Washington, DC), respectively, unless otherwise stated.

* Taken from Susan B. Carter et al., eds., *Historical Statistics of the United States: Earliest Times to the Present*, 5 vols. (Cambridge, 2006), pp. 610–11.

** Gilbert and Ellice Islands. They were separated into Tuvalu and Kiribati by 1980.

*** Consists of 2 for Papua and 4 for New Guinea.

**** New Hebrides.

***** Western Sāmoa.

****** Taken from Robert C. Schmitt, *Historical Statistics of Hawaii* (Honolulu, 1977), p. 544. Figure cited here is for 1974.

Between 1950 and 1974 84 to 99 per cent of 'exports' went to other parts of the United States and 'imports' became increasingly much larger than exports.

******* Taken from http://www.census.gov/foreign-trade/statistics/state/data/hi.html

Figures in square brakets do not include exports to other parts of the Unites States.

tourism. Since neither military-base-related transactions nor reve-
nues from tourism are well reflected in the export figures in Table
8.3, the overall post-war external influences must have been stronger
still. And these activities were as externally driven and vulnerable to
change as exports of primary products.

The environmental dynamics of the Pacific basin centres on the
sea, while industrial technology developed under the modern, land-
based system of territorial states and private property rights in the
West. To the extent that the system has not fully taken into account
the oceanic circulation of heat and water, and the movements of
plants, marine species and micro-organisms, it was harder for
modern forces to penetrate into the sea-based civilisation than into
the land-based parts of the Pacific economy.

Yet it was the distance unique to this ocean, which had limited the
volume of transoceanic trade for such a long time, that eventually
embraced the emergence of an industrialisation-driven trade and a
new centre of the world economy. Making the impact of economic
integration compatible with oceanic path dependency remains a
major challenge for the twenty-first century.

## Notes

1. Sidney Pollard, *Peaceful Conquest: The Industrialization of Europe, 1760–
   1970* (Oxford, 1981).
2. Figures on population and GDP in this chapter come from Angus
   Maddison, 'Statistics on World Population, GDP and Per Capita GDP,
   1–2008 AD (Horizontal file)' http://www.ggdc.net/maddison/ (made
   available in 2009, accessed 31 January 2013), unless stated otherwise.
   For estimates, see Notes of Table 8.1.
3. According to unadjusted population data, around 60 per cent of the
   population may have lived in the areas categorised as North East,
   North, East and South East (all along the coast) between 1819 and
   1957: Dwight H. Perkins, *Agricultural Development in China, 1368–1968*
   (Chicago, 1969), Appendix A, especially p. 212.
4. While some of the areas mentioned in footnote 3 are not directly
   connected to coastlines, per capita GDP in the littoral must have been
   higher than in the rest of China.
5. The proportions of residents in three US states facing the Pacific in the
   total US population were 1.4 per cent in 1860, 3 per cent in 1890, 5.5
   per cent in 1920, 10 per cent in 1950 and 15.7 per cent in 1990: Susan
   B. Carter, et al., eds., *Historical Statistics of the United States: Earliest
   Times to the Present*, 5 vols. (Cambridge, 2006), I, p. 38.
6. Dennis O. Flynn, Arturo Giráldez and James Sobredo, eds., *European Entry
   into the Pacific: Spain and the Acapulco–Manila Galleons* (Aldershot, 2001).

7. Man-Houng Lin, *China Upside Down: Currency, Society and Ideologies, 1808–1856* (Cambridge, MA, 2006); Maria Alejandra Irigoin, 'Gresham on Horseback: The Monetary Roots of Spanish American Political Fragmentation in the Nineteenth Century', *Economic History Review* 62 (2009), 551–75.

8. David Armitage and Alison Bashford, 'Introduction: The Pacific and its Histories', ch. 1 in this volume, p. 17.

9. Douglass North, *The Economic Growth of the United States, 1790–1860* (New York, 1996), pp. 99–100.

10. Barry Eichengreen and Marc Flandreau, 'The Geography of the Gold Standard', in Jorge Braga de Maredo, Barry Eichengreen and Jamie Reis, eds., *Currency Convertibility: The Gold Standard and Beyond* (London, 1996), pp. 117–43.

11. W. W. Rostow, *The World Economy: History and Prospect* (London, 1978), pp. 70–1, Appendix B.

12. John R. Hanson, II, *Trade in Transition: Exports from the Third World, 1840–1900* (New York, 1980), pp. 139–41.

13. Kaoru Sugihara, 'The Resurgence of Intra-Asian Trade, 1800–1850', in Giorgio Riello and Tirthankar Roy, eds. (with collaboration of Om Prakash and Kaoru Sugihara), *How India Clothed the World: The World of South Asian Textiles, 1500–1850* (Leiden, 2009), p. 159. The proportion of exports and imports going through the customs in the Pacific coast in the US total fluctuated from 2 to 9 per cent between 1860 and 1900. There was also a smaller percentage of Mexican border trade: US Department of Commerce, Bureau of Census, *Historical Statistics of the United States, Colonial Times to 1970*, Part 2 (New York, 1975), pp. 885, 897.

14. C. Knick Harley, 'Ocean Freight Rates and Productivity, 1740–1913: The Primacy of Mechanical Invention Reaffirmed', *Journal of Economic History* 48 (1988), 851–76.

15. League of Nations, *Network of World Trade* (Geneva, 1942), pp. 59–61.

16. M. H. Watkins, 'A Staple Theory of Economic Growth', *Canadian Journal of Economics and Political Science* 29 (1963), 145–6.

17. For a general discussion on the Americas, see Stanley Engerman and Kenneth Sokoloff, *Economic Development in the Americas since 1500: Endowments and Institutions* (Cambridge, 2012).

18. On containerisation, see Marc Levinson, *The Box: How the Shipping Container Made the World Smaller and the World Economy Bigger* (Princeton, 2006).

19. Jagdish Bhagwati, 'The Capital Myth: The Difference between Trade in Widgets and Dollars', *Foreign Affairs* 77, 3 (May–June 1998), 7–12.

20. Calculated from IMF, *Direction of Trade Statistics Yearbook*.

21. The APEC Summit 2012 took place in Vladivostok, Russia, which I have not included in calculating the Rim GDP and trade.

22. Damon Salesa, 'The Pacific in Indigenous Time', ch. 2 in this volume.

23. Ryan Tucker Jones, 'The Environment', ch. 6 in this volume.

# Part III: Knowledges

# 9

# Religion

## Bronwen Douglas

Geographically, this chapter bridges the vast zone of the globe that I call Oceania, stretching from the American west coasts to the Pacific Islands, the Philippines, Maluku, New Guinea, Australia and New Zealand.[1] Indigenous religion across this space – whether ancestral, Islamic or Christian – is best understood as local variations on a common pattern, each emergent within mobile historical, social and ecological settings. From this anthropological, rather than theological perspective, past and present Oceanian religions are not detached from worldly existence in a transcendent domain, as with much modern Christianity. Rather, religion is an embodied experience, encompassing human beings, gods or God, spirits, fauna, plants, places, rocks and other things within complex webs of relationship.[2] Tenacious but not unchanging, this pervasive practical religiosity supplies truths (ontology), knowledge (cosmology), explanations (aetiology) and ways of celebrating, influencing or controlling the world (ritual). In such contexts, there is neither justice nor logic in persistent evolutionist dichotomies which consign most of the world's populations to the 'non-West' and brand them negatively as 'backward' and 'superstitious', in opposition to the supposedly 'western' qualities of the 'modern' and the 'rational'.

We cannot be definitive about the religious beliefs and practices of the first modern human settlers of this immense zone because initial occupations might have spanned 60–70 millennia. Archaeologists, historical linguists and bioanthropologists estimate that Island Southeast Asia, Australia and Near Oceania (that is, New Guinea, the Bismarck Archipelago and Solomon Islands) were colonised from Asia at least 40–60,000 years ago and North America perhaps 15–20,000 years ago. From about 9,000 years ago, Austronesian-speaking seafarers left Taiwan, settled much of island Southeast Asia and many coastal areas of Near Oceania, and from about 4,000–5,000 years ago occupied all of previously uninhabited Remote Oceania (that is, Micronesia, southern Melanesia and Polynesia).[3]

It seems clear that, once established, communities were not 'primitive isolates' but were variously interdependent, linked by kinship or marriage, exchange or trade, alliance or emnity, tribute or domination. Persons, things, ideas and practices, including rituals, moved along often far-flung routes or networks, on sea and land.[4] However, the length and extent of isolation from the world beyond Oceania varied enormously in time and space. Bronze objects from Asia dated to more than 2,000 years ago were found in the Manus archipelago in Papua New Guinea (PNG), long inhabited by highly mobile maritime people.[5] With burgeoning international trade between India and Southeast Asia by the early first millennium CE, Hindu and Buddhist teachings reached the Indonesian archipelago. Indianised kingdoms emerged in the west before CE 400, though their religious life retained marked indigenous elements.[6] East and north, on the western margins of Oceania in Maluku and the Philippines, maritime-oriented coastal dwellers experienced Hindu and Chinese influences around CE 1000.[7] In contrast, with the land bridge to New Guinea submerged by about 8,000 years ago, Australia was effectively isolated until the late eighteenth century, apart from ongoing indigenous interactions across Torres Strait, fleeting seventeenth-century coastal visits by Dutch and English voyagers, and more protracted encounters with Macassan trepangers along the north and northwest coasts from the mid-seventeenth century.[8] Pacific Islanders made wide-ranging voyages within and between archipelagoes but were equally sequestered from the rest of the world until after the first crossing of the great ocean by Ferdinand Magellan in 1521 and the Spanish victories in Mexico in 1521 and Peru in 1532. In most Pacific Islands and the American northwest, subsequent outside encounters were non-existent or erratic before the mid-eighteenth century.[9] After 1760, European scientific voyages systematically criss-crossed the Pacific Ocean, stimulating whaling and trading expeditions from about 1790 and Protestant missionary activity in Polynesia from 1797. Permanent Russian trading posts were established in Alaska and further south from 1784 with effective Orthodox evangelisation in Alaska after 1794.[10] Spanish missionary colonisation of California was underway from 1769.[11] A century later, the coastal and insular mapping of Oceania was all but complete but most of the New Guinea Highlands and their inhabitants remained unknown to Europeans until the 1930s–50s.

Religious adherents tend to eternalise their own truths and rituals as immemorial. So-called 'primitive' religions are routinely stereotyped as timeless, superstitious and irrational by the self-styled 'civilised', including anthropologists for nearly two centuries after the late-eighteenth-century emergence of the discipline.[12] Social evolutionists positioned such beliefs and their holders at the earliest stages in a developmental sequence, typically running from magic to religion to science. Functionalists reduced ritual to a fixed reflex of social and economic institutions. Structuralists probed religion's relationships with other cultural elements within homeostatic total systems. Yet Oceanic worlds were neither closed nor stagnant. Historical comparison of Austronesian and Papuan languages reveals diverse degrees of conservatism or receptivity depending on the nature of encounters and the degree of bilingualism.[13] By analogy, ancestral religions in Oceania could also be variously hidebound or flexible, more or less open to innovation and liable to transformation in novel circumstances. Historians from the 1960s and anthropologists from about 1980 adopted practice-oriented approaches which acknowledge human agency in such processes – the potential to desire, choose and act strategically, within limits set by circumstance, status, gender, age or aptitude.[14]

Oral histories, myths and traditions, mostly recorded by missionaries and ethnographers, narrate how gods or ancestors formed and populated the world and how rituals or cults were dreamed and invented, borrowed, purchased, sold or exchanged, imposed, appropriated or rejected. Thus, in the generations following the introduction of the sweet potato to the Central Highlands of Papua New Guinea 300–400 years ago, the entire western region was criss-crossed by ritual tracks marking the movement of cults which people creatively inserted into existing ritual stocks to meet local goals.[15] In the Kimberley region of Western Australia, before and after colonisation, ritual complexes were similarly exchanged or traded for political and economic ends.[16] In Melanesia generally, altered states of consciousness – dreams, trances and possession – serve to introduce new knowledge, initiate or manage change, and cope with crises, natural disasters and modern challenges such as the onset of colonialism, Christianity, and decolonisation.[17] The fusion of traditionalist and Christian elements in so-called 'cargo cults' and millennial movements is best understood in similar terms.[18] When Europeans first visited Tahiti in the 1760s, the island's leading *ari'i* (chiefs) were enmeshed in bitter conflicts associated with the introduction of the cult of the war god 'Oro from neighbouring Ra'iatea, triggering the elaboration of more complex rank and political hierarchies.[19] Throughout Oceania, a widespread propensity for ritual innovation, whether top-down or popular or both, provided ontological templates for the reception and comprehension of global religions in the eight centuries after about CE 1200.

In hierarchical and egalitarian societies alike, people conceived their relationships with gods, ancestors or other spirits in terms of reciprocal dependence, not necessarily between equals. Ritual was thus an exchange and mundane outcomes confirmed the efficacy of spirits and rituals. Unsatisfactory spirits might be made irrelevant by denial of ritual offerings or abandoned and replaced by new ones. Thus, while the ancient Hawaiian gods were acknowledged to be powerful and capricious, they were also dependent on ritual recognition by human beings through sacrifices and prayers without which, it was said, they would die.[20] Perceived relative power was a key criterion of spiritual efficacy – known as *mana* or cognate terms. This, too, could be critical in indigenous engagements with the Islamic and Christian god.

Islam was established in Sumatra by the early thirteenth century and by 1500 had been embraced elsewhere in the Indonesian archipelago, including Maluku, and the Sulu Islands in southern Philippines.[21] However, since only fragmentary traces exist of these movements before the Portuguese arrival in 1511, I focus henceforth on the succeeding five centuries to the present. During this long period, the two great proselytising world religions ultimately won the general adherence of most indigenous communities in Island Southeast Asia, Latin America and the Pacific Islands while Christianity was more patchily adopted by Aboriginal Australians and North Americans. In the process, Islam and Christianity were variously indigenised. Until about 1970, conversion was conventionally explained as an external imposition on passive native recipients, whether by divine dispensation, missionary effort or local elite decision. Since then, scholars have increasingly acknowledged the agencies involved and the nuances of religious transformations. Without devaluing the pervasive sense of the divine and the sacred common to all Oceanian populations, 'conversion' in this pragmatic sense was a multifaceted individual or collective product of the interaction of myriad variables, depending on when, where, who and what were entailed – era, place, personalities, strategies, social and ecological settings, pre-existing beliefs, emotions and the perceived cosmological fitness or ritual power of new religions.

I identify three broad, overlapping phases of religious encounter, conversion and naturalisation in Oceania. The first two are 1511–1836 and 1788–1980, when religion was in varied association with different forms of colonial presence. The third, 1946 to the present, puts religion in relation to decolonisation and a now mostly postcolonial world. The staggered dates recognise the highly uneven chronologies of evangelism, colonialism and decolonisation in this vast, disparate zone. This strategy seeks to approximate the untidiness of actual human pasts by stressing overlap, commonality and subtle shifts over the sudden ruptures of clear-cut historical periodisation.[22] Four empirical vignettes illustrate and flesh out my schematic histories of the phases. Each relates religious innovation to unstable linkages between prior beliefs and practices; encounters involving local and foreign agents; missionary or elite authority; popular reception or appropriation; and, in the third phase, politics and custom.

## Phase 1: 1511–1836

During the first phase, religious proselytism and European colonial activities were confined to the western and eastern margins of the zone. In Maluku and the Philippines, Islam and Catholicism were widely worshipped in coastal areas by 1650. Local inhabitants sought, gave, changed or refused religious allegiance in the fluid, often nebulous contexts of Portuguese, Spanish and Dutch maritime imperialisms. These regimes attempted to monopolise trade via mercantile nodes, military superiority and local pacts rather than significant territorial control. Of the three, only the Spanish in the Philippines evangelised aggressively before the nineteenth century. Europeans became embroiled in alliance politics with indigenous rulers, some of whom adopted Islam or Christianity as weapons against enemies, rivals or foreign interlopers while others fought holy wars against infidels.[23] In the settlement colonies of Mexico and Peru and after 1668 in Guam (Marianas), Spanish Catholics had the mission field to themselves amid conquered populations traumatised by defeat, epidemic diseases and death.[24] In western California from 1769 to the 1830s, Spanish missionaries proselytised under military aegis in communities also undergoing serious depopulation.[25] Even in these dire situations, Christianity was not simply imposed but was appropriated, rejected or transformed according to indigenous understandings, to meet vernacular needs and desires. Franciscan friars from Peru also made an unsuccessful attempt to evangelise in Tahiti in 1774–5.[26]

### First vignette: Maluku and the Philippines

The sixteenth and seventeenth centuries saw both the advance and mutual antagonism of Islam and Counter-Reformation Catholicism in Maluku and the Philippines. The Portuguese apothecary Tomé Pires visited Sumatra and Java in 1513 and wrote a detailed report to his king on these and other islands he had heard about, particularly from *mouros* (Moors, Muslims) who had been there. 'Moor' was a pivotal term in sixteenth-century European lexicons, a marker of the importance of Islam in Iberian and Mediterranean political, economic and religious affairs over many preceding centuries. The word looms large in the travel accounts of Pires and the Venetian Antonio Pigafetta, chronicler of Magellan's expedition of 1519–22.[27] The centrality of religion in contemporary European worldviews is patent in their standard descriptors for the inhabitants of Maluku and the Philippines – 'moor' and its opposite 'gentile' (heathen, pagan, idolator, including Hindu). In practice, active proselytism was far less a goal of Lusitanian expansion than glorifying god and king by supplanting Moors and amassing wealth. Portuguese chronicles scarcely mention missionary activity or conversion in the fabled Spice Islands of Maluku.[28] Antonio Galvão, Portuguese captain there from 1536–9 and vaunted as 'Apostle of the Moluccas', wrote a history of the heroic saga of Iberian overseas discovery and conquest and a treatise on Maluku. Both works all but ignore Christian evangelism.[29]

Pires and Pigafetta suggest that, by the early sixteenth century, Maluku was a patchwork of small Muslim and non-Muslim kingdoms or chiefdoms but that Islam had not made significant inroads north of the Sulu archipelago. Both men heard that 'the beginning of the moors' in Maluku was 'about fifty years' before. Pires reported that the kings were Moors but were not heavily involved in the 'sect', many people were Muslim without being circumcised and overall the Moors were few while 'Gentiles' comprised three-quarters or more of the populace. Pigafetta cited examples of a pattern later common throughout Indonesia, that 'the moors live near the sea and the gentiles inland', and noted that the Spanish found Moors 'very much harder to convert than the gentiles'.[30]

Pires's interlocutors told him that the inhabitants of the 'Islands of the Luzons', named the Philippines by the Spanish in 1543, were 'nearly all Gentiles with no King' and were ruled by 'groups of elders'.[31] Pigafetta, in turn, identified as Gentiles every group directly encountered by Magellan's expedition in 1521 as it passed through the southeast of the archipelago en route to the Spice Islands, but everywhere he identified a *re* or *raya* (king or raja).[32] During a three-week stay in the island of Cebu, Magellan orchestrated a mass conversion to Christianity. Fortified by the conquistador's certainty of divine power and approval, he used a mixture of intimidation, bluff, a peace ceremony with formal alliance and exemplary Christian instruction to persuade the Gentile 'king' to accept baptism 'voluntarily'. The king, his 'queen' and 'eight hundred souls' were baptised in a single day, together with a visiting Moorish trader who served as an interpreter. They were no doubt encouraged by Magellan's promise that becoming Christian would enable the king to 'vanquish his enemies more easily' and by his threat to 'kill' recalcitrant 'chiefs' if they refused to obey 'the king or us'. When a chief of the nearby island of Mactan did so refuse, Magellan set out with a small armed party to teach him a lesson but received a fatal one himself from the tactically astute Mactan chief and his large force of warriors. Magellan and eight companions were killed and many others were wounded. The disaster evidently discredited the much-vaunted power of Magellan's god. A few days later, the newly 'Christian king' of Cebu lured more than 20 Europeans ashore, whereupon most were killed.[33] This fleeting encounter juxtaposes the potent blend of avarice, martial confidence and universalist religious conviction that impelled much Iberian colonial enterprise; and the pragmatic local-ised religiosity of indigenous maritime communities eager to extend their relations with the outside world.

For a century and a half after 1512, Maluku was the unstable setting for an intricate political, economic, imperial and religious quadrille which paired rival indigenous polities in expedient alliance or recurrent emnity with mutually hostile Portuguese, Spanish or Dutch colonial agents, avid for spices. In the process, local religions gave ground to widening adherence to Islam and, to a lesser extent, Christianity. The oscillating alliances of the adjacent sultanates of Ternate and Tidore are exemplary, as they sought to exploit or manage or resist the rapacious, often brutal presence of the Portuguese and their haphazard Catholic evangelism. In 1512, the sultan of Ternate invited several shipwrecked Portuguese to join him against Tidore. In 1522, the Portuguese built a fortress in Ternate after the sultan of Tidore sought a Spanish alliance with the remnants of Magellan's expedition.[34] The Portuguese were finally driven from Ternate in 1575 having murdered the sultan and so outraged his successor that for the next 30 years Ternate maintained an expan-sionist, aggressively Islamic, bitterly anti-Portuguese stance. Yet, far from joining a common Islamic cause against the infidels, the sultan of Tidore allowed the Portuguese to build a fortress on his island which they occupied until ousted from the region in 1605 by Ternate in alliance with the Dutch East India Company (VOC). Motivated mainly by economic and political priorities, the VOC was vigorously anti-Catholic but expediently neutral towards Islam. During two centuries as the dominant colonial presence in the East Indies, the VOC largely limited active Protestant evangelism in Maluku to non-Muslims or former Catholics.[35] The Spanish quickly filled the vacuum left by the Portuguese and maintained a foothold in Maluku until the 1660s, allied with Tidore against the Dutch-backed sultan of Ternate. But they reserved most of their missionary endeavour for the Philippines.

Both traditional Indonesian and academic histories usually represent Islamisation as a top-down process, instigated by authoritarian rulers, and attribute patchy adherence to Christianity to a combination of elite interest or initiative and missionary labour among kings and princes. In neither case is popular enthusiasm or agency much acknowledged, partly because their ephemeral traces are difficult to find, especially with respect to Islam.[36] Christianity made little headway in the sultanates of Ternate and Tidore where Portuguese greed and erratic, often violent behaviour probably discredited their religion.[37] However, from as early as the 1520s, many tens of thousands of people elsewhere in Maluku proclaimed themselves to be Christians, particularly in Ambon. Brett Baker's recent doctoral thesis provides convincing testimony that such conversions were largely popular, 'an indigenous-driven mission effort' mounted for varied local and personal reasons, at times in opposition to rulers. Jesuit missionaries, including Francis Xavier, were 'mere appendages' to the process of Christianisation, rather than its instigators and controllers in alliance with royal or chiefly supporters.[38] Following the Portuguese defeats in 1605, the Jesuits were expelled from areas under Muslim or Dutch control. The Catholic communities in Maluku either apostatised, were destroyed or identified as Protestant and ultimately forgot their ancestors' adherence to Catholicism.

The story of the acceptance of Catholicism in almost all lowland communities in the Philippines outside Sulu and Mindanao during the century after the first Spanish settlement in 1565 differs markedly from patterns of religious change in either Latin America or Maluku. Despite limited impact on Muslim communities in the south, Christianity kept Islam firmly and permanently at bay in Luzon and the Visayas. To avoid the widely condemned, lethal violence of Spain's American conquests, missionary orders rather than conquistadors were allowed to spearhead colonisation in the Philippines. They worked amongst mobile populations, long in contact with the outside world, and thus with some immunity to the diseases which ravaged indigenous Americans. As suggested by Cebuan responses to Magellan's heavy-handed evangelism, these maritime people might have been attracted by a religion promising wider efficacy than their own localised rituals and a god whose power outstripped that of demanding, unpredictable ancestors and local spirits.[39] Catholic historiography of the Philippines counterposes two eras. It celebrates two centuries of unbroken Christian progress until 1770, credited to rigorous missionary proselytism.[40] And it deplores a subsequent 'precipitous decline' into 'syncretism' – mindless mixing of pre-Hispanic and Catholic elements – blamed on a sudden, lasting reduction in the number and quality of priests leading to inadequate instruction or supervision of neophytes and converts.[41] A less Eurocentric perspective would look for continuities as well as rupture between the two eras and with what went before. Conversion presupposes an existing ontology which must help shape both the ways in which a new religion and its rituals are appropriated to meet present material and spiritual needs, as well as how they relate to enduring indigenous beliefs and practices.[42]

## Phase 2: 1788–1980

My second phase spans the nineteenth century and the first three-quarters of the twentieth, when the centre and the southern margins of Oceania entered global religious and geopolitical relations during an era of heightened imperial rivalry and eventual colonial encompassment of almost the entire zone.[43] The Aboriginal inhabitants of eastern, southern and southwestern Australia were colonised between 1788 and 1836 and those in more remote areas over the following century. Christian evangelisation was slow to start, uneven thereafter, always paternalist, and often heavy-handed. It has been argued that disjunction between Christian and Aboriginal religions made conversion to Christianity 'a virtual impossibility' unless 'the tribal ethic or structure has been destroyed'.[44] Yet recent studies (see Further Reading) show that Aboriginal people exercised considerable agency in their relationships with missionaries. Despite mutual miscomprehension and disruption of indigenous worlds, many Aboriginal Australians decided to become Christians on their own terms.

In nearly all of the Pacific archipelagoes, New Zealand, and some coastal areas of New Guinea, Protestant or Catholic missionisation preceded colonialism and had limited initial success amongst confident, independent populations. Comity agreements between Protestant denominations discouraged their overt competition and usually limited indigenous choice to a single Protestant mission and its Catholic rival. Sooner or later, most Islanders opted to identify as Christians because their leaders did so or because experience convinced them that Christian god and ritual were more powerful or effective than their own ancestral or other spirits. Colonial regimes date from the 1840s and 1850s in New Zealand, eastern

Polynesia and New Caledonia and from 1874 in Fiji. Between 1884 and 1906, New Guinea and most of the still independent archipelagoes were partitioned between contending European powers. In much of the New Guinea Highlands, formal colonisation preceded direct European contacts and missionaries followed 'pacification'. Moreover, the entire process was crammed into a few decades and sectarian differences proliferated from the outset. New evangelical or pentecostal groups competed with mainline denominations, encouraging both confusion and indigenous choice.

Established missionaries were often equivocal about the proclamation of colonial authority, though they usually aided its implementation by their own nation. On the one hand, they generally tried to protect their congregations from abuse by non-missionaries, including officials. On the other, they habitually infantilised local people, sometimes punished and exploited them, and almost always devalued 'paganism', which it was their vocation to transform or extirpate. Yet their pragmatic need to communicate and translate the gospel meant that they and their indigenous interlocutors were (and are) crucial co-producers of vernacular dictionaries, grammars and translations. Many missionaries made important contributions to anthropology while a few evinced sympathetic ethnographic interest in indigenous religion and sought to make acceptable beliefs and rituals a basis for familiarising Christian concepts and liturgical practices.

A critical reading of missionary texts, alert to ambiguous traces of indigenous agency, challenges the racialised stereotypes sometimes invoked – that mass conversions were rapidly imposed by chiefly fiat in advanced Polynesian societies, beginning in Tahiti in 1815; and that violent resistance or indifference to Christianity characterised the primitive, acephalous societies of Melanesia, epitomised in the killing of John Williams of the London Missionary Society (LMS) in south Vanuatu in 1839.[45] In popular imaginings, the typical nineteenth-century missionary was a driven, blinkered, bigoted European man. However, past actualities were more complex. Male missionaries themselves spanned a wide range of social and theological backgrounds, personalities, attitudes and approaches. But arguably the most critical elements, and certainly the main human interface in Christian mission in the Pacific Islands, were otherwise and twofold. Islander teachers, catechists, pastors and priests proselytised in their own or other places and brought vernacular or cultural expertise to the task of translating Christian words and ideas for local consumption. Women – mission sisters and wives, including Islanders, and female congregation members – did crucial work in the shadow of male authority, laying the groundwork for the earliest conversions and the ongoing embeddedness of Christian churches and beliefs in communities throughout the insular Pacific and New Guinea.

## Second vignette: Tahiti

This vignette is one of two featuring episodes in the great nineteenth-century movement of rival Christian denominations into the largely uncolonised Island Pacific. It spans the period from 1797, when the earliest Evangelical missionaries of the LMS arrived in Tahiti, to 1821 when the island's first Christian king died.[46] For 15 years, these 'godly mechanics' laboured with little spiritual success, heavily dependent on the patronage and protection of the emergent Pōmare dynasty and forced more than once to abandon their posts by the island's unsettled political state. From the 1770s, the highest-ranking *ari'i* Tu, later Pōmare I, and his son and successor Pōmare II engaged in a protracted struggle for unparalleled political domination of Tahiti and nearby Mo'orea. They combined old and new elements in a novel tactical armoury, skilfully exploiting ties of descent and marriage, waging ruthless war, and seeking to monopolise visiting or resident Europeans whose firearms and martial expertise were critical in several battles. By 1804, Pōmare II was effectively 'king'. From an indigenous perspective, worldly success at once required and demonstrated powerful spiritual backing. The 'present national religion', lamented the missionary John Davies, was 'so blended with the civil concerns, or the priviledges and authority of the chiefs, that they have no conception the one can stand without the other'. Until about 1810, Pōmare continued to sacrifice to 'Oro whose expanding cult underwrote the king's acknowledged ritual paramountcy. But so too did his opponents who united in 1808 in a successful general 'rebellion' against his despotism, rapaciousness, and escalating ritual programme of human sacrifices. When Pōmare's friend and 'Oro's *taura* (prophet) defected to the opposition, they were 'elated' and Pōmare's supporters much 'discouraged', since both groups saw it as 'the action of the *god* not of the *man*'. By 1809, dreading the 'anarchy' which seemed likely to succeed Pōmare's 'tyrany', the missionaries had fled to Mo'orea and contemplated abandoning the field altogether. They dared to warn Pōmare in a letter that the 'rebellion' and the 'death', 'war' and 'destruction' which afflicted Tahiti were proof of 'the displeasure and anger of God'. The statement no doubt resonated with Tahitians who shared certain aetiological principles with Evangelicals. But whereas a few years earlier it might have brought violent retaliation on the agents of the Christian God, it now reinforced growing doubts about 'Oro.[47]

Davies's history narrates the subsequent triumph of the Tahitian mission. By late 1811, Pōmare and his chiefly allies were 'vexed and angry' with the gods after successive defeats by the 'rebels' and the death of his mother's child, despite 'many prayers' and 'presents laid on the altars'. In July 1812, Pōmare announced publicly his resolve 'to forsake our false and foolish gods and worship Jehova' as the 'true God'. Jehovah's potency was undeniably proven when Pōmare and his allies achieved ultimate military victory over his 'Oro-backed enemies in November 1815. Equally impressive to 'the idolators' was the 'mildness, goodness and forbearance' of the new religion as shown by Pōmare's unprecedented 'lenity and moderation' towards the defeated, including 'Oro's prophet who had promised his supporters an 'easy victory'. Pōmare was less generous to the trappings of the old religion, ordering the wholesale destruction of *marae* (temples), altars, ritual paraphernalia and god images, including 'Oro's. He handed his own family gods to the missionaries who sent them as trophies to London. Within a few weeks, the profession of Christianity was 'national'.[48]

Before long, to the discomfort of straitlaced missionaries, the new religion became the spiritual arm of Pōmare's new paramountcy. As Congregationalists, they deplored his despotism which was less blood-thirsty but no less rapacious than his earlier pagan rule.[49] Years later, a vitriolic ex-missionary claimed that Pōmare had 'changed his Gods' only in the interests of 'consolidating his Government' and detailed his well-known moral failings: drunkenness, homosexuality and tyranny.[50] The missionaries called him an antinomian, 'one who sinned that the work of Grace would give the greater glory to God', while the king himself 'frequently evinced that he was under the influence of Antinomian notions'.[51] The coincidence of religion and government in Pōmare's eyes was patent in May 1819 when his baptism followed hard upon his public promulgation of the first Tahitian code of laws. The missionaries had prepared the code in consultation with the king. Their aim was to advance 'the good of the nation as a Christian community' but Pōmare ignored the laws when it suited him or made them serve the exercise of his own despotic power.[52]

Thus far, Davies's narrative of the Christianisation of Tahiti neatly fits the stereotype of Polynesian mass conversion by chiefly decree, for which indeed it is the model. However, his history of the crucial years 1812–15 also tells a more nuanced story. As early as 1807, he reported that hundreds of young people had learned a Tahitian catechism composed by the missionaries (with unmentioned local assistance) while some were beginning 'to spell, read, and write their own language'. Pōmare II was already completely literate in Tahitian but was careful 'to avoid anything of a religious nature'.[53] Late in 1812, Davies recommended his school among the mission's servants in Mo'orea and taught spelling 'by writing in sand'. A few months later, he noted a decrease in 'superstition and regard for the gods' in Mo'orea and widespread doubt everywhere 'about the efficacy' of prayer and sacrifice to them. In June 1813, an unprecedented crowd attended Sunday worship 'of their own accord' while striking news came from Tahiti, where no missionary was currently resident, that a group of young men had decided 'to cast off their gods, and bad customs, keep the Sabbath and worship Jehova alone', despite 'contempt and persecution'. In July, the missionaries recorded the names of 31 'professed worshippers of Jehova' in Mo'orea and soon after opened the school to all who agreed to renounce the old gods. Prudently (or cravenly according to critics), they decided to baptise no one before Pōmare himself. By April 1814, more than 80 persons, mostly adults, were attending the school and those now called the '*Bure atua* or praying people' (*pure atua*, pray-to-God) numbered 50. *Pure atua* were rapidly increasing in Tahiti where they were 'very ill used'. The first Christian marriage was celebrated in October and Pōmare added his name to the list of worshippers in January 1815. At this time, the missionaries estimated that between 500 and 600 people had 'renounced idolatry' throughout the archipelago, 'including most of the principal chiefs'. The priest of the district where the mission was based announced his considered decision to abandon the old religion and embrace the new. He subsequently burned 'his god'. With sickness and death rampant, fear of hellfire became a powerful motive to join the *pure atua*.[54]

This snowballing, internally driven popular commitment to Christianity was antecedent to Pōmare's victory and subsequent mass 'national' adherence to the new religion. It hints at common onto-logical grounds for conversion and problematises any tendency to reduce Christianisation in Polynesia to a shallow reflex of cynical chiefly autocracy. It also suggests threads of continuity between the beginnings of Christianity in the region and the profound Christian religiosity of modern populations.

### Third vignette: Island Melanesia

This vignette is a digest of episodes from my own research on encounters with Christianity in 'Western Polynesia' (Island Melanesia).[55] It challenges presumptions of general Melanesian nega-tivity towards missionaries or their religion and shows that broad

congruence of Oceanian ontologies did not preclude resort to very
different strategies during actual encounters. Modern Christian proselytism came late to this region. It began in 1839 with the LMS
martyr Williams and the Polynesian teachers he and his successors
left in several islands, including the adjacent Tanna and Aneityum in
south Vanuatu. Subsequent engagements with Christianity in these
islands diverged considerably. I argue that marked differences in attitudes and behaviour towards the new religion or its bearers were
partly shaped by subtle differences in the nature and expectations of
ritual relationships with spirits – exacerbated by deadly epidemics of
newly introduced diseases and diverse missionary approaches.

Presbyterian missionaries settled in Aneityum in 1848 and by the
mid-1850s could justly claim that the population was largely Christian.[56]
In contrast, in Tanna from 1840 until after 1865, periodic conditional
admittance of European or Islander missionaries ended in violence
against them and confident local assertions of ongoing adherence to
'our conduct'.[57] In Tannese cosmology, spirits did not oversee human
morality and only intervened in human affairs when compelled to do
so by ritual. Accordingly, Tannese explained disease as the result of the
ritual action of a human agent or sorcerer who alone could or would
cure the ailment, once propitiated. Illness or death commonly inspired
violence against an accused sorcerer.[58] In Aneityum, spirits were
believed to police human morality and act autonomously in human
affairs. They were approached through prayers, sacrifices and bargaining, rather than through coercive ritual as in Tanna, though sorcery
was by no means unknown. Aneityumese attributed disease to possession by 'selfish and malignant' spirits who either were offended by
human infringements or chose to respond to a sorcerer's ritual.[59]

In Tanna, where certain human actors were the equal of spirits they
controlled through ritual, missionaries were seen as rivals of the sorcerers. Because most Evangelical Christians attributed worldly ills to
divine judgement, missionaries repeatedly informed Tannese during
epidemics that their suffering was God's punishment for their sins.
They saw no valid logical link between this conviction and 'the deeply
superstitious notion that the missionaries and teachers possess and exercise the power of causing disease'.[60] But according to the Tannese
aetiology of disease and curing, a vengeful Christian God presupposed
malicious missionary sorcery. By contrast, in Aneityum, where the
'sacred men' were 'servants' of the spirits,[61] the contest was mainly
between competing spirits. Unusually for the era, the missionaries in
Aneityum stressed the Christian promise of salvation rather than the
threat of damnation. They pragmatically questioned the 'propriety and

prudence of denouncing temporal judgement' on the Islanders' 'idolatrous and wicked practices'.[62] Initially, Aneityumese blamed the
Christian god as 'the immediate cause of sickness and death'. Such
accusations were silenced in 1851 when an influenza epidemic caused
heavy mortality among the mission's opponents but most of the
Christian party recovered due, thought Islanders and missionary alike,
to the 'time[ly] use of medicine'.[63] This success enhanced the prestige
of Geddie's god and his own ritual reputation in Aneityumese eyes but
evidently did not entail the automatic Tannese corollary of a claim to
direct responsibility for the disease treated.

Differences between Tannese and Aneityumese aetiologies of
disease and their implications for mission security and success were
dramatically displayed in widely variant responses to an epidemic of
measles and dysentery which devastated the two islands in 1860–1.
Aneityumese reportedly viewed the calamity as 'the effects of sin' –
'a judgment on the island' for the recent burning of the church by an
arsonist – and responded with resignation and 'more than usual
attention to religion'. This interpretation was clearly not a simple
reflex of Christian teachings since their missionary explained their
suffering as 'trials' rather than punishment.[64] Tannese, on the other
hand, were said to attribute their troubles either to Jehovah, responding automatically to Christian ritual, or to local sorcerers anxious to
drive out their rivals. Some people shunned the missionaries. Some
interrupted services to prevent ritual communication with Jehovah.
Some threatened violence. By early 1862, escalating insecurity forced
the European missionaries to abandon Tanna again.[65]

In each case, indigenous understandings were significantly
informed by different assumptions about the ways in which spirits
intervened in human affairs. The Christian notion of an omnipotent
and inscrutable deity for whom propitiation was the only appropriate
ritual mode was more congruent with Aneityumese ideas of divinity
and ritual than with Tannese, making for readier mutual translatabil-
ity and integration of Christian concepts and ritual practices.[66]
Possibly because they conceived indigenous spirits as vengeful and
capricious, Aneityumese were attracted to a deity reputed to be both
'omnipotent' and 'kind', whose responses to human behaviour
seemed more predictable and reliable.[67] They claimed a kind of
human agency but it was the negative agency of sin which provoked
divine retribution. For more than twenty years, a discernible rhythm
saw Tannese call for teachers or missionaries during good times but
accuse them of sorcery and threaten or attack them when disease or
natural disaster struck. It was perhaps the Tannese assurance of active

agency – that men with appropriate ritual knowledge could control spirits for personal and collective benefit and to the detriment of rivals and enemies – that empowered them to engage with Christianity and modernity on their own terms, consistently challenging the imposition of external authority, whether missionary, colonial, or national.[68]

The dynamic processes by which particular Pacific Islanders made sense of particular missionaries' actions and words in specific island contexts produced complexes of actions and meanings which were sometimes labelled as dramatically opposed outcomes along racialised regional lines – as missionary success and Polynesian conversion, on the one hand; and as missionary failure and Melanesian 'barbarism', on the other. This superficial opposition is clearly inadequate. Everywhere in Oceania, indigenous religious ideas and ritual emphases were cardinal elements in encounters with foreign religions. New religious concepts and practices – like novelties in general – were unevenly and idiosyncratically domesticated, not only in 'conversion' but also during negative and ambivalent engagements with foreign religions and their bearers. Yet the widespread persistence, throughout Oceania, of instrumental notions of ritual and belief in ancestral and other local spirits, alongside devout faith in the Islamic or Christian god, underwrites the conception of conversion as 'indigenisation' and of Islam or Christianity as indigenous religious experience.

## Phase 3: 1946 to the present

During my final phase, the Philippines (1946), Indonesia (1949), most Pacific Islands states (1962–80), and Timor Leste (1999–2002) won or were granted independence. By this stage, most Protestant missions had already been transformed into local churches. However, colonialism has not entirely vanished. Mainly Islamic Indonesia is firmly entrenched in mainly Christian Papua. France clings to its former colonies in Polynesia and New Caledonia while granting some internal autonomy. In 1959, the already white-dominated territory of Hawai'i became a state of the United States which retains self-governing territories in American Sāmoa and much of Micronesia. Moreover, American (1776) and Peruvian (1821) independence, Canadian confederation (1867), Australian federation (1901) and dominion status in New Zealand (1907) did not mean autonomy for encompassed indigenous populations who remain more or less disadvantaged, mostly Christian minorities within multicultural nation-states.

Throughout Oceania, religion is of paramount importance to indigenous people, ontologically, socially and politically.[69] Religious commitment is far more mixed among non-indigenous residents, especially in the secular worlds of Australia, New Zealand, Canada and the United States. In Fiji, a significant Indian population – non-indigenous descendants of indentured labourers and thus formerly colonised but ambiguously decolonised – is unevenly split between Hindu and Islamic religiosity and secularism. Across the zone, in both Christian and Muslim contexts, the growing popular attraction of fundamentalism helps fuel serious religious and political tensions. While mainline churches are committed to ecumenism and relatively tolerant of indigenous custom, the proliferating evangelical and pentecostal groups may be highly sectarian, rigidly anti-custom and very politicised.[70] In Indonesia, there is sharp disagreement between pluralist Muslim traditionalists and reformists who seek to purge Islam of local practices or *adat* (custom). In Maluku, Muslim and Protestant sectarianism, entangled with entrenched local patronage politics, gang warfare and elite rivalry, erupted in bloody conflict in 1999–2004.[71]

In postcolonial Oceania, Islam and Christianity are neither foreign nor imposed nor separate existential domains but indigenised daily spiritual experience and powerful ritual practice with a distinctly local cast. Most people take for granted the efficacy of prayer and often mobilise it pragmatically to achieve private and public goals, including national ones. Such goals include managing relations with ancestors or neutralising malignant sorcery; curing disease, both introduced and local; combatting indigenous violence and disunity or ongoing colonial abuse; achieving salvation, protection, fellowship, material well-being or access to desired aspects of modernity and globalisation; reconstituting indigenous ideas of the person; punishing disapproved behaviour. The prayers that bracket most meetings, from sessions of Parliament to local fellowship groups, may seem low-key and pro forma but this does not mean they lack practical significance to people who communicate with their God on a regular, familiar, reciprocal basis. In a striking instance of the instrumental logic of Christian ritual in Oceania, employed publicly to punitive ends, many Papua New Guineans attributed the outcome of the 1997 election to a national ecumenical prayer movement called Operation Brukim Skru ('Bend the Knee') mounted 'for repentance and the election of a God-fearing government'.[72]

*Fourth vignette: Pacific Christianities*

Christianity is of great ideological and practical significance in nation-making in the Pacific Islands. Because colonial regimes left native schooling mainly to missions, most candidates for leadership in nascent states from the 1950s were professed Christians, sometimes priests or ministers. National constitutions typically enshrine Christianity in tandem with custom. Sāmoa is 'based on Christian principles and Sāmoan custom and tradition'. Papua New Guinea invokes 'our noble traditions and the Christian principles that are ours now'. Solomon Islands brackets 'the wisdom and the worthy customs of our ancestors' with 'the guiding hand of God'. Vanuatu appeals to 'traditional Melanesian values, faith in God, and Christian principles'. In these national charters, the terms 'tradition' and 'custom' themselves encode Christian values since they refer to indigenous practices deemed acceptable by mainline Christians. Yet custom and Christianity are ambiguous bases for nationhood. The abstract, sanitised concept of national custom is shorn from diverse, place-specific customary practice – long treated by Christian missions and churches with at best qualified tolerance and often blanket rejection. Christianity itself is doubly resistant to nationalist appropriation. Experientially, it is parochial and grounded in congregations. On the other hand, it has long offered Islanders membership in transnational moral communities that transcend the often dubious legitimacy of colonial and national states.

Intersecting global and local dimensions of Christianity were highlighted in several ethnographies of apocalypticism in PNG where ambivalent citizens confronted the legacies of colonialism, the paradoxes of modernity, the frustration of unmet desires in an ineffective, corrupt state and the threat and promise of a global millennium. Thus the Urapmin, a remote Highlands group, practise a largely home-grown version of charismatic Christianity and yet see themselves as participating more or less equally in a global Christian millennialism. The anthropologist Joel Robbins argued that they combine a 'strong' sense of national identity and self-recognition as 'inescapably citizens of Papua New Guinea' with extremely 'negative feelings' about the 'black' nation of PNG and a strong positive sense of Christian identity 'that connects them with a white transnational community far more powerful than the nation'.[73]

The ideological significance of Oceanic Christianity has a critical practical counterpart in the core contributions long made by missions and churches to education, health and welfare services. Moreover, the churches were acknowledged as a major force for moderation, conflict resolution and reconciliation during fierce civil conflicts in Bougainville (1988–97) and Solomon Islands (1998–2003). In Bougainville, organised groups of Christian women went into the bush to seek out alienated young Bougainville Revolutionary Army men. In Solomon Islands, the Solomon Islands Christian Association worked tirelessly for peace while members of the Melanesian Brotherhood – an Anglican order of young, unmarried male evangelists – intervened physically between warring militants, assisted victims and energetically promoted peace. In the process, seven were kidnapped and murdered by a rebel leader. In Solomon Islands, too, Christian women made organised efforts to alleviate the massive human cost of the conflict and help broker peace. Women from both sides cooperated in the volunteer, ecumenical Women for Peace group, across the faultlines of ethnicity, religion, age, class and politics and in the face of intimidation or violence from militants affronted by opposition and criticism.

The potential for churches to help avert conflict in the first place is unclear. But there are anecdotal hints from the PNG Highlands that Christian belief and church membership may provide effective local strategies to combat the endemic breakdown of internal security. The home-grown millenarian God Tri Wan (Holy Trinity) movement mobilised independent or grassroots Catholic spirituality 'to secure prosperity ... by ceasing all tribal fighting and introducing an era of peace'.[74] The Seventh-day Adventist Church has grown rapidly because persons wanting 'to end their consumption of beer' found that, by converting, 'they gained the strength to oppose the pressures from non-Adventists to drink'. Alcohol, banned by the Adventist Church, is a financial millstone for individual drinkers and their families and a serious social problem, heavily implicated in sexual and domestic violence, criminal activity and tribal fighting.[75] Its abandonment is an incalculable social, familial and personal benefit.

## Conclusion

The themes of indigenous agency and appropriation weave through my discussion of Oceanian encounters with foreign religions and diverse positions adopted by local people in relation to them – including the conversion of most Oceanian populations to either Christianity or Islam, with parallel indigenisation of the world religions themselves. The concepts of agency and appropriation decentre Europeans and other outsiders and disrupt the stereotype that conversion was a disastrous external imposition on romantic but helpless natives. This approach also has general moral and theoretical implications. It contests widespread assumptions that 'the local' is necessarily subsumed and dominated by 'the global'. It problematises any tendency to take Christianity for granted as an objective basis for evaluating other varieties of a universalised human spirituality. And by probing the entanglement of the sacred and the profane in mundane religious experience, it challenges modernist ideology that compartmentalises 'religion' as a reified separate domain, along with 'society', 'politics' and 'the economy'.

## Notes

1. For economy and clarity, I use modern place-names throughout this chapter.
2. Damon Salesa, 'The Pacific in Indigenous Time', ch. 2 in this volume.
3. Patrick V. Kirch, 'Peopling of the Pacific: A Holistic Anthropological Perspective', *Annual Review of Anthropology* 39 (2010), 131–48.
4. Salesa, 'The Pacific in Indigenous Time'.
5. W. R. Ambrose, 'An Early Bronze Artefact from Papua New Guinea', *Antiquity* 62 (1988), 483–91.
6. S. Supomo, 'Indic Transformation: The Sanskritization of *Jawa* and the Javanization of the *Bharata*', in Peter Bellwood, James J. Fox and Darrell Tryon, eds., *The Austronesians: Historical and Comparative Perspectives* (Canberra, 1995), pp. 309–32.
7. Benito Legarda Jr., 'Cultural Landmarks and their Interactions with Economic Factors in the Second Millennium in the Philippines', *Kinaadman (Wisdom)* 23 (2001), 29–36.
8. Günter Schilder, *Australia Unveiled: The Share of the Dutch Navigators in the Discovery of Australia*, trans. Olaf Richter (Amsterdam, 1976); Regina Ganter, 'Muslim Australians: The Deep Histories of Contact', *Journal of Australian Studies* 32 (2008), 482–6.
9. Joyce E. Chaplin, 'The Pacific before Empire, *c.* 1500–1800', ch. 3 in this volume.
10. Lydia Black, *Russians in Alaska, 1732–1867* (Fairbanks, AK, 2004), pp. 222–53.
11. Stephen G. Hyslop, *Contest for California: From Spanish Colonization to the American Conquest* (Norman, OK, 2012).
12. Johannes Fabian, *Time and the Other: How Anthropology Makes its Object* (New York, 1983); Stanley Jeyaraja Tambiah, *Magic, Science, Religion, and the Scope of Rationality* (Cambridge, 1990).
13. Andrew Pawley and Malcolm Ross, 'Austronesian Historical Linguistics and Culture History', *Annual Review of Anthropology* 22 (1993), 448–52.
14. Bronwen Douglas, *Across the Great Divide: Journeys in History and Anthropology* (Amsterdam, 1998), pp. 1–25.
15. Polly Wiessner and Akii Tumu, 'A Collage of Cults', *Canberra Anthropology* 22 (1999), 34–65.
16. Thomas Widlok, 'Practice, Politics and Ideology of the "Travelling Business" in Aboriginal Religion', *Oceania* 63 (1992), 114–36.

17. For example, Edward L. Schieffelin, 'The Unseen Influence: Tranced Mediums as Historical Innovators', *Journal de la Société des Océanistes* 33 (1977), 169–78; Michele Stephen, 'Dreams of Change: The Innovative Role of Altered States of Consciousness in Traditional Melanesian Religion', *Oceania* 50 (1979), 3–22.

18. Kenelm Burridge, *New Heaven, New Earth: A Study of Millenarian Activities* (Oxford, 1969); Peter Lawrence, *Road Belong Cargo: A Study of the Cargo Movement in the Southern Madang District, New Guinea* (Carlton, Vic., 1964).

19. Douglas L. Oliver, *Ancient Tahitian Society*, 3 vols (Canberra, 1974), II, pp. 674–87, 890–964, 1121–32.

20. Valerio Valeri, *Kingship and Sacrifice: Ritual and Society in Ancient Hawaii*, trans. Paula Wissing (Chicago, 1985), pp. 103–4.

21. M. C. Ricklefs, *A History of Modern Indonesia since c. 1200*, 4th edn (Stanford, CA, 2008), pp. 3–16.

22. Compare Adam McKeown, 'Movement', and Kaoru Sugihara, 'The Economy since 1800', chs. 7 and 8 in this volume.

23. Ricklefs, *History*, pp. 26–32, 69–79.

24. Vicente M. Diaz, *Repositioning the Missionary: Rewriting the Histories of Colonialism, Native Catholicism, and Indigeneity in Guam* (Honolulu, 2010); Alan Durston, *Pastoral Quechua: The History of Christian Translation in Colonial Peru, 1550–1650* (Notre Dame, IN, 2007).

25. Hyslop, *Contest for California*.

26. Bolton Glanvill Corney, *The Quest and Occupation of Tahiti by Emissaries of Spain during the Years 1772–1776*, 3 vols (London, 1913–19).

27. Antonio Pigafetta, *Magellan's Voyage around the World*, trans. and ed. James Alexander Robertson, 3 vols (Cleveland, 1906); Tomé Pires, *The Suma Oriental of Tomé Pires*, trans. and ed. Armando Cortesão, 2 vols (London, 1944).

28. Brett Charles Baker, 'Indigenous-Driven Mission: Reconstructing Religious Change in Sixteenth-Century Maluku' (PhD thesis, Australian National University, Canberra, 2012), pp. 12–27.

29. Antonio Galvão, *Tratado ... de todos os descobrimentos antigos & modernos* (Lisbon, 1563), fol. 68v; Galvão, *A Treatise on the Moluccas (c. 1644)*, ed. Hubert Th. Th. M. Jacobs (Rome, 1971), pp. 296–9.

30. Pigafetta, *Magellan's Voyage*, I, p. 156; II, pp. 68, 76, 112, 148; Pires, *Suma Oriental*, II, pp. 443–4.

31. Pires, *Suma Oriental*, II, p. 462.

32. Pigafetta, *Magellan's Voyage*, I, pp. 99–193.

33. Pigafetta, *Magellan's Voyage*, I, pp. 132–82.

34. Galvão, *Treatise*; Pires, *Suma Oriental*, II, p. 144; Pigafetta, *Magellan's Voyage*, II, pp. 64–74.

35. Jan Sihar Aritonang and Karel Steenbrink, eds., *A History of Christianity in Indonesia* (Leiden, 2008), pp. 19, 28–31, 103, 108.

36. For example, Adolph Heuken, 'Catholic Converts in the Moluccas, Minahasa and Sangihe Talaud, 1512–1680', in Aritonang and Steenbrink, eds., *History of Christianity in Indonesia*, pp. 23–71; Anthony Reid, 'Islamization

and Christianization in Southeast Asia: The Critical Phase, 1550–1650', in Reid, ed., *Southeast Asia in the Early Modern Era: Trade, Power, and Belief* (Ithaca, NY, 1993), pp. 152–4; Ricklefs, *History*, pp. 14–16.

37. Heuken, 'Catholic Converts', pp. 49–52.

38. Baker, 'Indigenous-Driven Mission'.

39. Reid, 'Islamization', pp. 159, 168–72; see Robin Horton, 'African Conversion', *Africa* 41 (1971), 101–7.

40. Pedro Murillo Velarde, *Historia de la Provincia de Philipinas de la Compañia de Jesus* ... (Manila, 1749).

41. John N. Schumacher, 'Syncretism in Philippine Catholicism: Its Historical Causes', *Philippine Studies* 32 (1984), 251–72.

42. Vicente L. Rafael, *Contracting Colonialism: Translation and Christian Conversion in Tagalog Society under Early Spanish Rule* (Durham, NC, 1988); Terence Ranger, 'Christianity and Indigenous Peoples: A Personal Overview', *Journal of Religious History* 27 (2003), 255–71.

43. Compare Nicholas Thomas, 'The Age of Empire in the Pacific', and Robert Aldrich, 'Politics', chs. 4 and 14 in this volume.

44. Aram A. Yengoyan, 'Religion, Morality, and Prophetic Traditions: Conversion among the Pitjantjatjara of Central Australia', in Robert W. Hefner, ed., *Conversion to Christianity: Historical and Anthropological Perspectives on a Great Transformation* (Berkeley, 1993), pp. 234–6.

45. For example, George Turner, *Nineteen Years in Polynesia: Missionary Life, Travels, and Researches in the Islands of the Pacific* (London, 1861), pp. 1–4, 82–5.

46. Oliver, *Ancient Tahitian Society*, III.

47. John Davies, *The History of the Tahitian Mission 1799–1830*, ed. C. W. Newbury (Cambridge, 1961), pp. 103, 118 (original emphasis), 120, 133.

48. Davies, *History*, pp. 138, 153, 192–5, 197–200.

49. Davies, *History*, pp. 233–4; Niel Gunson, 'Pomare II and Polynesian Imperialism', *Journal of Pacific History* 4 (1969), 67–9.

50. John Muggridge Orsmond, 1849, quoted in Davies, *History*, pp. 349–50.

51. William Pascoe Crook, 6 February 1821, 22 December 1821, in Richard Lovett, *The History of the London Missionary Society 1795–1895*, 2 vols (London, 1899), I, p. 227, 231; Gunson, 'Pomare II', 81.

52. Davies, *History*, pp. 203, 216; William Ellis, *Polynesian Researches during a Residence of Nearly Eight Years in the Society and Sandwich Islands*, 2nd edn (London, 1831), III, p. 137; Lovett, *History*, I, pp. 219–23.

53. Davies, *History*, p. 102.

54. Davies, *History*, pp. 152–90.

55. Douglas, *Across the Great Divide*, pp. 227–61.

56. John Geddie, 3 October 1854, *Missionary Register of the Presbyterian Church of Nova Scotia* (hereafter *MR*) (1855), 125, 135–6.

57. John G. Paton, 10 June 1861, *Reformed Presbyterian Magazine* (1862), 38.

58. Paton, 11 October 1861, *Home and Foreign Record of the Presbyterian Church of the Lower Provinces of British North America* (hereafter *HFR*) (1862), 100; Turner, *Nineteen Years*, pp. 18–19, 89–92.

59. John Inglis, *In the New Hebrides: Reminiscences of Missionary Life and Work, Especially on the Island of Aneityum, from 1850 till 1877* (London, 1887), pp. 30–2.

60. Turner, *Nineteen Years*, p. 18; Henry Nisbet, 'Voyage of the "John Williams" to the New Hebrides and New Caledonia Groups ...', *Samoan Reporter* 5 (1847), 4.

61. John Geddie, July 1849, in George Patterson, *Missionary Life among the Cannibals being the Life of the Rev. John Geddie, D.D.* (Toronto, 1882), p. 206.

62. Geddie, 20 August 1861, *HFR* (1862), 36.

63. John Geddie, *Misi Gete: John Geddie, Pioneer Missionary to the New Hebrides*, ed. R. S. Miller (Launceston, Tas., 1975), p. 90.

64. Geddie, 3 April 1861, *HFR* (1861), 248–9; 26 August, 12 December 1861, 23 May 1862, *HFR* (1862), 40, 159, 293.

65. Ron Adams, *In the Land of Strangers: A Century of European Contact with Tanna, 1774–1874* (Canberra, 1984), pp. 116–49.

66. Inglis, *In the New Hebrides*, p. 31.

67. Geddie, 29 November 1854, *MR* (1855), 167–8.

68. Joël Bonnemaison, *The Tree and the Canoe: History and Ethnogeography of Tanna*, trans. Josée Pénot-Demetry (Honolulu, 1994).

69. For example, Helen James, ed., *Civil Society, Religion and Global Governance: Paradigms of Power and Persuasion* (London, 2007).

70. Manfred Ernst, ed., *Globalization and the Re-shaping of Christianity in the Pacific Islands* (Suva, 2007).

71. Gerry van Klinken, 'The Maluku Wars: Bringing Society Back In', *Indonesia* 71 (2001), 1–26; Christopher R. Duncan, 'The Other Maluku: Chronologies of Conflict in North Maluku', *Indonesia* 80 (2005), 53–80.

72. Philip Gibbs, 'The Religious Factor in Contemporary Papua New Guinea Politics', *Catalyst* 28 (1998), 33–6, 40.

73. Joel Robbins, *Becoming Sinners: Christianity and Moral Torment in a Papua New Guinea Society* (Berkeley, 2004), pp. 170–9.

74. Jan Bieniek and Garry W. Trompf, 'The Millennium, not the Cargo?', *Ethnohistory* 47 (2000), 124–6.

75. George Westermark, 'History, Opposition, and Salvation in Agarabi Adventism', *Pacific Studies* 21 (1998), 54, 58.

# 10

# Law

## Lisa Ford

Many and diverse peoples have clung to the shores of the Pacific Ocean casting their laws seaward. Indigenous North Americans, Pacific Islanders and the peoples of the Indonesian archipelago all created complex legal regimes governing coast-dwellers and regulating the harvesting of resources in their proximate seas. Few, however, imagined legal regimes that spanned the Ocean. Ocean-faring Polynesian peoples shared trade routes and rules in vast seas bounded by invisible markers, by proximate archipelagoes, and, sometimes, by distant continental shores.[1] The vast tributary empire of China claimed jurisdiction over all the world including its oceans, but it exercised suzerainty no further into the Pacific than Japan.[2] If the polities that crowded around the rim of the Indian Ocean understood the sea to be a 'common' or free space linking trading ports, then most Pacific peoples saw the ocean as a border, as interwoven smaller seas or as coastal fisheries.[3] Accordingly, legal histories of the Pacific have been many and disconnected – determined, variously, by the geography of its continental coastlines and archipelagoes and by the myriad political, cultural and material technologies produced by their inhabitants.[4]

In order to tell an interconnected legal history of the Greater Pacific, this chapter eschews these rich regional histories of law. It focuses instead on trans-oceanic legal regimes in the Pacific from the Treaty of Saragossa (1529) to modern international law, describing how changing European ideas about claiming and governing distant territory and oceans were refined in Pacific encounters. While, as Damon Salesa points out, this approach threatens to reproduce colonial relationships by privileging western law over its Pacific interlocutors, it also rests on a frank acknowledgement that, to some degree, the Pacific basin was constituted as an entity by imperial law carried on the first ships to cross and recross it regularly.[5] Empires, however, were not the only producers of trans-Pacific law. This chapter ends by noting two contradictory legal inversions: the deployment by new Pacific states of now ubiquitous languages of territorial sovereignty and their appeal to international maritime law to enclose huge swathes of the world's largest ocean even as their territorial sovereignties are eroded by the rising sea.

## Early modern claims in the Pacific

In 1513, in what must have been a comical performance, Vasco Núñez de Balboa crossed the Isthmus of Panama from the Caribbean Sea, planted the Spanish flag in the surging tidal waters of the Pacific, and claimed 'these austral seas and lands and coasts and islands with every-thing annexed to them' for the monarchs of Aragon and Castile.[6] Ferdinand Magellan crossed the Pacific from the Indian Ocean just a few years later, claiming islands indiscriminately for Spain and losing most of his crew in the process.[7] It took decades longer for any semblance of a trans-Pacific imperial order to emerge; legal claiming in the sixteenth century was, after all, an aspirational business.

Spain's claims mattered in 1513 because existing inter-European agreements about overseas exploration dealt only with the Atlantic world. In 1493, the Pope – mobilising the universal pretensions of the Roman Emperor and the doctrine of Papal infallibility – granted Spain exclusive rights to explore and to claim the 'islands' and 'main lands' west of an imaginary line in the Atlantic Ocean.[8] While many Catholic princes and lawyers thought the Papal Bull outlandish,[9] it formed the basis of bilateral treaties among Spain, Portugal and a few other European kingdoms, most notably the Treaty of Tordesillas (1494).[10] Balboa's claim to the Pacific sought to define its antemeridian, helping Spain to stretch its sphere westwards towards Asia, the global centre of manufacturing and commerce. In the end, it helped only a little: the 1529 Treaty of Saragossa completed Spain and Portugal's dissection of the globe, drawing a line 17° east of the Moluccas, and leaving the China trade and the Spice Islands firmly in Portugal's ambit.[11] Of course, these European negotiations had no bearing what-soever on engagements among European states and Pacific peoples.

Not content to be excluded from eastern cornucopias, Spain wrested control of a foothold in the Philippine Islands in 1571 in notionally Portuguese waters.[12] Thereafter, as far as Europeans were concerned, the greater part of the Pacific Ocean became a 'Spanish Lake', and, indeed, Spanish jurists produced the first legal regime professing to have trans-Pacific scope: the *Leyes de Indias* (1573) and the *Recopilación de las leyes de los reinos de Indias* (1680). The latter sought to construct a trans-Pacific code out of piecemeal legislation governing

Spanish colonies from New Mexico to the Philippines. The former laid down what eventually became a pan-European programme for establishing firm 'possession' (a term adapted from Roman law) of New World territories.[13] It enjoined Spanish settlers to fortify convenient coastal ports, to settle permanent strategically placed towns, and, most importantly, to 'pacify' indigenous people on the Pacific Rim.[14]

Both legal codes posited a fiction of legal uniformity that was beyond the reach of any early modern European state. Even the most 'pacified' of Spain's New World territories was legally plural. In conquered Mexico, the Tlaxcalan people used their collaboration with Cortés to bargain for exemption from the *encomienda* system (which gave individual conquistadors limited jurisdiction to extract tribute from indigenous people), to claim tempered political autonomy, and to bargain for special rights as Spanish subjects.[15] Moreover, for centuries Spain's hold on Chile and the Philippines was tenuous; and it neither visited nor mapped most of the islands in 'its' parts of the Pacific.[16]

If Spanish trans-Pacific law was aspirational, Portugals left a still lighter legal footprint in 'its' western Pacific. Portuguese legal claims and military efforts in the Indian Ocean were bent on monopolising ocean access rather than accruing territorial holdings – though the two converged in Portugal's brutal seizure of the Straits of Malacca in 1511.[17] By contrast, in the Pacific, Portugal simply slotted into China's tributary empire. From 1557, it tendered yearly tribute in return for access to Macau. There, the Chinese claimed jurisdiction to regulate trade, and to control both Chinese people and Portuguese–Chinese conflict. Again, the reality was messier. By the eighteenth century, Chinese administrators established mixed courts, or ordered Portuguese administrators to punish wayward Portuguese subjects. Meanwhile, Portuguese residents evaded Qing jurisdiction either by deliberately mistranslating Chinese decrees or by bribing local officials to evade prosecution. So ambiguous was the arrangement that Portugal later argued that it had purchased Macau, giving it territorial sovereignty over the city.[18] Portugal negotiated access to Japan in 1571 on similarly ambiguous terms, but was expelled in 1640 for the contentious proselytising efforts of Portuguese Jesuits.[19]

The Netherlands was the first European state to challenge Spain and Portugal in the Pacific – and, in the process, it refined legal technologies and arguments that played a pivotal role in the history of the region. Their most important legal technology was the colonial corporation: weak European states, including the Netherlands, England and, later, Russia and Germany, devolved broad sovereign powers to chartered companies to trade, treat and conquer in the

Pacific. The Dutch East India Company (VOC) deployed its powers to sign a series of unbalanced treaties with rulers in Penang and the Spice Islands committing them to trade exclusively with the Company, and to ally with it against the Portuguese. Building on Spanish scholastic arguments about the sovereignty of non-Christian indigenous peoples, company jurist Hugo Grotius argued that Asian polities could sign, and were obliged to honour, solemn treaties with Christian nations.[20] The Company then used treaty breaches as a pretext to seize Batavia and Amboina, to massacre thousands of people in the Banda Islands, and eventually to wrest control of key trading posts in the island archipelago, giving it effective control of the waterways of the Spice Islands. While Roman law vested sovereignty and *dominium* in conquerors, the profit-oriented VOC had limited interest in and capacity to transform the legal administration of the polyglot and politically divided archipelago. So it established 'direct rule' only in key ports and settlements (like Batavia), policed strategic coastal waters and left most of the islands to govern themselves under 'indirect' supervision which could, nevertheless, be transformative of local legal orders. This system set a pattern of colonisation which was followed by the British and the French in Southeast Asia in the nineteenth century.[21]

Grotius also penned the influential doctrine of free seas in defence of the company. In *Mare Liberum* (1609), he argued that the seizure of a Portuguese Ship by the VOC in the Straits of Malacca was a legitimate act of war, given Portugal's illegal attempt to monopolise the ocean. Natural law demanded free navigation of the seas, according to Grotius, because free seas facilitated friendly trade among nations, while the vastness and fluidity of the oceans made their meaningful possession unnatural. Grotius's notion of the free sea was far more constrained than is often acknowledged. In *Mare Liberum*, Grotius conceded that states could cast their *imperium* over the ocean in order to protect their subjects or to punish crimes on their ships. In his larger work on the subject, *De Jure Praedae*, Grotius argued that jurisdiction over proximate seas might be a natural consequence of effective control of coastlines.[22] Small differences thus distinguished Grotius from his antagonists Serafim De Freitas (of Portugal) and John Selden (of England) whose arguments that treaty and customary law could abrogate free navigation and resource exploitation in the ocean have had a long afterlife in modern international law.[23]

Grotius's notion of the free seas came late to the greater Pacific Ocean. Spain's stranglehold on the Straits of Magellan meant that most European visitors to the Ocean from the Atlantic came with

Spanish acquiescence.[24] Activity slowly increased in the eighteenth century. From the Western Pacific, the Dutch found, named and half-heartedly claimed New Guinea, 'New Holland' (Australia), Tasmania and New Zealand.[25] In the 1710s, the British South Sea Company won a short-lived concession from the British East India Company's 'monopoly' to trade in the South Pacific. Also, between 1713 and 1760, Russian trading companies quietly discovered a sea route to Kamchatka and commenced company-based fur trading with the Alaskan Inuits.[26] However, these interlopers were late to challenge Spain's claims in the region. Thus, Spain found itself urging what Benjamin Keene (British envoy to Spain in the 1740s) had called its 'whimsical notions of exclusive rights' to the Pacific Ocean well into the 1780s.[27] When Spain seized a privately owned British ship trading with Indians in Nootka Sound in 1789 on the basis of discovery and Papal donation, Britain forced the weakened empire to sign the first Nootka Sound Convention of 1790. This Convention laid down the nineteenth-century legal status quo: that party states would not claim Pacific lands that they had not actually occupied and would respect each other's rights to navigate the free seas.[28]

## Law and the Pacific in the long peace

Sovereign treaties, free seas and the emerging mantra of free trade proved to be powerful legal technologies in the Pacific for most of the nineteenth century, fuelled, not least, by European investment in maintaining the long peace established by the end of the Napoleonic Wars in 1815. Whereas the early modern Atlantic was beset by inter-minable inter-European war, punctilious legalism enabled nine-teenth-century European competitors to explore and exploit the Pacific more or less amicably.[29] At the same time, the American Revolution, the Napoleonic Wars and then the struggles for inde-pendence fought throughout Spanish America produced new articu-lations of state sovereignty that weakened respect for customary law, strengthened legislative power and pegged sovereignty increasingly to exercises of territorial jurisdiction.[30] This transition was embod-ied, in part, in Emer de Vattel's enormously successful compendium, *The Law of Nations* (1758). Vattel not only posited an international law predicated on sovereign self-interest; he also popularised Lockean arguments that sovereignty and, indeed, private property accrued only to farming peoples.[31] Finally, two tightly enmeshed impulses produced transformative legal structures of encounter in the Pacific: stadial development theory, then Darwinian science, relegated Asian peoples, Pacific Islanders, and the world's hunter-gatherers to lesser stages of human development than Europeans, while evangelical humanitarians demanded the protection and 'improvement' of lesser peoples, often through intrusive applications of European law.[32]

These legal conjunctures produced peculiar innovations in the new Anglophone settler polities emerging on the southwestern and north-eastern continental littorals of the Pacific Ocean. In 1788, Britain sent a few thousand convicts and marines to the eastern coast of New South Wales to establish an outpost and a dumping ground.[33] The settlement was a legal oddity from the outset, because colonial officials made no attempt to conquer or treat with Australian Aborigines for land, in marked departure from their practice in eighteenth-century North America.[34] Stuart Banner has argued that the British instantiated a post-Vattelian colonial project in Australia, predicated on the notion that hunter-gatherers had no sovereignty, no land rights and no law. Whether or not the British arrived in Australia in 1788 with this very modern legal agenda, Vattel *was* deployed explicitly by courts and legal officers in the 1820s and 1830s to justify land claims, taxation and even criminal jurisdiction over indigenous people.[35] In addition, humanitarian lawyers in Britain and Australia argued that the rejection of indigenous law was essential to indigenous civilisation and protection. In reality, of course, rejecting indigenous law and property rights legitimated their forcible dispossession from almost all arable and pasture lands in the continent by 1930. Further, even though Aboriginal law persisted on the peripheries of settlement and in settler courts into the twentieth century, this legal logic of non-recognition and protection articulated into a very peculiar legal subjecthood for indigenous Australians.[36] State-based legislative regimes from the 1860s until the 1970s controlled indigenous peoples' rights to move, to associate and to raise children in order to facilitate either their separation from or their integration into settler society.[37]

The confluence of logics that produced this extreme legal regime in Australia also determined the fate of indigenous people on the West Coast of North America after 1840. When the United States acquired California after the Mexican–American War, its representatives signed treaties with local hunter-gatherers for their land, but these were never ratified, in part on the grounds that Indian hunter-gatherers were 'very little less degraded and uncivilisable than the blacks of New South Wales'.[38] Likewise, no treaties were signed with the Inuit of Alaska after its acquisition by the United States from Russia in 1867. Treaty-making was abandoned in British Columbia in 1854; from 1859, indigenous reserve lands were held on trust for the welfare of indigenous people.[39] Indian and Aboriginal reserves in Western North America became places of coercive confinement in the late nineteenth century, where indigenous people were surveilled, starved and their children forcibly assimilated.[40]

Meanwhile, English, French and American traders and whalers had very different legal aspirations elsewhere – producing different constellations of nineteenth-century legal technologies. At least at first, their home states deployed a combination of the 'natural laws' of the freedom of the seas, free trade and an increasing investment in the 'rule of law' to protect the commercial interests of their subjects. In 1839, when China exercised what all parties agreed was its sovereign right to control the sale and consumption of opium in Canton, Britain used the seizure of British opium and the expulsion of foreign consuls by Chinese officials as a pretext for war. It argued that, while China could control trade within its borders, it had not exercised that jurisdiction consistently. Britain declared war cynically to uphold what it asserted was an international rule of procedural fairness. When Britain blockaded the Yangtze River with an iron warship, China was forced to sign the first of dozens of unequal treaties with European states, America and Japan removing trade restrictions and divesting criminal and civil jurisdiction over foreign traders in Chinese territory.[41] Similar arrangements were forced on Japan and Korea after 1870.

While extraterritoriality had been part of Chinese and European trade policy before 1850, mid-century Pacific geopolitics changed its character and its function. Treaties ending the Opium Wars (1839–42; 1856–60) created an unprecedented profusion of foreign jurisdictions on Chinese soil – an enormous (if treaty-based) derogation of Chinese sovereignty that tended to give European sojourners opportunities to both evade and exploit law, even as it occasionally provided new forums and favourable outcomes for Chinese litigants. The difference was not only one of scale. The new extraterritoriality was built on stadial logic: East Asian legal systems were deemed unready and unfit to regulate Europeans. Japan alone negotiated an end to extraterritorial jurisdiction in its treaty ports only after adopting a new constitution and penal code between 1868 and 1882 modeled on western legal systems.[42]

In the Pacific Islands and, to a lesser degree, in the trading principalities of Southeast Asia,[43] the convergence of hardening sovereignty and legal ideologies of protection produced very different but connected legal encounters. Myriad legal systems had been developed and shared among the Pacific Islands – many Melanesian societies were governed by clan-based law loosely affiliated under weak tribal chiefs, while Polynesian peoples tended to have more hierarchical structures of governance, some of which, like that operating in Hawai'i, reposed ultimate title in a single ruler. Despite their differences, island peoples were gardeners as well as fishermen and hunters, with well-articulated claims to land and sea. These claims varied markedly from European tenure but were nevertheless difficult to ignore. Accordingly, the same legal ideologies that led to wholesale dispossession in North America and Australia required Europeans to treat Pacific Islanders, for a time, as sovereign peoples. This approach was bolstered by the fact that Britain, France and the United States were not interested in collecting Pacific Islands. Such a project promised to be prohibitively expensive and, for the Americans, morally unpalatable. (A notable exception, of course, was the United States' mania for collecting uninhabited and undisputed islands under the Guano Islands Act of 1853 – a curious piece of legislation that was used later to justify Congressional rule without constitutional rights in Puerto Rico, Guam and the Philippines.)[44] Instead, the chief legal interest of *arriviste* states was the protection and control of their subjects and property in the islands. This was a difficult project, not least because some European whalers and traders seeking trepang, sandalwood and pearls were unscrupulous troublemakers.[45]

Most European states began the project of policing trade by deploying a combination of naval jurisdiction, consular extraterritoriality and force. For example, Britain expanded old legislation extending jurisdiction over crimes committed under its flag on the high seas to crimes committed by its subjects on Pacific Islands (46 Geo. III, *c.*54). Naval warships were to arrest British miscreants and to inflict war-like punishment on island communities for destroying British property and massacring British crews. This apparently neat solution was little more than a licence for disorder: few warships patrolled the region, the nearest court with Admiralty jurisdiction was in Ceylon, and the act could not effectively police disputes among sojourners of different nationalities. Later, Britain joined France and the United States in signing treaties establishing consulates in many islands (for example, in Tahiti, Sāmoa and Fiji) charged with administering extraterritorial jurisdiction. However, these suffered from the same practical difficulties. In frustration, Britain's consul in Tahiti negotiated to lead indigenous courts exercising broad jurisdiction over transactions between locals and traders, but his efforts ended in his expulsion and the annexation of Tahiti by France.[46]

By mid-century, consular extraterritoriality had articulated into dubious treaties of cession, whereby island rulers gave European states sovereignty and jurisdiction over islands. These treaties were increasingly deemed secondary to intra-European conversations about who could exploit resources and what moral responsibilities were owed to Pacific peoples. In the Treaty of Waitangi (1840), Māori tribes gave Britain a contested degree of sovereignty in New Zealand, while in 1842 France treated with Queen Pōmare to establish a protectorate in Tahiti. Eleven years later, France declared sovereignty over the Melanesian islands of New Caledonia *before* signing a very dubious treaty (1853) with Noumean chiefs for territory and sovereignty on that island.[47] Likewise, the United States responded to the intrigues of American sugar planters in Hawai'i by annexing the islands in 1897 – an act legitimated by a disputed treaty. By the time the Berlin Conference to regulate the colonisation of Africa met in 1884, treaty-making with so-called 'backward peoples' was at best a formality.[48] European powers used the language of protection to justify a range of imperial legal engagements spanning from indirect rule to the assumption of territorial sovereignty – all 'in the interests' of Africans and Pacific Islanders.

Legal protection operated in reality to transfer wealth and, often, to mask extremely oppressive labour regimes. Wholesale transfers of land were not always the product of imperial cynicism. In Hawai'i, the transfer of land to Americans was facilitated by Hawaiian efforts to simplify tenure (the Māhele).[49] Injustice also resulted from the inability of western law to deal with the complexities of Pacific Island tenures. In New Zealand, dedicated land courts sought to locate Māori landowners and purchase their land in order to minimise settler land fraud. However, the system failed to do justice because the court could not (and arguably would not) come to terms with the complexities of Māori tenure. Māori – like many Pacific islander societies – had multilayered land tenures. In contrast to Lockean models of ownership and possession, Māori gardeners seldom had exclusive rights to their plots. Rights to garden, hunt, gather, fish and visit a single plot of land could be reposed in many different users. Prior users might also mount competing claims, and chiefs rarely possessed power to transfer land. The Land Court's failure, and the series of wars it caused, resulted in the reduction of Māori landholdings to seven million acres by 1911, and to the effective shelving of the Treaty of Waitangi until the 1970s.[50]

European 'protectors' imposed oppressive policing and labour regimes in a variety of Melanesian islands and Papua New Guinea, where indigenous peoples were allocated very low status both by stadial theory and also by emergent Darwinian science. In 1887, after a series of local uprisings, the French passed coercive laws called the *indigénat* controlling the movement of indigenous New Caledonians, imposing curfews and regulating their labour. In the mid-1890s, they imposed a 'head tax' that basically forced New Caledonians into contracts of indenture.[51] The French were not unique in this regard. Germans implemented repressive labour codes predicated on fines and corporal punishment for multiracial labourers in New Guinea – laws adapted, they said, to 'the low level of cultural development of Melanesians, Malays and Chinese' and their experience, from childhood, with 'corporal and other severe punishments'.[52] Australian colonies not only tolerated the imposition of similarly exploitative labour regimes over indigenous Australians – northern cane-growers participated actively in the kidnapping and indenture of Islanders after 1850, and Australian administrators imposed extremely harsh regimes in its protectorates and mandates in New Guinea from 1900.

The legal absurdities involved in regimes of 'legal protection' in the Pacific are most clearly evident in the French and British Condominium in the New Hebrides (Vanuatu). This joint arrangement reposed broad jurisdiction over the islands in a French and a British High Commissioner, each with their own police force, exclusive jurisdiction over their countrymen, and limited jurisdiction over other sojourners who had to choose to which national jurisdiction they would submit. Indigenous customary law was to prevail among indigenous people when not deemed 'contrary to the maintenance of order and the dictates of humanity'.[53] The system paid lip service to indigenous customary law, but operated instead to exclude indigenous people from the benefits of British or French citizenship and from participation in local representative institutions. British and French commissioners had power to pass ordinances binding on the tribes, and a European-run condominium court had jurisdiction to determine disputes about indigenous tenure and civil and criminal matters involving indigenous and non-indigenous people. This left New Hebrideans effectively stateless and vulnerable, particularly when the confounded court threw up its hands and vested land tenure in anyone who could demonstrate exclusive possession for three years or more.[54]

Meanwhile, the inherent instability of protection as a legal ideology for Pacific colonisation became painfully apparent after the First World War, when former German colonies in the Pacific were placed under the mandatory administration of Britain, Japan and the newly independent and expansionist Australia and New Zealand. Under the League of Nations settlement, Pacific Islands were declared C-Class mandates on account of the 'backwardness' of their indigenous populations.

C-Class mandatory powers were invested with 'full power of admin-istration and legislation over the territory' on the condition that they used that power 'to promote to the utmost the material and moral well-being and the social progress' of its inhabitants. They were required to abolish the slave trade, prevent traffic in arms, and prohibit the sale of alcohol to 'natives'. They could only interfere in local reli-gion for 'the maintenance of public order and public morals'.[55] This language of protection was drawn in part from the Berlin Conference of 1884–5, but it also deployed practices of colonialism developed in the Pacific littoral. Similar rules were used to control indigenous peoples in Canada, Australia and, particularly, in the post-1830s United States (a key player in the drafting of the mandate system).

While the League had no mechanisms for enforcement, manda-tory powers were required to give yearly reports on the progress of the mandates, and, at least on paper, were committed to eventual island self-government. Most importantly, yearly meetings provided a forum for Islanders and outsiders to complain about abuse by mandate holders – a model continued in the toothless UN Human Rights Committee after 1945. So when Australia continued the punitive labour laws implemented by Germany in New Guinea, Sir Herbert Murray, the 'paternalistic governor of Australia's ... Papua', complained to the League's Commission. His complaints pressured the Australian government to give him control of the mandated territory.[56] Indigenous complainants were not so fortunate: Sāmoan calls for independence resulted in committee support for New Zealand's massacre and deportation of dissidents.[57] The mandate system was largely ineffective, but its logic of protection, combined with rhetorical commitment to the eventual sovereign independence of the Pacific Islands, operated to undermine the normative ground of European and, increasingly, of Japanese colonisation in the Pacific in ways that came to fruition after the Second World War.[58]

## International law and the rise of maritime sovereignties

Since the Second World War, the Pacific region has become an impor-tant testing ground for the regime of international law instantiated by the United Nations from 1945: a regime that eschews empires, and deals almost exclusively with modern states wielding Vattelian territorial sovereignty. Indeed, the region exemplifies the 'contagion of sover-eignty' in the late twentieth century.[59] China emerged from the war free of Japanese colonisation and western unequal treaties. The 'conta-gion of sovereignty' hit Southeast Asia in the immediate post-war era, delivering Indonesia, Indochina, the Philippines, Malaysia and Singapore to independence between 1945 and 1960. Whether they became democratic or dictatorial, most Southeast Asian states wrote and passed constitutions and built institutions explicitly crafted to exercise Eurocentric sovereignty. Indeed, many East and Southeast Asian states are now engaged in neocolonial legal encounters with separatist peripheries (Tibet), ethnic minorities (Chinese Malays), and, increasingly, newly assertive indigenous peoples (Formosans) all of whom are seeking some combination of sovereignty, self-determination, jurisdiction or tenure which their host states argue derogates unacceptably from their territorial sovereignty.[60]

Sovereignty came somewhat later to the Pacific Islands. Sāmoa, Nauru, Tonga, Fiji, Papua New Guinea, the Solomon Islands, Tuvalu, Kiribati, Vanuatu, the Marshall Islands, Micronesia and Palau were decolonised slowly between 1962 and 1986, many without struggles for independence.[61] Though the Pacific States have produced a wide array of state structures, from monarchy to oligarchy, most have passed very democratic, Westminster-style constitutions, with the notable exception of Fiji which has tried to limit the access of its large Indian population to representation and resources since 1970.[62] However, decades of colonialism, mining, plantation farming, and, more recently, the emigration of many Pacific Islanders have left most with highly dependent economies, opening them to political and legal intervention by former colonial powers.[63] Meanwhile, some parts of the Pacific have not been decolonised. France still holds Tahiti and New Caledonia and uses them as strategic outposts, making the Pacific one of the last bastions of European colonialism.[64]

In North America, New Zealand and Australia, indigenous peoples have succeeded only very slightly, if at all, in their long struggle for recognition of their rights as individuals and political communities. The UN Declaration of Human Rights in 1945 had little to do with these modest successes.[65] Australia, Canada, New Zealand and the United States contend that indigenous rights should be adjudicated only within national sovereignties and by local democratic processes rather than international law.[66] In New Zealand, a political effort to honour the Treaty of Waitangi has not resulted in shared sovereignty with Māori tribes, but it has produced a national, political commitment to biculturalism that would have been unthinkable without the relatively large population of Māori people in the islands.[67] Since the 1970s, registered tribes in the United States have been able to exercise a tempered jurisdiction over their reserve lands, though this 'domestic dependent sovereignty' has been constantly eroded by aggressive state legislation and the US Supreme Court.[68] Courts and legislatures in Australia have steadfastly refused to make any space for indigenous sovereignty and jurisdiction – an insistence reinforced recently by federal legislation limiting the access of remote Aborigines to alcohol, controlling their expenditure of welfare and subjecting them to quasi-military policing.[69] In contrast, settler democracies have proved more ready to honour indigenous treaty rights to land, and, occasionally, to waterways. Māori peoples have been given a multi-billion-dollar stake in the islands' seabeds and foreshores under the Treaty of Waitangi.[70] And, though no land treaties were signed in Australia, a combination of state legislative regimes, and the *Mabo* decision in 1992, has placed nearly one-third of the continent under some sort of indigenous tenure.[71]

The most interesting product of post-war international law in the Pacific, however, has been the deployment of the language of territorial sovereignty by decolonised Pacific states to assert both ancient and modern claims to oceanic space. In the second half of the twentieth century, new naval technologies fed widespread calls for the expansion of territorial waters from the customary three nautical miles (the early modern standard) to a maximum of 12 nautical miles – a rule now embodied in the 1982 UN Convention on the Law of the Sea (UNCLOS). These rules have caused particular problems in the Pacific where key straits and passages are effectively enclosed by territorial waters. UNCLOS provides transit passage through enclosed straits and territorial waters, but there is deep dispute in Southeast Asia about whether military aircraft and naval vessels should be included in this rule – dispute grounded in the region's often-violent colonial history. Some signatory states to UNCLOS have argued that only signatories to the treaty can enjoy passage rights. The United States, a non-signatory, and the world's leading naval power, argues that transit passage has become a part of international customary law.

A number of Pacific countries, including Australia, Cambodia, China, South Korea and Vietnam, have used a rule developed to classify the fjords of Norway as territory to expand their sovereignty out from a straight baseline drawn around their coastlines. Many include submerged reefs within their 'coastlines' while Vietnam and Cambodia draw their baseline around isolated cays 50 nautical miles offshore.[72]

Indonesia, along with other island clusters in the Pacific, took a leading role in creating the legal concept of the archipelagic state. From 1954, it argued that all water within 12 miles of a line drawn around the low-water mark of its outermost islands fell within its territorial sovereignty. After much resistance from the Netherlands and the United States, Indonesia managed to have this formula adapted in the UNCLOS Convention, drawing 2.8 million kilometres of the Pacific into its jurisdiction, subject to a right of innocent passage on approved routes in the 'normal mode'.[73] The United States and the archipelagic states of the Pacific still argue about whether submerged submarines engage in a 'normal mode' of passage.[74]

Chile and other Pacific States were also pivotal in the creation of Exclusive Economic Zones vesting exclusive rights to exploit and 'jurisdiction to protect and preserve' maritime resources within 200 miles of a sovereign state.[75] Under UNCLOS, virtually all of the South Pacific Ocean falls within the EEZ of island states. Indeed the sale of rights to fish and mine EEZs is an important source of income for marginal island economies – though their limited capacity to police, combined with ever-improving technologies for extraction, may threaten their food security. At the same time, island sovereignties have provided avenues for the subversion of international laws regulating the merchant marine. Some modern multinational shipping companies register their ships under the sovereignty of Pacific Islands in return for generous licensing fees. 'Flags of convenience' allow shipping companies all of the benefits of marginal state infrastructure: loose safety legislation, exploitative labour contracts, and poor regulation reduce costs for shipowners, while making working on a ship in the Pacific one of the most dangerous jobs one can do.[76]

The EEZ has become a particularly contentious rule of international law in the Pacific. Some states purport to exercise territorial-like jurisdiction in their EEZ; for instance, China forbids military surveillance within 200 nautical miles of its shores. Most importantly, however, the enormous incentives provided by the EEZ to claim islands (even tiny, uninhabitable ones) has caused increasing instability in the busy South China Sea. Early modern rituals of possession are performed daily by contenders for the Diaoyu (or Senkaku), Spratly and Paracel Islands – the seabeds of which contain rich mineral and gas deposits. Taiwan, claiming to be the legitimate heir to the Republic of China, claims the Spratlys on the bases that Chinese fisherman frequented the islands and China's tributary empire exercised sovereignty over the entire South China Sea. Mainland China mounts the same historical claim, relying also on a contested reading of an 1887 Convention with France (dividing territorial claims in the region), and on the treaty of surrender signed by Japan in 1945. Vietnam bases its claims to the islands on post-1800 Vietnamese maps that showed the islands to be under its control, and on a different reading of the 1887 French–Chinese Convention.

The Philippines claims the islands by first occupation according to the doctrine of *res nullius* (through a series of declarations and symbolic acts performed between 1956 and 1978) and through the 1982 UNCLOS that gives sovereignty over uninhabited cays within overlapping EEZs to the proximate state. Malaysia mounts similar claims, melding the doctrine of *res nullius* with the novel claim that the islands form part of its continental shelf. These controversies show how shared languages of sovereignty and of early modern claiming, refracted through much newer international conventions, are being deployed to close the Pacific Ocean.[77]

Meanwhile, however, the oceans are rising – causing acute crises in the ocean of islands that is the Pacific. The peoples of Kiribati and Tuvalu face imminent crises of water supply, erosion and soil salination that will render their islands uninhabitable. Relocation has deep roots in many Pacific Island cultures, but in the twenty-first-century world of territorial sovereigns, the rising waters of the Pacific pose particular challenges. The first is the proliferation of hard borders, regulating interstate migrations with increasing inflexibility since the late nineteenth century, and of soft borders, restricting the forced migrations of refugees despite international conventions protecting refugees (1951) and stateless people (1954 and 1961). Secondly, the gradual inundation of islands will create peoples of a character scarcely contemplated by international law: peoples with polities but without inhabitable land. It is still unclear whether the peoples of uninhabitable islands will be considered sovereigns without territory: Indonesia has offered to rent islands to displaced Pacific Islanders, and some scholars argue that they could trade access to their EEZs for the right to exercise self-governance in a federal state like Australia. Most likely, however, these island communities face mass migration and integration into proximate Pacific states at great cost to their culture and society.[78]

## Conclusion

I have told the legal history of the Pacific Ocean here as a series of imperial and international legal regimes casting law over land, peoples and ocean. While many of the chapters in this volume speak of dispersal and difference in the Pacific Basin, this story has traced a convergence of sorts. Highly speculative medieval and early modern claims gave way from 1800 to uniform modes of claiming, uniform assumptions about state sovereignty and jurisdiction, and, among Europeans, a shared discourse of cultural superiority that enabled them to compete peacefully for access to the wealth of the region. The disruption of imperial legal ideologies in the twentieth century in turn facilitated the globalisation of the sovereign state as a universal legal construct – a convergence that has, in turn, facilitated great political and economic diversity in the basin. Though scholars write increasingly about the erosion of state sovereignty by globalisation, nation-states still dominate the legal history of the Pacific. To this day, Pacific states deploy the ubiquitous language of territorial sovereignty to cast their laws further than ever before into the world's largest, and deepening, ocean.

## Notes

Many people helped me to craft this chapter: I owe particular thanks to Edward Cavanagh, Alison Bashford, David Armitage, the other contributors to this volume and the members of both the NYU Colloquium in Legal History and the Princeton Workshop in American Studies. Parts of it were produced with the support of the Australian Research Council, DE120100593.

1. See Damon Salesa, 'The Pacific in Indigenous Time', ch. 2 in this volume.
2. Li Zhaojie (James Li), 'Traditional Chinese World Order', *Chinese Journal of International Law* 1 (2002), 27; Ulises Granados, 'The South China Sea and its Coral Reefs During the Ming and Qing Dynasties: Levels of Geographical Knowledge and Political Control', *East Asian History* 32 (2006), 109–28.
3. Philip E. Steinberg, *The Social Construction of the Ocean* (Cambridge, 2001), pp. 50–60.
4. Donald B. Freeman, *The Pacific* (London, 2010), p. 65; J. Arthur Lower, *Ocean of Destiny: A Concise History of the North Pacific, 1500–1978* (Vancouver, BC, 1978), p. 8.
5. Salesa, 'The Pacific in Indigenous Time'.
6. Kathleen Romoli, *Balboa of Darién, Discoverer of the Pacific* (Garden City, NY, 1953), p. 162.
7. Ricardo Padrón, 'A Sea of Denial: The Early Modern Spanish Invention of the Pacific Rim', *Hispanic Review* 77 (2009), 8; Joyce Chaplin, 'The Pacific before Empire, *c.* 1500–1800', ch. 3 in this volume.
8. *European Treaties Bearing on the History of the United States and its Dependencies*, ed. Frances G. Davenport, 4 vols (Washington, DC, 1917), I, p. 62; Lauren Benton, 'Possessing Empire: Iberian Claims and Interpolity Law', in Saliha Belmessous, ed., *Native Claims: Indigenous Law against Empire, 1500–1920* (New York, 2012), p. 21; Philip E. Steinberg, 'Lines of Division, Lines of Connection: Stewardship in the World Ocean', *Geographical Review* 89 (1999), 254–8; Steinberg, *The Social Construction of the Ocean*, pp. 75–83.
9. Cardinal of Toledo to Charles V, 27 January 1541, quoted in Paul E. Hoffman, 'Diplomacy and the Papal Donation 1493–1585', *The Americas* 30 (1973), 161.
10. Davenport, *European Treaties,* I, pp. 93–100.

11. Davenport, *European Treaties,* I, pp. 2, 148, 159–68.
12. Lauren Benton and Benjamin Straumann, 'Acquiring Empire by Law: From Roman Doctrine to Early Modern European Practice', *Law and History Review* 28 (2010), 19.
13. Benton and Straumann, 'Acquiring Empire by Law', 20–5.
14. On the contested notion of pacification, see Tamar Herzog, 'Conquista o integración: Los debates entorno a la inserción territorial (Madrid–México, siglo XVIII)', in Michel Bertrant and Natividad Planas, eds., *Les sociétés de frontière: de la Méditerranée à l'Atlantique, XVIᵉ–XVIIIᵉ siècle* (Madrid, 2011), pp. 149–64.
15. R. Jovita Baber, 'Law, Land, and Legal Rhetoric in Colonial New Spain: A Look at the Changing Rhetoric of Indigenous Americans in the Sixteenth Century', in Belmessous, ed., *Native Claims*, p. 48; Tamar Herzog, 'Colonial Law and "Native Customs": Indigenous Land Rights in Colonial Spanish America', *The Americas* 63 (2013), 303–21.
16. O. H. K. Spate, *The Spanish Lake* (London, 1979), pp. 157–62, 220–3; Freeman, *The Pacific,* pp. 85–7; K. R. Howe, *Where the Waves Fall: A New South Sea Islands History from the First Settlement to Colonial Rule* (Sydney, 1984), pp. 74–8; David Joel Steinberg, *The Philippines: A Singular and a Plural Place*, 3rd edn (Boulder, CO, 1994), pp. 57–8.
17. Philip E. Steinberg, 'Lines of Division, Lines of Connection: Stewardship in the World Ocean', *Geographical Review* 89 (1999), 258; Adam Clulow, 'European Maritime Violence and Territorial States in Early Modern Asia, 1600–1650', *Itinerario* 33 (2009), 72–94.
18. Pär Cassel, *Grounds of Judgment: Extraterritoriality and Imperial Power in Nineteenth-Century China and Japan* (Oxford, 2011), pp. 41–3.
19. O. H. K. Spate, *Monopolists and Freebooters* (London, 1983), pp. 39, 68–9.
20. Gough, *Distant Dominion*, pp. 15–16; Arthur Weststeijn, 'Empire by Trade: Treaties in Seventeenth-Century Dutch Colonial Expansion' (paper presented at the Empire by Treaty Symposium, University of New South Wales, August 2012).
21. John G. Butcher, 'Resink Revisited: A Note on the Territorial Waters of the Self-Governing Realms of the Netherlands Indies in the late 1800s', *Bijdragen tot de Taal-, Land- en Volkenkunde (BKI)* 164 (2008), 1–12; H. J. Leue, 'Legal Expansion in the Age of Companies: Aspects of the Administration of Justice in the English and Dutch Settlements of Maritime Asia, c. 1600–1750', in W. J. Mommsen and J. A. de Moor, eds., *European Expansion and Law: The Encounter of European and Indigenous Law in 19th and 20th-Century Africa and Asia* (Oxford, 1992), pp. 129–58.
22. Hugo Grotius, *The Free Sea*, ed. David Armitage (Indianapolis, 2004); Martti Koskenniemi, 'International Law and the Emergence of Mercantile Capitalism: Grotius to Smith' (unpublished paper): http://www.helsinki.fi/eci/Publications/Koskenniemi/MKMercantileCapitalism.pdf, 21; Benton and Straumann, 'Acquiring Empire by Law', 21–6.
23. Mónica Brito Vieira, '*Mare Liberum* vs *Mare Clausum*: Grotius, Freitas, and Selden's Debate on Dominion over the Sea', *Journal of the History of Ideas* 64 (2003), 361–77.

24. Spate, *Monopolists and Freebooters*, pp. 190–200.

25. Freeman, *The Pacific*, pp. 85–7.

26. Spate, *Monopolists and Freebooters*, pp. 189–94, 244–9.

27. Benjamin Keene, cited by Glyndwr Williams, 'The Pacific: Exploration and Exploitation', in P. J. Marshall, ed., *The Oxford History of the British Empire*, II: *The Eighteenth Century* (Oxford, 1998), p. 555.

28. Alan Frost, 'Nootka Sound and the Beginnings of Britain's Imperialism of Free Trade', in Robin Fisher and Hugh Johnson, eds., *From Maps to Metaphors: The Pacific World of George Vancouver* (Vancouver, BC, 1993), pp. 104–27.

29. Eliga H. Gould, 'Zones of Law, Zones of Violence: The Legal Geography of the British Atlantic, circa 1772', *William and Mary Quarterly* 3rd ser., 60 (2003), 471–510.

30. James Sheehan, 'The Problem of Sovereignty in European History', *American Historical Review* 111 (2006), 1–15.

31. Ian Hunter, 'Vattel in Revolutionary America: From the Rules of War to the Rule of Law', in Lisa Ford and Tim Rowse, eds., *Between Indigenous and Settler Governance* (London, 2013), pp. 12–23.

32. Jane Samson, *Imperial Benevolence: Making British Authority in the Pacific* (Honolulu, 1998).

33. Alan Frost, *Convicts and Empire: A Naval Question,* (Oxford, 1980); Mollie Gillen, 'The Botany Bay Decision, 1786: Convicts Not Empire', in Gillian Whitlock and Gail Reekie, eds., *Uncertain Beginnings: Debates in Australian Studies* (St. Lucia, Qld., 1993), pp. 25–36.

34. Daniel K. Richter, 'To "Clear the King's and Indians' Title"': Treaty-Making and North American Land in England's Restoration Era' (paper presented to the Empire by Treaty Symposium, University of New South Wales, August 2012); Lisa Ford, *Settler Sovereignty: Jurisdiction and Indigenous People in America and Australia, 1788–1836* (Cambridge, MA, 2010), pp. 26–9. On the Batman Treaty (1835), see Bain Attwood, *Possession: Batman's Treaty and the Matter of History* (Carlton, Vic., 2009).

35. Stuart Banner, *Possessing the Pacific: Land, Settlers, and Indigenous People from Australia to Alaska* (Cambridge, MA, 2007), pp. 13–46.

36. Heather Douglas and Mark Finnane, *Indigenous Crime and Settler Law: White Sovereignty after Empire* (Basingstoke, 2012).

37. Anna Haebich, *Broken Circles: Fragmenting Indigenous Families, 1800–2000* (Fremantle, 2000).

38. Scottish traveller J. D. Borthwick, quoted by Banner, *Possessing the Pacific,* p. 165, more generally, see ibid., pp. 163–94.

39. Banner, *Possessing the Pacific,* pp. 195–230, 293–314.

40. Amanda Nettelbeck and Robert Foster, 'Food and Governance on the Frontiers of Colonial Australia and Canada's Northwest Territories', *Aboriginal History* 36 (2012), 21–41; Margaret Jacobs, *White Mother to a Dark Race: Settler Colonialism, Maternalism, and the Removal of Indigenous Children in the American West and Australia, 1880–1940* (Lincoln, NE, 2010).

41. Cassel, *Grounds of Judgment.*

42. Cassel, *Grounds of Judgment*, pp. 29–38.

43. Nicholas Tarling, 'The Establishment of Colonial Regimes', in Tarling, ed, *The Cambridge History of Southeast Asia,* III: *From c. 1800 to the 1930s* (Cambridge, 1999), pp. 49–55; Carl Trocki, 'Political Structures in the Nineteenth and Early Twentieth Centuries', in *The Cambridge History of South East Asia,* III, pp. 75–126.

44. Christina Duffy Burnett, 'The Edges of Empire and the Limits of Sovereignty: American Guano Islands', *American Quarterly* 57 (2005), 779–803.

45. For a complex account, see Dorothy Shineberg, *They Came for Sandalwood: A Study of the Sandalwood Trade in the South-West Pacific, 1830–1865* (Melbourne, 1967).

46. John M. Ward, *British Policy in the South Pacific, 1786–1893: A Study in British Policy towards the South Pacific Islands Prior to the Establishment of Governments by the Great Powers* (Sydney, 1948).

47. Colin Forster, 'French Penal Policy and the Origins of the French Presence in New Caledonia', *Journal of Pacific History* 26 (1991), 135–50.

48. C. H. Alexandrowicz, *The European–African Confrontation: A Study in Treaty Making* (Leiden, 1973).

49. Banner, *Possessing the Pacific*, pp. 128–62; Donald D. Johnson, *The United States and the Pacific: Private Interests and Public Policies, 1784–1899* (Westport, CT, 1995), pp. 79–112, 145–64.

50. R. G. Crocombe, *Land Tenure in the Cook Islands* (Melbourne, 1962); Banner, *Possessing the Pacific*, pp. 84–127.

51. Adrian Muckle, 'Troublesome Chiefs and Disorderly Subjects: The *Indigénat* and the Internment of Kanak in New Caledonia (1887–1928)', *French Colonial History* 11 (2010), 131–60.

52. Peter G. Sack, 'Law, Politics and Native "Crimes" in German New Guinea', in John A. Moses and Paul M. Kennedy, eds., *Germany in the Pacific and Far East, 1870–1914* (St Lucia, Qld, 1977), p. 266.

53. Quoted by Linden A. Mander, 'The New Hebrides Condominium', *Pacific Historical Review* 13 (1944), 152.

54. Greg Rawlings, 'Statelessness, Citizenship and Annotated Discriminations: Meta Documents, and the Aesthetics of the Subtle at the United Nations', *History and Anthropology* 22 (2011), 461–79; Rawlings, 'Statelessness, Human Rights and Decolonisation: Citizenship in Vanuatu, 1906–80', *Journal of Pacific History* 47 (2012), 45–68.

55. 'Status of Islands in Pacific Ocean', US Naval War College, *International Law Studies Series* 29 (1929), 50–1.

56. Susan Pedersen, 'The Meaning of the Mandates System: An Argument', *Geschichte und Gesellschaft* 32 (2006), 575.

57. Patricia O'Brien, 'Massacres in the 1920s Pacific: Australia, New Zealand, and the League of Nations' (paper presented at the Australian Historical Association Biennial Conference, Adelaide, July 2012); Susan Pedersen, 'Samoa on the World Stage: Petitions and Peoples Before the Mandates Commission of the League of Nations', *Journal of Imperial and Commonwealth History* 40 (2012), 231–61.

58. Antony Anghie, *Imperialism, Sovereignty and the Making of International Law* (Cambridge, 2004), pp. 115–95.

59. David Armitage, *The Declaration of Independence: A Global History* (Cambridge, MA, 2007), p. 103.

60. Benedict Kingsbury, 'Indigenous Peoples as an International Legal Concept', in Christian Erni, ed., *The Concept of Indigenous Peoples in Asia: A Resource Book* (Copenhagen, 2008), pp. 103–58.

61. Contrast Sāmoa.

62. Robert Aldrich, 'Politics', ch. 14 in this volume.

63. Geoff Leane and Barbara Von Tigerstrom, 'Introduction', in Geoff Leane and Barbara Von Tigerstrom, eds., *International Law Issues in the South Pacific* (Aldershot, 2005), pp. 2–3.

64. Yash Ghai, 'Constitution Making and Decolonisation', in Ghai, ed., *Law, Government and Politics in the Pacific Island States* (Suva, 1988), pp. 1–105. On France, see Robert Aldrich, *France and the South Pacific since 1940* (Honolulu, 1993).

65. Samuel Moyn, *The Last Utopia: Human Rights in History* (Cambridge, MA, 2010).

66. Miranda Johnson, 'Reconciliation, Indigeneity and Postcolonial Nationhood in Settler States', *Postcolonial Studies* 14 (2011), 187–201.

67. Kirsty Gover, 'Indigenous Jurisdiction as a Provocation of Settler State Political Theory: The Significance of Human Boundaries', in Ford and Rowse, eds., *Between Settler and Indigenous Governance*, pp. 187–99.

68. For example, Katherine J. Florey, 'Indian Country's Borders: Territoriality, Immunity and the Construction of Tribal Sovereignty', *Boston College Law Review* 51 (2010), 595–668.

69. See generally, Jon Altman and Melinda Hickson, *Coercive Reconciliation: Stabilise, Normalise, Exit Aboriginal Australia* (Melbourne, 2007).

70. F. M. Brookfield, 'Māori Customary Title in Foreshore and Seabed', *New Zealand Law Journal* 34 (2004), 34–48; Abby Suzko, 'The Marine and Coastal Area (Takutai Moana) Act 2011: A Just and Durable Resolution to the Foreshore and Seabed Debate?', *New Zealand Universities Law Review* 25 (2012), 148–79.

71. Jon Altman, 'Land Rights and Development in Australia: Caring for, Benefiting from, Governing the Indigenous Estate', in Ford and Rowse, eds., *Between Indigenous and Settler Governance*, pp. 121–34.

72. Scott Davidson, 'The Law of the Sea and Freedom of Navigation in Asia Pacific', in Leane and von Tigerstrom, eds., *International Law Issues in the South Pacific,* p. 140.

73. Robert Cribb and Michele Ford, 'Indonesia as an Archipelago: Managing Islands, Managing the Seas', in Cribb and Ford, eds., *Indonesia beyond the Water's Edge: Managing an Archipelagic State* (Singapore, 2009), pp. 1–7; John G. Butcher, 'Becoming an Archipelagic State: The Juanda Declaration of 1957 and the "Struggle" to Gain International Recognition of the Archipelagic Principle', in Cribb and Ford, eds., *Indonesia beyond the Water's Edge*, pp. 28–48.

74. Davidson, 'The Law of the Sea and Freedom of Navigation in Asia Pacific', in Leane and von Tigerstrom, eds., *International Law Issues in the South Pacific,* pp. 132–9.

75. Francisco Orrego Vicuña, *The Exclusive Economic Zone: Regime and Legal Nature under International Law* (Cambridge, 1989), pp. 3–6.

76. Alastair Couper, *Sailors and Traders: A Maritime History of the Pacific Peoples* (Honolulu, 2009), pp. 186–206.

77. Xavier Furtado, 'International Law and the Dispute over the Spratly Islands: Whither UNCLOS?', *Contemporary Southeast Asia* 21 (1999), 386–404.

78. Jane McAdam, '"Disappearing States", Statelessness and the Boundaries of International Law', in Jane McAdam, ed., *Climate Change and Displacement: Multidisciplinary Perspectives* (Oxford, 2010), pp. 105–30.

# 11

# Science

## Sujit Sivasundaram

There is a consensus about how to interpret the history of science in the Pacific. Accordingly, the vastness of the ocean has served as a scientific opportunity, presenting the possibility of testing the newest scientific ideas ranging from astronomy in the eighteenth century by James Cook to the relation of species in the nineteenth century by Charles Darwin and on to nuclear physics in the midst of the Cold War. This scientific opportunity has lain in the alleged isolation of each of the constituent tracts of land which are found within this vast ocean. The Pacific island has been a productive terrain for the scientific thought of intruders: it has been possible to calibrate peoples, animals, fauna and the Earth itself in these spaces, because of the smallness of islands and their supposed lack of interest in the strategic games of empire and decolonisation. The historiographical consensus is well expressed as follows: the Pacific Ocean has been 'a laboratory for scientific methods and mentalities', 'a veritable school for science, and a vast classroom for educating the European mind'.[1]

Yet this view of the 'Pacific laboratory' misses something. For it takes the region as static – a terrain which allows science to be done, from which data and specimens are extracted and against which theories are tested. In some such accounts, science is a bundle of things or practices which comes fully formed or with great intentional force to intrude into the Pacific periphery. Following this view, the prime subjects of historical study are the European gaze and European technologies which document the Pacific and these need to be understood in relation to the evolution of traditions far away, in the heartlands of the West. The idea of the Pacific as a laboratory borrows from past practitioners of science and could lead at times to the assumption that this maritime world was inert, sterile or controlled, like everything in a scientific work station.[2] The Pacific has changed the course of science rather more meaningfully than by letting itself be subjugated by structures such as the European ship or the European gentlemanly

237

traveller. When searching questions were asked in this region, the Pacific had a role to play in the answers that emerged. Such an argument also provides a more robust view of how science is made: science is not formed in full in Europe, it develops through fluid encounters in a range of sites of interaction.

The Pacific is and has always been alive. This is the starting point of the argument laid out in this chapter. Energetic processes of evolutionary, migratory and climatic change have been witnessed here. Yet for many outsiders – or Outlanders as they are called by Pacific peoples – this ocean has signified something dead: the end of the Earth, the inversion of the natural and a vast expanse of emptiness. In order to destabilise such representations I urge the dynamic role of the living Pacific in scientific theorisations of this sea. The pattern of islands across a vast expanse of water, changing over time, with people moving over vast distances, showing modes of connection and disconnection across this large space, has served as a context for the shaping of science undertaken here. The changeability of the Pacific kept interrupting the thought patterns of thinkers from all perspectives. This is not to make the Pacific a unit or even an organism which has a defined boundary separating it from its neighbours, but rather to highlight that the living Pacific becomes visible in its engagement with human travellers and inhabitants. This argument follows in the wake of a series of revisionist approaches to the global history of science that have stressed the role of intermediaries and brokers in making it possible for science to move on a global scale.[3] Importantly, the living Pacific includes the people who have lived here as well as the ocean and land.

One way of shoring up such claims in a rather literal sense is to point to the persistent obsession with a set of questions across cultural divides and across time, amongst philosophers and scientists in the Pacific, namely issues of cosmology related to the origin, relationship and distribution of land and sea. The foci of this chapter – from islander chants to the records of Darwin's voyage, and from fears surrounding nuclear tests to recent predictions of climate science – demonstrate that the Pacific has been a site for thinking about what happens when land rises or sinks. This concern has oftentimes veered into religious debates and discussion of the status of the human in relation to nature. This study of land and sea has also been inseparable from accounts of migration, ethnicity and culture, which have had a scientific base.[4]

What follows is an episodic history of thinking about nature – or science, broadly construed. It connects up events across the centuries and can only be suggestive in the material that it weaves together. It is by no means comprehensive as an account of science in the Pacific. This is also an attempt to undertake a project of what I have elsewhere called 'cross-contextualisation', the reading of the archival and material remains of European science within and against material that is not normally considered part of the scientific canon.[5] By stretching the category of science across cultural perspectives and across different genres of recording and thinking, it is possible to appreciate the distinctive features of the history of science in the Pacific, and to take indigenous knowledges seriously. The discussion therefore begins with a set of unorthodox, but highly revealing sources to the historian of science – genealogical texts concerned with earth history and geology – before it moves on to sources emerging from European voyages.

★ ★ ★

Throughout the Pacific region, islanders have long told accounts of their origin and descent in genealogical fashion. In these histories, the origin of things is often connected to the emergence of land and sea. It is sometimes plotted in relation to travel across the ocean to arrive at a home island or travel from the sky down to the land. In some narratives islands disappear into the sea or rise from it. There is a great deal of naturalism in these histories – as ancestors are said to arrive on whales or coconuts, or a giant octopus or turtle.[6] As Margaret Jolly writes of these indigenous representations, '[t]he land is seen as active not inert, as possessed of people, living and dead'. For her, this is particularly borne out by the fact that the word for land in Austronesian languages is the same as that for placenta, 'and a person's attachment to place is secured by the planting of the placenta soon after birth'.[7] These genealogical histories were often the preserve of the initiated, and were recited with accompanying bodily and verbal gestures in order to convey their meaning. They were political stories, in the sense that they were aimed at legitimating the standing of particular chiefs or peoples, and could take on anti-missionary or anti-colonial sentiments.

One particularly good example of such a genealogical text is the chant of *Kumulipo*, from Hawai'i, which is a prayer of about two thousand lines providing the genealogical history of the hereditary chiefs or *ali'i* of Hawai'i.[8] *Kumulipo* is literally 'Beginning-in-darkness', and the chant is divided into seven sections, which are times of darkness, which gave way to nine sections, which are times of daylight. In its content the *Kumulipo* links the origins of the earth to the chief Lonoikamakahiki and leads on from there to King Kalākaua (r. 1874–91), under whose patronage it was published as *He Pule Ho'ola Ali'i* (A prayer to consecrate

[an] Ali'i) in 1889. As the Hawaiian scholar Lilikal'a Kame'eleihiwa writes: 'Hawaiian identity is in fact derived from the Kumulipo, the great cosmogonic genealogy... Conceived in this way, the genealogy of the Land, the Gods, Chiefs and people intertwine with one another'.[9] The publication of this text came when Kalākaua appointed a 'Board of Genealogy of Hawaiian Chiefs' to collect genealogies and to revise, correct and record such narratives, given some concern about his ancestry and legitimacy, and in the context of the encroachment of foreign powers. Later, a translation undertaken by Queen Lili'uokalani, Kalākaua's sister and successor, was published in Boston in 1897, after her exile there following the annexation of Hawai'i by the United States: the intention again was to underline Hawai'i's long-standing cultural traditions.[10]

The opening section of *Kumulipo* is as follows and bears out its narration of the deep history of the earth:

> At the time when the earth became hot
> At the time when the heavens turned about
> At the time when the sun was darkened
> To cause the moon to shine
> The time of the rise of Pleiades
> The slime, this was the source of the earth
> The source of the darkness that made darkness
> The source of the night that made night
> Nothing but night.
> The night gave birth
> Born was Kumulipo in the night, a male
> Born was Po'ele in the night, a female
> Born was the coral polyp, born was the coral came forth
> Born was the grub that digs and heaps up the earth, came forth
> Born was his [child] an earthworm, came forth
> Born was the starfish, his child the small sea cucumber came forth...[11]

The chant is full of reproductive energy; indeed, its content has been termed 'evolutionary'.[12] The heavens warm the earth by rubbing against it and producing a slimy substance; female and male forces, Kumulipo and Po'ele, are involved in the creation of life and the gods give birth to creatures that inhabit both the sea and the land. The fecund character of this poem is fitting for the period of its publication, where concerns of depopulation were rife in Hawai'i. As one commentator writes: 'cosmogenesis is equated with anthropogenesis, and the latter with the ontogenesis of an individual human'.[13] Critically for a later episode covered in this chapter there is an understanding that corals are born, are alive, and so give rise to land. This would become a key puzzle that vexed European scientists into the twentieth century.

The publication of this text at the end of the nineteenth century came not only from a need to assert Hawaiian identity and heritage in the context of western intrusion, but was born also as a result of an engagement with western science. The report of the board of genealogy established by Kalākaua sought to align the discoveries of oceanographic science with genealogical histories: it serves as a revealing example of an explicit and self-aware comparison between tradition and science. This engagement with marine surveying came from a desire amongst Hawaiians to demonstrate that what they had known all along was verified by the new findings of science, at a time when indigenous traditions were being disparaged.[14] In addition to collecting and classifying genealogical narrations, the Board also acquired some maps and soundings undertaken by scientists, from the Surveyor General's Department of Hawai'i, including soundings emerging from the *Challenger* expedition which we will turn to later. In quoting contemporary views about the possibility that there had been continents in the Pacific Ocean and also in taking on board theories of migration, the Board noted: 'the evidence deduced from these soundings is of great value to the Board in solving many points and theories already advanced by writers of the history of the Polynesian Races'. It held to the view that the 'atollic formation of Islands' can 'only be accounted by the many transformations of the earth's surface at its most remote period'. However, it sought to privilege 'ancient folklore' and divest itself 'of all quotations from other sources', in order to place the origin of the peoples of Hawai'i at a date 'long anterior to those given by any of the historians that have written upon this subject'.[15] The first text it turned to for evidence was the *Kumulipo* and the seven periods that occurred before the appearance of humans. It then proceeded to announce that the origins of the Hawaiians predated the settlement of Tahiti and Sāmoa.

The role of missionaries and converts in transcribing some of these texts has led to a debate about the extent to which they indicate a Christianised rendition of genealogical tradition.[16] Indeed the Board's report went on to the question of the evidence for a universal deluge. It also noted the work of David Malo (1793?–1853), who had been trained by the leading genealogist of the reign of Kamehameha I, and who converted to Christianity and then went on to be regarded as 'the universal authority' on Hawaiian lore in the mid-nineteenth century.[17] In political terms Malo has been described as both a critic of western intrusion as well as a conduit for it.[18] If this is so, a similar claim can be made for his contradictory engagement with diverse traditions of natural and scientific knowledge. His book,

*Figure 11.1* 'David Malo, a Native of the Hawaiian Islands', in Charles Pickering *The Races of Man, and Their Geographical Distribution* (London, 1849). The image is titled 'U.S. Exploring Expedition', indicating that it arises from Charles Wilkes' expedition of 1838–42, on which Pickering was a naturalist, and also 'Malayan Race Plate III'.

*Moolelo Hawaii*, was translated by Nathaniel Emerson, with the title *Hawaiian Antiquities* in 1898. This text reads as a critical engagement with Hawaiian traditions alongside the latest science. The section that bears out most fully the contradictory placement of Malo's views in-between genealogy and geology appears in the second chapter, which was translated in the nineteenth century as follows:

5. In the genealogy of Wakea it is said that Papa gave birth to these islands. Another account has it that this group of islands were not forgotten, but really made by the hands of Wakea himself.

6. We now perceive their error. If the women in that ancient time gave birth to countries then indeed would they do so in these days; and if at that time they were made by the hands of Wakea, doubtless the same thing would be done now...

9. In these days certain learned men have searched into and studied the origin of the Hawaiian islands, but whether their views are correct no one can say, because they are speculations.

10. These scientists from other lands have advanced a theory and expressed the opinion that there was probably no land here in ancient times, only ocean; and they think that islands rose up out the ocean as a result of volcanic action.

11. Their reasons for this opinion are that certain islands are known which have risen up out of the ocean and which present features similar to Hawaii nei. Again a sure indication is that the soil of these islands is wholly volcanic... Such are their speculations and reasoning...[19]

These two extracts indicate how Malo was weighing up both genealogy and geology and yet preventing himself from a full commitment to either. Genealogists like Malo undoubtedly reshaped their narratives over time, by engaging with waves of new knowledge, religion and culture. Therefore, genealogical histories should not be interpreted as unchanging or as coming into first contact and dramatic encounter with science in this period. Rather, Malo's text is a prime indicator of the confluence of cosmological traditions and ways of knowing nature which characterised the Pacific.

Studying Hawaiian genealogical traditions in the broader context of Pacific accounts of the deep history of the Earth can usefully serve as the point of reference for the science of the great voyages of European discovery. This is because European travellers were also working within oral and sensory customs connected with the origin of things.

Often the emergence of a science of empire not just in the Pacific but on the global stage is linked to the three epic voyages of Captain Cook, given the navigator's instructions to observe the transit of Venus and find the North West Passage. Yet there is a longer history of European natural knowledge which encroached upon the Pacific and the link between those earlier voyages and the genealogical histories just discussed lies in their shared attention to the contours of land and sea.

The idea of a missing southern continent was pivotal to early European voyages to the Pacific, prior to the arrival of Cook.[20] If the 'Pacific' as a term denoting the region was in all probability born with Ferdinand Magellan, this navigator's circumnavigation of the globe between 1519 and 1522 accelerated the idea of a southern continent.[21] That there was a mass of land in the southern hemisphere, which, according to one cosmographic thesis, would counterbalance the continents in the northern hemisphere, had been held since the days of antiquity. It is apparent in the work of Pythagoras or Ptolemy. The longevity of this conception bears out the way mythic tradition worked as an organising principle in western thought about the southern seas: the idea was recited down the generations as a norm of geographical knowledge, and repeated voyages fitted their findings around it. Why should this traditional knowledge be marked out as distinct from the Hawaiian genealogical chant? In fact the legacy of the idea of missing continents would not disappear with the arrival of Cook, lasting well into the nineteenth century.

In sixteenth-century Portuguese and Spanish visions emphasis was placed on the outcrops of this southern continent: Tierra del Fuego, the New Hebrides, Java and New Guinea were such entry points. Even as the Pacific emerged in a cartographic sense it was as the first plottings of land rather than sea; observers seemed convinced that more land would be found. The Ocean was mythologised as paradisiacal and utopian: Paradise lay in the southern hemisphere. One creature that focussed such a view was the paradise bird: five arrived in Seville on the *Victoria*, the only vessel of Magellan's contingent that returned to Europe in 1522. In the official account of Magellan's voyage written by Antonia Pigafetta, the bird was described in a manner consistent with the natural historical style which would dominate European travel accounts of the Pacific into the nineteenth century:

> These birds are as big as thrushes, with a small head and a long beak. Their legs are the length of a palm and thin as a pen. In place of wings they have long multi-coloured plumes, resembling great panaches, whereas the feathers of the rest of the body are bronze-colored... This explains why they would have come from the Earthly Paradise; because they call them 'bolondivita', which means 'birds of God.'[22]

Accompanying the maps and atlases there appeared beautifully coloured drawings of the birds of paradise in the sixteenth century. In these engagements with the Pacific Europeans were playing out their own account of cosmology, and they too, like the Islanders, were interested in separating out land and sea, in the quest to chart a Judaeo-Christian history of humankind. In this sense the notion of the missing continent fed into a cosmological history.

The gaze of European travellers in the Pacific might also be termed cosmographic to signal the incorporation of the project of science in a broader need to work out the observer's placement in the universe. A visual trope that was utilised a great deal in these voyages was the coastal profile, as land rising up literally from nowhere, and this is evident in Portuguese sources, as well as in Dutch voyages.[23] For instance, Dutch navigators, working out of Batavia and the Netherlands, were particularly keen to determine the coast of Australia in the seventeenth century. One example of this is a delicate set of watercolours drawn by Victor Victorszoon, the son of a painter, which are amongst the earliest depictions of the coast of Australia. These arose from the voyage of the ex-whaler Willem de Vlamingh in 1696–7, undertaken with direction from the man of science, director of the Dutch East India Company (VOC), and mayor of Amsterdam, Nicolaas Witsen (1641–1717). Watercolours were drawn by Victorszoon as profile views to supplement a manuscript chart of 'T'ZUYDLANDT', which is numbered to denote the site of each of the coastal paintings. It is important to note that there is no sea in these watercolours, simply the line of the coast in shades of blue, brown or grey, sometimes curved to indicate the hemispheric horizon, and indicating elevation upwards. The text accompanying the first profile view of Rottnest Island, off the Australian coast is as follows:

Anchored at the north side of Rottnest Island a half mile from the shore at the depth of 10 fathoms on a sandy bottom. With the centre of the island to the south south west of us, the island appeared as is indicated by figure no. 1.[24]

This profile shows a horizontal concentration of low-lying shrub land, with a series of islands off Rottnest (see Figures 11.2 and 11.3). As indicated by the description, it is a rendition of what it meant to sit on a 'sandy bottom' out at sea and gaze towards land; the sea and the ship disappear in an anthrocentric act. Victorszoon engages directly with the visual experience of land, with the sand beneath him.

These watercolours are not part of the paradisiacal cosmogony of land. There was one word that recurred in the middle of Victorszoon's

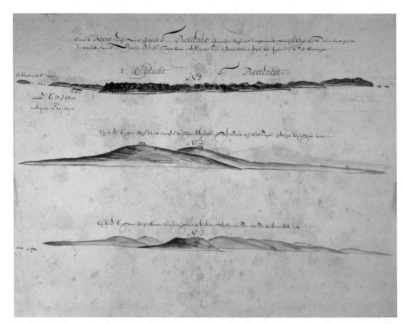

*Figure 11.2*   Coastal profile views numbered 1, 2 and 3, accompanying a manuscript chart of 'T'ZUYDLANDT' drawn by Victor Victorszoon in 1697. The first coastal profile reads: 'Anchored at the north side of Rottnest Island a half mile from the shore at a depth of 10 fathoms on a sandy bottom. With the centre of the island to the south south west of us, the island appeared as is indicated by figure no.1.'

rather clipped textual annotations to his maps: 'barren'. Of Rottnest Island, the voyager's patron, Witsen, wrote: 'They found a crowd of woodrats about as big as cats, having a bag beneath their throat, in which one can plunge one's hand without being able to discover for what purpose Nature had shaped the animal in this way.'[25] These quokka were soon taken as indicators of 'antipodean inversion', a regular trope in the study of the natural history of the Pacific.[26] Importantly, no people were sighted near the Swan River estuary, and only a few elsewhere on the coast of Southland: 'however carefully we inspected everything, we found no people'.[27] The people who were sighted did not welcome the Dutchmen who had landed on their shores. In tracing origins, the cosmographic gaze could thus veer from the notion of paradise to emptiness, and sometimes tempestuousness, in a matter of years and even lines. Three profiles shaded in the type of blue usually used for the ocean documented a territory described by De Vlamingh as follows: 'here the shore is steep and rough everywhere, no growth and very steep right to the

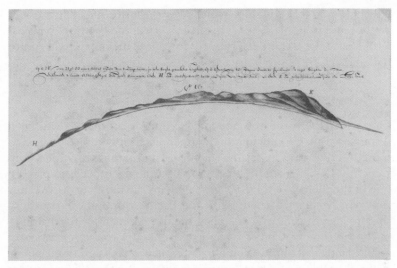

*Figure 11.3* Coastal profile view numbered 15 indicating hemispheric horizon accompanying a manuscript chart of 'T'ZUYDLANDT' drawn by Victor Victorszoon in 1697. The text reads: 'Anchored in a bay at the north end of the Southland at the southern latitude 21° 33' at a depth of 10 fathoms ¾ of a mile from the shore, the land appears as is indicated below. Letter H the most easterly land, a white point, letter K the most westerly land, a high point.'

top, as if it has been cut off with an axe, no beach at its foot and big breakers which are wonderful to look at'.[28]

It is apposite to point to the impact on James Cook of these earlier voyages. For instance, he took with him summary accounts of Dutch voyages – especially those undertaken by Vlamingh's predecessor Abel Janszoon Tasman. Cook's voyages are said to have finally put to rest the obsession with the existence of a southern continent. Regardless, Cook still puzzled over origins, and a great deal of his time was spent determining the boundary of sea and land, or in other words of pretending to be on land when he was on sea. He put his training in land surveying to good use. His technique of coastal surveying was to trace the coastline as the ship proceeded around it, in a running survey, by taking a series of measurements in relation to the position of coastal landmarks which were visible from on board. In practice this meant an estimation of the coastline from the track of the ship. As Richard Sorrenson writes in an influential article: 'With such a method he could construct a map by using the ship to probe and skirt around, yet never touch the coastline.'[29] Even the arch-empiricist Cook therefore had to undertake some dream work in order to set on paper a line which demarcated land and sea, and which meant that his ship, which was the platform of his vision, disappeared from the result. The materiality of the Pacific also played a role here: the terrain determined how close his ships could run to the land and therefore impacted on the resulting maps.

★ ★ ★

Once the thesis of the missing southern continent had been dismissed, Europe's fascination fragmented, as it became attached to more discrete geographical spaces – to paradise islands, which were sometimes taken as indicators of lost continents. Indeed, to pick up one of the themes of the *Kumulipo*, perhaps the most pervasive question which engaged scientists in the Pacific through the course of the nineteenth century concerned the development of coral atolls.

By the time of Cook's voyages, the question of the formation of coral islands had already come to prominence as a significant philosophical problem amongst Europeans in the Pacific.[30] The German Lutheran naturalist Johann Reinhold Forster, who accompanied Cook on his second voyage, devoted a chapter in his *Observations Made During a Voyage Round the World* (1778) to a 'Theory of the Formation of Isles'. The chapter was placed in a section devoted to 'changes in the globe', and this signals the broader intellectual context in which this puzzle was located through the course of the century to follow. Working out how small fragments of land rose and fell became central to working out the dynamics of the earth's crust, and deciding between gradualist and catastrophist theories. Forster spent a good deal of space describing the action of volcanoes, after observing an erupting volcano at Tanna, and noted how volcanoes were often placed close to the sea. The volcano at Tanna was causing 'a great revolution', 'the soil of the whole island had been altered by the continued fall of ashes'.[31] Forster also speculated on changes in the level of the sea. He divided islands into two classes: those that were low-lying and those which reached a higher altitude. He asserted that low-lying islands emerged as a result of the work of sea creatures, 'the polype-like animals forming the lithophytes'. As shells, weeds, sand and coral accumulated, according to Forster, a bird or the sea vegetated such a reef. Meanwhile, higher islands were formed by earthquakes and volcanoes. Pacific traditions played a role in Forster's formulation. He cited the 'mythology' of the Pacific to show how islanders also held that catastrophes had been critical to the formation of islands: 'they have not forgotten that their habitations formerly were parts of a great continent, destroyed by earthquakes, and a violent flood, which [their account of] the dragging of the land through the sea seems to indicate'.[32]

More than fifty years later, when Charles Darwin was voyaging through the Pacific, he inherited these intellectual contours. The experience of travel and the changing tides of sea and land shaped the kinds of questions that Darwin asked and led him to the deep history of the whole earth and its peoples. Darwin did not bring with him a fully worked-out scientific agenda and this allowed the living Pacific to direct his course. As with Forster, witnessing natural catastrophes had a decisive impact on Darwin's geological ramblings. Darwin observed the effect of earthquakes along the coast of Chile. In January 1835, he witnessed Mount Osorno erupting, and about three months later in Concepción, a tidal wave damaged most of the buildings: '[t]he ruins of Concepción is a most awful spectacle of desolation'.[33] In the aftermath, in Concepción, his companion Captain Robert FitzRoy repeated a survey that he had previously undertaken to find that the land had been raised. It was these experiences in South America and the stimulus they gave to Darwin's attempt to imagine the geological structure of the whole subcontinent that led him in the end to the question of the formation of Pacific islands. In travelling through the Pacific, Darwin was struck by the absence of land. For instance, after the voyage, in December 1837, he wrote to the geologist Charles Lyell: 'People's ideas of the Pacific are most false. – In the thick archipelagos – in a long days sail, you will often only see one or two islands...But then there are spaces of some hundred miles without an island of any kind.'[34] Given the proximity of South America to the Pacific, Darwin was led to a set of paired ideas: if land was rising in the former, it was surely sinking in the latter.

Lyell held that coral reefs were structures rising on slightly submerged volcanoes. Darwin grew sceptical about this claim, and in 1836 he wrote to his sister that it was a 'monstrous hypothesis'.[35] In response to Lyell's views, Darwin developed the hypothesis that fringing reefs, barrier reefs and atolls were the evolutionary stages of islands, indicating not the rise in land but the descent of the seabed beneath (Figure 11.4).[36] In an account framed later in life, he explained how he came to this theory:

> No other work of mine was begun in so deductive a spirit as this; for the whole theory was thought out on the west coast of S. America before I had seen a true coral reef. I had therefore only to verify and extend my views by a careful examination of living reefs.[37]

Yet this retrospective explanation obscures his practical methods of observation and how his views were forged in situ. His theoretical work was neither fully deductive nor inductive. One critical stop in the development of his ideas of coral reefs was at Cocos-Keeling atoll

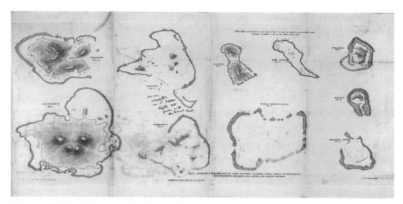

*Figure 11.4* 'Shewing the Resemblance in Form Between Barrier Coral-Reefs Surrounding Mountainous Islands and Atolls or Lagoon-Islands', in Charles Darwin, *The Structure and Distribution of Coral Reefs* (London, 1842). This image is from Darwin's own copy and shows an annotation made by him in the centre of the plate, which reads: 'Since Completed in the 2o voyage. Depth not given in the historical part.'

in the Indian Ocean. In writing about the appearance of the atoll, he noted the need to see in a different way: 'It is not a wonder which at first strikes the eye of the body, but rather after reflection, the eye of reason.' Darwin gave an example of how the eye needed to work:

> Hence we must consider this Isl$^d$ as the summit of a lofty mountain; to how great a depth or thickness the work of the Coral animal extends is quite uncertain ... We see certain Is$^{ds}$ in the Pacifick, such as Tahiti & Eimeo, mentioned in this journal which are encircled by a Coral reef separated from the shore by channels & basins of still water ... Hence if we imagine such an Island, after long successive intervals to subside a few feet, in a manner similar, but a movement opposite to the continent of S. America; the coral would be continued upwards, rising from the foundation of the encircling reef. In time the central land would sink beneath the level of the sea & disappear, but the coral would have completed its circular wall. Should we not then have a Lagoon Island? – Under this view, we must look at a Lagoon Is$^d$ as a monument raised by myriads of tiny architects, to mark the spot where a former land lies buried in the depths of the ocean.[38]

The kind of vision that is entailed here is at least triangulated: in the sense that it reached out from Cocos-Keeling to South America and Tahiti, to set up a three-point contrast. Indeed his published journal sought to link a whole array of other spots in the mind as he consolidated his theory about how the 'inter-tropical ocean', can be 'divided into linear and parallel bands' which denote elevation and subsidence.[39] Looking at an island from out at sea is still significant to the practice of vision. Yet looking at an island requires a calibration of what it looked like in time, and over long intervals. It is suggestive to interpret Darwin's manner of looking at islands alongside the seeing practised by those in search of the missing continent in the South Seas. Indeed, his views continued to be debated alongside theoretical speculations that the islands of the Pacific had been connected in bygone eras by missing continents, and that this was the only way to explain some similarities in the natural history of the islands. This was a view that Darwin – in the end – did not accept: '... why not extend a continent to every island in the Pacific & Atlantic oceans!'[40]

If this bears out the intricacies of sight involved in Darwin's *Beagle* voyage, this does not yet support the argument that such a style of thought was cosmological. The broader context of debate about coral islands which drew in more religious questions of human origins is helpful in adding a further layer to these claims. Darwin's views on coral reefs certainly came to dominate geology, especially after his publication of *The Structure and Distribution of Coral Reefs* (1842). Arguably, the reception of this work fell alongside a popular and religious fascination with corals in Britain in this period.[41] The link between Darwin and religion in the Pacific lies with his interaction with missionaries.[42] It is worth noting that the naturalist's first publication, together with FitzRoy, was a defence of the missionaries of the South Pacific.[43] One key text written by these South Pacific missionaries and which became a bestseller was John Williams' *A Narrative of Missionary Enterprises* (1837). Williams served as an informant for Darwin.[44] The first edition of Williams's book came out two years before he was killed in Erromango, Vanuatu. After his martyrdom, sales rocketed as a 'People's Edition' was issued. In *A Narrative,* Williams classified the islands as volcanic, crystal and coral, and commented on the views of the geologists William Buckland and Lyell. Ideologically, he sought to twin scripture with the new science of geology. Referring explicitly to the 'little coral insect', that creature of recurring scientific interest, he noted: 'if we come to the study of natural phenomena, with minds unchilled by scepticism or infidelity, we shall be led to sublime religious contemplations ...'[45] He concluded that the islands remained in the same way that they had been left after the Biblical deluge, and that corals were formed by insects who moulded the carbonate of lime from evaporated salt water. Elsewhere in *A Narrative*, the improving possibilities held out by corals were aptly illustrated. One of the most memorable passages related to how coral

could be burnt to lime, which could then be used to plaster missionary buildings in white, a significant achievement given the colour
coding of Christian salvation as a 'whitening' process. Williams wrote
of the reaction of the people of Raiatea:

> Early on the next morning, they all hastened to see this wonderful
> sight. The chiefs and common people, men, women, and children,
> hurried to the spot: and when the covering was removed a sheet of
> beautifully white plastering was presented to their astonished view. All
> pressed forward to examine it; some smelling it, some scratching it,
> whilst others took stones and struck it, exclaiming, as they retired,
> 'Wonderful, wonderful! The very stones in the sea, and the sand on
> the shore, become good property, in the hands of those who worship
> the true God and regard his good word.'[46]

Despite the religious furore that erupted around Darwin's works, out
in the Pacific and in works concerned with this ocean, science and
religion could interact in this manner.

The cosmological strain – wanting to find oneself and one's place in
time and space by engaging with the Pacific – was sustained in the
work of later scientists of the Pacific, who responded to Darwin's views
well into the end of the nineteenth century. Directly in Darwin's wake
came the first American-government-led exploration of the Pacific,
the US Exploring Expedition under the command of Lieut. Charles
Wilkes, with the geologist James Dwight Dana on board. Dana
published a competing text to Darwin's work on corals titled *On Coral
Reefs and Islands* (1853), which came out in a new edition in 1872.
Fundamentally, Dana agreed with Darwin's theory, but they disagreed
on some minor points; Dana insisted that there had been recent uplift
on coral reefs where there had been subsidence in the past and that sea
temperature was a controlling factor in the distribution of coral reefs.[47]
After becoming a more zealous Christian in 1837, Dana sought to
place his geology in the light of a scriptural history of the earth. He
postulated that the geological shape of continents was related to the
distribution of oceans: '[m]ost plainly that the extent and positions of
the oceanic depressions have some way determined, in a great degree,
the features of the land; that the same cause which originated in one,
impressed particularities on the other; that the two had a parallel
history through past time – the oceanic depressions tending down-
ward, the continents upward'.[48] His explanation of this patterning
bore the strains of natural theology – the contemporary argument of
nature's artifice by a deity – the patterning had arisen from the effect
of 'a systematic untiring force', 'a unity of cause' and 'a common system

of structure'.[49] In this manner, Dana's Pacific travels set the context for a theory of 'the characteristics of our globe', which was cosmological.

Interest and discord over reefs carried through into the third quarter of the nineteenth century. The debate widened in the aftermath of the contentions of the oceanographer John Murray on the British *Challenger* expedition to the Pacific from 1872 to 1876, which fed into the efforts of the Board of Genealogy of Hawai'i, and who held that stable islands lay beneath corals. This led to an appeal on Darwin's part for borings to be made in the Pacific to determine once and for all how coral islands were formed, and three expeditions were sent to Funafuti. The reason why so much attention was given to coral atolls was because a solution could publicise the explanatory power of Darwinism.[50] Yet it was only in 1952, in the context of preparations for nuclear bomb testing by the US Atomic Energy Commission, with drillings deeper than four thousand feet, in the Enewetak atoll in the Marshall Islands, that the scientific puzzle was finally 'solved' in Darwin's favour.[51]

The long-running coral reef question emerged out of attempts to place the Pacific Ocean against adjoining landmasses. It picked up Judaeo-Christian concerns through the course of the century – and its theorisation was not simply the work of empiricism, but about seeing things in a certain way. Throughout these long decades the physical changes and make-up of the Pacific were critical in shaping science and taking thinkers down routes they did not anticipate.

\* \* \*

Looking into the twentieth century, the Pacific Ocean has not only been a place where the human and global past is worked out, but where the future of the planet is fought over, and, in part, determined. Critically, advances in science and technology have meant that humans have amassed the power to change the shape of islands in the Pacific. They have also become more aware of their effect on the islands and the seas, and the long-term consequences those effects bring. Of course, science has always been an instrumental concern for peoples and theorists in the Pacific – witness the writing of the missionaries – but that instrumentality has intensified.

At 7.15 a.m. on 1 November 1952, a detonation on the Marshall Islands code-named 'Mike' burst into the sky.[52] This was the world's first test of a hydrogen bomb, and it was the eighth of 43 nuclear tests at Enewetak 'that transformed a placid atoll into a moonscape'.[53] Mike was 693 times more powerful than the bomb dropped on Hiroshima, and a cloud of secrecy surrounded it because of the US Presidential elections three days later. Mike totally vapourised the coral island of Elugelab. In its place there appeared a huge hole – 6,240 feet across and 164 feet deep – in the reef. More islands disappeared in March 1954, when the largest US nuclear explosion code-named Bravo was conducted again in the Marshall Islands, in Bikini atoll. As one commentator put it: 'Years later, some Bikinian leaders would return to Bikini and weep openly at the sight of sandbars and open water, all that remained of the islands destroyed by the Bravo shot. They would declare that the islands had "lost their bones".'[54] The Marshallese have not recovered from these tests, and their health continues to be grievously tainted by them.[55] Ironically, a tomb to Elugelab was created in the late 1970s, after a clean-up of Enewetak atoll. It contains 110,000 cubic yards of contaminated material stuffed into the hole created by the bomb and cased in cement, where it remains as Runit Dome.

The race for nuclear testing in the Pacific was run between a series of states – the United States, Britain and France. At its core was the idea of the Pacific as isolated and empty: nuclear weapons could be conveniently tested here, away from the gaze of the world and without creating victims. Yet this has been a myth, for the Pacific explosions have undoubtedly changed our world in physical terms. They have left a stamp on our bodies. This transformative power is as significant as their political legacy in the Cold War. In visual terms, the way in which these explosions were said to remake the world can be traced through their most common trope, the mushroom cloud. In April 1954 *Time* magazine published a black and white image of the Mike explosion on its cover, and colour images followed. *Life* magazine also ran images of the explosion. *Time* wrote of how people watched the '100-mile wide cauliflower' blaze from planes and ships. What did this explosion conjure to its observers, if for us it is an image of horror? The very fact that people were watching it is significant – for an argument can be made that these photographs neutralised the public view of the bomb, they were meant to create a spectacle and so to erase the tragic environmental consequences and to nullify the significance of the physical site of the Pacific in which the explosions took place.[56] The iconography of the spectacular which operated here was a cosmic one: explosions were interpreted as procreative, in harnessing the fundamental powers of the universe, whilst at the same time holding the awful potential to extinguish the earth.[57] The islands of the Pacific had once again become a site for playing out of a game of destiny. The represented materiality of the Pacific was central to why these events took place in that location – and yet the materiality of the sea of islands was itself being changed as never before.

The thread from Darwinian thought to the late twentieth-century age of science in the Pacific also lies in another set of concerns which congeal around issues of environmental vulnerability. The discussion of the level of the sea, which engaged Darwin and Dana, carries on in scientific work about global warming. Coral reefs and the states located on them are especially vulnerable to rises in carbon dioxide and temperature that accompany this new era of the Earth, as well as the more intense pressures of fishing and other human activity.[58] As one recent group of scientists has written: 'A major concern is that the accelerating rate of environmental change could exceed the evolutionary capacity of coral ... to adapt.'[59] Scientists forecast that many low-lying states such as Tuvalu and Kiribati, where land rarely exceeds two metres above sea level, will become uninhabitable, and the category of 'climate refugees' is increasingly applied to some Pacific peoples. For instance, in 2001 the Earth Policy Institute based in Washington, DC, wrote that Tuvalu was 'the first country where people are trying to evacuate because of rising seas'.[60] This discursive view of Pacific peoples as weak and vulnerable is also evident in initiatives arising out of Australia and New Zealand, where calls have been heard for the inhabitants of Tuvalu to 'sink or swim'. Of course, both Australia and New Zealand have long histories of receiving reluctant migrants from environmentally devastated islands, even as Australia's ratification of the Kyoto Protocol was delayed until 2007. With this plight facing the Pacific, Islanders have spoken on the predicament of their future. They have objected to the view that their homes can be sacrificed and that they themselves can move elsewhere. They have called on the world not to give up on the possibility of reversing the consequences of climate change and not to take the sovereignty of island states too lightly. Tuvaluans have rejected the discourses that have been applied to them both by industrialised polluting states and climate activists. In the words of one Pacific ambassador to the UN: 'We are not going to go quietly.'[61]

★ ★ ★

In these encounters about climate change, the Pacific has become a place of the future, inasmuch as it had earlier served as a site where the Earth's deep history had been contemplated. Throughout this history, the Pacific has been a space for working out the relations between land and sea. This links all the episodes which I have covered, an intentional choice which illustrates the continuity of contours of thought in and about the Pacific. Such continuity hints at the role of the Pacific as a living agent. Debates have come and gone – such as the search for the missing continent or questions of subsidence and elevation – but throughout these intellectual tussles, humans from different times and cultural positions have sought to comprehend themselves and humankind in the Pacific. Sight has been critical here – and seeing, like thinking, has been cosmological. We have witnessed theorists engaging in an intensely subjective manner with the shores they have encountered. The reason why this kind of deep intellectual work has happened here is not because the Pacific is blank, waiting for ideas from the outside to be painted over it. Rather, the materiality of the Pacific has framed and directed these forms of work, by determining modes of surveying, geology and physics, and taking thinkers into lines of thought they did not anticipate. In these ways, the Pacific has played a critical role in birthing science, not in a singular site but in the range of its islands and beaches, chapels and *marea*, craters and reefs.

This is not an essentialist argument about the character of the Pacific as a unit in the history of science, but an attempt to respect its own materiality in narratives of intellectual history. Such materiality lies in its patterning of islands separated by a vast sea, and in its human and non-human life tied as they are to long-term genealogy. Importantly, given the argument this chapter seeks to displace, the Pacific is an inhabited materiality. Of course, other regions of the world – such as the Caribbean or the Arctic – have also generated quests for origin, and I do not aim to raise the Pacific above its rivals, but rather to point to the particularity and persistence of the questions which have been asked here.[62] This materiality has not been static: rather the dynamism of geological, climatic and evolutionary change has been critical for the work undertaken here. At the same time the productive placement of this materiality in human thinking has changed over time. It is undeniable that as time has passed increasing powers have been wielded over the living Pacific by science and technology. Nuclear bombs, fishing and industrial pollution, within the region and far away, are starting to impact on the Pacific as never before. While the Pacific has always changed, these alterations are of a different order. Even then, it is important in thinking of these new challenges to avoid objectifying or victimising the expansive Pacific world.

## Notes

For particularly close and insightful readings of this chapter, I thank Simon Schaffer, James A. Secord, Alistair Sponsel and my graduate students.

1. Roy MacLeod and Philip F. Rehbock, eds., *Nature in its Greatest Extent: Western Science in the Pacific* (Honolulu, 1988), pp. 1 ff. For more on the historiographical consensus and the need to attend to indigenous knowledges, see the introduction to Tony Ballantyne, ed., *Science, Empire*

*and the European Exploration of the Pacific* (Aldershot, 2004); compare Damon Salesa, 'The Pacific in Indigenous Time', ch. 2 in this volume.

2. This claim should be qualified. There has undoubtedly been substantial reflection already on how the Pacific impacted on scientific thought: see, for instance, Janet Browne, *Charles Darwin: Voyaging* (London, 2003) or Iain McCalman, *Darwin's Armada: Four Voyages and the Battle for the Theory of Evolution* (London, 2010).

3. Simon Schaffer, Lissa Roberts, Kapil Raj and James Delbourgo, eds., *The Brokered World: Go-betweens and Global Intelligence, 1770–1820* (Sagamore Beach, MA, 2009). See also the work on Tupaia and his engagement with James Cook: David Turnbull, '(En)-Countering Knowledge Traditions: The Story of Cook and Tupaia', in Ballantyne, ed., *Science, Empire and the European Exploration of the Pacific,* pp. 225–46.

4. The concern with cosmology on all sides has also recently been highlighted in Simon Schaffer, 'In Transit: European Cosmologies in the Pacific', in Kate Fullagar, ed., *The Atlantic World in the Antipodes: Effects and Transformations since the Eighteenth Century* (Newcastle upon Tyne, 2012), pp. 70–93.

5. Sujit Sivasundaram, 'Sciences and the Global: On Methods, Questions and Theory', *Isis* 101 (2010), 146–58.

6. See, for instance, Niel Gunson, 'Understanding Polynesian Traditional History', *Journal of Pacific History* 28 (1993), 139–58.

7. Margaret Jolly, 'Imagining Oceania: Indigenous and Foreign Representations of a Sea of Islands', *The Contemporary Pacific* 19 (2007), 515.

8. This account of *Kumulipo* relies primarily on Noenoe K. Silva, *Aloha Betrayed: Native Hawaiian Resistance to American Colonialism* (Durham, NC, 2004), esp. pp. 97–104, and *The Kumulipo: A Hawaiian Creation Chant*, ed. and trans. Martha Warren Beckwith (Chicago, 1951).

9. Lilikalʻa Kameʻeleihiwa, *Native Land and Foreign Desires: How Shall We Live in Harmony?* (Honolulu, 1992), p. 3.

10. Queen Liliʻuokalani, *An Account of the Creation of the World According to Hawaiian Tradition* (Boston, 1897).

11. *The Kumulipo*, pp. 58–9.

12. Valero Valeri, *Kingship and Sacrifice: Ritual and Society in Ancient Hawaii*, trans. Paula Wissing (Chicago, 1985), p. 5.

13. Valeri, *Kingship and Sacrifice*, p. 6.

14. Silva, *Aloha Betrayed*, p. 97.

15. *Hoike a ka Papa Kuauhau o na Alii Hawaii* = *Report of the Board of Genealogy of the Hawaiian Chiefs* (Honolulu, 1884), pp. 12, 14–15.

16. For more on this see Gunson, 'Understanding'.

17. David Malo, *Hawaiian Antiquities (Moolelo Hawaii)*, trans. Nathaniel Bright Emerson (Honolulu, 1898), p. viii. See also *The Kumulipo*, p. 2, for Malo's training.

18. Jon Kamakawiwoʻoele Osorio, *Dismembering Lāhui: A History of the Hawaiian Nation to 1897* (Honolulu, 2002), pp. 14–15.

19. Malo, *Hawaiian Antiquities*, pp. 3–4. Note that this is Nathaniel Emerson's translation.

20. This section relies heavily on William Eisler, *The Furthest Shore: Images of Terra Australis from the Middle Ages to Captain Cook* (Cambridge, 1995).
21. O. H. K. Spate, '"South Sea" to "Pacific Ocean": A Note on Nomenclature', *Journal of Pacific History* 12 (1977), 205–11.
22. Quoted in Eisler, *Furthest Shore,* p. 34.
23. Günter Schilder, *The Southland Explored: The Voyage of Willem Hesselsz. de Vlamingh in 1696–97, with the Coastal Profiles and a Chart of Western Australia in Full-size Colour Reproduction* (Alphen aan den Rijn, 1984), p. 18.
24. Schilder, *The Southland Explored,* p. 27.
25. Schilder, *The Southland Explored,* pp. 13–14.
26. Günter Schilder, 'New Holland: The Dutch Discoveries', in Glyndwr Williams and Alan Frost, eds., *Terra Australis to Australia* (Melbourne, 1988), p. 111.
27. Cited in Schilder, *The Southland Explored,* p. 14.
28. Schilder, *The Southland Explored,* pp. 15–16.
29. Richard Sorrenson, 'The Ship as Scientific Instrument', *Osiris* 2nd ser., 11 (1996), 230.
30. For the long history of coral reef formation, see David R. Stoddart, 'Darwin, Lyell and the Geological Significance of Coral Reefs', *British Journal for the History of Science* 9 (1976), 199–218. The following discussion of coral reef science up to Dana also draws on David R. Stoddart, '"This Coral Episode": Darwin, Dana and the Coral Reefs of the Pacific', in Roy MacLeod and Philip F. Rehbock, eds. *Darwin's Laboratory: Evolutionary Theory and Natural History in the Pacific* (Honolulu, 1994), pp. 21–48.
31. J. R. Forster, *Observations Made during a Voyage Round the World* (London, 1778), p. 145.
32. Forster, *Observations,* p. 159.
33. Charles Darwin to W. D. Fox, [7–11] March 1835, Christ's College Library, Cambridge, Fox 47, in *The Correspondence of Charles Darwin,* gen. eds. Frederick Burkhardt and Sydney Smith, 19 vols. to date (Cambridge, 1985– ), I, p. 433.
34. Charles Darwin to Charles Lyell, 19(?) December 1837, American Philosophical Society, Philadelphia, APS 9, in *The Correspondence of Charles Darwin,* II, p. 65.
35. Charles Darwin to Caroline Darwin, 29 April 1836, Cambridge University Library, CUL: DAR 223:34, in *The Correspondence of Charles Darwin,* I, p. 495.
36. This draws on a short essay by Frederick Burkhardt, 'Darwin's Early Notes on Coral Reefs', republished online as 'Darwin & Coral Reefs', Darwin Correspondence Project, http://www.darwinproject.ac.uk/darwin-coral-reefs, accessed 13 February 2013.
37. Charles Darwin, 'Recollections of the Development of my Mind and Character', Cambridge University Library, CUL: DAR26.1–121, p. 76.
38. Charles Darwin, *Charles Darwin's Beagle Diary,* ed. Richard Darwin Keynes (Cambridge, 1988), p. 418 (entry for 12 April 1836).

39. Charles Darwin, *Journal and Remarks, 1832–1836*, in Robert FitzRoy and Darwin, *Narrative of the Surveying Voyages of His Majesty's Ships Adventure and Beagle, Between the Years 1826 and 1836*, 4 vols (London, 1839), III, p. 569.

40. Charles Darwin to Charles Lyell, 16 June 1856, American Philosophical Society, AP 131, in *The Correspondence of Charles Darwin*, VI, p. 144. For Darwin on missing continents, see E. Alison Kay, 'Darwin's Biogeography and the Oceanic Islands of the Central Pacific, 1859–1909', in MacLeod and Rehbock, eds. *Darwin's Laboratory*, pp. 49–69.

41. Katharine Anderson, 'Coral Jewellery', *Victorian Review* 34 (2008), 47–52.

42. Janet Browne, 'Missionaries and the Human Mind: Charles Darwin and Robert FitzRoy', in MacLeod and Rehbock, eds. *Darwin's Laboratory*, pp. 263–82.

43. Robert FitzRoy and Charles Darwin, 'A Letter, Containing Remarks on the Moral State of Tahiti, New Zealand, &c.' (28 June 1836), in *Charles Darwin's Shorter Publications, 1829–1883*, ed. John van Wyhe (Cambridge, 2009), pp. 15–31.

44. Sujit Sivasundaram, *Nature and the Godly Empire: Science and Evangelical Mission in the Pacific, 1795–1850* (Cambridge, 2005).

45. John Williams, *A Narrative of Missionary Enterprises in the South Sea Islands* (London, 1837), p. 25

46. Williams, *Narrative of Missionary Enterprises,* p. 76.

47. The summary of Dana draws on Stoddart, '"This Coral Episode"'; see also David Igler, 'On Coral Reefs, Volcanoes, Gods, and Patriotic Geology: Or, James Dwight Dana Assembles the Pacific Basin', *Pacific Historical Review* 79 (2010), 23–49.

48. James Dwight Dana, 'Plan of Development in the Geological History of North America with a Map', republished in Dana, *Science and the Bible: A Review of "The Six Days of Creation" of Prof. Tayler Lewis* (Andover, MA, 1856), pp. 4–5.

49. Dana, 'Plan of Development', p. 5.

50. Roy MacLeod, 'Imperial Reflections in the Southern Seas: The Funafuti Expeditions, 1896–1904', in MacLeod and Philip F. Rehbock, eds., *Nature in its Greatest Extent: Western Science in the Pacific* (Honolulu, 1988), pp. 159–94.

51. MacLeod, 'Imperial Reflections'.

52. For more on the context for nuclear test explosions in the Pacific, see Mark D. Merlin and Ricardo M. Gonzàlez, 'Environmental Impacts of Nuclear Testing in Remote Oceania, 1946–1996', in J. R. McNeill and Corinna R. Unger, eds., *Environmental Histories of the Cold War* (Cambridge, 2010), pp. 167–202; see also Ryan Tucker Jones, 'The Environment', ch. 6 in this volume.

53. This is to quote the award-winning journalist who researches and writes on this topic, Beverly Deepe Keever, 'Un-Remembered Origins of "Nuclear Holocaust": World's First Thermonuclear Explosion, November 1, 1952' originally published by *Honolulu Weekly*, now online at: www.wagingpeace.

org/articles/2004/05/24_keever_origins–nuclear–holocaust.htm, accessed
15 August 2012.

54. Richard N. Salvador, 'The Nuclear History of Micronesia and the Pacific'
online at: www.wagingpeace.org/articles/1999/08/00_salvador_microne-
sia.htm, accessed 15 August 2012.

55. See Keever, 'Un-Remembered Origins'.

56. This is the argument of Scott Kirsch, 'Watching the Bombs Go Off:
Photography, Nuclear Landscapes and Spectator Democracy', *Antipode* 29
(1997), 227–55.

57. For some thought on this see Peggy Rosenthal, 'The Nuclear Mushroom
Cloud as Cultural Image', *American Literary History* 3 (1991), 63–92.

58. For a very valuable overview of the changing idea of coral reefs in science
from 'mysterious, powerful and resilient' to 'fragile', see Alistair Sponsel,
'From Cook to Cousteau: The Many Lives of Coral Reefs', in John Gillis
and Franziska Torma, eds., *Fluid Frontiers: Exploring Oceans, Islands, and
Coastal Environments* (forthcoming).

59. T. P. Hughes, et al. 'Climate Change, Human Impacts and the Resilience
of Coral Reefs', *Science* 301 (2003), 930.

60. Karen Elizabeth McNamara and Chris Gibson, '"We do not want to leave
our land": Pacific Ambassadors at the United Nations Resist the Category
of "Climate Refugees"', *Geoforum* 40 (2009), 478; Carol Farbotko and
Heather Lazrus, 'The First Climate Refugees? Contesting Global
Narratives of Climate Change in Tuvalu', *Global Environmental Change* 22
(2012), 382–90.

61. Quoted in McNamara and Gibson, '"We do not want to leave our
land"', 481.

62. For treatment of the Caribbean along these lines, see Richard Drayton,
'Maritime Networks and the Making of Knowledge', in David Cannadine,
ed., *Empire, the Sea and Global History: Britain's Maritime World, c. 1760–c. 1840*
(Basingstoke, 2007), pp. 72–82.

# Part IV: Identities

# 12

# Race

## James Belich

Historically meaningful oceanic 'worlds' require a human filament to connect their islands and beaches. The Pacific first became such a world with the voyages of the Polynesians, beginning several thousand years ago. Polynesian long-range voyaging had declined by 1500 CE, but at its peak it linked most of the great ocean, from the sub-Antarctic Auckland Islands in the south to Hawai'i in the north. Research is now confirming that Polynesians reached South America too, and one might add that a cousin culture reached East Africa – a staggering Neolithic globalisation.[1] A second Pacific world was inaugurated soon after 1500, when Iberians appeared on the eastern and western Pacific coasts, and connected the two from 1571 with the annual voyages of the Manila galleon from the Philippines to Mexico. Over the next three centuries, the islands and beaches of the Pacific were increasingly linked together and to the rest of the world. Europeans instituted these linkages, but Asians, Amerindians and Pacific Islanders used them too. Did Europeans bring racism into this Pacific world, like a snake into the garden? Was it with them when they arrived, or did it emerge thereafter, perhaps with the help of their Pacific experience? How important was the Pacific to racism, and racism to Pacific history?

Racism is the delusion that cultures have natures, combined with the ranking of these natures with one's own on top. Hard racism opines that the natures and rankings never change, except in cosmetic or trivial ways. Soft racism allows that both can 'improve', implying that all humans are prospective equals. Some feel that this is not racism at all. But racial equality was often a distant prospect, dangled in front of aspirants like the hare in front of a racing greyhound. It required that 'inferior' races become more like 'superior' races, 'improving' solely in the judgement of the latter.

Many scholars argue that, until about 1800, Europeans used the term 'race' to mean simply lineage or descent group, and that this was not necessarily racist.[2] On the other hand, a new strand of scholarship is suggesting that one could have racism without 'race'. Here, it is useful to distinguish between racial theory, a realm of the intellectual history of ideas, and racial ideology, a matter of the social history of ideas. Racial theories emerged among European savants around 1775, and flowered between about 1840 and 1945. Their grip on the public varied from substantial to minimal, and their claims to be science were often risible in their own present, let alone ours. But they did seek to explain, even predict, relations between peoples, and paid lip service to such things as evidence and consistency. Racial ideology, popular value-laden preconceptions about the natures of cultures, began earlier and lasted longer. It was not concerned about science or logical consistency; it tended to be driven by its utility in particular historical contexts; and it allied with theory when convenient. One might assume that ideology flowed from theory, but history suggests that the reverse was the case. Scholars who focus exclusively on racial theory, the discourse of elites, deal only with the tip of an iceberg.

Racial ideology seems to have emerged in Spain in the fifteenth century, in the shape of the idea of 'impurity of blood'.[3] Muslims and Jews had long been seen as inferior, dangerous and deluded, but salvageable through conversion and assimilation, at least over several generations. In the fifteenth century, their vice and inferiority came to be seen as intrinsic and eradicable, resulting in their expulsion, converted or not. During the sixteenth century, in an illogical but useful slippage typical of racial ideology, the idea of 'impurity of blood' was gradually transferred to Native Americans and black Africans. 'In the course of the first century of colonization, mixed parentage, such as being mulatto, came to be viewed in the New World as a "stain" akin to having Jewish ancestors.[4] As always, racial stereotypes worked both ways. The impure were cursed by vice and inferiority across the generations, while the pure were blessed with virtue and superiority, also in the long run – even if only their great-grandparents had been born in Europe. A measure of the social grip of this idea is the degree of insistence on female endogamy. Whatever European men might do, this thinking went, European women should breed with European men only, so preserving the 'purity of the blood' and the 'European-ness' of settler societies.

On this argument, racist ideology arrived on the Pacific shore, in Spanish America in 1513, well before racist theory. But were Europeans the Pacific's only racists? From the nineteenth century, peoples such as the Japanese certainly adopted racism when it seemed useful, but did it exist earlier, independent of Europeans? I am uncertain about Aztec and Inca societies, but racism seems absent from the traditional tribal societies of the Pacific's coasts and islands. These peoples had their prejudices, and their self-defining denigrations of Others, and a few adopted select European racial ideas from the nineteenth century, though with less dire consequences than the Japanese. But they were typically happy to adopt strangers into their communities, temporarily or permanently, without bias against the offspring.

The most numerous inhabitants of the second Pacific world were the Chinese, and they were always important players in it – as consumers and producers, as migrants, and, in Taiwan and the South China coast, as settlers. Scholarship on their 'racial' attitudes suggests a long-standing categorisation. First came Han or Han-like Chinese, the blessed inhabitants of the Middle Kingdom. Second and third came two categories of barbarians: 'cooked' or semi-civilised, who were quite Han-like, and 'raw' or uncivilised, who were not. This seems similar to the Polynesian tendency to divide their world into kin, neighbour and stranger zones, and is compatible with soft racism at worst.[5]

> Chinese racialism drew sharp distinctions between peoples, and almost always assumed a hierarchy of superiority and inferiority. Unlike much modern Western racism, however, these distinctions did not have to be based on skin colour or physiognomy, and did not invoke genetic inferiority or pretensions to science. This racialist perspective had more environmental than genetic foundations.[6]

But it transpires that the Chinese story is more complicated. Recently, scholars have documented moments of hard racism in Chinese writings, especially with regard to certain barbarians on the Yunnan frontier. These peoples refused to be cooked and resisted the oven violently and vigorously. The Yao, in particular, mounted a stubborn resistance to the Ming Dynasty between the 1440s and the 1560s, and continued to resist Sinicisation thereafter. In response, some Chinese officials dismissed them as uncookable – intractable savages who had to be driven off or exterminated. 'Their natural disposition already set, they cannot be transformed by teaching.'[7] Here we have ideological hard racism, triggered by stubborn resistance. The situation changed with the advent of the Manchu or Qing dynasty in the midseventeenth century. Technically barbarians themselves, they were sensitive to the idea that some barbarians were uncivilisable, and tried to suppress it – an intriguing anti-racist imperialism. But some Chinese officials proved as stubborn as the Yao.[8]

China might have lacked much in the way of racial theory; it did have hard racial ideology. But it differed from Europe in that its racism was not exported very far. There is no doubt that when Europe began to spread in the fifteenth century, its capacity for global expansion was far exceeded by that of China. The seven remarkable voyages of Zheng He between 1405 and 1433, once neglected, are now a compulsory vignette in global histories, and they deserve to be. Long-range voyages ceased thereafter and, implausible theories aside, never extended far into the Pacific. But China remained a key player in the Pacific world. Europeans used expansion to integrate space; the Chinese preferred magnetic attraction. Until the nineteenth century, China was the leading manufacturer of prime trade goods, notably silk and porcelain. They had no use for other peoples' manufactures in exchange, and instead wanted silver or luxuries from the wild, such as shark fin and sea cucumber, pearls and furs. Chinese proxies probed quite deep into the Pacific in search of these luxuries. From the sixteenth century, the Chinese allowed Europeans and their slaves to do the global dirty work. Europeans were happy to oblige, and diligently shipped furs, silver and American biota to Canton and Macau in return for silk, porcelain and, later, tea. As early as 1600, the Chinese had acquired American sweet potatoes, maize and peanuts, together with much of the output of American silver mines. The route from Acapulco to Mexico City was known as 'the China Road', and broken porcelain served as currency along it.[9] In the 1790s, Russians slaughtering sea otters in the sub-Arctic Pacific, and Anglos slaughtering fur seals in the sub-Antarctic had a market in common: China. You did not need to move to globalise.

The Chinese did migrate, but they preferred to return home to be buried with their ancestors, women migrants were few, and the total numbers were tiny compared to the home population. At the peak, 30 million Chinese migrated in the nineteenth and early twentieth centuries.[10] But of these, 25.4 million went to nearby Manchuria, and of these, in turn, 16.7 million returned home.[11] Earlier Chinese migration, to Southeast Asia for example, had more expansive potential. It was small in scale but this was also true of early European migration. It created one overseas neo-China, in Taiwan from the seventeenth century, and could have created others if more women had migrated, and metropolitan support had been forthcoming. But it was not. When Chinese merchants were attacked by locals in Vietnam in 1076, the Sung state 'was prepared to offer limited financial assistance to refugees', but only 'once they returned to the empire'.[12] In the seventeenth century, the Qing Dynasty faced a similar issue when Chinese merchants were again under threat in Southeast Asia. Chinese abroad, the Qing decided, were 'not different from the native barbarians' and would get no help.[13] If people were silly enough to leave the Middle Kingdom, that was their problem. 'in the eyes of the Chinese government – and perhaps in the eyes of the people – the Chinese diaspora who abandoned ancestral graves to live abroad in violation of imperial law was not Chinese at all'.[14] Neither racism nor expansion was peculiar to Europeans. Their speciality was combining the two.

★ ★ ★

The history of European racial theory is familiar enough to permit a brief retelling. To the mid-eighteenth century, standard monogenism dominated the Christian worldview. All peoples were siblings, descended from a single pair, Adam and Eve, and had developed their differences in the 6,000 years of human history inferred by some Biblical commentators. From mid-century, voyages of scientific exploration, the research branch of the Enlightenment, began pumping back evidence of biological diversity that made six millennia and one original pair seem too few. The newer world of the Pacific featured large here. It was hard to see how Ainu and Tasmanian had sprung from Adam so fast, or imagine the tuatara and the platypus descending from the Ark, two by two. Monogenism was forced into conceptual gymnastics to retain credibility. Peoples had progressed or degenerated with remarkable rapidity, and both civilisation and colour became quite plastic. As early as 1749, a French woman 'upon being rudely insulted in the street, developed a black skin'.[15]

Like its hard racist rivals, polygenism and Social Darwinism, monogenism took partners as it sought to dance its way to influence, in its case humanitarianism and evangelism. These movements have the abolition of slavery to their credit, together with numerous acts of benign, if sometimes misguided, altruism. At its peak in the 1830s, humanitarianism actively discouraged official British intervention in the Pacific. But it seldom succeeded for long, and missionary intervention was another matter. From 1800, missionaries were very slow to fully ordain Pacific converts and slower still, when Protestant, to marry their daughters to them. Tribal peoples had to remain savage enough to urgently require salvation or they did not need missionaries. Still, monogenism was less malign than polygenism, which in its pure form held that different races were different species, whose core characteristics would never change. Such views can be dated back to Paracelsus in the early sixteenth century: 'it is impossible to conceive that the newly-found peoples are of Adam's blood'.[16] But it only developed theoretical momentum from the 1830s, partly in reaction to what it saw as the pipe-dreams of unrealistic evangelists.

Pure polygenism was a marginal creed, easily disproved even in its day. The infertility of cross-breeds was the standard test of speciation, and cross-breeds of all races bred like rabbits. But many scholars under-estimate the influence of polygenism. It lost the battle on race-as-species, but won the war on race as immutable type.[17] This was useful for the defence of slavery and was also helped by a mid-century turn against monogenist claims of savage salvageability. Like the Chinese turn against the Yao, this stemmed from perceived instances of barbarians biting the hand that fed them and refusing – or only pretending – to be saved. Historians emphasise the Indian Mutiny of 1857 and the Jamaica Rebellion of 1865, but Pacific cases were also influential. Māori resistance in New Zealand in the 1860s, the Kanak rebellion in New Caledonia in 1878, and determined Aboriginal resistance in Queensland around these dates, which killed a thousand settlers, are examples. The savage, it was thought, had shown his true colours, which were indelible.[18]

All racial theories ordained roles for the 'superior' as well as the 'inferior'; they were as much about 'Us' as about 'Them'. Polygenism urged white races to fulfil their destiny, which for Anglo-Saxons was rule of at least the temperate zones of the world. 'To build up within a lifetime at the extremity of the globe such communities as those of Victoria, New South Wales, Tasmania and New Zealand require faculties conceded by Providence to the Anglo-Saxon race alone.' 'A profound and ardent faith in the destiny of our race' is 'our second nature, our national religion.' Both quotes are from London newspapers of 1860, reprinted the same year in the *Sydney Morning Herald*, for whom 'our' was the key word.[19]

Social Darwinism, the last of our three theories, is better described as racial Darwinism but the former has become common usage. It involved the belief that the racial conflict was inevitable in the 'struggle for existence', and that the fittest races would survive, expand and exterminate or absorb the less fit. Social Darwinism was a mutant hybrid of Charles Darwin's theory of 1859 and a pre-existing ideology known as Fatal Impact. Fatal Impact was the idea that natives of new worlds faded away at European contact, by a law of Nature or Providence, however much one might try to salvage them. This might be regretted, but it underwrote the notion that Europeans were destined by nature to inherit their earth. It was based, of course, on a misunderstanding of epidemiology and immunity that was almost universal before 1900. Fatal Impact thinking dates to the Spanish Caribbean around 1520, when smallpox struck Hispaniola, but also surged in the Pacific from about 1800, with the depopulation of societies in Tahiti, Australia and New Zealand. In 1805, a genteel European visitor to New Zealand lamented that '[t]he lowest profligate of

Europe fancies himself a superior being, and treats the untaught native of a peaceful isle, as an animal almost unworthy his consideration'. He noted that 'neither the appearance or accounts of the natives indicate the prevalence of disease', but himself regretfully predicted a future of 'Fatal Impact'. 'In a few generations, in all probability, how great will be the change – children of diseased parents, they will grow up a puny race; and in many instances, both miserable and disgusting; in no respect resembling the hardy inhabitants of the island previously to their unhappy communications with civilized man.'[20] In the words of another visitor in 1834:

> It seems to me that the same causes that depopulated the Indian Tribes are doing the same all over the World. In New Zealand the same as in Canada or North America, And in Southern Africa the Hottentots are a decreasing people and by all accounts the Islands of the South Seas are the same. Rum, Blankets, Muskets, Tobacco and Diseases have been the great destroyers; but my belief is the Almighty intended it should be so or it would not have been allowed, Out of Evil comes Good.[21]

This view emerged completely independently of Darwin, who was touring the Pacific aboard the *Beagle* at the same time. Darwin himself shared it, but he did not mention it in the *Origin of Species* in 1859 and it was not part of his theory of evolution. This maintained that *competition within* groups drove natural selection. The Social Darwinist mutation turned this into *conflict between* groups. But rubbing the sticks of Fatal Impact ideology and the theory of evolution produced the fire of Social Darwinism without need for further theoretical intervention. Nine months after reading the *Origin*, New Zealand settler-soldier Arthur Atkinson wrote: 'I find one lies in wait to shoot Māoris without any approach to an angry feeling – it is a sort of scientific duty.'[22] In the appropriate ideological contexts, such as the mid-nineteenth settler Pacific, Social Darwinism took no longer to gestate than a human embryo, and its numerous theorists in the later nineteenth and earlier twentieth centuries were mere boosters. Thus Social Darwinism was in fact the merger of a sixteenth-century idea – Fatal Impact – and the misunderstanding of a nineteenth-century theory about the origin of all species.

Social Darwinism's ideological partner was Aryanism, a broader church than Anglo-Saxonism. Hitler was not the only one to argue that everything good in human history could be traced to the Aryan master-race, which was destined to win the struggle for existence and inherit the earth. Late-nineteenth-century settlers in Oklahoma and

New Zealand had been there before him.[23] On this view, the twentieth-century world wars were the World Cup Final of the struggle for
existence, in which the two greatest Aryan cousins, Anglo-Saxons and
Germans, slugged it out.

European racial theory remains important, in the Pacific as elsewhere, especially from about 1840. But it needs to be studied in
tandem with racial ideology. The two interacted with each other, and
together interacted with perceived realities. They made racism a real
force in Pacific history – we will look later at their contribution to a
'White Pacific'. They also created a set of stereotypes or lenses
through which Europeans viewed Pacific peoples. Not all involved
denigration. Until 1800, European savants admired Chinese civilisation at a distance, though those actually dealing with Chinese were
irritated by both their sense of superiority and their actual superiority
in the balance of trade. From 1800, Chinese civilisation came to be
seen as static, doomed to be overhauled by progressive Europeans.
Attitudes deteriorated further from 1850. A strange moral panic
emerged, whereby tiny numbers of Asian migrants in European
settler societies were seen as forerunners of a 'Yellow Peril'. From the
mid-eighteenth century, the idea of the 'Noble Savage', which can be
traced to the Roman historian Tacitus, was applied to some Pacific
island peoples, notably the Tahitians. It owed as much to a European
desire for an external angle from which to criticise their own society
as to Pacific realities. A 'Grey' or 'Dying Savage' stereotype also
emerged, as we have seen, blending with Social Darwinist theory
from 1859. But the most basic stereotypes were the 'White' and
'Black' Savage. White Savages were seen as more European-like, both
willing and able to convert to Christianity and civilisation. Black
Savages were seen as inferior to them, more hostile to Europe, and less
able to convert. Monogenism and Polygenism buttressed these stereotypes, but here again theory both followed and reinforced ideology.

From the 1820s, Europeans developed a pernicious distinction
between the Blacker Savages of the western Pacific islands, including
Australia, and the Whiter Savages of the east, including New Zealand.
The former became known as Melanesians, from the Greek for 'black',
and the latter as Polynesians, the people of many islands.[24] The distinction developed in concert with a surge in racial theory, and in turn
provided grist for the mills of racial theorists. But the idea can be traced
back to at least the late sixteenth century, when the Spanish named
New Guinea, 'which they saw as inhabited by "Negroes" like those of
African Guinea'.[25] In 1595, Spanish visitors to the Marquesas Islands
in the eastern Pacific found the locals friendly, attractive and almost

white.'Respecting their complexion, if it cannot be called white, it is nearly white.'[26] Almost two centuries later, the German scientist J. R. Forster, travelling with Cook in the 1770s, began the merging of this idea with racial theory by positing what amounted to the Melanesian–Polynesian distinction. But the ideological influence persisted, featuring utility and malleability rather than theoretical consistency. Unlike xenophobia, which denigrated all Others equally, racism ranked 'inferior' Others, so helping it to divide and rule, or divide and convert. When evangelism or colonialism was thwarted in Melanesia, Black Savagery was blamed, and efforts shifted to the Whiter Savages of Polynesia. But when Polynesians bit the hand that was trying to feed them, they too could suddenly become Black. This blithe capacity for paradox was a hallmark of racial ideology, not theory, and it even had a good side. Individuals could be exempted from racial prejudice. Whalers and sailors might be racist ashore and non-racist afloat, valuing and even obeying their Pacific Island crewmates.

\* \* \*

Racism could hinder imperial projects. It could lead to dangerous delusions about the limited capacity of non-European peoples, notably in war. Europeans expensively underestimated the resistance capacity of Tlingit, Nez Perce, Modoc, Yacqi and Mapuche peoples along America's Pacific coast; of the Māori of New Zealand and the Aborigines of Tasmania and Queensland; and of the Tahitians and Sāmoans, among others. But, in general, racism was more help than hindrance to European expansion, in several ways, including war. Convictions of intrinsic superiority – not just intellectual and technological but also moral and even physical – steeled Europeans in their wars of conquest and made them confident of victory. Europeans always won in the end. If they did not, it was not the end. Roman or Chinese empires might have walled out the peoples who most stubbornly and successfully resisted expansion, such as the Mapuche of Chile, who quite properly ate their first two governors. Instead, Europeans kept trying to conquer them for over three hundred years until they finally succeeded in the 1880s.

This was only the beginning of racism's utility for expansion. A central problem for European colonial elites was how to get 'poor whites' to side with them against indigenes and imported non-white labour, free or unfree. This was especially acute where white labour was unfree too, or had been until recently. The seventeenth-century Caribbean plantations, which initially used indentured white labour, and the nineteenth-century convict colonies of New South Wales and

Van Diemen's Land are examples. Here whites as well as non-whites were subjected to slave-like exploitation, including the lash. Proclaiming a shared religion or nation could not provide the necessary cement, because many of the relevant whites were Catholic Irish. Shared 'whiteness' did the job. Seventeenth-century Barbadian elites were at pains to point out that white was 'the general name for Europeans'.[27] The capacity of race to incorporate select non-nationals, notably Germans in the United States, also massively reinforced settler societies.

Racism enhanced the growth of settler societies and their capacity to remain 'Neo-European' – separate from both indigenous hosts and imported non-white labour. It helped them to be seen as 'virtual metropolitans'. From the sixteenth century to the nineteenth, some metropolitan Europeans believed that settlers degenerated abroad. In late sixteenth-century Lima, locally-born Spanish Jesuit cadets had to wait until age 20 to be inducted, while the Spanish-born were taken on at 18. American-born Spanish struggled for parity of status with Spanish-born throughout the colonial period.[28] From 1685, a strand of French thinkers argued that everything, including human intellects, became smaller in the Americas, eliciting indignant denials from the likes of Benjamin Franklin and Thomas Jefferson.[29] The same was feared for Europeans in Australia. By 1858, it was 'already apparent' that in Australia, 'Anglo-Saxons and Celts in a few generations must deteriorate both mentally and physically'.[30] For settler societies this was serious slander. Attracting desirable immigrants was never easy, and a reputation for degeneracy made it harder still. But if race was hard-wired into settlers, and not subject to particular environments, then they could claim persisting parity and metropolitan-like standing.

The keys to creating and maintaining a settler society that considered itself racially European and was accepted as such by metropolitans, were the presence of women settlers and the ideology of female endogamy. At one extreme, where white women were absent, European men interbred with the locals. If the European presence was tiny or temporary, the offspring simply merged back into the indigenous population. Whalers are the classic Pacific case. Whaling ships entered the Pacific in the eighteenth century and by the nineteenth it was their main hunting ground. The number of American whaling ships alone exceeded 700 in 1846. Indigenous peoples from Alaska to New Zealand therefore share a dash of Nantucket, to no great effect.

If the male European lodgement was long-term, as in Portuguese Macau, a mixed race or *métis* group could emerge, especially if it had official encouragement. Male-only Portuguese establishments were particularly good at developing such groups. This was more a matter of their shortage of manpower and lack of womanpower than of some special immunity to racism as their 'white legend' has it. Portuguese attitudes were very different in Brazil, where female settlers were quite numerous. The process of incorporation was cumulative: the 400 Portuguese who settled Macau in the 1550s were accompanied by half-Portuguese from earlier establishments in Goa and Melaka.[31] Where Europeans were particularly few, as in Macau and marginal parts of the Spanish, Dutch, and British possessions in Southeast Asia, nominal Europeans could come pretty close to the standing and function of the real thing.[32] Hence we occasionally find 'genuine' Black Portuguese and Black Dutch and Black English, literally operating as white. More often, the *métis* group was privileged relative to the enslaved or indigenous mass of the population, but only if they bought into a racial hierarchy with 'pure' Europeans on top. Thus Europeans bred their own collaborators and, ironically enough, retained their loyalty through shared racism.

At the other pole were migrations with substantial minorities of European women. Here racialism supplied the ideology of female endogamy that enabled settlers to retain their racial identity. Again, genetic reality could be trumped by perception. In Latin America, and for a time in some US states, a person with a black great-grandmother still counted as white, even officially.[33] But genetic reality did help racial fiction. Because they were a minority and land was abundant, settler women married earlier and bred more than their metropolitan sisters. The numerous men without white wives were surplus to racial reproductive requirements, and could therefore be expended on risky but profitable trades, hunts and wars, yet another race bonus. Such men (and husbands on the sly) interbred with non-whites, and *métis* groups emerged here too, but they were less necessary to white dominance, less valued and less privileged relative to the mass of the population than in the male-only settler scenario.

Where indigenous populations were thin, and made thinner still by new diseases, and imported slaves were few or absent, white settlers became the absolute majority. By 1900, this was the situation around much of the Pacific littoral: in Australia, New Zealand, American California, the Pacific Northwest, British Columbia and Siberia. These societies were built on racial ideology, and continued to rely on it for their identity and their claim to virtual 'European-ness' – even though they often believed their own 'lesser races' were dying out, and even though most had gained independence or autonomy from their metropolis. Independence, indeed, may have increased reliance on race to allege European-ness because formal links no longer existed. In purely practical terms, it helped attract European migrants and capital, both of which were much more attracted by racially European environments. An interesting example of the difference between male and mixed European migrations can be found in Russian Pacific expansion. Siberia was a relatively balanced settler society in terms of gender, and over 80 per cent Russian in 1914; mixed-race people were not needed as a caste and do not feature prominently in the records. Alaska, on the other hand, was a male-only settlement and the vital 'half-castes' or 'Kreols' feature large.[34]

Between these two poles were various gradations, and Latin America encompassed most of them. Recent studies suggest that race here was complex, shifting and contested, involving a rapid (though perhaps not instant) transfer of metropolitan Iberian concerns about 'purity' and 'stains'.[35] Where and when settlers were so few that the collaboration of indigenous elites was essential, their status could be quite high, but was translated into the language of racial purity. In a somewhat bizarre but telling example, in 1697 the new seminary in Mexico City explicitly opened its doors to 'caciques [chiefs], but only if they were "untainted by any stains or bad races of Moors, Indians, and heretics." In other words, native nobles had somehow ceased to be (unclean) "Indians."'[36] Again, we see that logical consistency was not a strong point of racial ideology.

Mestizo (Amerindian-European) and mulatto (African-European) groups emerged in numbers comparable to 'pure' Indios and Africans, but their ranking varied. Africans, for example, technically ranked lowest but also featured as soldiers, foremen and skilled labourers with authority over other Others. More white settlers could diminish the need for Indio or Mestizo cooperation and so lower their standing, and the African contribution could be written out. In Mexico, just before independence in 1821, the population was categorised as 18 per cent white, 22 per cent mixed and 60 per cent Indio.[37]

Racial character might be seen as constant, but one could shift racial categories in Latin America. Depending on your random luck in skin colour, you could promote yourself up the shifting hierarchies, especially if you went somewhere where your parentage was unknown. For a time, 'facial hair was central to Iberian forms of self-identification' and a decent beard could transform an Indio into a mestizo, or even a white if his skin was light.[38] Families could 'breed back' to whiteness, or even change *casta* in their own lifetime. 'Individuals altered the legal classification of their descendants by "whitening" them through strategically chosen marriages. People migrated in the course of everyday life from one category to another, depending upon the context of interaction.'[39]

Yet being malleable and negotiable made race more important, not less. 'Rather than indicating the irrelevance of "race," this anxious ambivalence demonstrates how such fluidity and imprecision worked to make "race" and racial categories even more socially charged and potent.'[40] The very shifts in the currency ensured that people had constantly to deal in it. Race was less rigid in Latin America than in Anglo-America, as the former's legends claim, but it was not necessarily less important.

After independence, especially from the late nineteenth century, racial reinventions occurred in the Latin Pacific, now with some help from racial theory. Some Chileans retrospectively transformed their Celtiberian forebears into Visigothic Aryans, aided by a race-detecting sixth sense. 'Through the various portraits and descriptions of the conquerors of Chile with which I am familiar, I can assure you that not more than ten per cent of them show signs of racial mixing with the autochthonous race of Spain... The rest of them are of pure Teutonic blood... the Latin peoples have nothing in common with the Chilean race', wrote Nicolás Palacios in 1904.[41]

Echoing the racial theorist who attributed Inca civilisation to a European washed ashore on a log, Peru and Mexico took another route, whitening chiefly Incas and Aztecs into suitable co-ancestors.[42] This lent a distinctive golden tinge to the new nations without undercutting whiteness. New Zealand settlers adopted a similar strategy. From 1885, they increasingly convinced themselves that the Māori were in fact sun-tanned Aryans, whose symbols were suitable for a new Better British nation. Some, in New Zealand and elsewhere, argued that all Polynesians, as against Melanesians, were Aryans, and Polynesian intellectuals themselves sometimes bought into this. The distinguished Māori ethnologist Peter Buck was a 1930s case in point, describing the Polynesians as 'The Vikings of the Pacific' in a famous book, and even convincing two congressmen from the US South. 'The job was to show that the Sāmoan was a Polynesian of Caucasian descent and quite distinct from the negroid division of mankind. The two democrats were duly converted.'[43]

Our final gradation of settler racism, or perhaps racial settlerism, involves the small planter or rancher elites who established themselves, in the wake of missionaries, on several of the larger Pacific islands during the nineteenth century – Americans in Hawai'i, British in Fiji and French in New Caledonia. These elites acquired just enough white wives to perpetuate their whiteness, but were unable to force or persuade the indigenous peoples to work for them on slave-like terms. They attributed this to the regrettable decline or innate laziness of their own natives, and imported what they hoped would be sturdier or less recalcitrant labourers. This may have been one of several motives for the French despatch of some 20,000 white convicts to New Caledonia between 1864 and 1897,[44] but most labour imports were non-white. From the mid-1860s to about 1914, British, French and Peruvian ships began to raid various Pacific islands for labour, a practice known as 'blackbirding'. 'Despite a history of increasing regulation, to the very end the obtaining of "recruits" by trickery, lying and outright force remained a feature of the trade.' New Caledonia and Fiji were joined as destinations by mainland plantations, in North Queensland for example. There was a comparable trade in Amerindians in California in the 1860s,[45] and such semi-slaveries outlasted the official kind, which disappeared in the United States in 1865 and in Latin America by the 1880s.

But harvesting declining island populations was never going to be enough, and in the later nineteenth century the plantation colonies of the Pacific turned to indentured Asian labour. This modest flow of Asians into the Pacific joined two others. Chinese and Filipino migration across the Pacific, via the Manila galleons, dates back to the 1570s, and Indian and Southeast Asian crewmen were common on European ships from much the same early time. But anti-Asian sentiment in the form of Sinophobia does not seem to have flowered until the third small influx during the Pacific gold rushes of the mid-nineteenth century. Between 1849 and 1861, hundreds of thousands of people poured into the new goldfields of California, Victoria, New Zealand and New South Wales. Most were European, but they were accompanied by a persistent trickle of adventurous Chinese. Despite the small numbers, Sinophobia flared on the goldfields, perhaps because the Europeans were themselves a mixed bag who needed a unifying anti-type.

For a decade or so after the gold rushes, labour shortages sometimes made Chinese migration acceptable. Official opinion in New Zealand, Australia and the United States favoured it at some points between 1861 and 1871.[46] But from that time on Sinophobia surged. It became entrenched in the Anglophone Pacific from the 1890s, extended to Japanese as well, and infected Latin America and Siberia in the 1900s.[47] What makes 'Yellow Peril' moral panics so strange is that Asian migration was never large, that antagonism to it sometimes fell as well as rose, that these variations seldom correlate with variations in Asian numbers, and that the antagonism predates even the remotest actual possibility of Asian invasion. Like the gold miners, the 'White Pacific' was worried about its whiteness, and needed a unifying anti-type, reinforcing neo-Europeaness by stigmatising its perceived opposite. If the Yellow Peril had not existed, the settler Pacific would have had to invent it, which, indeed, it did.

In Yunnan and Hokkaido, the Yao and Ainu might have felt that the Chinese and Japanese deserved everything they got. My impression is that Japanese racism was not prominent until the mid-nineteenth century, at least in the sense that the Japanese disliked all outsiders equally. This changed as the Japanese began to expand from the 1870s, when older beliefs about Japanese exceptionalism were blended with European-style racial theory. Ironically, the Japanese were helped in this by a sudden promotion. Europeans watched in amazement as Japan industrialised, militarised, defeated China and Russia in 1894–5 and 1904–5, and acquired an empire including Taiwan, Korea and, informally, Manchuria. Only Europeans were supposed to do this kind of thing and for some European thinkers the solution was to find a European origin for the Japanese. In 1907, one announced that 'White men, belonging to the great Aryan family ... were the first Japanese.'[48] In another irony, there may have been a tiny kernel of truth in this in the shape of the oppressed Ainu minority, who are thought to have had Indo-European ancestral links.

Just how the Japanese themselves felt about becoming white I do not know, but they did engage to some extent with Social Darwinism, and with a home-grown idea of themselves as chosen people or master-race, superior to other Asians.[49] Their attitudes in practice towards conquered Koreans and Chinese were notorious, and racism would have enhanced the cohesion of their substantial attempts at settlement in Taiwan and Manchuria. The number of Japanese in the latter peaked at 1.5 million in 1945.[50] On the other hand, claiming racial kinship with the Chinese and other East Asians, as with the proposed establishment of the 'East Asian Co-prosperity Sphere', may have seemed a more profitable alternative. But it is no accident that Japanese racism and expansion flowered together. The Japanese used the proven European software of expansion – race – as well as the hardware.

Saying that racism is about collective Self as well as collective Other is commonplace among scholars, yet the former receives much less analysis. Another commonplace is to note that, until about 1800, the word 'race' did not carry a racist loading. It was used for a group of people presumed to share descent, and often as a synonym for nation. Yet, well before the mass advent of race theory in the mid-nineteenth century, 'race' and 'nation' had diverged.[51] 'Anglo-Saxon race' was more *transferable* than 'English nation'. This lay at the heart of racism's utility for expansion through reproduction – the creation of settler societies. The reproduction itself was race-guided, through European female endogamy. Racism enabled settlers to perpetuate their European-ness over generations, and to claim continuing parity with and connection to their metropolis. Along with legitimating the subordination of many indigenous peoples, and enabling the co-option of a few, this was racism's main legacy in the Pacific. In the late nineteenth and earlier twentieth centuries, when settler whiteness seemed threatened, 'Great White Walls' of immigration restrictions were built to buttress it.[52] It has been suggested that these restrictions were motivated not by racism but by a desire to avoid swamping by Asians and to retain cultural cohesion.[53] This is untrue. Swamping was not a realistic threat at the time. An illiterate Gaelic-speaking Scots fisherman was generally preferred to an Anglo-Indian lawyer, despite the fact that the former clearly contributed less to 'cultural cohesion'. The 'Great White Walls' survived in Australia and New Zealand to the 1970s, and continue to haunt the post-settler societies of the Pacific.

## Notes

1. Harilanto Razafindrazaka, et al., 'Complete Mitochondrial DNA Sequences Provide New Insights into the Polynesian Motif and the Peopling of Madagascar', *European Journal of Human Genetics* 18 (2010), 575–81; Atholl Anderson, 'Subpolar Settlement in South Polynesia', *Antiquity* 79 (2005), 791–800; Alice A. Storey, et al., 'Pre-Columbian Chickens, Dates, Isotopes, and mtDNA', *Proceedings of the National Academy of Sciences of the United States of America* 105, 48 (December 2008), E99.

2. For example, Bronwen Douglas, 'Slippery Word, Ambiguous Praxis: "Race" and Late-18th-Century Voyagers in Oceania', *Journal of Pacific History* 41 (2006), 1–29.

3. Miriam Eliav-Feldon, Benjamin Isaac and Joseph Ziegler, 'Introduction', in Eliav-Feldon, Isaac and Ziegler, eds., *The Origins of Racism in the West* (Cambridge, 2009), pp. 1–31.

4. Joanne Rappaport, '"Asi lo paresçe por su aspeto": Physiognomy and the Construction of Difference in Colonial Bogotá', *Hispanic American Historical Review* 91 (2011), 601–31.

5. James Belich, 'Myth, Race, and Identity in New Zealand', *New Zealand Journal of History* 31 (1997), 9–22.

6. Peter C. Perdue, 'Nature and Nurture on Imperial China's Frontiers', *Modern Asian Studies* 43 (2009), 254. Also see Mu-chou Poo, *Enemies of Civilization: Attitudes towards Foreigners in Ancient Mesopotamia, Egypt and China* (Albany, NY, 2005).

7. S. B. Miles, 'Imperial Discourse, Regional Elite, and Local Landscape on the South China Frontier, 1577–1722', *Journal of Early Modern History* 12 (2008), 99–136.

8. Charles Patterson Giersch, *Asian Borderlands: The Transformation of Qing China's Yunnan Frontier* (Cambridge, MA, 2006).

9. Luke Clossey, 'Merchants, Migrants, Missionaries, and Globalization in the Early-Modern Pacific', *Journal of Global History* 1 (2006), 41–58.

10. Adam McKeown, 'Global Migration, 1846–1940', *Journal of World History* 15 (2004), 156–60.

11. James Reardon-Anderson, *Reluctant Pioneers: China's Expansion Northward, 1644–1937* (Stanford, CA, 2005), p. 98.

12. Hugh R. Clark, 'Frontier Discourse and China's Maritime Frontier: China's Frontiers and the Encounter with the Sea through Early Imperial History', *Journal of World History* 20 (2009), 1–33.

13. John L. Cranmer-Byng and John E. Wills, Jr., 'Trade and Diplomacy with Maritime Europe, 1644–c.1800', in Wills, ed., *China and Maritime Europe, 1500–1800: Trade, Settlement, Diplomacy, and Missions* (Cambridge, 2011), p. 191.

14. Clossey, 'Merchants, Migrants, Missionaries'.

15. William B. Cohen, *The French Encounter with Africans: White Responses to Blacks, 1530–1880* (Bloomington, IN, 1980), p. 83.

16. Paracelsus, quoted in Annemarie de Waal Malefijt, *Images of Man: A History of Anthropological Thought* (New York, 1974), p. 42.

17. Michael Banton, *The Idea of Race* (London, 1977); Banton, *Racial Theories* (Cambridge, 1987).

18. See, for example, Kay Anderson and Colin Perrin, 'How Race Became Everything: Australia and Polygenism', *Ethnic and Racial Studies* 31 (2008), 962–90.

19. *Sydney Morning Herald* (11 April 1860, 17 April 1860), quoting the *Times* and the *Daily News*.

20. John Savage, *Some Account of New Zealand; Particularly the Bay of Islands, and Surrounding Country* (London, 1807), pp. 88–90.

21. Edward Markham, *New Zealand or Recollections of It*, ed. E. H. McCormick (Wellington, NZ, 1963), p. 83.

22. A. S. Atkinson, Journal, 5 June 1863, in Guy H. Scholefield, ed., *The Richmond–Atkinson Papers*, 2 vols. (Wellington, NZ, 1960), II, p. 49.

23. Edward Tregear, *The Aryan Maori* (Wellington, NZ, 1885); *El Reno Democrat* (23 April 1892), quoted in B. H. Johnson, 'Booster Attitudes of Some Newspapers in Oklahoma Territory – "The Land of the Fair God"', *Chronicles of Oklahoma* 43 (1965), 242–64; Tony Ballantyne, *Orientalism and Race: Aryanism in the British Empire* (Basingstoke, 2002).

24. Bronwen Douglas, '*Terra Australis* to Oceania: Racial Geography in the "Fifth Part of the World"', *Journal of Pacific History* 45 (2010), 179–210.

25. Serge Tcherkézoff, 'A Long and Unfortunate Voyage Towards the "Invention" of the Melanesia/Polynesia Distinction 1595–1832', trans. Isabel Ollivier, *Journal of Pacific History* 38 (2003), 175–96.

26. *The Voyages of Pedro Fernandez de Quiros, 1595–1606*, ed. Clements Markham (London, 1904), p. 27.

27. Russell R. Menard, *Sweet Negotiations: Sugar, Slavery, and Plantation Agriculture in Early Barbados* (Charlottesville, 2006), p. 119.

28. Anthony Pagden, 'The Peopling of the New World: Ethnos, Race and Empire in the Early-Modern World', in Eliav-Feldon, Isaac and Ziegler, eds., *Origins of Racism in the West*, p. 298.

29. C. J. Jaenen and D. Standen, 'Regeneration or Degeneration? Some French Views of the Effects of Colonization', *Proceedings of the Annual Meeting of the French Colonial Historical Society* 20 (1994), 1–10.

30. Arthur Thomson, *The Story of New Zealand: Past and Present – Savage and Civilized*, 2 vols. (London, 1859), II, p. 309.

31. Roderich Ptak, 'The Demography of Old Macao, 1555–1640', *Ming Studies* 15 (1982), 27–35.

32. Toby Green, *The Rise of the Trans-Atlantic Slave Trade in Western Africa, 1300–1589* (Cambridge, 2012).

33. Massimo Livi Bacci, *Conquest: The Destruction of the American Indios* (Cambridge, 2008), p. 17; George M. Fredrickson, 'Mulattoes and Métis: Attitudes Toward Miscegenation in the United States and France Since the Seventeenth Century', *International Social Science Journal* 57 (2005), 103–12.

34. On Siberia see Anna Reid, *The Shaman's Coat: A Native History of Siberia* (London, 2002); Yuri Slezkine, 'The Sovereign's Foreigners: Classifying the Native Peoples in Seventeenth-Century Siberia', *Russian History* 19 (1992), 475–85; on Alaska, Andrei V. Grinev, 'A Fifth Column in Alaska: Native Collaborators in Russian America', trans. Richard L. Bland, *Alaska History* 22 (2007), 1–21; Gwenn A. Miller, *Kodiak Kreol: Communities of Empire in Early Russian America* (Ithaca, NY, 2010).

35. María Elena Martínez, *Genealogical Fictions: Limpieza de Sangre, Religion, and Gender in Colonial Mexico* (Stanford, 2008).

36. Peter B. Villella, '"Pure and Noble Indians, Untainted by Inferior Idolatrous Races": Native Elites and the Discourse of Blood Purity in Late Colonial Mexico', *Hispanic American Historical Review* 91 (2011), 633–63.

37. P. J. Bakewell, *A History of Latin America: Empires and Sequels 1450–1930* (Oxford, 1997), p. 298.

38. Rappaport, "Asi lo paresçe por su aspeto".

39. Ibid., 604.

40. Alexandra Minna Stern, 'Eugenics and Racial Classification', in Ilona Katzew and Susan Deans-Smith, eds., *Race and Classification: The Case of Mexican America* (Stanford, 2009), p. 152.

41. Nicolás Palacios, *Raza chilena: libro escrito por un chileno i para los chilenos* (Valparaiso, 1904), p. 4, quoted in Michela Coletta, 'The Role of Degeneration Theory in Spanish American Public Discourse at the *Fin de Siècle*: Raza Latina and Immigration in Chile and Argentina', *Bulletin of Latin American Research* 30 (2011), 97–8.

42. Richard Whately, 'On the Origin of Civilisation', in Whately, *Miscellaneous Lectures and Reviews* (London, 1861), p. 35.

43. Peter Buck (Te Rangi Hīroa), in M. P. K. Sorrenson, ed., *Na to hoa aroha = From Your Dear Friend: The Correspondence between Sir Apirana Ngata and Te Rangi Hīroa, 1925–50*, 3 vols (Auckland, 1986–88), II, p. 78.

44. New Caledonia's neo-French grew into a substantial minority, but except for convicts did not supply much manual labour. See Alice

Bullard, '"Becoming Savage?"': The First Step toward Civilization and the Practices of Intransigence in New Caledonia', *History and Anthropology* 10 (1998), 319–74, and David A. Chappell, 'Frontier Ethnogenesis: The Case of New Caledonia', *Journal of World History* 4 (1993), 307–24.

45. M. Magliari, 'Free Soil, Unfree Labor: Cave Johnson Couts and the Binding of Indian Workers in California, 1850–1867', *Pacific Historical Review* 73 (2004), 349–90.

46. In New Zealand a commission of inquiry in 1871 favoured Chinese migration, as did a US–Chinese treaty in 1868, while the Australian colonies repealed their restrictions on it between 1861 and 1867.

47. Eva-Maria Stolberg, 'The Siberian Frontier between "White Mission" and "Yellow Peril", 1890s–1920s', *Nationalities Papers* 32 (2004), 165–81.

48. W. E. Griffis, quoted in Morris Low, 'The Japanese Nation in Evolution: W. E. Griffis, Hybridity and the Whiteness of the Japanese Race', *History and Anthropology* 11 (1999), 203–34.

49. Hiroshi Unoura, 'Samurai Darwinism: Hiroyuki Katō and the Reception of Darwin's Theory in Modern Japan from the 1880s to the 1900s', *History and Anthropology* 11 (1999), 235–55; Ken Ishida, 'Racisms Compared: Fascist Italy and Ultra-Nationalist Japan', *Journal of Modern Italian Studies* 7 (2002), 380–91.

50. Mariko Asano Tamanoi, 'Introduction', in Tamanoi, ed., *Crossed Histories: Manchuria in the Age of Empire* (Honolulu, 2005), p. 9. Also see Yoshihisa Tak Matsusaka, *The Making of Japanese Manchuria, 1904–1932* (Cambridge, MA, 2001); Sandra Wilson, 'The "New Paradise": Japanese Emigration to Manchuria in the 1930s and 1940s', *International History Review* 17 (1995), 249–86; R. M. Myers and M. R. Peattie, eds., *The Japanese Colonial Empire, 1895–1945* (Princeton, 1984).

51. Nicholas Hudson, 'From "Nation" to "Race": The Origin of Racial Classification in Eighteenth-Century Thought', *Eighteenth-Century Studies* 29 (1996), 247–64.

52. Charles Price, *The Great White Walls are Built: Restrictive Immigration to North America and Australasia, 1836–1888* (Canberra, 1974).

53. For example, Matthew Jordan, 'Rewriting Australia's Racist Past: How Historians (Mis)Interpret the "White Australia" Policy', *History Compass* 3 (2005), 1–32; Daniel Gorman, 'Wider and Wider Still? Racial Politics, Intra-Imperial Immigration, and the Absence of an Imperial Citizenship in the British Empire', *Journal of Colonialism and Colonial History* 3, 3 (2002), 1–24.

# 13

# Gender

## Patricia O'Brien

Gender – culturally constructed identities, roles and sexualities for men and women – is vital to understanding the cultural kaleidoscope of the Pacific. Gender deepens understandings about how Pacific peoples were impacted by the waves of historical forces and events following the region's incorporation into a global economy of commerce, ideologies and humanity from the sixteenth century. The Pacific's 'European era' commenced along the cultural and commercial highways of Southeast and East Asia and, after the Magellan voyage, from the Americas. The frontiers of European contact continued to be forged through to the 1930s when peoples in Highland New Guinea became the last to be ushered into the European era following the intrusion of Australian gold-seekers. Through centuries of exploration and commercial contact, of resource harvesting and mining, of plantation and pastoral economies, of colonial governance and settlement, and of war and travel, gendered systems shaped Pacific history.

As gender was both pervasive and central to the making of this history, there are a multiplicity of ways in which its impact on history can be explored. Here, we will investigate gender in the Pacific through the framework of power and its overlapping frames of racial ideologies and conceptions of sexuality and bodies. Though European colonialism was a global phenomenon, its coalescence with indigenous and extant cultures in and around the Pacific formed new societies or layered existing ones with altered ideas about gender that gave this region's history a distinctive cast. Genders extended beyond complementary constructions of men and women, encompassing a range of alternatives, often determined by sexual preference and embodied in a variety of ways. Though this chapter focuses upon women and constructions of femininity, examining such ideas necessarily says a great deal about men and masculinities. The historical impacts of gender occurred in ways so diverse that this chapter will explore illustrative case studies from China, Japan, Oceania, the Pacific littoral and Australia, where we begin.

In 1976, the ashes of a woman were scattered into the waters of the D'Entrecasteaux Channel off the coast of Tasmania. Since her death one hundred years earlier, the woman's remains had been as contested as had her extraordinary life, lived through the brunt of Britain's imperial expansion into the Pacific. The woman's name was Trugernanna and she was born on Bruny Island off the southeast coast of Van Diemen's Land around 1812, almost 25 years after Britain colonised Port Jackson, present-day Sydney (see Figure 13.1). Aiming to replace lost American colonies, Britain established a base for maritime and commercial connections with Chinese and other Asian ports and as a beachhead for a new settler society destined to extend British control over the vast continent of what became known as Australia, but was then New Holland. Though Dutch and French explorers had indelibly marked the place where Trugernanna was born on European maps, it was the frontiers of British empire that wrenched Trugernanna's life into its extraordinary shape.

After British and French explorers had mapped and described Trugernanna's people and country some decades before her birth, the next wave of intruders arrived as sealers plundering the coast of Van Diemen's Land. Sailing south from Port Jackson, the sealers set up remote communities near their quarry where they could process seal skins for one of Australia's first export products – merchandise to offer China in the colossal Anglo-Chinese trade imbalance. The sealers not only raided seal populations; they also kidnapped women and girls from coastal communities on the mainland and Van Diemen's Land. The women were taken to live on remote islands in Bass Strait where they worked as hunters of seals and muttonbirds, preparers of skins and feathers, and domestic helpers and they also became mothers of the surviving indigenous peoples of Van Diemen's Land, the Palawa peoples. From 1803, Van Diemen's Land became the second node of British imperial expansion in the South Pacific. Like Port Jackson, this settlement was a penal colony designed for permanent ongoing occupation. Palawa lands were coveted for live-stock pasture and soon the pressures for land and resources erupted into a violent and increasingly brutal struggle. Into this world, Trugernanna was born.

Her first encounters with white men were with sealers, whalers and foresters who killed, kidnapped and raped women. In order to survive in this transformed world, Trugernanna may have sold sex at sealers' camps. During these encounters she may have produced children and also contracted venereal diseases, as would so many other women across the Pacific. When she met a missionary tasked with finding a

*Figure 13.1*    Trugernanner *c.*1866

solution to the costly frontier wars that intensified in the 1820s due to
the upsurge in pastoralism, Trugernanna acted as an emissary for the
'Friendly Mission' aimed at encouraging beleaguered warring tribes to
surrender and accept relocation away from settler farms to a 'safe' environment on a remote island in Bass Strait. Due to her role in the
'Friendly Mission', Trugernanna became a prominent historical character and was painted into iconic colonial images of the history of Van
Diemen's Land, and would later be photographed when that technology evolved. In 1834, Trugernanna moved with her people to Flinders
Island, a place safe from settler violence but not from the ravages of
disease or the pressures of Christian evangelism that aimed to fundamentally alter her traditional culture, not least through imposing new
gendered systems onto Aboriginal women and men. When Charles
Darwin arrived in Van Diemen's Land in 1836, he was impressed that
in thirty years 'all the aborigines have been removed to an island in

Bass Strait, so that Van Diemen's Land enjoys the great advantage of being free from a native population'.[1]

When the Van Diemen's Land colony expanded across Bass Strait, Trugernanna travelled there too, and ended up on trial for the murder of a whaler along with two men and two other Aboriginal women. The men were hanged, the first public executions in present-day Melbourne, whilst Trugernanna and the other women were freed to return to Flinders Island in 1842.[2] In 1847, Trugernanna and those members of the community that had not perished in the unhealthy conditions on Flinders Island were returned to the Tasmanian mainland. As more of this community continued to perish at alarming rates, Trugernanna's fame began to hinge on her status as a surviving remnant of a 'dying race', and then she fallaciously became known as the last of her people.[3]

When she died in 1876, she was buried against her express wish, as she feared her bones would be disinterred and sold as a scientific specimen like many before her: fears that were realised. Her skeletal remains were on display in the Tasmanian Museum from 1904 to 1947, a macabre trophy of white triumph over 'unfit' indigenous people. It was not until the century of her death approached that campaigns to have her remains released and cremated succeeded, and her ashes were scattered by Palawa people, the descendants of Aboriginal women and sealers.

The scattering of Trugernanna's ashes launched her on another journey. She became a part of the immense and ongoing project of recovering the histories of women and non-Europeans that was transforming Pacific history from the 1970s onwards. Thus as Trugernanna's ashes washed through the waters of the Pacific, she became connected with other Pacific women, part of the project of unearthing and investigating how gender impacted their lives and the course of history since the coming of Europeans. Trugernanna has been likened to a 'spectre', haunting white Australia's history of race relations with its Indigenous peoples.[4] For gender historians, her story goes to the heart of tensions that arise in writing gender history with its implicit or explicit attempt to explode assumptions that women were not historical actors but universal victims to external male-driven forces: assumptions that applied manifold to women who did not belong to European elites. The challenge for gender historians has been to render their subjects as full-fledged historical actors who had 'agency' over their lives but at the same time not to lose sight of the overwhelmingly negative impacts of colonialism on non-European communities. One interpretation of Trugernanna portrayed her as using her sexual wiles to betray her people.[5] Another rendered her story in the context of brutal colonial violence, asserting that she survived through pragmatism, holding onto traditional culture whilst making 'her own adjustments on her own terms' to colonial intrusion.[6] Trugernanna's story shares much with the history of the Americas and mainland southern Australia where colonialism came fast and the asymmetries of military power, population size, disease and an overwhelmingly male intruding population forced rapid realignments and accommodations. In other parts of the Pacific – Oceania, South-east Asia and the Pacific littoral of mainland Asia – the story of colonialism played out differently, with many regions yet to be so disrupted by colonial intruders.

Colonial historical layers sat atop existing indigenous systems where gender was a central organisational category of every society, but in varying ways. Though heterosexual genders dominated, in Polynesian cultures for instance there was cultural space of additional genders, men who dressed and lived as women – *fa'fafines* in Sāmoan – whose lives were a widely accepted and normalised expression of gender. Colonial disruptions to these existing systems varied in degree and pace across the region, leaving uneven, divergent and sometimes unexpected outcomes over place and time. In the Sinic world, gender was shaped by Confucian ideas about hierarchies based on social rank, gender and age.[7] In these societies, 'righteous' behaviour was conveyed through 'moralizing tracts and biographies' promoting ideals for 'woman as submissive, chaste, hard-working, and obedient to her parents, husband and senior relatives'.[8] Colonial contacts were heavily restricted in northeast Asia until the middle of the nineteenth century. The 1842 Opium War forced the signing of unequal treaties between China and Britain, a colonial tactic replicated in 1854 when the United States's 'Black Ships' entered Japanese waters and forcibly 'opened' them to all manner of western influences. Before this period, Europeans had been permitted 'to cross' the barriers of China and Japan, but the 'severest restrictions' applied. Dynastic China required these foreigners to adopt Chinese dress and to be strictly confined to their own precincts. They were 'never permitted to return home': for instance, the Jesuit priests (with their vows of chastity) were permitted access to the Chinese court from the latter part of the sixteenth century, though they adhered to strictly policed racial and gender divisions. This contrasted greatly to the Portuguese colony of Macau (territory rented by China in the 1550s), where foreign men mixed more freely with local Chinese people.[9] The lack of contact with women through these heavily mediated encounters spurred colonial stereotypes of the region that centred on mysterious and sequestered women with practices such as foot-binding taking a central place in the orientalist gaze. This orientalist gaze increased in utility and intensity along with imperial designs and activities from the 1840s, depicting Imperial China as corrupt and corroding, exemplified through the treatment of women. But were Chinese women universally oppressed as the stereotype of an ignorant, economically parasitic and cloistered existence suggested? Gender scholars have been at pains to show that interpretations of Chinese women as universally passive ignore the considerable maternal power that women wielded within the family and also the economic contributions women in all classes made to their households in the pre-Communist era.[10] Communism from the late 1940s claimed to 'liberate' women from Confucian constraints, supposedly empowering them through negating gender differences and the rigid hierarchies built around such ideas, and freeing women from a life of domestic vassalage. Evaluating such claims has produced a major body of work.[11]

In terms of colonial impact, gender in the Sinic Pacific was shielded from the effects of increasingly large numbers of incoming peoples excepting colonies like Macau and, from the 1840s, Hong Kong, where Chinese and incoming peoples commingled and formed fusion societies and cultures. A 'closed' Northeast Asia contrasted diametrically with other areas of the Pacific which, to western eyes, were saturated with femininity. In the Polynesian Pacific, women and their sexual accommodations of European men reached mythic proportions.[12] Originating in accounts generated by the first three voyages of James Cook (1768–71, 1772–5, 1776–9), these myths came to define the South Pacific. European myths of 'free love' akin to legendary ancient Greece and Rome abounded, but they were erroneous, obscuring the complex system of obligation and reciprocity that accompanied intimate relations. Nevertheless, these differing manifestations of sexual cultures and the accessibility of local women to European men, formed the basis for demarcations of civilisation across the region, that carried with it potent valences that significantly impacted the course of history.

From the archipelagic Pacific and the Pacific littorals of Asia, the Americas and Australia, European cultural descriptions teem with references to gender and the way societies organised around male and female roles. This literature, which can be broadly described as 'anthropological', was based upon (supposedly) objective observations by westerners upon 'primitive' or 'static' cultures. Once anthropology became professionalised in the twentieth century, fieldwork became the standard method for gaining an 'insider view' into Pacific cultures being studied and described. The works of Margaret Mead from the 1920s, for instance, investigated gender, adolescence and sexual cultures in Sāmoa, New Guinea and Bali. Her most famous work, which launched her career and came to define sexual cultures not only in Sāmoa but also in the wider region, was *The Coming of Age in Samoa: A Psychological Study of Primitive Youth for Western Civilization,* first published in 1928. Based on the confessions of girls about their unfettered sexual freedoms during adolescence, the book spurred the ideal of 'free love' that underlay the West's 'sexual revolution' of the late 1960s. Mead's findings about the sex lives of Sāmoan girls have since been challenged, if not debunked.[13] Bronisław Malinowski likewise drew increased international attention to sexuality and the Pacific with his 1929 classic work of sexology, *The Sexual Lives of Savages,* based upon fieldwork undertaken in the Trobriand Islands when it was under Australian colonial rule.[14]

Descriptions of 'the Other' were often blended with chronicles of European contact. The interaction between anthropology and history in both the generation of sources and in the academic work on the region is important – as it is in other regions – and the borders between the disciplines are blurred. Both disciplines were framed on the notion that western observers provided impartial vistas into Pacific societies, cultures and the past, as in the case of Mead. Since the 1970s such notions of objectivity have been exposed by postcolonial scholars as deceits and another form of imperial control and empowerment. The pitched battle of the 1990s between Gananath Obeyesekere and Marshall Sahlins over Cook's death in Hawai'i invigorated the postcolonial pushback against the colonising gaze of the disciplines of anthropology and history, with global repercussions.[15] This was reworked twofold within Pacific history, by postcolonial and feminist scholars, forming a specific branch of gender history.

The prominence of gender in Pacific historical texts has spurred much academic work. In addition to textual readings, investigations of visual representations have played a particularly prominent role. This is most apparent in the work on the South Pacific – Pacific Islands and Australia – where anthropology and history, text and visual representation have marked studies of gender to a striking extent.[16] Postcolonial scholars, who objected to scholarly practices that perpetuated colonial hierarchies and concepts, emerged internationally, though voices from the Pacific have also had a considerable impact in shaping studies of gender in Pacific history. Scholars from a mix of intellectual traditions – art history, history of science, anthropology, film studies, postcolonialism and feminist studies, as well as history – have variously studied representations of racialised femininity and masculinity, demonstrating how regional particularities, such as Polynesia versus Melanesia, have had considerable cultural and historical importance.[17]

Examining the historical impact of colonial stereotypes and how greatly Pacific women's lives diverged from colonial stereotypes has also provided a rich vein of historical investigation. Linking studies of representation with the lives of historical figures shows how women defied simplistic archetypes. In many areas of the Pacific – Polynesia, for example – women have historically held considerable political power. Ka'humanu, *kuhina-nui* to King Kamehameha of Hawai'i, was an influential figure at the outset of American missionary activity. Missionaries attempted to prevent young Hawaiian women from engaging in sexual commerce with legions of US whalers who arrived in Hawaiian ports from the 1820s expecting the legendary 'refreshment' that island women were supposed to bestow willingly on male crews. The missionary quest to curtail sexual connections between Hawaiian women and New England whalers would have had no effect were it not for Ka'ahumanu imposing a *kapu* on young women, preventing their interaction with whaling crews. This action both preserved Ka'ahumanu's chiefly authority and protected the women from an exploitative exchange with the US crewmen, some of whom turned to violence to express their displeasure at the attack upon their perceived rights to sex.[18] Ka'humanu's influence was critical to the introduction of Christianity, a turning point in Hawaiian history on many levels; not least of which entailed a layering of ancient Hawaiian notions of masculinity and femininity with additional and often antithetical ideas about how men and women should act and be valued in society.

These machinations of imperial power and competing notions of imperial masculinity, Pacific femininity and Christian ideals of gender had a dramatic impact on 1840s Tahiti. Here Queen Pōmare IV was confronted by French Admiral Abel Aubert Dupetit Thouars' gunboat diplomacy aiming to extend French control over the islands. The encounter between Dupetit Thouars and the young queen, who was supported by British missionaries, is replete with gendered and racialised dimensions. French sources condemned Queen Pōmare as drunk, sexually lascivious and disorderly in body and habit, whilst British sources focused upon her feminine suffering and maternal virtue, portraying her as a Pacific Queen Victoria (see Figure 13.2). Dupetit Thouars and the other Frenchmen involved were meanwhile cast as brutish violators of her realm. The iconography of Queen Victoria also featured in the overthrow in the 1890s of Hawaiian Queen Lilioukalani by American planters.[19] The projected virtue of

*Figure 13.2*   George Baxter, *Pomare Queen of Tahiti, the Persecuted Christian Surrounded by her Family at the Afflictive moment when the French forces were landing, 1845*

the Queen stood for the worth of her people and the justice of their cause: protecting indigenous rights and lawful political processes. US economic and strategic interests in the islands nonetheless overrode this, and Hawai'i was annexed to the United States in 1898.

These high-ranking women, along with other similar examples, received their authority through traditional systems of familial prestige and hereditary power. Once imperial zones had been established across the region by the turn of the twentieth century, women organised in innovative ways to challenge the excesses of colonialism.

Within two years of the publication of Margaret Mead's classic *The Coming of Age in Samoa*, which cast Sāmoan women both sexually and apolitically, Sāmoan women in the Mandated Territory of Western Sāmoa had formed an arm of the nationalist movement opposed to New Zealand rule. Following the massacre by New Zealand forces of Mau leaders who espoused non-violent resistance in Apia on 28 December 1929, the New Zealand military then raided homes in search of other Mau men who had fled into the steep and heavily vegetated hills behind the town. New Zealand was accused in this new phase of waging a 'war on women and children'. In the wake of these developments, the wives of four Mau leaders – Ala Tamasese, Rosabel Nelson, Faamusami Malietoa (wife of High Chief Faumauina) and Paisami Tuimalealiifano – formed the Women's Mau along with significant numbers of other women who were affected by this violent turn of events (see Figure 13.3). The New Zealand administrator's report to the League of Nations on this development described those who had formed the Women's Mau as 'dissolute', thereby aligning women's political activism with being 'public women' or 'prostitutes' – a connection which had been made both

*Figure 13.3* 'Leaders of the Women's Mau', 1930

before and since by detractors of women's involvement in the political realm, but was here compounded by racial inferences of ingrained sexual 'immorality'. This accusation enraged Sāmoan nationalists. The leaders of the Women's Mau demanded a public apology from the administrator that was never proffered.[20]

Forty years after this episode of Sāmoan women's involvement in political protests against New Zealand, an eighty-year-old Māori woman, Whina Cooper, became the figurehead for the civil rights movement for Māori throughout the country. In a powerful and symbolic protest, in 1975 Cooper led the thirty-day Māori Land March, 700 miles down the length of New Zealand's North Island to the nation's capital of Wellington (see Figure 13.4). The march drew thousands and focused international attention on inequities and injustices endured by Māori through breaches of the 1840 Treaty of Waitangi. Arguably, the scarf-wearing Whina Cooper is as iconic a figure in New Zealand history as was Rosa Parks in the 1960s struggle for Civil Rights in the United States. Cooper's life had been characterised by community leadership 'gifted' by hereditary factors and *mana* (authority and power). She became the first president of the Māori Women's Welfare League which gave her a national profile in indigenous affairs. Cooper's activism was not aimed at rights for Māori women over that of Māori men, but rather for justice along racial lines between indigenous Māori and the Pakeha [European] majority: this was an objective shared by many anti-colonial women activists around the region, who perceived the main barrier to social equity to be not the oppression of all women by men (as western feminists did), but rather the oppression of racial minorities, of which they were a part.[21]

The historical function of gender and power was concentrated when hybrid Pacific communities founded by Pacific women and incoming men were created throughout the region. An investigation of the histories of these communities provides many insights into how Pacific women defied the passivity of colonial stereotypes. From Pitcairn Island to Ngatik Island in Micronesia and in sealing and whaling communities from Bass Strait, New Zealand to the Bonin Islands in the Okhotsk Sea, and in 'Eurasian' communities across the region from Batavia, Macau and French Indochina, it was the seemingly most unremarkable historic events that have had the most considerable historical legacy. The intimate commingling of colonial peoples (usually men) and indigenous people (usually women) generated *mestizo* populations across the region. Yet in traditional historical narratives, which have been preoccupied with the public deeds of

*Figure 13.4* 'Whina Cooper addressing Māori Land March at Hamilton', 1975

white men, this aspect of colonial history has received the least historical attention.[22]

Despite their prevalence throughout the region, mixed populations were the focus of attention, sometimes for their perceived 'degeneracy', and at other times as drivers of racial improvement.[23] The intermingling of white male whalers and traders with Māori communities in New Zealand began in the late eighteenth century in the far north, before spreading gradually throughout the country following the

establishment of sealing, timber getting and other extraction industries. European men learnt that marriage to highborn Māori women
brought with it numerous advantages of social prestige and land
entitlements, though this entailed considerable reciprocity. Pakeha-
Māori, as they were known – white men who had entered Māori
communities through marriage – accrued different powers than their
counterparts across the Tasman Sea in Australia or in other settings
where women were extracted from their familial networks and
protections. In New Zealand, white observers were struck by the
seeming prestige that Māori women held in their societies.[24] In this
they were correct: Māori women's *mana* was retained to a far greater
degree than in other colonial scenarios around the region. A critical
difference in New Zealand was that white men were absorbed into
Māori communities to a far greater extent making these men subject
to extant power and gendered systems that preserved the social status
of women and curtailed that of colonial men.

Ideas about racial superiority and inferiority played an important
role in shaping intimate relations throughout the region. In tropical
beachcomber communities, foreign men melded into nineteenth-
century tropical island societies according to their political utility.
Beachcombers often married local women, gained access to land and
then acted as traders and go-betweens for local people and European
merchants. Some of the intimate relationships between island women
and beachcombers were affectionate and were regarded as marriages.
Yet the intervention of racial views in these intimate connections
compounded the inherent inequality between men and women in
nineteenth-century marriage, so that many beachcombers considered their marriages as versions of a master–servant relationship.[25]

Relations in Australia's twentieth-century colony of Papua were
shaped by anxieties about the perceived sexual threats by Papuan men
to the growing number of white women in the colony. Accordingly,
the colonial administration passed the White Woman's Protection
Ordinance in 1926 which was based on unfounded fears that the
influx of greater numbers of white women into the territory was
leading to an upsurge in sexual violence against them by Papuan
men. Such anxieties were common in other colonial settings, divert-
ing attention away from the most significant instance of predatory
sexual behaviour; that perpetrated by white men towards local
women. In the Papuan case, the presence of a significant 'half-caste'
population (admitted by colonial administrators), identified the more
pervasive story of cross-racial sexual exploitation of Papuan women
by white men, though these relationships were largely hidden and

illicit.[26] The discretion that Papuan women had in entering these relationships was limited, a number of historians have concluded, citing an acknowledgment by Australia's administrator of the neighbouring New Guinea territory that 'a few years ago ... it was practically impossible to find a white man, except the Missionaries, who had not his mary [an indigenous woman], and that in the procuring of the mary her like or dislike was not of the least importance'.[27]

In northern Australia, the politics of intimacy and the mixing of races played out in intriguing ways. In the pastoral economy that dominated northern Australia in the twentieth century, Aboriginal women operated as vital workers, prized for their skills on horseback, and as intimate partners of many white men employed in the industry. Such intimate relationships and the resulting mixed-race community, were so prevalent and troubling to government authorities that legislation was introduced in the Northern Territory in 1911 to make such liaisons unlawful. To skirt this legislation, the practice of dressing Aboriginal women to appear as men became widespread. As was the case in Papua, violence and force were highly significant factors in white men's gaining access to Aboriginal women, yet, even within these circumstances, women were able to exercise some self-determination.[28]

Intimacy in Pacific history also involved domestic service relationships. Domestic service was a dominant mode of interaction between colonial men and women and indigenous peoples, mostly women, across the region. It involved cooking, cleaning and childcare and often also included sexual relations too, initiated within the asymmetric power relationships inherent in domestic service that were compounded by the dynamics of colonialism.[29] Racial dynamics operated in some unique and draconian ways. In twentieth-century Australia, governments attempted to solve a number of 'problems' through linking the domestic service needs of middle-class, white families with the government practice of removing Aboriginal children, in this instance girls, from their mothers. (Aboriginal boys were also removed for their families and hired out as farm labourers.) It was hoped that removed girls, who would be exposed to affluent white society, would spurn relationships with Aboriginal men in favour of white partners, thus 'diluting' or eradicating Australia's indigenous 'problem' along eugenic reproductive principals. A number of Aboriginal-authored accounts, such as Margaret Tucker's *If Everyone Cared* (1977), Glenyse Ward's *Unna You Fullas* (1991) and Doris Pilkington's story of her mother and aunts, *Follow the Rabbit Proof Fence* (1996), detailed the effects of being a young girl caught up in this grand scheme to preserve race and gender orders.[30] Rather than revealing the benefits of the scheme, these accounts and others reveal the inhumanity these girls experienced in institutions and in white homes, where paragons of white femininity sometimes brutalised the young girls in their charge, and they were routinely sexually abused by the men of the household. A high number of girls left domestic assignments pregnant.[31]

These twentieth-century views of white women in suburban Australia are part of the long history of European women's presence in Pacific history. Wherever they appeared, white women added layers of complexity to this gendered history. The first European women to enter Pacific history were involved in Portugal's colony, Macau, and then the Spanish colony of the Philippines from 1565.[32] European women were present in small numbers. Donna Ysabel Barretos, for example, was the wife of Spanish captain Don Alvaro de Mendaña who attempted to establish a Spanish colony in the Solomon Islands, the supposedly fabled Biblical lands, in 1595.[33] The short-lived experiment ended in a disastrous loss of life (with about three-quarters of the colonisers having perished) due to attacks from locals and tropical diseases. When Don Alvaro died, Donna Ysabel was made the governor of the settlement, though the Solomon settlement was soon abandoned, with the remnants of the population limping into Manila. There, Donna Ysabel married the governor's cousin three months later.[34] Yet such lives were rare: European men greatly outnumbered European women in Iberian Pacific colonies, resulting in substantial *mestizo* populations.

The presence of white women in the Pacific has produced some interesting arguments. Many male-centred studies of empire argued that the late arrival of white women in colonial arenas increased the distance and tensions between imperial men and colonised people, as they came between the intimate colonial bonds white men had forged with Indigenous women and their communities. In the Pacific, such views were challenged by studies that tested the view that 'idle white ladies' poisoned harmonious colonial situations through their demanding, moralistic and racist presence.[35] The colonial society of Fiji offered one such setting in which these empire-wide questions about the effect of white women's presence were deliberated. Fiji was a plantation economy where a small, white population presided over Indigenous Fijians and indentured labourers imported from British India to work the sugar plantations. In one account, white women were defended and absolved of the accusation that it was their presence that eroded good relations between whites, Indians and Fijians in the late nineteenth century when there was an increase in the numbers of white women. Instead, a sentimental picture of racial harmony, especially between white women and their Fijian servants, was proposed. This cross-racial bonding of women, a case of universal sisterhood, was posited upon shared female experiences of marriage, birth and childrearing that transcended race: a view that can rarely be sustained in a colonial setting. Critics of this account pointed to the lack of attention given to the historical views of Fijian or Indian servants, who no doubt had quite divergent views about the sentimental relationships between white women and their household staff.[36]

The presence of white women had significantly different historical outcomes in tropical colonies such as Fiji than it did in temperate settler societies. For example, the key to the success of the British settler empire, with its Pacific concentration in Australia, New Zealand, Canada and the United States, was the presence of substantial numbers of European women amongst the ranks of settlers. Their reproductive work not only produced biologically European offspring, but these women also kept a British culture and identity relatively intact.[37] From the formative works in Australian women's history there has been a steady stream of scholarship on convict women as founding mothers. In differing ways, these works have enriched understanding about the lives of convict women and their purpose in the grand scheme of Britain's imperial outreach. They have stressed the factors of work, sexuality and the reproductive intent behind the transportation of thousands of women to Australia between 1788 and the 1840s, comprising about one-sixteenth of the transported population. Other historians have highlighted the story of convict women who rejected the seemingly mandatory heterosexual and reproductive destiny in favour of homosexual relations.[38]

There were considerable gender imbalances in Pacific populations, compounded by mid-century gold rushes in California and southeast Australia. The relative absence of women troubled authorities who feared the results of masculine frontiers. Pervasive homosexual relations among men was a leading concern, and part of the rationale for a push to 'domesticate' the frontiers in the form of Selection Acts (in Australia) or Homestead Acts (in the United States) from the 1860s onwards; such policies sought to break up large landholdings into smaller family-run farms. In the Australian case, these acts were complemented by female immigration schemes. The re-creation of a different frontier society based upon family units, it was hoped, would shift the character of the frontier from one dominated by 'marauding men' to one that was tamed by women with their 'civilising' Christian virtues and tender concerns of childrearing. Such ideas strongly drove suffrage campaigns that were successful first in New Zealand and Australia. Taming the excesses of white working-class masculinity, with its stereotyped alcoholic and violent tendencies directed at women in the home, was a political agenda for middle-class white women.[39]

It is telling that British officials initially contemplated bringing women from China and the Pacific Islands to be wives and mothers of antipodean working-class stock in the planning stages of the Port Jackson colony in the late eighteenth century. The abandonment of this plan set this antipodean settler society on a different racial course towards aspirationally white-only societies. The influx of substantial numbers of Chinese miners, who were almost exclusively male, prompted the redefinition of the United States and Australia as 'white men's countries'. New Zealand followed suit after their first gold rush in the 1860s.[40] Chinese men were being pushed out of China into these increasingly hostile societies because of the deterioration of the Qing Dynasty and accompanying economic hardships intensified by the financial terms of unequal treaties. This situation was compounded by the Taiping Rebellion (1850–64) which aimed to overthrow traditional systems of governance and cultural structures, particularly of Confucian gender hierarchies. The rebellion proclaimed the equality of men and women, and 'Taiping armies included women's battalions and women soldiers'. Despite this seemingly radical departure from the status quo, ultimately the 'Taiping Rebellion could not break free of feudal ideology' with its axiomatic gender hierarchy of men over women, in spite of all protestations to the contrary.[41]

In white settler nations the movement of large numbers of Chinese men, pushed by internal disruptions and attracted to the booming mining economies, was met by restricted immigration laws that set race-based criteria upon who could enter these 'white countries', though Chinese men, and other nationalities, circumvented restrictions in various ways.[42] The establishment of plantation economies throughout the region coincided with the expansion of the mining frontiers that expanded into western Pacific Islands in the second half of the century in French-run New Caledonia and New Guinea 'shared' by the Netherlands, Britain and Australia and Germany from the 1880s. Indentured labour, again overwhelmingly male, and originating mainly in Asia, and especially from China, France's Indo-Chinese colonies and also from the Pacific Islands provided the labour force for these two colonial economies. The overwhelmingly masculine make-up of these non-European migrant populations (with the major exception of Indian men and women brought to Fiji to be workers on the sugar plantations) prompted not only further race-based restricted immigration policies, but also a grotesque cultural shift.

The sexual threat to white women posed by Indigenous men that had been such an important (and largely imagined) anxiety in settler frontier mythologies was recalibrated and Asian men were now portrayed in sexually threatening ways as peddlers of opiates and seducers of vulnerable white women, thereby polluting the purity of the white races. Articulations of gendered and racial anxieties can be found across the cultural spectrum, with political cartoons being an especially virulent means of communicating cultural fears. The work of US-born cartoonist Livingston Hopkins, who published cartoons in the stridently racist *Bulletin* magazine in Sydney, epitomised the monstrous dimensions of miscegenation anxieties – especially in his 1902 cartoon *Piebald Possibilities – a Little Australian Christmas Family Party of the Future*.[43] Briton Robert Fletcher likewise encapsulated the perceived perils of racial death and the depletion of white masculinity through cross-racial relations in *His Native Wife* (1924). In this novel, Fletcher provided a fictionalised account of his real-life experience as a plantation overseer in the New Hebrides when he 'succumbed' to a relationship with a local woman, Onéla Kohkonne. In *His Native Wife*, the leading male character endures the erosion of masculinity and self-worth, finally sacrificing himself to sharks: his death was a metaphor for white racial extinction occasioned by the crossing of races.[44]

The upsurge in colonial activity in the Pacific and the accompanying denigration of non-Europeans in the second half of the nineteenth century was challenged in many ways. In Japan, these forces were met with a unique response that would have a far-reaching impact on the region, culminating in the Pacific theatre of the Second World War and beyond. The traumatic intrusion by the United States into Japanese territory and history from 1853 set Japan on a path of rapid political reform involving the restitution of the Meiji Emperor, the westernisation of its institutions and the swift industrialisation of its economy. In its effort to westernise and modernise at a remarkable pace, there was also questioning about the status and role of women. The leading educator and social critic Fukuzawa Yukichi is credited with being the first to grapple with questions about women, gender and what aspects of Japanese tradition should be jettisoned or retained regarding women. Fukuzawa made key gendered prescriptions he considered crucial to modernising Japanese society, arguing against polygamy, for the education of girls regardless of rank or wealth (noble women had been receiving education before the Meiji reform period), for greater equality between the sexes, a higher social status to be assigned to women as well as greater attention paid to improving women's health. Some of Fukuzawa's ideas were adopted promptly, whilst others would take longer to break entrenched ideas about women and their subordinate status.[45] It was not until 1947, when the Japanese Constitution, written during the Allied Occupation, was enacted, that gender equality was given the protection of the law.

Japan's modernisation also entailed militarisation. In order to fend off European domination, Japanese leaders mimicked many European strategies to advance national power, particularly in relation to imperial expansion. In Korea (annexed in 1910) Japan commenced a programme of settler colonialism, with mass migrations of Japanese to Korea and the implementation of numerous assimilationist policies designed at blending Japanese settlers with Koreans, not the least of which was the promotion of intermarriage between the two groups. Despite public acclaim for couples that entered into such marriages, rates of intermarriage remained low, due to 'mutual contempt and antagonism'.[46] The effects of denigrating racial and gendered ideas were brutally apparent when Imperial Japan launched its attack against the Chinese nationalist capital in 1937, unleashing sexualised violence against the people of Nanjing, an atrocity that became known as 'Rape of Nanking'. After this shocking incident, the system of 'comfort women' was expanded throughout Japan's imperial zone as Japanese officials excused the sexual violence as a consequence of the pent-up frustrations of soldiers who 'required' sexual access to women. This system of sexual slavery had a particular impact on Korean women but also engulfed women throughout Imperial Japan's range. Though this scheme of ensuring sex for soldiers was not unique to Japan (previously France and Britain had devised similar systems in imperial arenas) it remains one of the most challenging legacies of the Second World War with all its unprecedented horrors, as does the Rape of Nanking, marking an apogee of colonial rule saturated with gendered power.[47]

The impact of the war upon the Pacific is immeasurable, in every respect.[48] The war disrupted gendered ideas about femininity and masculinity, transforming notions of gendered work, societal roles, sex and political ambitions, not to mention colonial orders. Marriages between Allied servicemen and Asian wives were the first to test rigid restricted immigration laws. The end of the Second World War was quickly followed by anti-Communist wars that were also heavily influenced by anti-imperial ambitions. The Korean War, and the Vietnam War in particular, transformed the countries where the wars were fought and on the homefronts of combatant countries, further breaking down Asian immigration barriers into white settler societies, and increasing social prejudices against intermarriages. The 1960s and 1970s sparked numerous 'revolutions': decolonisation and power struggles in newly independent countries, civil rights movements targeting race, feminist ones targeting gender inequalities, sexual revolutions, globalisation, educational, economic and technological ones.

All of these vast changes have had an untold impact on Pacific people and, in many instances, have had a multitude of positive effects on 'closing the gaps' for life opportunities and living standards for men and women across the region. But these vast changes have come unevenly, and many Pacific peoples still live in poverty, the majority of them being women who do not have adequate access to health, education, employment opportunities and personal security in regions of conflict.[49]

Gendered hierarchies have changed, but nonetheless remain in place. Political and economic power remains predominantly a male province, notwithstanding relatively recent examples of female heads of government throughout the region from the Philippines, Indonesia and South Korea to New Zealand and Australia. As power shifts in the Pacific away from the West and towards China, perhaps one of the most significant challenges in the region will emerge from that nation's marked gender imbalance. Hawaiians have a saying that 'the past is in front of us' and historians of gender in the Pacific will continue to have much material to work with as they explain historical continuities and changes, and evaluate how gender continues to shape the region's history in profoundly important ways.

## Notes

1. Charles Darwin, quoted in F. W. Nicholas and J. M. Nicholas, *Charles Darwin in Australia* (Cambridge, 2002), p. 97.
2. Lyndall Ryan, *Tasmanian Aborigines: A History Since 1803* (Sydney, 2012), p. 197.
3. Ryan, *Tasmanian Aborigines*, pp. 268–70.
4. Bernard Smith, *The Spectre of Truganini* (Sydney, 1980).
5. Vivienne Rae Ellis, *Trucanini: Queen or Traitor?* (Canberra 1981).
6. Lyndall Ryan and Neil Smith, 'Trugernanner (Truganini) (1812?–1876)', *Australian Dictionary of Biography*, 18 vols (Melbourne, 1966–2007), VI, p. 305.
7. Vivian Lee Nyitray 'Confucian Complexities: China, Japan, Korea and Vietnam', in Teresa A. Meade and Merry E. Wiesner-Hanks, eds., *A Companion to Gender History* (Oxford, 2006), pp. 281–2.

8. Barbara Watson Andaya, 'Gender History, Southeast Asia and the "World Regions" Framework', in Meade and Wiesner-Hanks, eds., *A Companion to Gender History*, p. 324.

9. *The Qianlong Emperor's Edict on the Occasion of Lord Macartney's Mission to China* (September 1793): http://afe.easia.columbia.edu/ps/china/qian-long_edicts.pdf, accessed 30 January 2013.

10. Gail Hershatter, 'State of the Field: Women in China's Long Twentieth Century', *The Journal of Asian Studies* 63 (2004), 992.

11. Gail Hershatter and Wang Zheng, 'Chinese History: A Useful Category of Gender Analysis', *American Historical Review* 113 (2008), 1404–21.

12. Patty O'Brien, *The Pacific Muse: Exotic Femininity and the Colonial Pacific* (Seattle, 2006).

13. Margaret Mead, *Coming of Age in Samoa: A Psychological Study of Primitive Youth for Western Civilization* (New York, 1928); Mead, *Growing Up in New Guinea: A Comparative Study of Primitive Education* (London, 1931); Mead, *From the South Seas: Studies of Adolescence and Sex in Primitive Societies* (New York, 1939); Derek Freeman, *Margaret Mead and Samoa: The Making and Unmaking of an Anthropological Myth* (Cambridge, MA, 1983).

14. Bronisław Malinowski, *The Sexual Life of Savages in North-Western Melanesia: An Ethnographic Account of Courtship, Marriage, and Family Life among the Natives of the Trobriand Islands, British New Guinea* (London, 1929).

15. Gananath Obeyesekere, *The Apotheosis of Captain Cook: European Mythmaking in the Pacific* (Princeton, 1992); Marshall Sahlins, *How 'Natives' Think: About Captain Cook, For Example* (Chicago, 1995).

16. Bernard Smith, *European Vision and the South Pacific* (Oxford, 1960).

17. See, for example, Bernard Smith, *Imagining the Pacific: In the Wake of Cook* (Melbourne, 1992); Teresia Teaiwa, 'Bikinis and other S/pacific N/oceans', *The Contemporary Pacific* 6 (1994), 87–109; Haunani-Kay Trask, *From a Native Daughter: Colonialism and Sovereignty in Hawai'i* (Honolulu, 2012).

18. O'Brien, *The Pacific Muse*, pp. 109–10; Noelani Arista, 'Captive Women in Paradise 1796–1826: The *Kapu* on Prostitution in Hawaiian Historical Legal Context', *American Indian Culture and Research Journal* 35 (2011), 39–55.

19. Patricia O'Brien, 'Think of Me as a Woman: Queen Pomare of Tahiti and Anglo-French Imperial Contest in the 1840s Pacific', *Gender and History* 18 (2006), 108–29; Viviane Fayaud, 'A Tahitian Woman in Majesty: French Images of Queen Pomare', *History Australia* 3 (2006), 121–6; O'Brien, *The Pacific Muse*, pp. 209–10.

20. *Mandated Territory of Western Samoa Tenth Report of the Government of New Zealand on the Administration for the Year ended the 31st March 1930* (Wellington, NZ, 1930), p. 5; Faamu Faumuina, Paisami Tuimalealiifano and Ala Tamasese to the Administrator of Western Samoa, 10 September 1930, Archives New Zealand, IT1 41 EX1/23/8, part 19.

21. Michael King, *Whina: A Biography of Whina Cooper* (Auckland, NZ, 1983), pp. 8, 216.

22. O'Brien, *The Pacific Muse*, pp. 115–64; Jean Gelman Taylor, *The Social World of Batavia: European and Eurasian in Dutch Asia* (Madison, WI,

1983); Ann Laura Stoler, *Race and the Education of Desire: Foucault's History of Sexuality and the Colonial Order of Things* (Durham, NC, 1995).

23. Damon Salesa, *Racial Crossings: Race, Intermarriage, and the Victorian British Empire* (Oxford, 2011).

24. Patricia Grimshaw and Helen Morton, 'Theorizing Māori Women's Lives: Paradoxes of the White Male Gaze', in Robert Borofsky, ed., *Remembrance of Pacific Pasts: An Invitation to Remake History* (Honolulu, 2000), pp. 269–86; Patricia Grimshaw, 'Interracial Marriages and Colonial Regimes in Victoria and Aotearoa/New Zealand', *Frontiers: A Journal of Women Studies* 23 (2002), 12–28.

25. Caroline Ralston, *Grass Huts and Warehouses: Pacific Beach Communities of the Nineteenth Century* (Canberra, 1977), pp. 20, 137–8.

26. Amirah Inglis, *Not a White Woman Safe: Sexual Anxiety and Politics in Port Moresby 1920–1934* (Canberra, 1974), pp. 12–20.

27. A. E. Wisdom to J. G. McLaren, 9 July 1924, cited in Roger C. Thompson, 'Making a Mandate: Australia's New Guinea Policies 1919–1925', *Journal of Pacific History* 25 (1990), 74–5.

28. Ann McGrath, *Born in the Cattle: Aborigines in Cattle Country* (Sydney, 1987).

29. Ann Laura Stoler, *Carnal Knowledge and Imperial Power: Race and the Intimate in Colonial Rule* (Berkeley, 2002).

30. Margaret Tucker, *If Everyone Cared* (Sydney, 1977); Glenyse Ward, *Unna You Fullas* (Broome, 1991); Doris Pilkington (Nugi Garimara), *Follow the Rabbit Proof Fence* (St Lucia, Qld., 1996).

31. Victoria Haskins, *One Bright Spot* (New York, 2005).

32. George Brian Souza, *The Survival of Empire: Portuguese Trade and Society in China and the South China Sea, 1630–1754* (Cambridge, 1986), p. 14.

33. O'Brien, *The Pacific Muse*, pp. 22–3.

34. Miriam Estensen, *Terra Australis Incognita: The Spanish Quest for the Mysterious Great South Land* (Sydney, 2006), p. 15.

35. Claudia Knapman, *White Women in Fiji 1835–1930: The Ruin of Empire?* (Sydney, 1986), pp. 4–9; John Young, 'Race and Sex in Fiji Re-Visited', *Journal of Pacific History*, 23 (1988), 214–22.

36. Jane Haggis, 'Gendering Colonialism or Colonizing Gender?', *Women's Studies International Forum* 13 (1990), 111–12.

37. James Belich, *Replenishing the Earth: The Settler Revolution and the Rise of the Anglo-World, 1783–1939* (Oxford, 2009).

38. Joy Damousi, *Depraved and Disorderly: Female Convicts Sexuality and Gender in Colonial Australia* (Cambridge, 1997).

39. Marilyn Lake, 'Frontier Feminism and the Marauding White Man', *Journal of Australian Studies* 20 (1996), 12–20.

40. Marilyn Lake and Henry Reynolds, *Drawing the Global Colour Line: White Men's Countries and the International Challenge of Racial Equality* (Cambridge, 2008).

41. Wang Qingshu, 'The History and Current Status of Chinese Women's Participation in Politics', in Shirley Mow, Tao Jie and Zheng Bijun, eds., *Holding Up Half the Sky: Chinese Women Past, Present and Future* (New York, 2004), pp. 93–5.

42. Compare Adam McKeown, 'Movement', ch. 7 in this volume.

43. See Geoffrey Dutton, *White on Black: The Australian Aborigine Portrayed in Art* (Melbourne, Vic., 1974), plate 147.

44. O'Brien, *The Pacific Muse*, pp. 227–8.

45. *Fukuzawa Yukichi on Japanese Women: Selected Works*, ed. Eiichi Kiyooka (Tokyo, 1988); Martha Tocco, 'Made in Japan: Meiji Women's Education', in Barbara Molony and Kathleen Uno, eds., *Gendering Modern Japanese History* (Cambridge MA, 2005), p. 39.

46. Jun Uchida, *Brokers of Empire: Japanese Settler Colonialism in Korea, 1876–1945* (Cambridge, MA, 2011), pp. 375–6.

47. Elisa Camiscioli, *Reproducing the French Race: Immigration, Intimacy and Embodiment in the Early Twentieth Century* (Durham, NC, 2009).

48. Compare Akira Iriye, 'A Pacific Century?', ch. 5 in this volume.

49. Kathy E. Ferguson and Monique Mionesco, eds., *Gender and Globalization in Asia and the Pacific: Method, Practice, Theory* (Honolulu, 2008).

# 14

# Politics

## Robert Aldrich

The states of the Pacific, island and littoral, display dramatically varying political institutions and ideologies. On the marches of the Pacific, an emperor reigns in Japan, Thailand and Cambodia enthrone kings with a semi-divine status, Malaysia has a rotating monarchy; in Tonga, too, a crowned head of state rules. In Singapore, Australia, New Zealand and Canada, as well as several island nations, the Westminster system of government represents a British imperial legacy. The People's Republic of China, North Korea, Vietnam and Laos espouse a Marxist ideology. The United States forms a federal republic, with most of the Central and Latin American states unitary presidential republics. France, the United States, New Zealand and Australia administer non-contiguous territories in Oceania. Such diversity results from centuries of change during which indigenous forms of politics were challenged by colonialism, reacted to it, and eventually blended with ideas and institutions from outside.

In 1983, the Paris-based Institut du Pacifique heralded the Pacific as the 'new centre of the world'.[1] Though not suggesting that the Pacific, ocean and land, formed a Braudelian unity, the institute pointed to linkages that it claimed justified a regional analytical approach corresponding to a geopolitical reality. The position provoked critiques about the proposed dense grid of connections and about definitions of where the Pacific begins and ends, alongside reminders that already a century earlier, geopolitical theorists (and colonial lobbyists) had prophesied the advent of the Pacific as the political and commercial centre of a new world order.[2] Commentators have continued to voice reservations about the Pacific as a 'Mediterranean in the making'.[3] Some have nevertheless identified aggregated zones within the Pacific, one of the most useful being a 'Pacific Asian region'.[4]

In strategic and military politics, certain lines can indeed be drawn across the Pacific, both past and present, from Spanish colonialism in Mexico and the Philippines in the 1500s to American expansion (and later claims to military hegemony) across a rectangle bounded by Alaska, Hawai'i, Sāmoa and Micronesia, extending to contemporary defence alliances with Japan, Taiwan, Australia and New Zealand. In terms of political institutions and philosophies, unifying traits prove more difficult to discern, although in today's Pacific world, there exist evident commonalities: the omnipresence of written constitutions, parliamentary institutions, state-to-state relations conducted within the framework of the so-called 'Westphalian' system and growing cooperation through regional and global organisations.

In exploring the structures and ideologies of politics around a fragmented, indeed balkanised, Pacific, this chapter underlines the obvious, but essential, differences in precolonial political formations, though pointing out that some political systems (China and its tributary states, for instance) provided centripetal nodes. Secondly, it suggests that colonialism – both rivalry for territory and the imposition of new forms of rule – provides the pivot in the political transformation of the Pacific, though in varying circumstances and outcomes: one key difference is between settler societies in the eastern Pacific and Australasia, on the one hand, and the states of Pacific Asia, on the other. Furthermore, the chapter argues that, in anti-colonialist and nationalist campaigns, and in the postcolonial successor states, there occurred a hybridisation of political perspectives, old and new. Imperialist powers effaced precolonial political formations, but did not wipe them out completely. Political experiments, regime changes and turmoil in the years since decolonisation evidence the difficult *métissage* of political philosophies and structures; arguably, nowhere in the world have ructions proved so explosive as in the western Pacific. Perhaps contemporary systems of governance (and opposition) that with constitutions, legislatures and alliance systems appear globally familiar, but which possess distinct particularities, can best be seen as a landscape of political isomorphism around the Pacific rather than a terrain of political identity conjoining a 'Pacific world'. Similarities in form meld with underlying differences in culture that shape political life. Given the disunity of the Pacific, a regional approach allows for exploration of these landscapes, and since Lisa Ford's chapter in this volume explores issues of international law and politics, especially in regard to colonial possession, the particular focus here is on institutions and ideologies inside polities.[5]

## Colonialism and decolonisation in the Eastern Pacific

The end of the eighteenth century provides a convenient starting point before the final colonial partition of Southeast Asia and Oceania, the disaggregation of the Chinese imperial system and the transformation of Japan substantially redrew political maps. By the 1780s, such change had already started: the Netherlands was an established colonial power in the East Indies and Spain in the Philippines, the British established their first settler colony on the Australian continent, Russians moved across the Bering Strait, explorers reconnoitred islands between the Asian and American landmasses, and the United States' independence ushered in its continental expansion. Throughout the Americas, North and South, anti-colonialists inscribed ideas of the Enlightenment and the French Revolution – constitutionalism, parliamentarianism, republicanism – into manifestoes of independence.

The coastal regions of Central and South America had come under Spanish rule in the 1500s, and Spanish dominion still covered part of the northeastern Pacific. A monarchical state with a highly influential Catholic Church, Spain ruled its outposts through viceroys, though with rising friction between peninsular administrators and a settler class of *criollos* and *mestizos* of mixed Spanish and Native American ancestry. The Spanish had largely done away with the indigenous institutions, dynasties and political philosophies of the Aztecs, Incas and other polities, and marginalised the 'full-blooded' native population. Missionaries had converted most Amerindians to Catholicism, although precolonial cultural values remained resistant. The weakening of Spain, increasing strength of *criollos* and dissemination of ideas of self-government promoted liberation movements. During the early and mid-1800s, 10 new nations emerged along the Pacific – Mexico, Guatemala, El Salvador, Honduras, Nicaragua, Costa Rica, Colombia, Ecuador, Peru and Chile; Panama's independence came later.

In addition to the search for sovereignty, several issues dominated politics in these states in the long nineteenth century. One was conflict over territory, exemplified by the expansionist ambitions of Peru and Chile that culminated in the War of the Pacific of 1879–83. Chile's victory brought loss of territory to Peru and Bolivia (the latter ceding its Pacific littoral); Chile's booty, and expansion towards the Straits of Magellan, made it the dominant power of western South America. Experiments with different political systems, and violent regime transitions, marked the Hispanophone states. In Mexico, an emperor reigned briefly in the 1820s, followed by a dictatorship and then a liberal revolt in the 1850s; civil war and European intervention led to the establishment in 1864 of a French-sponsored empire under an Austrian archduke. After his overthrow, another dictator, Porfirio Díaz, held power from 1876 until revolution in 1910. Fission and fusion of polities meanwhile dominated Central America. Contests between conservatives and liberals – boiling over into occasional civil war – marked politics in several South American states.

The United States had established a more enduring form of government with powers divided between national and state institutions, though with conflicts that reached a paroxysm in the Civil War of the 1860s. Forty years earlier, the United States set out to fulfil a self-appointed 'Manifest Destiny' to extend from the Atlantic to the Pacific, and perhaps onwards. This meant conquest of the American continent south of Canada and north of Mexico, armed battle against Native American populations and confinement of 'Indians' into reservations under colonial-style rule. The large-scale destruction of Native institutions, earlier accomplished by the Spanish in Latin America, was repeated under the North Americans. Though Native American peoples and cultures proved resilient, their political institutions disappeared as part of national political life. The expansion of American settler society and federalist government also involved war against Mexico in the 1840s, taking the United States to the Pacific coast. Peripheral territories, initially ruled as conquered lands, could earn statehood, as was the case for California (1850), Oregon (1859) and Washington (1889).

American rule over the '48 States' achieved, Washington found further opportunity to expand commercially and, eventually, politically: the trade of sailing and whaling ships in the Pacific, based in such ports as San Francisco, opened entrée to Oceania and Asia. The California gold rush of the 1840s and 1850s drew settlers and focussed attentions on America's Pacific frontier – and across the Ocean. Gunboat diplomacy forced open Japan in the 1850s; in later decades Americans promoted an 'Open Door' policy in China that served its own interests. In 1867, the United States bought Alaska; the investment paid off with the Klondike Gold Rush in 1896. In the 1880s Washington added eastern Sāmoa, in the South Pacific, to its colonial portfolio. Planters, traders and missionaries instigated takeover of the Hawaiian Islands in 1897. The following year, the United States went to war against Spain, and as prize, claimed the Philippine islands and Guam. In Central America, Washington in 1903 acquired land for the Panama Canal, opened in 1914. In little more than half a century, the United States had become a continental and Pacific empire. Only two other empires – the Spanish and the British – boasted such reach across the Pacific. American sovereign territories remain more widely scattered throughout the Pacific than those of any other power.

Britain's interests in western Canada, anchored by trading posts, brought it into conflict with both the United States and Spain in the early 1800s. In 1858 Britain took over, from the Hudson's Bay Company, the city of Vancouver and its huge hinterland, and in 1869 it also purchased the Northwest Territories. The new province of British Columbia in 1871 joined the Dominion of Canada, which had been established four years earlier; London devolved most administrative and political power to settler elites. As elsewhere, the native populations, later termed First Nations, were allowed little role in politics. As subjects of the British monarch, Canadians were drawn into an international colonial and settler network. Trans-Pacific ties among Canada, Australia (federated in 1901) and New Zealand ran along lines of kinship and imperial loyalties with increasing and stable self-government in the dominions.

## Politics before colonialism: Asia and Oceania

The most complex changes in the Pacific from the late 1700s onwards occurred in Pacific Asia. Conquest, regime change, dynastic disputes and shifting borders make generalisations about precolonial Asian politics hazardous. However, a starting point is the absence of a system of separate, sovereign and nominally equal states as had evolved in Europe. Such Enlightenment and revolutionary notions as representative government, equality of citizens (or indeed the very notion of the citizen) and the separation of secular and ecclesiastical power were unknown. Western views concerning Asia indulged in stereotypes of colourful rajahs, sultans and other potentates, obsequious and scheming courtiers, and masses of impoverished peasants subject to autocratic rule: a situation that western intervention might set aright. Political realities, not surprisingly, were more complicated.

Several great political systems appeared in eastern Asia, though tribal populations and areas such as Siberia (still incompletely brought under tsarist control by the late 1700s) lay outside them. One found its origin in China, and extended to Korea, Japan and Vietnam; another was most evident in Buddhist polities that now cover much of mainland southern Asia, while the third encompassed the Islamic sultanates of the Malay world.

In the China of the Qing Dynasty (1644–1911), the emperor – charismatic and numinous, though largely invisible in the Forbidden City – reigned as hereditary and absolute sovereign. Especially important was the performance of the rites that guaranteed the beneficence of heaven. The court formed the locus of the power that the emperor exercised as the Son of Heaven. If his actions were insufficiently meritorious, if he failed in the primary task of maintaining a stable social order, the mandate would be lost. Politics was intertwined with Confucianism, harnessed by the imperial government to legitimate authority and induce public support. Virtue – benevolence, propriety, filial piety and loyalty – in theory secured social harmony. This involved obedience by subjects to rulers, wives to husbands, children to fathers, the young to elders, and pupils to teachers. Social order demanded respect, submission and homage, culminating in fealty to the emperor. However, Confucian literati sometimes took radically critical stands against abuse of imperial power, with recurrent tensions between the political leadership and the cultural elite.[6]

To govern the huge and populous Middle Kingdom, the ruler relied on a corps of administrators. The training of public servants had no parallel in Europe. The public service was open to all, designed (in principle) as a meritocracy. After many years of preparatory study candidates proved their capabilities in local, provincial and national examinations, based on the Chinese classics. Success earned postulants appointment to the administration and enormous status. Officers of the six ministries of the central government, and local administrations, were moved around, promoted and demoted according to competence and the needs of the state. China had no elected assemblies or political parties, and little possibility for political activism by the masses existed short of rebellion.

Chinese authorities saw little need for wide-ranging diplomatic relations with distant powers that lived bereft of the benefits of Chinese civilisation and the emperor's rule, though merchants traded widely in the eastern Asian region, and ventured further afield. China was self-sufficient, its relations with neighbours structured as a tribute system. Though imperial China did not seek to conquer other countries or impose its culture by force, it expected neighbours to acknowledge the supremacy of the emperor as embassies arrived to kowtow and present tribute. In return, the emperor invested local rulers with authority represented by an imperial seal, allowing autonomous government and trade with China. Such rulers held secondary position to the emperor in Beijing but enjoyed the imperial imprimatur, peace with China, commerce and the blessings of Chinese civilisation. The system did not always work so neatly in practice, as evidenced by sporadic conflicts between China and its neighbours and Beijing's difficulty in controlling frontier provinces. Yet rulers from as far south as Malacca paid tribute to the Son of Heaven.[7]

Some countries neighbouring China adopted a merit-based system for the appointment of bureaucrats by competitive examination, with ministries parallelling those of China. Korea, the most Sinified country, held the highest status among tribute nations. Vietnam, and in particular its northern and central regions, was also considerably Sinified with a corps of mandarins and an imperial court in Hué mirroring the one in Beijing. Japan, which had taken much from Chinese culture, was politically less tied to the Chinese and for only a limited period acted as an official tribute state. With a network of provincial feudal lords (*daimyō*) and class of warriors (*samurai*), the Japanese social structure differed substantially from that of China, and under the Tokugawa regime (1603–1868), political power was concentrated in the shogun in Edo (Tokyo), while the emperor (in Kyoto) reigned as a ceremonial and divine figure.

In southeastern Asia, a second great political tradition derived from brahminical and Buddhist traditions in India. Milton Osborne schematises political power in China as a pyramid, with the emperor at the apex, then ministers and court officials in the capital, provincial officials, prefects and sub-prefects, and communal officials. By contrast, he represents power in the Buddhist polities as a series of concentric circles of palace and capital, inner provinces and outer provinces, and border regions on the edge.[8] Osborne's conceptualisation links to O.W. Wolters' theory about political power as a set of 'mandalas'. He argued that the notion of 'kingdom' or 'state' is inappropriate for this region. In the early history of southeastern Asia, a plethora of rulers emerged, with succession based on cognatic relationships rather than direct inheritance, and with little emphasis on strictly delimited territory. With Indian influence, rulers styled themselves part of a Shiva-cult; 'men of prowess', in Wolters' phrase, exercised spiritual and political leadership, power legitimised with semi-divine status and ability to mobilise supporters. The mandala formed a 'network of personal loyalties rather than a territorial unit' with no fixed boundaries nor a formal bureaucracy.[9] A ruler designated his heir, often in his dying days, among numerous sons or brothers; aspiring rulers could also seize power. The link between religion and the monarchy was strong, the ruler a *devaraja* who enacted spiritual and secular power. Mandala governance led to shifting frontiers and rivalries – vassals could pay tribute to one or another ruler, or several, over time or simultaneously – punctuated by military conquests, extension and contraction of zones of effective control, and the rise and fall of dynasts, but without state formation in the western or Chinese mould and without mass political participation.

Buddhism and Hinduism structured politics in Insulindia and the Malay peninsula, from the fourteenth century overlaid by Islam and the greater or lesser adoption of *shari'ah*. Islam indeed became a defining feature of the politically fragmented Malay world with its changing political frontiers. New entities appeared, merged or divided, though some, such as the sultanate of Brunei, remained remarkably stable.

Societies were hierarchically ordered with sultans or rajahs at the top, the ruler's power residing not so much in territory controlled or wealth amassed, but the labour that he could mobilise. The 'Shadow of God on Earth', the raja or sultan, what Anthony Milner calls 'the lynchpin of the system', stood apart from the rest of society through language, clothing, court splendour; the peasant majority remained in a state of subjection.[10] Especially important was the ceremonial of power (in what Clifford Geertz famously called, in the case of Hinduised Bali, the 'theatre-state').[11] The 6,000 islands of the East Indies, and Muslim sultanates in southern Thailand and the Philippines, showed particularities of rule.

In the islands of Oceania, several political systems existed before the arrival of the Europeans. Polynesian societies were highly structured, often divided into strata of chiefs, landowners and commoners. A chief held power on the basis of hereditary rights as well as conquest or the defeat of rivals. Certain islands hosted several chiefs; in other cases, as in Tahiti, a chief's domain extended over multiple islands. By contrast, in the southwestern Pacific or Melanesia, societies were less stratified, chiefly rights were generally not hereditary, and a chief (or 'big man', as anthropologists later termed him) attained status through individual prowess and wealth. Decision-making, in practice, relied on consensus reached by discussion among chiefs and elders.[12] More than in Polynesia, society was fragmented into varying and competing villages, language and culture groups, and political entities; in New Guinea, with a population speaking thousands of languages, disaggregation remained intense.

## Colonial politics after the scramble for the Pacific

The modern process of political transformation induced by colonialism began far earlier in Asia than in Oceania with the European search for the prized commodities of the spice trade. The Portuguese led the way in the early 1500s, largely displaced by the Dutch in the 1600s; both generally limited their domains to coastal enclaves. The Spanish, sailing from South America, entrenched themselves in the Philippines. The Dutch and Spanish enjoyed privileged positions in southeastern Asia until the British East India Company mounted a challenge, taking over Penang in 1786, Singapore in 1819 and Malacca in 1824. By the end of the nineteenth century, Britain controlled the whole Malay peninsula. The acquisition of Hong Kong in 1842 greatly advanced the British sphere of political and commercial influence. The French, their main colonial rivals, in vain sought a toehold in eastern Asia until the late 1850s, when they took over southern Vietnam (Cochinchina), to which they added central and northern Vietnam (Annam and Tonkin) by the mid-1880s, as well as Cambodia (in the 1860s) and Laos (in the 1890s). Japan after the Meiji restoration entered the race for expansion, annexing the Ryukyu Islands in the 1870s, Taiwan in the 1890s and Korea in the first decade of the twentieth century. The United States captured the Philippines in 1898. Britain, France, Japan and other powers in the early 1900s secured 'concessions' in China – most famously the International Settlement and the French Concession in Shanghai – where they enjoyed extraterritorial legal privileges, trading rights and near-colonial domination.

The Pacific Asian seaboard and its hinterland, from the Indonesian archipelago to Hong Kong, thus came under European control by the late 1800s, with Japan soon in possession of an insular and continental empire further north, and variegated concessions dotting the Chinese coast. Russia meanwhile consolidated its rule over Siberia, founding Vladivostok in 1860; tsarist expansionism brought Russia head to head with Japan in Manchuria in 1904–5.

Colonial control effected immense change, especially in coastal zones, even if interior regions remained more marginally concerned.[13] Several generalisations about the shape of politics remoulded by colonialism are crucial. One is the new cartography: colonisers drew lines on maps, the entities they created eventually becoming the nation-states of the contemporary globe. Colonialism fixed political borders that had earlier been far more vague and mutable: the Dutch brought together thousands of islands to form the Netherlands Indies, while Borneo was divided between the Dutch, the British and an adventurous 'white rajah' of Sarawak. The vagaries of international conflict saw later alteration in imperial maps, as the Japanese, Americans, New Zealanders and Australians took over German colonies in the island Pacific after the First World War, and the United States succeeded Japan as the administrator of Micronesian islands after the Second World War. If colonial boundaries remained largely stable, the militancy of postcolonial secessionist movements – for example, in Maluku, Aceh and West Papua in the East Indies – testifies to the arbitrary delineation of boundaries.

Colonialism also brought migrants, both European overlords and subaltern populations whose presence upset demography and the balance of political power; migration also led, as Adam McKeown points out in his chapter, to the closing of some borders after the 1870s as both Americans and Australians feared contamination by Asians.[14] In Australia, New Zealand, Hawai'i and New Caledonia, white settlers established permanent political authority at the expense of indigenous populations with land despoliation, political disenfranchisement and efforts at cultural assimilation. In Asia and Oceania, though full colonial dominion proved relatively short-lived, demographic transformation endured: Indians became the majority in Fiji and a major presence in the Malay states; diasporic Chinese gained commercial and political sway in Indonesia, Malaysia and the Philippines, and formed the majority in Singapore. Large numbers of Japanese settled in Manchuria, though most left after 1945. Chinese, Japanese and Portuguese mixed in with Polynesian and American mainland populations in Hawai'i. Such cosmopolitanism, added to the precolonial ethnic mix of most Asian regions (and some Pacific archipelagoes), fuelled political tensions that outlived colonialism. In Pacific Asia, the colonisers' departure nevertheless restored political supremacy to Asians, though leaving it concentrated in the hands of dominant ethnic groups (such as the Javanese in Indonesia).

Another change was introduction of western institutions and ideologies, perhaps the key political legacy of imperialism. In colonised Asia, Europeans occasionally abolished existing dynasties, as with the Japanese in Korea in 1910. Elsewhere at least some political institutions remained in place – the sultanates of the Malay world, the royal house of Vietnam – though colonisers reduced sovereigns to puppet figures, deposing them if they became recalcitrant (as occurred thrice in Vietnam) and undermined the ideological and cultural order on which their rule rested.

The Europeans constructed a new edifice of rule, exercised through governors and district agents, law codes and decrees, taxes and *corvées,* armies and police forces. Pith-helmeted proconsuls ran the gamut from brutal and racist potentates to dedicated representatives genuinely interested in the well-being of their subjects, all still convinced of the beneficence of the civilising mission. The mass of natives saw themselves deprived of political participation except for small groups of westernised individuals (tellingly called *évolués* in the French empire) incorporated as public servants and members of consultative councils. Political structures followed the lines of the colonising power, with, for instance, greater devolution and indirect rule in the British empire compared to more centralised administration in French and Japanese colonies. The Dutch, in particular, continued to make great use of East Indian sultans, though they brutally crushed those who resisted, as happened with the war in Aceh (on Sumatra) that began in 1873 and the extension of Dutch suzerainty in Bali in the early twentieth century.[15] Colonial rule remained arbitrary, with actual or potential

violence a constant. Pacification meant suppression of resistance movements, whether opposition against initial incursions or in the form of
new nationalist movements that developed in the early 1900s. The
erection of grandiose government houses and law courts as well as
gaols in Batavia (Jakarta), Hanoi and Taipei provided solid proof of the
colonisers' intention to stay put.

Colonial rule was not immutable. Britain, as already mentioned,
transferred day-to-day political power to settler elites in Canada,
Australia and New Zealand in the late 1800s, though unwilling to do
so for colonies with largely non-European populations. (London never
instituted universal suffrage in Hong Kong.) In the early 1900s, the
French moved from 'assimilation' – naïvely envisaging the creation of
black, brown and yellow Frenchmen in territories integrated into the
Third Republic – to one of 'association' with more limited objectives.
The Dutch introduced a new 'ethical policy' proclaimed a more
humanitarian expression of rule. Even in the islands of Oceania,
considered the most backward of all colonies, by the 1950s and 1960s,
colonialists set up councils with selected indigenous representatives. A
change of colonial master also brought political alterations, though in
the Philippines, the Americans proved no less reluctant to stamp out
resistance after 1898 than the Spanish had been. Each ruler brought its
baggage of colonial policies and practices; the Japanese, who replaced
the Germans in Micronesia after 1918, introduced Japanese language
and education, the cult of the emperor and Shinto religion. Policies
were never consistent and empires never unitary – the Japanese ruled
Taiwan as a colony, while they incorporated Korea into Japan, and set
up a puppet-ruler (the reinstated last Qing emperor) in Manchukuo,
occupied Manchuria, in 1932.

Countries not colonised by foreigners also imported political institutions and practices, as was strikingly the case in Japan with the Meiji
restoration of 1868. The emperor began to dress in a western-tailored
uniform, and public buildings were constructed in European style. The
government adopted a written constitution and set up a parliament, the
Diet, in 1889; Tokyo remodelled the public service and the military
along western lines.[16] After unsuccessful attempts by modernisers to
introduce reforms in imperial China, the revolution of 1911 overthrew
the Qing Dynasty and instituted a republic, though with destructive
fractiousness among competing warlords over the next decades. On the
Pacific periphery, Siam (Thailand), which had restructured certain
public institutions in the late 1800s, then experienced dramatic transition from an absolute to a constitutional monarchy in 1932.

## The decolonisation of Australasia

European political institutions predictably took root in the British settler colonies, where the move to decolonisation was gradual.[17] No single date marks the independence of Australia, New Zealand or Canada, although the Statute of Westminster of 1931 recognised the equality of Britain and its dominions. Political life replicated the structures of Westminster, with a move to federation the major dynamic in Australian colonies in the late 1800s. Regular elections punctuated political life, accompanying spirited debate in parliamentary chambers and organisation of political parties. Extraparliamentary politics also resembled those of Britain. Labour unions did not hesitate to engage in industrial action, though in Australia a system of arbitration for labour and wage disputes was hailed as an innovative approach, even favourably branded 'socialism without doctrines' by one French commentator.[18]

Australians and New Zealanders proudly paid allegiance to the Crown (though Irish migrants, often sympathetic to Home Rule, did not always share such loyalty), and institutions – the Anglican Church, universities, civic organisations – reproduced ones of the country many still called 'home'. Race, as James Belich points out in his chapter, was primordial both for formulation of 'native policy' and for the development of a sense of neo-European identity; Patricia O'Brien, in her contribution here, moreover provides a reminder about fears of miscegenation.[19] Aborigines, seen as a primitive people destined for extinction, remained largely excluded from political life except as objects of paternalistic and racialist policies imposed by colonial, then federal and state authorities. Activism to secure indigenous Australians equal rights, to make amends for ill treatment and to recognise native land title was largely a phenomenon of the late twentieth century.

In New Zealand, a different political situation prevailed. Chiefs of the Māori population signed the Treaty of Waitangi with the British in 1840; for the British, though not for later generations of Māori, the agreement relinquished sovereignty to the Crown. The British accorded the Māori reserved seats in parliament, and the Māori – a larger proportion of the total population than native peoples in Canada and Australia, and one with a largely homogeneous language and culture – retained a greater place in political life than indigenous populations in other dominions. Politics in New Zealand, however, otherwise looked similar to other British settler territories.

## Anti-colonialism and decolonisation in Asia and Oceania

Although resistance to European interventions had initially rallied around precolonial dynasties, western ideas of constitutionalism, parliamentarianism and nationalism, and more radical ones of Marxist socialism, increasingly gained traction in Pacific Asia. Reformist and radical ideas circulated through the press, education and intelligentsia networks, already challenging European overlordship in the late 1800s – from Madrid to Havana to Manila, for instance, where José Rizal was executed for leading a revolt in the dying years of Spanish overlordship.[20] Japan, staving off foreign takeover to become an imperial power itself after victory over China in 1894–5, served as model for those disaffected with European colonialism; from the Meiji Restoration, under a slogan of 'Enrich the country, strengthen the army', with economic growth and international assertion, Japan offered a template for adaptation and modernisation. Japan's signal defeat of Russia took on inestimable importance. As Pankaj Mishra puts it, 'The contemporary world first began to assume shape in May 1905'.[21] Anti-colonial nationalists throughout Asia lauded Japan's triumph. Chinese, Vietnamese and Indian theorists and practitioners of anti-colonialism gathered in Tokyo to study the Japanese achievement, looking to Japan for revitalisation of 'Asia for the Asians'. Their mission, in the memorable words of Okakura Kakuzo (counterpoising it with western paranoia about the 'yellow peril'), was to overturn the 'White Disaster' of imperialism.[22] Thus, says Mishra, 'the central event of the last century for the majority of the world's population was the intellectual and political awakening of Asia and its emergence from the ruins of both Asian and European empires'. In this volume, Akira Iriye has underlined the importance of 'cultural internationalism', with the transnational movement of missionaries (including Japanese Buddhists and Korean Christians), students, intellectuals and political actors, as well as artists and athletes who contributed to exchange of ideas, cultures and ways of life.[23]

Non-traditional political ideas vied for support. In China, 'new terms and concepts eclectically derived from Confucianism, Buddhism, and Western science and commerce (especially utilitarianism)…could be used to make sense out of a rapidly changing world'.[24] The 1911 revolution brought to the fore, in the person and philosophy of Sun Yat-sen, ideas of the nation and republic that owed much to western, specifically British, concepts. In Vietnam, early-twentieth-century literati such as Phan Boi Chau and Phan Chu Trinh, schooled in both Confucian and French philosophy (and with links to Japan, where the former lived in exile), catalysed ideas of liberty, equality and fraternity derived from the revolution of 1789. The most famous Vietnamese revolutionary, Ho Chi Minh, found inspiration for emancipation in his experiences in Boston, Paris and Moscow, and his reading of western treatises on nationalism and Marxism. In the post-First World War world, buoyed by the 'Wilsonian moment' (though hopes for decolonisation through self-determination proved illusory), militant nationalist ideas and strategies gained strength.[25] The Chinese Communist Party was founded (in the French Concession in Shanghai) in 1921; in 1927, Sukarno in the East Indies established an independence party, and three years later Marxist groups coalesced into the Indochinese Communist Party under Ho. In a different fashion, the right-wing turn of Japanese politics in the 1930s took on board precepts of western imperialism, militarism and racialism.

The Second World War provided the turning point in Asian politics as Japan overran British and Dutch territories in southeastern Asia after establishing dominion over much of eastern China; the Japanese also forced collaboration from the Vichy-allied government of Indochina. Despite its brutality, that rule helped to sever European ties and gave succour to independence movements; though only a political expedient, Japanese promotion of nationalists and recognition of independence in former colonies (as in Vietnam in the last months of the war) shored up demands for change not silenced with Japan's defeat. Restoration of the *status quo ante bellum* proved impossible despite colonialists' best efforts.

Several eastern Asian countries moved to independence over the decade following Japan's defeat: the Philippines in 1946, Indonesia effectively in 1945 though with Dutch recognition waiting until 1949. The Dutch battled independence forces unsuccessfully in the East Indies, and the French likewise resisted in Indochina. Paris recognised an 'associated state' of Vietnam under a new constitution in 1946; it first negotiated with Ho Chi Minh, then engaged in a war against the Viet Minh that lasted until Ho's army defeated the French at Dien Bien Phu in 1954. The Geneva Accords divided Vietnam into a Communist north and a western-aligned south. There followed twenty years of efforts by Ho against the southern state and, from the 1960s, its American and other allies, before unification in 1975. The Malay states also saw violence with a decade-long 'Emergency' in which the British faced down Communist insurgents, a situation that extended beyond the independence of Malaysia in 1956.

The map nevertheless continued to change. Singapore broke away from Malaysia in 1965, and the sultanate of Brunei gained independence from Britain only in 1984. The Melanesian-populated western half of New Guinea remained under Dutch control until ceded to Indonesia (after a fraudulent referendum) in 1969. When the Portuguese withdrew from East Timor – one of the smallest and oldest colonial possessions in Asia – in 1974, Indonesia occupied the territory, Jakarta's violent colonial rule sparking enduring resistance until independence in 2002. Further north, the Chinese mainland and Taiwan went their separate ways in 1949, Taiwan's anti-Communist government first dominated by the military but now a stand-out democracy in Asia. Beijing had more success in incorporating British Hong Kong in 1997 and Portuguese Macau in 1999.

Political disputes wracked eastern and southeastern Asia from the 1940s through the 1970s, with one characteristic being extreme political experimentation under authoritarian regimes. The victory of Mao Zedong over Chiang Kai-shek in 1949 was cataclysmic, leading to wholesale restructuring, at great cost, of China according to principles adapted from Marx and enshrined for a time in Mao's 'Little Red Book'. Revolution brought nationalisation of property and assets, one-party rule, the purging of dissidents, repressive actions by the Red Army and the state police, the Great Leap Forward towards economic development, then the bloodthirsty Cultural Revolution which raged for a decade until Mao's death in 1976. Recent decades have seen phenomenal economic development not matched by political transformation, as evidenced by suppression of the Tiananmen Square protests in 1989.

The struggle between Communists and non-Communists that split China and Vietnam (and the Cold War in which they played a part), also sundered Korea into two countries in the early 1950s. The northern state pursued Communism largely in isolation from the rest of the world, its policy changing little under three generations of the Kim dynasty. For several decades South Korea had an authoritarian government but, like Taiwan, it has metamorphosed into a multi-party democratic state – meaning that the Koreas now display radically divergent models of governance and politics. Vietnam meanwhile remained orthodox in ideology until adoption of reformist *doi moi*, and the establishment of a socialist market-oriented economy in 1986. On the Pacific periphery, in Cambodia, Pol Pot's Khmer Rouge established a genocidal regime in 1975, its terror ended by Vietnamese invasion in 1979 with subsequent restoration of the monarchy in 1993; the year 1975 also saw the victory of Marxists in a civil war in Laos. Insurgent campaigns broke out in various regions of the Indonesian archipelago after independence. Conflict between Communists and opponents led to a coup in 1965; military rule lasted until 1998, with the country now democratised. Similarly, Ferdinand Marcos ruled the Philippines as strongman from 1965 to 1986.

While dramatic regime changes have been the lot of many countries in Pacific Asia, Japan offers a rare example of continuity since the adoption of its 1947 constitution. The Korean War, the Indochinese and

Vietnam/American war, and other armed conflicts, as well as violent domestic insurrections, otherwise marked the political history of a region that was a battleground for ideological warfare. As Cold War tensions have disappeared, other geopolitical, ideological and cultural contests have replaced them; ethnic disputes appear one of the major political challenges of postcolonial states. Continuing and violent clashes, for instance, involve minority Muslims in the southern Philippines and in Thailand. Some dissident groups, such as Islamist movements, reject westernised principles of government. Other critics lament restrictions on human rights, even in those countries with democratic and parliamentary regimes.

In Oceania, decolonisation arrived later and, in general, more peacefully than in Asia. Colonial authorities believed the islands to be too small and poor, and their populations too primitive, perhaps ever to sustain independence. An indigenous push for self-government occurred to a far smaller degree than in Asia; indeed, in the case of British, Australian and New Zealand outposts, colonial powers themselves promoted as much as resisted decolonisation. Sāmoa led the way to independence from New Zealand in 1962, then Fiji (from Britain) in 1970, though with ethnic clashes between indigenous islanders and the majority Indo-Fijians. Britain disengaged from the Solomon Islands in 1978, and from Kiribati and Tuvalu in 1979. Australia meanwhile withdrew from Papua New Guinea in 1975. The islands of Micronesia, under American administration, worked out diverse constitutional statuses by the 1980s – independence-in-association with the United States in the case of several countries. Washington retained sovereignty over American Sāmoa and Guam, and in 1959 made Hawai'i its fiftieth state. (Another former American Pacific colony, Alaska, had become the 49th state with a 1958 law, joining the union in 1959.)

Paris resisted independence for French Polynesia, New Caledonia and Wallis and Futuna, territories whose residents possess full citizenship rights in the French Republic. In French Polynesia, an independence movement, active since the 1950s, ebbs and flows in popularity. In the mid-1960s, the French began testing nuclear weapons there, sparking large-scale regional and local opposition. The testing did not conclude until the mid-1990s, its cessation confirming the reliance of Tahiti and the outer islands on French subsidies but without resolving political status. An independence movement based in the indigenous Melanesian population emerged in New Caledonia in the 1970s; during the following decade, confrontation intensified between Melanesians (Kanaks) and a coalition of descendants of French settlers (Caldoches), French metropolitan migrants and Polynesian workers.

The Front de Libération Nationale Kanak et Socialiste combined ideological perspectives derived from Melanesian culture, French constitutionalism and a communitarian socialism with civil resistance and guerrilla manoeuvres. The pro- and anti-independence groups eventually agreed a modus vivendi, and New Caledonia remains an 'overseas country' of France with plans for a vote on sovereignty in the coming years.

Pacific islands have not escaped postcolonial political disputes, though seldom of the magnitude of Asian upheavals (or those of Latin America in the 1800s). For more than two decades Islanders on Bougainville waged an unsuccessful secessionist struggle against the central government of Papua New Guinea. Violence between different Islanders in the Solomons led to intervention by an international police force in 2003. Fiji has experienced several violent racially based coups, and periods of authoritarian military rule since the 1980s. Opposition groups press for greater democratisation in Tonga, where the royal family and nobility dominate politics.

In eastern Asia and Oceania – unlike Australasia and the Americas – the major political question of the post-Second World War period, especially between 1945 and the mid-1970s, was the form of government: colonial or independent, monarchical, republican, Communist (with varying sorts of Communism proposed) or military. Not every alternative was essayed everywhere, but the record chronicles many twists and turns, with political disputes revolving around sovereignty, ideology and the structure of government, as well as more quotidian debates of political life. Conflicts between ethnic groups, elites and masses, centres and peripheries, and proliferating political factions interlace with these debates.

A key overarching theme has been the variety of political experiments since decolonisation, especially in Pacific Asia. This contrasts with the cases of Australasia and North America, though there is a parallel in some parts of Pacific South America, such as the coming to power in Chile of the Marxist Salvador Allende in 1970 and his overthrow, and death, three years later by Augusto Pinochet, whose dictatorship then lasted until democratisation in 1990. Countries such as Panama and Nicaragua have also experienced dictatorships, violent changes in regimes with disparate ideologies, and foreign intervention.

Another characteristic of postcolonial politics, pronounced in Asian and Oceanic countries, is the syncretism of western political institutions and ideologies with local and precolonial legacies. Reverence for the emperor of Japan connects contemporary politics with a veteran dynasty – a Japanese sovereign's genealogy goes back a millennium and, in legend, to the Moon Goddess – and with the principles of Shinto. (The persistence of the traditional monarchy in Thailand and Cambodia is also noteworthy.) In Tonga, notions of kingship exercised by a monarch who now styles himself very much in the western mode connects with ideas of Polynesian chieftainship. Sun Yat-sen's 'three principles' – of the ethnic nation, the people's rights and the well-being of the people – were occulted by the People's Republic, but are enshrined in Taiwan. Beijing has rehabilitated Confucius with the establishment of Confucius Institutes around the world, quotations from his works intoned at the 2008 Olympics Opening Ceremony, and the erection of a giant statue of the sage near Mao's mausoleum in Tiananmen Square three years later.

Elsewhere, as well, politicians have hybridised the local with the global, the indigenous with the western. In 1945, President Sukarno in Indonesia proclaimed the doctrine of *pancasila* – a fivefold belief in God, unity, democracy, social justice and a civilised humanity – to provide a political and ethical philosophy for his compatriots under a western-style parliamentary system. Ho Chi Minh reworked nationalist precepts and Marxist principles to relocate them to peasant societies, guerrilla warfare and anti-colonial struggles, but the Vietnamese have also evoked early episodes of Vietnamese history – resistance to the Chinese by the Trung sisters in the first century BCE and Le Loi in the early 1400s – to inspire patriotism. Leaders in Oceania in the 1960s and 1970s, such as Kamisese Mara in Fiji, spoke of a 'Pacific way' of consensual decision-making that could be merged with parliamentary democracy,[26] while southeastern Asian statesmen such as Lee Kuan-Yew in Singapore and Mahathir Mohamad in Malaysia in the 1980s espoused 'Asian values'. A foundational principle of Mahathir's dominant political party in Malaysia was the promotion of the rights of the indigenous people (*bumiputra*, the people of the land). Proponents of the rights of Kanaks, Aborigines, Māori, ethnic Fijians, native Hawaiians and First Nations people in the Americas have asserted the primacy of first occupants of their lands.

Non-western heritage retains a large presence in Pacific Asia and Oceania (if less so in Australasia and the Americas), interwoven with the institutions of presidents, prime ministers and parliaments, electoral campaigns and party politics. Buddhism richly infuses the culture and public sphere in parts of southeastern and eastern Asia, just as Islam in Indonesia and Malaysia, and Catholicism in the Philippines, and Protestantism in the South Pacific. Old elites may have lost status with colonialism and post-independence transformations, but the *zaibatsu* dynasties of Japan, the hereditary Malay sultans and traditional chiefs in

Oceania have not relinquished status and influence. Ancestral institutions, beliefs and elites have not vanished with colonialism and postcolonial, globalising change, and old layers of the palimpsest reappear in new ways. And foreign ways became localised. Bronwen Douglas, elsewhere in this volume, for instance, outlines three overlapping phases in connections between Oceanic peoples and Christianity: encounter, conversion and – very importantly – naturalisation, the final phase in which Christianity becomes indigenised as part of the heritage of Islanders.[27] The boundaries, in culture and in politics, between a before and after, us and them, old and new, are indeed porous.

## Politics in the twenty-first century

In the early twentieth-first-century world, the countries of the Pacific face several common political problems. Border disputes fester, most recently with competing claims in the South China Sea involving China, Taiwan, Japan and Southeast Asian countries. At stake are not only maritime territory and uninhabited islands, but potential mineral resources, geopolitical advantage and nationalist pride. The mighty growth and ambitions of China as a commercial, military and political power cause concern around the Pacific. States of the Pacific, both large and small, can be more immediately touched by the rise of China, and reactions to it, than those more distant. The United States has meanwhile asserted its role in the Pacific anew, with Russia increasingly interested in the region on its eastern frontier.

Domestically, ethnic tensions inflame passions in southeastern Asia and parts of Oceania, and encompass remonstrances by Aborigines and Torres Strait Islanders in Australia, Māori in New Zealand, and Amerindians on the other side of the Pacific. Irregular migration has become a major political issue in Australia, and refugees are a concern almost everywhere. Secessionist movements do not abandon hopes of creating new nation-states. Islamist groups agitate for laws and social norms in conformity with their version of religion. The Pacific has not been immune from terrorism, such as the attacks in Bali in 2002. Resource issues linked to mining, fishing rights and Exclusive Economic Zones trouble policy-makers everywhere, as do environmental concerns – from pollution and the effects of mining to climate change and global warming. The after-effects of the global financial crisis pose questions about relations between the state and private enterprise, and about social entitlements whose provisions vary widely around the Pacific. Corruption remains widespread. Though dictatorial governments are increasingly scarce, democratic systems with multi-party elections, the rule of law and free public debate have not been secured in many countries; political transitions do not always occur easily. Social problems of disaffected youth, alcohol and drugs beset even remote islands. Despite high standards of living – among the world's highest in Canada, the United States, Australia, New Zealand, Japan, Singapore, Taiwan and South Korea – pockets of grim poverty exist, with endemic diseases, illiteracy and legal systems and cultures that discriminate against women and minorities.

The study of politics in the Pacific world maps a fragmented rather than a united hemisphere, offering a corrective to simplistic ideas about construction of a 'new centre of the world' anchored in the United States, China or another fulcrum. Yet isomorphic developments, and past and present events, suggest further consideration of parallels not yet fully investigated, such as comparisons between Anglophone and Francophone settler societies in the South Pacific, the War of the Pacific in South America and the Sino-Japanese War and Russo-Japanese War on the other shore, the revolutions in Mexico and China, the dynamism of Marxism in both southeastern Asia and South America in the 1960s and 1970s, and the mechanisms of state formation following the dissolution of the great empires on both sides of the ocean.

The political history of the Pacific underlines the impact of colonialism in transforming political cultures, but provides a reminder that the postcolonial outcomes – regimes, institutions and ideologies – display their own character: the survival of precolonial elements, sometimes in transmuted alloys of indigenous, western liberal and Marxist beliefs. Deep-seated cultural affiliations and practices have not been abandoned despite the adoption of western-style parliamentary systems and discourses of governance. Violence, within states and occasionally between states, gives proof that the Pacific is not always pacific. There is, for the moment, no 'end of history', no great convergence of political systems, in the Pacific sphere; but the historic mixing and melding of ideas, people and practices offers hope that a tectonic clash of civilisations will not rock the Pacific of the future.

### Notes

1. Jean-Pierre Gomane, et al., eds., *Le Pacifique: 'nouveau centre du monde'* (Paris, 1983).
2. Robert Aldrich, 'Rediscovering the Pacific: A Critique of French Geopolitical Analysis', *Journal de la Société des Océanistes* 87 (1989), 57–71; Aldrich, 'Le Lobby colonial de l'Océanie française', *Revue Française d'Histoire d'Outre-Mer* 76 (1989), 411–24.

3. Paul W. Blank, 'The Pacific: A Mediterranean in the Making?', *The Geographical Review* 89 (1999), 265–77.
4. Chris Dixon and David Drakakis-Smith, 'The Pacific Asian Region: Myth or Reality?', *Geografiska Annaler* 77 (1995), 75–91.
5. Lisa Ford, 'Law', ch. 10 in this volume.
6. Peter K. Bol, *Neo-Confucianism in History* (Cambridge, MA, 2008), pp. 144–52.
7. David C. Kang, *East Asia before the West: Five Centuries of Trade and Tribute* (New York, 2010), esp. chs 2, 4.
8. Milton Osborne, *Southeast Asia: An Introductory History* (Sydney, 1995), ch. 3.
9. O. W. Wolters, *History, Culture and Region in Southeast Asian Perspectives*, rev. edn (Ithaca, NY, 1999), p. 117.
10. Anthony Milner, *The Malays* (Oxford, 2011), esp. ch. 3.
11. Clifford Geertz, *Negara: The Theatre-State in Nineteenth-Century Bali* (Princeton, 1980).
12. Douglas L. Oliver, *Oceania: The Native Cultures of Australia and the Pacific Islands* (Honolulu, 1989).
13. James C. Scott, *The Art of Not Being Governed: An Anarchist History of Upland Southeast Asia* (New Haven, 2010).
14. Adam McKeown, 'Movement', ch. 7 in this volume; see also McKeown, *Melancholy Order: Asian Migration and the Globalization of Borders* (New York, 2008).
15. See Colin Newbury, *Patrons, Clients and Empire: Chieftaincy and Over-Rule in Asia, Africa, and the Pacific* (Oxford, 2003).
16. Takashi Fujitani, *Splendid Monarchy: Power and Pageantry in Modern Japan* (Berkeley, 1998).
17. See Deryck M. Schreuder and Stuart Ward, eds., *Australia's Empire* (Oxford, 2008).
18. Albert Métin, *Le socialisme sans doctrines: la question agraire et la question ouvrière en Australie et Nouvelle-Zéland* (Paris, 1901).
19. James Belich, 'Race', and Patricia O'Brien, 'Gender', chs 12 and 13 in this volume.
20. Benedict Anderson, *Under Three Flags: Anarchism and the Anti-Colonial Imagination* (London, 2008).
21. Pankaj Mishra, *From the Ruins of Empire: The Revolt Against the West and the Remaking of Asia* (London, 2012), p. 1.
22. Quoted in Mishra, *From the Ruins of Empire*, p. 221.
23. Mishra, *From the Ruins of Empire*, p. 8; Akira Iriye, 'A Pacific Century?', ch. 5 in this volume.
24. Peter Zarrow, *After Empire: The Conceptual Transformation of the Chinese State, 1885–1924* (Stanford, 2012).
25. Erez Manela, *The Wilsonian Moment: Self-Determination and the International Origins of Anticolonial Nationalism* (Oxford, 2007).
26. Kamisese Mara, *The Pacific Way: A Memoir* (Honolulu, 1997).
27. Bronwen Douglas, 'Religion', ch. 9 in this volume.

# Afterword: Pacific Cross-currents

## Matt K. Matsuda

The challenge of Pacific History has been fundamentally straightforward: 'the Pacific' cannot be written about as a subject. Rather, the Pacific is a subject that needs to be defined. What are its boundaries? What are the ranges of spatial – and temporal – extension? In many ways, *Pacific Histories: Ocean, Land, People* has been about these questions.[1]

In some ways, it is easier to underscore what this volume on 'the Pacific' is not. It is not a collection of erudite studies of nations, nor even of particular peoples. It is not based upon the monographic expertise of specialist studies famed in Oceanic island studies, nor the national or postnational interrogations of Asia and the Americas. It could have been, but is not, a collection by specialists with an expert chapter apiece on Japan, China, Hawai'i, Indonesia, Tonga or Australia.

Rather, 'the Pacific' has been here imagined in some of the ways that early seafarers and later explorers might have experienced it – not as a region, or even an idea to be described, but as an overlapping set of actors, transits and shifting boundaries. The Pacific here is less described than made and defined, and the essays in this volume have approached their subjects by thematically wrestling with the currents, flows and markers of adjacent, intersecting, colliding cultures rather than selecting and isolating particular countries, islands or littoral societies.

The keystone of the collection has been its emphasis on histories of connection and interaction. All contributors were invited to underscore local cases with global reach, and to define what is 'specific' to working in and on the Pacific that contributes to other historiographies and disciplines. Each of the contributors has pursued a daunting task, launching from his or her own scholarly expertise and examples, yet each also connecting to the others over as vast a span of historical times and geographical regions as are imaginable.

The assembled works have focused on categories and case studies that engage with broader questions, as well as example-oriented research that is conceptually more theoretical and methodological in orientation. Thus, at the core of each essay has been a key idea, 'religion', or 'gender' or 'knowledges'. To anchor these, citations proliferate of Melanesian encounters, Hsiao Liang-lin's foreign trade statistics, figures like Tevita Mara, Trugernanna, Ho Chi Minh, or ports from Manila to Macau to Acapulco.

All of these figures and places have their own scholars, but one would not necessarily think that they could be so juxtaposed in a single collection. For generations 'Pacific Studies' as a field has developed through the multiple domains of specialists: Asian studies experts who did not necessarily share perspectives with researchers in Oceanian and Pacific Island studies, who in turn might be unconcerned with the work of Americanists or distant from the world-systems approach of many global historians. What would a scholar of early modern China find of common interest with an ethnohistorian from the Polynesian and Melanesian Islands of the mid-Pacific, a marine scientist specialising in ocean temperature or a student of Latin American economics? The Pacific as a domain of historical study has long been seen as lacking unifying narratives such as the search for the New World, the 'Columbian Exchange', 'Atlantic Revolutions' or an organising system like the triangular trade.[2]

Grand narratives do emerge: the economic and cultural work of the galleons that connected Canton, Macau, Nagasaki, Guam and Acapulco across centuries; Asian and Islander migrations stretching from China to Australia, Fiji, Hawai'i and California. Yet, rather than seek a world-system analysis or an encompassing explanatory framework for 'the Pacific', the essays collected here tack back and forth between a wealth of historiographies and the particularities of experiences and practices. In this way, the volume has opened up dialogue with other disciplines that have very much been at the heart of Pacific History, including crossover approaches from anthropology, performance studies, political activism and marine science and maritime archaeology.[3] The aim has been an expression of Pacific History as staggeringly diverse in both method and subject.

Still, what might a generation ago have seemed parallel tales of interesting but disconnected scholarly pursuits have surprising resonance, and offer hints of future directions for the study of the Pacific. An evident touchstone for the changes can readily be found, for example, in Ryan Jones's reading of the Pacific as a place of energy distribution, the movement of winds, currents and tides, and the ultimate pursuit and extraction of that energy by human populations chasing fish and marine mammals and rendering sea creatures into fat, flesh, oils and fuel.[4] These are conceptualisations that come to life in the volume, to see how talk about 'the Pacific' is to imagine that Fijian traders would find common cause with Australian commercial agents to supply marine creatures to China and Japan, while gathering crews from Vanuatu and transiting on a circuit from the Hawaiian Islands to the Canadian and Ecuadorian coastlines, driven by knowledge of winds and tides.

The contributors have launched from their areas of speciality to widely imagine how what they know from Cold War policy, Kanak villages, silver exchange rates or colonial protection ordinances can shape a 'Pacific' developed in multiple depths and interlocking currents. These are like the seas and ocean they describe, capturing at once a fast-moving surface, a vibrant and changing pelagic region, and a deep benthic zone, transected by attentive focus to 'environment', 'movement', 'gender', 'race' or 'law'. Through this presentation of cross-currents, the discussions of environment are clearly glossed also by science and by navigation. Religion, race and politics are all but inseparable; gender, law, and immigration are so connected that to offer distinct chapters might even seem contrived.

Still, this is a collected set of works on the Pacific, and to be more than a mere anthology of erudite pieces, or demarcated essays, a structure must emerge. In keeping with the project, that structure need not be rigidly architectural. Rather, as suggested by Damon Salesa, it can be well understood as a braided and interwoven series of genealogical strands. One thinks here of Sāmoan author Albert Wendt's 'Inside Us the Dead', a poem of long pasts borne by ancestors from a multiplicity of civilisations, embodied in and carried down through the teller's family line to become his own flesh and history.[5] The molecular combinations sequenced together from canoe-voyagers, Islander fathers and mothers, European traders and outlander missionaries reflect on and embody a geneticist's/genealogist's language by which traits and mutations in the history of an organism are 'expressed' or 'silenced' across the generations.

Where, then, are these expressions and silences connected in this volume? Salesa leads by situating the arguments in multiple registers of indigenous time that frame history, often manifested through genealogical research and both oral as well as written and performed traditions that also shape 'placeness' in a *Vasa Loloa*, a sea of stories.[6] These explorations find strong reflections in Akira Iriye's grand overview of the economics, politics and immigration strategies of Cold War geopolitics, and, above all, his central idea that what most marks Japan, Korea and China is a 'shared memory' of both cultural borrowings and conflict to explain the contemporary Pacific. So the Pacific has not a single past, but many pasts intertwined, part genealogy, part memory.[7] It is less a space with an abstract boundary than a series of interconnected places filled with lives and tales.

This 'sharing' is thus about commonalities, but also about widely divergent politics and militancy about visions of the past. It is this fractured yet joined set of intertwined histories that animates the volume. So it is that the 'memory' question is also expressed in Joyce Chaplin's peregrination through the cartographies of proud European 'discoveries' and encounters. Hers is a study that intersects with figures like Jorge de Menezes and Tupaia, but is also fundamentally a telling of histories that 'did not take place', often indigenous or non-European experiences that have struggled for recognition, a lens upon rich, complex worlds and cultures before imperial narrative. It is also a critique of the tendentious imposition of precolonial and postcolonial demarcation of Pacific time. As Chaplin cogently points out, the early modern European history of the Pacific is hardly a tale of incipient mastery. Rather, it can probably best be rendered as 'almost three centuries of overwhelmingly passive and decidedly inconclusive events'. [8]

Nicholas Thomas also very much sails against the current of conventional historiography. His essay, dedicated to the Age of Empire, is framed by obligatory overviews of British, French, Dutch and Spanish authority in Oceania, but his reading of 'empire' pays little attention to governors and administrative systems, and focuses instead on a kaleidoscopic array of contingent missions, collected artefacts and cultural exchanges, and shared knowledge between Islanders and outlanders. Labour migrations for sandalwood and *bêche-de-mer*, navigators like Omai, James Cook's systematic energy for mapping and Islanders' 'reverse collecting' of iron, fabric, mirrors and books indicate an 'empire' defined less as a series of European hegemonic projects, and more as an array of unevenly dominated exchanges and mutual exploitations. [9]

Bronwen Douglas picks up these threads of appropriations, countersigns and exchanges in and out of western chronologies through her elucidation of the webs of encounter that wove spiritual traditions from worlds of gods and fauna and natural deities to Islam and Buddhism, to Christianity, especially as adapted to local spirituality in Tanna. Her multiple interrogations of agency, local gods, island teachers and syncretic beliefs play out in registers of encounter, conversion and naturalisation, so that worlds of transformed faith, at times in tension, yet allied, develop across generations. [10]

Notably, Sujit Sivasundaram, in what might seem a distinct interrogation of 'science', follows a somewhat parallel course – by troubling the lines between regimes of knowledge. He neither begins nor ends with assumptions about what constitutes scientific knowledge, though he does address the natural history and some of the chemistry, physics and biology of coral reef theory, nuclear fallout and climate change.

But this is no tale of aggregate positive knowledge. Rather, he frames his analyses around oceans and islands not as experimental domains, nor as static 'laboratories' for investigation, but as fluid realms that also integrate ancestral animals, and readings of cosmology, geography and oceanography through traditional tales. Darwin and oceanographic missions are part of the story, but so is a detailed study of the legendary Hawaiian sacred narrative, the *Kumulipo*.[11]

In parallel, Robert Aldrich frames his extraordinarily wide-ranging survey of Pacific politics and states by giving strong emphases to inter-woven pasts with his subregional, indigenous, colonial and syncretic studies of political regimes across Asia and Oceania. By detailing not just regimes, but their own attractions to 'kastom' (custom) practices and heritage and sovereignty struggles, he underscores the connections and legitimation of contemporary politics with 'veteran dynasties' and assertions of tradition from Singapore's neo-Confucian capitalists to customary claims by Kanak and Aboriginal peoples in New Caledonia and Australia.[12]

It becomes easy to see how this telescoping of past and present becomes manifested in Lisa Ford's legal research, ranging over claims of possession from the papal Treaty of Tordesillas to the continuing rein-terpretations of Aotearoa/New Zealand's Treaty of Waitangi, and the force of control under the law from Spanish territories to indigenous and customary sea tenure, to Exclusive Economic Zones for strategic, mineral and fishing rights. Perhaps most critical is Ford's elucidation of the way that legal conventions operate to abet and restrict immigration and migration – the question of who can go where.[13]

This finds substantial reinforcement in Adam McKeown's studies of movement, and the fragile hubs he traces across the Pacific, from the ancient migrations of the Polynesians to slaves and galleon crews from the Philippines to Mexico, to staggering numbers of Chinese out-migrants, settling in Southeast Asia, the Pacific Islands and the Americas. By intersecting statistical knowledge of both bodies and capital flows, the work illustrates lives initially framed by numbers, yet bounded by entangling webs of opportunities, discrimination, contracts for labour and trans-oceanic cultures.[14]

The web of interconnections across the Pacific is rendered in struc-tural form by Kaoru Sugihara's work on the oceanic economy. Here, almost overly familiar terms like 'bilateral' and 'multilateral' suddenly take on new meanings when employed to describe the sophisticated integration of the 'Pacific Rim' through the circulation of silver and gold, export and import materials such as tea, rubber and guano, and luxury goods like silk. As with the other essays, Sugihara eschews national studies to focus on the shifting dependencies of China and Japan in the textile trade, Latin America and the Philippines through the galleons, and – at the end of the twentieth century – the new era of both labour- and capital-intensive industries in consumer-driven technical and cultural fusions. These create new markets, generate new East–West tastes and styles and ignite labour movements around the Pacific.[15]

These trajectories are then also those of the women and men of Patricia O'Brien's gendered histories, following the life of Trugernanna of Tasmania, at the frontier of the British empire, to representations and realities of Polynesian, Aboriginal and Melanesian women. The discussions draw together the intimate and working lives of servants and labourers in Chinese households, Spanish notables like Donna Ysabel Barretos and migrants across Asian and Oceanian societies. The narrative equally encompasses the roles of both war brides and Asian feminists, shaping the Pacific with a politics of struggle and opportunity. In surveying both popular literature and statist policy for the affective and the administrative, the stories keenly demonstrate the roles of colonial institutions in building populations by validating and prohibiting marriages and liaisons, encouraging immigration and emigration, and facing challenges to authority brought by lineages of activism from Queen Pōmare Vahine to Whina Cooper to Haunani Kay-Trask.[16]

Notably, these lines of law and jurisdiction and gender are also tendered by James Belich, whose considerations of 'race' examine the differential and hierarchical organisation and concomitant regimes of power deployed to identify and rule peoples from New Zealand to Hong Kong to Manila, Macau, China, Japan and the Anglo and Hispanic worlds of the Pacific. His essay is a challenge to tidy ideas and easy ascriptions, parsing out distinctions between 'race', 'racialism', and 'racism', and casting an eye upon the prejudices yet accommodations of Islander societies, the created Han identity of China, and the blood distinctions of Indios, Mestizos, Whites and Africans in Latin America. His chronicle ranges across and connects peoples of many cultures, colours and faiths, and illustrates both their integrations, and fractures in racially saturated conflicts from 1857 in India to the 1860s and 1870s in the lands of the Māori, Kanak and Aboriginal Australian peoples. The vision is strongly bonded to the essays of O'Brien, Ford and Aldrich in law, gender and politics.[17]

The essays are each unique, and form set-pieces, yet each is also the 'expression' of multiple historical-genealogical strands, drawn from innumerable Asian, Oceanian and American experiences. Where they overlap, they are tangled together like the dense lower branches of superimposed family trees. It is those connections which define the newness of the project overall. Rather than an anthology of contributors working tightly in their specialisations, McKeown's studies of migration are framed by Ford's understandings of law and jurisdiction; Chaplin's cartographies of strangers on different shores illustrate Belich's monogenetic and polygenetic analyses of race; Sivasundaran's readings of rising seas and hydrography navigate within Jones's knowledge of cyclonic energy and wind cycles; O'Brien's political women are parts of Aldrich's narratives of sovereignty; both converge in Iriye's and Salesa's and Douglas's understandings of multiple times and memories shaping past and present.

The works here have, overall, been interested in transnational, global, indigenous and other perspectives, with emphases on connectivity, diaspora and knitted-together worlds across time and space. The chapters do not take the Pacific as an absolute space to be filled by every single monograph, but rather as an invitation to rethink the history of interconnected domains from transnational or regional perspectives.

Newer works will continue to develop along these lines, with interests connecting Asia and islands, and aims that reach not only East–West, but also North–South. Evolving research also incorporates Siberian/Alaskan/Canadian indigenous peoples and links them to coastal cultures in Asia and the Americas. In this, perspectives from Latin America and Southeast Asia will be even more strongly integrated. Much of this is developed with perspectives on Iberian engagements in the Pacific, and connections with the Chinese and Malay worlds by way of Asian and Oceanian islands, with their emphases on commerce, pirates, state-building and transnational maritime networks.[18]

Also expanding is what might be correctly called 'underwater history' that engages narratives of maritime voyaging and through the prism of disciplines like marine science, ichthyology and meteorology. Such works propose histories of the Pacific 'from below the waves' as well as on the surface. Some of the work is not typically archival in nature but developed by scholars who are research explorers and divers, in the field and under the water. Such works increasingly capture audiences moving towards environmental and biosystems approaches to historical thinking.[19] These dimensions of Pacific History are very much in line with important developments in the field of environmental history – a field incorporated here that continues to become a very lively arena for global and transnational approaches.

Taken together, the essays have explored the transitions and boundaries between different places, spaces and historical times of the Pacific through disciplinary engagements as they express moments that illustrate globality. The idea of the Pacific has been the pursuit of a place of mutual and multiple entwining of stories of both local detail and resonant inter-connections across generations that have long been facing the waves.

## Notes

1. Paul W. Blank and Fred Spier, eds., *Defining the Pacific: Opportunities and Constraints* (Aldershot, 2002); Donald Freeman, *The Pacific* (London, 2010); Matt K. Matsuda, *Pacific Worlds: A History of Seas, Peoples, and Cultures* (Cambridge, 2012).

2. David Armitage and Michael J. Braddick, eds., *The British Atlantic World, 1500–1800*, 2nd edn (Basingstoke, 2009); Armitage and Alison Bashford, 'Introduction: The Pacific and its Histories', ch. 1 in this volume; Karen Ordahl Kupperman, *The Atlantic in World History* (New York, 2012).

3. See also Arif Dirlik and Rob Wilson, eds., *Asia-Pacific as Space of Cultural Production* (Durham, NC, 1996); Greg Dening, *Performances* (Chicago, 1996); Hans K. Van Tilburg, *Chinese Junks on the Pacific: Views from a Different Deck* (Gainesville, 2007).

4. Ryan Tucker Jones, 'The Environment', ch. 6 in this volume; see also J. R. McNeill, ed., *Environmental History in the Pacific World* (Ashgate, 2001).

5. Albert Wendt, *Inside Us the Dead: Poems, 1961–1974* (Auckland, NZ, 1976).

6. Damon Salesa, 'The Pacific in Indigenous Time', ch. 2 in this volume; compare Salesa, 'Remembering Samoan History', in Tamasa'ilau Suaalii-Sauni, I'uogafa Tuagalu, Tofilau Nina Kirifi-Alai and Naomi Fuamatu, eds., *Su'esu'e Manogi—In Search of Fragrance: Tui Atua Tupua Tamasese Ta'isi and the Samoan Indigenous Reference* (Apia, 2008), pp. 215–28.

7. Akira Iriye, 'A Pacific Century?', ch. 5 in this volume; see also Iriye, *Global and Transnational History: Past, Present, and Future* (Basingstoke, 2013).

8. Joyce E. Chaplin, 'The Pacific before Empire, c.1500–1800', ch. 3 in this volume; see also Chaplin, *Round About the Earth: Circumnavigation from Magellan to Orbit* (New York, 2012).

9. Nicholas Thomas, 'The Pacific in the Age of Empire', ch. 4 in this volume; see also Thomas, *Islanders: The Pacific in the Age of Empire* (New Haven, 2010).

10. Bronwen Douglas, 'Religion', ch. 9 in this volume; compare Douglas, 'From Invisible Christians to Gothic Theatre: The Romance of the Millennial in Melanesian Anthropology', *Current Anthropology* 42 (2001), 615–50; Douglas, *Science, Voyages and Encounters in Oceania, 1511–1850* (Basingstoke, 2014).

11. Sujit Sivasundaram, 'Science', ch. 11 in this volume; see also Sivasundaram, *Nature and the Godly Empire: Science and Evangelical Mission in the Pacific, 1795–1850* (Cambridge, 2005).

12. Robert Aldrich, 'Politics', ch. 14 in this volume; compare Aldrich, *Greater France: A History of French Overseas Expansion* (Basingstoke, 1996); Aldrich, ed., *The Age of Empires* (London, 2007).

13. Lisa Ford, 'Law', ch. 10 in this volume; see also Ford, *Settler Sovereignty: Jurisdiction and Indigenous Peoples in America and Australia, 1788–1836* (Cambridge, MA, 2010).

14. Adam McKeown, 'Movement', ch. 7 in this volume; compare McKeown, *Chinese Migrant Networks and Cultural Change: Peru, Chicago, Hawaii, 1900–1936* (Chicago, 2001).

15. Kaoru Sugihara, 'The Economy Since 1800', ch. 8 in this volume; compare Sugihara, ed., *Japan, China and the Growth of the Asian International Economy, 1850–1949* (Oxford 2005); Sugihara, 'Oceanic Trade and Global Development, 1500–1995', in Sølvi Sogner, ed., *Making Sense of Global History: The 19th International Congress of the Historical Sciences Oslo 2000 Commemorative Volume* (Oslo, 2001), pp. 55–70.

16. Patricia O'Brien, 'Gender', ch. 13 in this volume; see also Lenore Manderson and Margaret Jolly, eds., *Sites of Desire, Economies of Pleasure: Sexualities in Asia and the Pacific* (Chicago, 1997); Jolly, 'Women of the East, Women of the West: Region and Race, Gender and Sexuality on Cook's Voyages', in Kate Fullagar, ed., *The Atlantic World in the Antipodes: Effects and Transformations since the Eighteenth Century* (Newcastle upon Tyne, 2012), pp. 2–32.

17. James Belich, 'Race', ch. 12 in this volume; compare Belich, *The New Zealand Wars and the Victorian Interpretation of Racial Conflict* (Auckland, NZ, 1986); Belich, *Making Peoples: A History of the New Zealanders: From Polynesian Settlement to the End of the Nineteenth Century* (Auckland, NZ, 1996).

18. See, for example, Ryan Tucker Jones, 'A "Havock Made among Them": Island Biogeography, Empire, and Environmentalism in the Russian North Pacific, 1741–1810', *Environmental History* 16 (2011), 585–609; David Igler, *The Great Ocean: Pacific Worlds from Captain Cook to the Gold Rush* (Oxford, 2013); Tonio Andrade, *How Taiwan Became Chinese: Dutch, Spanish, and Han Colonization in the Seventeenth Century* (New York, 2008); Andrade, *Lost Colony: The Untold Story of China's First Great Victory over the West* (Princeton, 2011); Rainer Buschmann, *Defending the Spanish Lake: Iberian Visions of the Pacific Ocean, 1507–1899* (Basingstoke, 2014).

19. For example, Ryan Tucker Jones, 'Running into Whales: The History of the North Pacific from Below the Waves', *American Historical Review* 118 (2013), 349–77; Shankar Aswani, 'Socioecological Approaches for Combining Ecosystem-Based and Customary Management in Oceania', *Journal of Marine Biology* 2011 (2011), 1–13.

# Further Reading

## 1 Introduction: The Pacific and its Histories

The best one-volume surveys of the Pacific and its histories are now Donald B. Freeman, *The Pacific* (London, 2010) and Matt K. Matsuda, *Pacific Worlds: A History of Seas, Peoples, and Cultures* (Cambridge, 2012). Dennis O. Flynn and Arturo Giráldez, eds., *The Pacific World: Lands, Peoples and History of the Pacific, 1500–1900*, 17 vols. (Aldershot, 2001–9), provides a wide-ranging library of previously published articles and chapters on the Pacific in all its dimensions before the twentieth century. The first volume in that series – Paul W. Blank and Fred Spier, eds., *Defining the Pacific: Opportunities and Constraints* (Aldershot, 2002) – offers useful overviews, especially of the physical Pacific. O. H. K. Spate, *The Pacific since Magellan*, I: *The Spanish Lake*; II: *Monopolists and Freebooters*; III: *Paradise Found and Lost* (London, 1979–88), remains the classic treatment of the Pacific basin between European contact and the early nineteenth century.

Pacific History is part of the broader history of oceanic regions, on which see Jerry H. Bentley, 'Sea and Ocean Basins as Frameworks of Historical Analysis', *Geographical Review* 89 (1999), 215–24; '*AHR* Forum: Oceans of History', *American Historical Review* 111 (2006), 717–80, especially Matt K. Matsuda, 'The Pacific', *American Historical Review* 111 (2006), 758–80; and Rila Mukherjee, ed., *Oceans Connect: Reflections on Water Worlds across Time and Space* (New Delhi, 2013). For a Braudelian comparison between the Pacific and the Mediterranean, see Paul W. Blank, 'The Pacific: A Mediterranean in the Making?', *Geographical Review* 89 (1999), 265–77. Katrina Gulliver, 'Finding the Pacific World', *Journal of World History* 22 (2011), 83–100, and Damon Salesa, 'Afterword: Opposite Footers', in Kate Fullagar, ed., *The Atlantic World in the Antipodes: Effects and Transformations since the Eighteenth Century* (Newcastle upon Tyne, 2012), pp. 283–300, offer contrasting attempts to connect the histories of the Atlantic and the Pacific. Ben Finney, 'The Other One-Third of the Globe', *Journal of World History* 5 (1994), 273–97, and Damon Salesa, 'The World from Oceania', in Douglas Northrop, ed., *A Companion to World History* (Chichester, 2012), pp. 391–404, diagnose the reasons for the relative absence of the Pacific from global and transnational history.

On the unfolding historiography of the island Pacific, see J. W. Davidson, 'Problems of Pacific History', *Journal of Pacific History* 1 (1966), 5–21; H. E. Maude, 'Pacific History – Past, Present and Future', *Journal of Pacific History* 6 (1971), 3–24; Malama Meleisea, 'Pacific Historiography: An Indigenous View', *Journal of Pacific Studies* 4 (1978), 5–43; Brij V. Lal, ed., *Pacific Islands History: Journeys and Transformations* (Canberra, 1992); Doug Munro, ed., *Reflections on Pacific Island Historiography*, Special Issue, *Journal of Pacific Studies* 20 (1996); Lal and Munro, eds., *Texts and Contexts: Reflections in Pacific Islands Historiography* (Honolulu, 2006); and Teresia K. Teaiwa, 'On Analogies: Rethinking the Pacific

335

in a Global Context', *The Contemporary Pacific* 18 (2006), 71–88. Greg Dening, 'History "in" the Pacific', *The Contemporary Pacific* 1 (1989), 134–9 is a classic brief account of the challenges of Pacific History; it is reprinted with other germinal articles in David Hanlon and Geoffrey M. White, eds., *Voyaging through the Contemporary Pacific* (Lanham, MD, 2002). For a valuable collection of pedagogical perspectives, see Paul D'Arcy, Stewart Firth, Teresia Teaiwa, Anne Perez Hattori, Anita Smith, Greg Dvorak, Jane Samson and Max Quanchi, 'Forum: The Teaching of Pacific History', *Journal of Pacific History* 46 (2011), 197–256.

Changing geographical and geopolitical visions of the Pacific can be traced in Ricardo Padrón, 'A Sea of Denial: The Early Modern Spanish Invention of the Pacific Rim', *Hispanic Review* 77 (2009), 1–27; Rainer Buschmann, *Defending the Spanish Lake: Iberian Visions of the Pacific Ocean, 1507–1899* (Basingstoke, 2014); Marcia Yonemoto, 'Maps and Metaphors of the "Small Eastern Sea" in Tokugawa Japan', *Geographical Review* 89 (1999), 169–87; Bronwen Douglas, '*Terra Australis* to Oceania: Racial Geography in the "Fifth Part of the World"', *Journal of Pacific History* 45 (2010), 179–210; Margaret Jolly, 'Imagining Oceania: Indigenous and Foreign Representations of a Sea of Islands', *The Contemporary Pacific* 19 (2007), 508–45; Ryan Tucker Jones, 'Running into Whales: The History of the North Pacific from Below the Waves', *American Historical Review* 118 (2013), 349–77; David Igler, 'On Coral Reefs, Volcanoes, Gods, and Patriotic Geology: Or, James Dwight Dana Assembles the Pacific Basin', *Pacific Historical Review* 79 (2010), 23–49; Tomoko Akami, *Internationalizing the Pacific: The United States, Japan and the Institute of Pacific Relations in War and Peace, 1919–45* (London, 2002); Alison Bashford, 'Karl Haushofer's *Geopolitics of the Pacific Ocean*', in Fullagar, ed., *The Atlantic World in the Antipodes*, pp. 120–43; Pekka Korhonen, 'The Pacific Age in World History', *Journal of World History* 7 (1996), 41–70; Peter A. Gourevitch, 'The Pacific Rim: Current Debates', *Annals of the American Academy of Political and Social Science* 505 (1989), 8–23; and Arif Dirlik, ed., *What Is In a Rim? Critical Perspectives on the Pacific Region Idea*, 2nd edn (Lanham, MD, 1998).

Examples of new histories using a Pacific frame include Stuart Banner, *Possessing the Pacific: Land, Settlers, and Indigenous People from Australia to Alaska* (Cambridge, MA, 2007); Bruce Cumings, *Dominion from Sea to Sea: Pacific Ascendancy and American Power* (New Haven, 2009); John Price, *Orienting Canada: Race, Empire, and the Transpacific* (Vancouver, BC, 2011); Kornel S. Chang, *Pacific Connections: The Making of the US–Canadian Borderlands* (Berkeley, 2012); Gregory T. Cushman, *Guano and the Opening of the Pacific World: A Global Ecological History* (Cambridge, 2013); and David Igler, *The Great Ocean: Pacific Worlds from Captain Cook to the Gold Rush* (Oxford, 2013).

## 2   The Pacific in Indigenous Time

'Indigenous' is a prickly term, one well explored in Pacific Island scholarship: see especially 'Native Pacific Cultural Studies on the Edge', a special issue of *The Contemporary Pacific* 13, 2 (Fall 2001), edited by Vicente Diaz and J. Kēhaulani Kauanui; Ty Tengan, *Native Men Remade: Gender and Nation in*

*Contemporary Hawaii* (Durham, NC, 2008); and Vicente Diaz, *Repositioning the Missionary: Rewriting the Histories of Colonialism, Native Catholicism, and Indigeneity in Guam* (Honolulu, 2010). *The Contemporary Pacific* is the leading journal in Pacific studies and is much engaged with these concerns.

Indigenous historians have been writing since at least authors such as Te Rangikaheke (published, heavily modified and unacknowledged) as Sir George Grey, *Ko Nga Moteatea me Nga Hakirara Maori* (Wellington, NZ, 1853) or the Lahainaluna students (often given as David Malo) *Ka Mooolelo Hawaii: The History of Hawaii* (Lahainalua, 1838; reprinted Honolulu, 2006). More recently, important and innovative attempts to engage mainstream historical scholarship with local/indigenous forms of historical knowledge include: Lilikalā Kame'eleihiwa, *Native Lands / Foreign Desires: Pehea La e Pono ai?* (Honolulu, 1992); Noenoe Silva, *Aloha Betrayed: Native Hawaiian Resistance to American Colonialism* (Durham, NC, 2004); Tamasa'ilau Suaalii-Sauni, I'uogafa Tuagalu, Tofilau Nina Kirifi-Alai and Naomi Fuamatu, eds., *Su'esu'e Manogi – In Search of Fragrance: Tui Atua Tupua Tamasese Ta'isi and the Samoan Indigenous Reference* (Apia, 2008); Keith Camacho, *Cultures of Commemoration: The Politics of War, Memory and History in the Mariana Islands* (Honolulu, 2011); Greg Dening, *Islands and Beaches: Discourse on a Silent Land: Marquesas, 1774– 1880* (Carlton, Vic., 1980); Serge Tcherkézoff, *First Contacts in Polynesia – the Samoan Case (1722–1848): Western Misunderstandings about Sexuality and Divinity*, new edn (Canberra, 2008); Klaus Neumann, *Not the Way it Really Was: Constructing the Tolai Past* (Honolulu, 1988).

Indigenous Pacific intellectuals have challenged some of the norms of history writing. See indicative works by Bernard Narokobi, *The Melanesian Way: Total Cosmic Vision of Life* (Port Moresby, 1980); Albert Wendt, 'Historians and the Art of Remembering', in Anthony Hooper, et al., eds., *Class and Culture in the South Pacific* (Auckland, NZ, 1987), pp. 78–91; Epeli Hau'ofa, 'Our Sea of Islands', *The Contemporary Pacific* 6 (1994), 147–61; and I. Futa Helu, *Critical Essays: Cultural Perspectives from the South Seas* (Canberra, 1999).

Regarding what are here called 'native seas' one should begin with David Lewis, *We, the Navigators: The Ancient Art of Landfinding in the Pacific* (Honolulu, 1994). Anthropologists have been most revealing: for example, William Alkire, *Lamotrek Atoll and Inter-Island Socioeconomic Ties* (Urbana, 1965) or the most studied example, Massim: see 'The History and Anthropology of the Massim, Papua, New Guinea', Special Issue, *Journal of Pacific History* 18, 1/2 (January/ April 1983). Pacific archaeology has also often been crucially engaged with indigenous tradition and practice. See Janet Davidson, et al., eds., *Oceanic Culture History: Essays in Honour of Roger Green* (Dunedin, NZ, 1996) or Patrick V. Kirch and Roger Green, *Hawaiki: Ancestral Polynesia: An Essay in Historical Anthropology* (Cambridge, 2001).

Decolonisation in the Pacific was a catalyst not just for new national histories, but also new kinds of historical practice. Pacific History, founded as an interdisciplinary enterprise in Canberra after the Second World War, explicitly aimed to centre its history on Islanders. See the key works of J. W. Davidson, *Samoa mo Samoa: The Emergence of the Independent State of*

*Western Samoa* (Melbourne, 1967); Davidson and Deryck Scarr, eds., *Pacific Island Portraits* (Canberra, 1970); and the retrospective volume by Brij Lal, ed., *Pacific Islands History: Journeys and Transformations* (Canberra, 1992). See also the 25 titles published by the University of Hawai'i Press since 1983 in the Pacific Islands Monograph Series: an outstanding example is David Hanlon, *Upon a Stone Altar: A History of the Island of Pohnpei to 1890* (Honolulu, 1988).

From the 1970s onwards a handful of indigenous historians gained their doctorates, most notably Sione Latukefu, *Church and State in Tonga: The Wesleyan Methodist Missionaries and Political Development, 1822–1875* (Canberra, 1974), John Dademo Waiko, *A Short History of Papua New Guinea* (Melbourne, 1992) and the path-breaking work of Malama Meleisea, *The Making of Modern Samoa: Traditional Authority and Colonial Administration in the History of Western Samoa* (Suva, 1987). Allied to this were a series of collectively authored volumes of new national histories, produced by teams of Island experts and leaders, with consulting academic historians. Important examples are Hugh Laracy, et al., *Tuvalu, a History* (Suva, 1983), Maihetoe Hekau, et al., *Niue: A History of the Island* (Suva, 1982), Malama Meleisea, et al., *Lagaga: A Short History of Western Samoa* (Suva, 1987) and the trilingual book by Walter Lini, et al., *Vanuatu: Twenti Wan Tingting Long Team Blong Independents* (Suva, 1980).

For insights into the diasporic, transnational histories that Islanders are now part of, see Steve Tupai Francis and Helen Lee, eds., *Migration and Transnationalism: Pacific Perspectives* (Canberra, 2009), Sean Mallon, Kolokesa Māhina-Tuai and Damon Salesa, eds., *Tangata o le Moana: New Zealand and the People of the Pacific* (Wellington, NZ, 2012) and Cluny Macpherson and La'avasa Macpherson, *The Warm Winds of Change: Globalisation in Contemporary Samoa* (Auckland, NZ, 2009).

## 3   The Pacific Before Empire, *c*.1500–1800

To understand the nature and significance of early modern global travel in broader chronological and geographic perspectives, readers might profitably consult Stephen Gosch and Peter N. Stearns, *Premodern Travel in World History* (New York, 2007) and Felipe Fernández-Armesto, *Pathfinders: A Global History of Exploration* (New York, 2006). See Raymond John Howgego, ed., *Encyclopedia of Exploration*, 5 vols. (Sydney, 2003–13) and Joyce E. Chaplin, *Round about the Earth: Circumnavigation from Magellan to Orbit* (New York, 2012), for, respectively, a catalogue of Pacific voyages (among others) and analysis of the Pacific segments of round-the-world voyages.

The earliest European voyages into the Pacific are covered in George E. Nunn, 'Magellan's Route in the Pacific', *Geographical Review* 24 (1943), 615–33; J. C. Beaglehole, 'Pacific Exploration before Cook', *Endeavour* 27 (1968), 18–22; Norman J. W. Thrower, ed., *Sir Francis Drake and the Famous Voyage, 1577–1580: Essays Commemorating the Quadricentennial of Drake's Circumnavigation of the Earth* (Berkeley, 1984); Anton Gill, *The Devil's Mariner: A Life of William Dampier, Pirate and Explorer, 1651–1715* (London, 1997); and Glyndwr Williams, *The*

*Great South Sea: English Voyages and Encounters, 1570–1750* (New Haven, 1997). On Spain's Pacific-spanning empire, see O. H. K. Spate, *The Spanish Lake* (London, 1979); Dennis O. Flynn, Arturo Giráldez and James Sobredo, eds., *European Entry into the Pacific: Spain and the Acapulco–Manila Galleons* (Aldershot, 2001); and Mercedes Maroto Camino, *Producing the Pacific: Maps and Narratives of Spanish Exploration (1576–1606)* (Amsterdam, 2005). On the Dutch, see Günter Schilder, *Australia Unveiled: The Share of the Dutch Navigators in the Discovery of Australia*, trans. Olaf Richter (Amsterdam, 1976). On the slow European entry into east Asian trade, see the relevant essays in Ernst van Veen and Leonard Blussé, eds., *Rivalry and Conflict: European Traders and Asian Trading Networks in the Sixteenth and Seventeenth Centuries* (Leiden, 2005).

Several works have considered how the experience of voyaging the Pacific, or sojourning on its islands, confounded the majority of European travellers. See Greg Dening, *Islands and Beaches: Discourses on a Silent Land: Marquesas, 1774–1880* (Carlton, Vic., 1980); David A. Chappell, *Double Ghosts: Oceanian Voyagers on Euroamerican Ships* (Armonk, NY, 1997); Jonathan Lamb, *Preserving the Self in the South Seas, 1680–1840* (Chicago, 2001); Joyce E. Chaplin, 'Earthsickness: Circumnavigation and the Terrestrial Human Body, 1520–1800', *Bulletin of the History of Medicine* 86 (2012), 515–42. In their *Great Map of Mankind: British Perceptions of the World in the Age of the Enlightenment* (London, 1982), P. J. Marshall and Glyndwr Williams compare European descriptions of the Pacific to those for other parts of the world.

On Cook and his near-contemporaries, see John Dunmore, *French Explorers in the Pacific: The Eighteenth Century* (Oxford, 1965); Dunmore, *French Explorers in the Pacific: The Nineteenth Century* (Oxford, 1969); J. C. Beaglehole, *The Life of Captain James Cook* (London, 1974); N. A. Ivashintosov, *Russian Round-the-World Voyages, 1803–1849* (Kingston, Ont., 1980); Greg Dening, *Mr. Bligh's Bad Language: Passion, Power, and Theatre on the Bounty* (Cambridge, 1992); Londa Schiebinger, 'Jeanne Baret: The First Woman to Circumnavigate the Globe', *Endeavour* 27 (2003), 22–5; Anne Salmond, *The Trial of the Cannibal Dog: The Remarkable Story of Captain Cook's Encounters in the South Seas* (New Haven, 2003); Salmond, *Bligh: William Bligh in the South Seas* (Berkeley, 2011); and Vanessa Smith, *Intimate Strangers: Friendship, Exchange and Pacific Encounters* (Cambridge, 2010).

The ecological consequences of European empires, including in the Pacific, are discussed in Alfred W. Crosby, *Ecological Imperialism: The Biological Expansion of Europe, 900–1900* (New York, 2004); Richard H. Grove, *Green Imperialism: Colonial Expansion, Tropical Island Edens, and the Origins of Environmentalism, 1600–1860* (Cambridge, 1995); J. R. McNeill, 'Of Rats and Men: A Synoptic Environmental History of the Island Pacific', *Journal of World History* 5 (1994), 299–349; and Jennifer Newell, *Trading Nature: Tahitians, Europeans, and Ecological Exchange* (Honolulu, 2010).

On imperialism and scientific activities, see Harry Woolf, *The Transits of Venus: A Study of Eighteenth-Century Science* (London, 1959); Roy MacLeod and Philip F. Rehbock, eds., *Nature in its Greatest Extent: Western Science in the Pacific* (Honolulu, 1988); Robin Fisher and Hugh Johnston, eds., *From Maps to*

*Metaphors: The Pacific World of George Vancouver* (Vancouver, BC, 1993); William Eisler, *The Furthest Shore: Images of Terra Australis from the Middle Ages to Captain Cook* (Cambridge, 1995); David Philip Miller and Peter Hanns Reill, eds., *Visions of Empire: Voyages, Botany, and Representations of Nature* (Cambridge, 1996); Tony Ballantyne, ed., *Science, Empire, and the European Exploration of the Pacific* (Aldershot, 2004); Harry Liebersohn, *The Travelers' World: Europe to the Pacific* (Cambridge, MA, 2006); and Ian R. Bartky, *One Time Fits All: The Campaigns for Global Uniformity* (Stanford, 2007). For the closely related topic of indigenous experts and informants, see Glyndwr Williams, 'Tupaia: Polynesian Warrior, Navigator, High Priest – and Artist', in Felicity Nussbaum, ed., *The Global Eighteenth Century* (Baltimore, 2003), pp. 38–51; Jocelyn Hackforth-Jones, 'Mai', in Hackforth-Jones, ed., *Between Worlds: Voyagers to Britain, 1700–1850* (London, 2007), pp. 44–55; and Simon Schaffer, Lissa Roberts, Kapil Raj and James Delbourgo, eds., *The Brokered World: Go-betweens and Global Intelligence, 1770–1820* (Sagamore Beach, MA, 2009).

## 4   The Age of Empire in the Pacific

The themes of contact, commerce, evangelism, colonial annexation and early administration were addressed by the Canberra-based Pacific historians of the 1960s and 1970s and by their students and associates. Important studies were published through the *Journal of Pacific History* from 1966 onwards, and in two anthologies: J. W. Davidson and Deryck Scarr, eds., *Pacific Islands Portraits* (Canberra, 1970) and Davidson and Scarr, eds., *More Pacific Islands Portraits* (Canberra, 1978). While many monographs were island- or archipelago-focused, important comparative studies from this period included Peter Corris, *Passage, Port and Plantation: A History of Solomon Islands Labour Migration, 1870–1914* (Carlton, Vic., 1973); Niel Gunson, *Messengers of Grace: Evangelical Missionaries in the South Seas, 1797–1860* (Melbourne, 1978); Caroline Ralston, *Grass Huts and Warehouses: Pacific Beach Communities of the Nineteenth Century* (Canberra, 1977); and Dorothy Shineberg, *They Came for Sandalwood: A Study of the Sandalwood Trade in the South-west Pacific, 1830–1865* (Melbourne, 1967).

   Greg Dening, in his *Islands and Beaches: Discourse on a Silent Land: Marquesas, 1774–1880* (Carlton, Vic., 1980), challenged the conventional empiricism of the 'Davidson school' and advocated a cultural, cross-disciplinary and 'reflective' approach, animated by what he called the 'artifice' of historical writing. Over the same period, anthropologists such as Marshall Sahlins became interested in the workings of 'structure' over time: see, for example, Sahlins, *Islands of History* (Chicago, 1985) and Sahlins, *Apologies to Thucydides: Understanding History as Culture and Vice Versa* (Chicago, 2004). Pacific historical scholarship came to have diverse and experimental expressions, stimulated by anthropology, literary and performance studies, feminism, the South-Asian focused Subaltern Studies group, and other movements in the 'new humanities' of the 1980s and 1990s. Important examples of this cross-disciplinary turn included Margaret Jolly and Martha Macintyre, eds., *Family and Gender in the Pacific: Domestic Contradictions and the Colonial Impact* (Cambridge, 1989), Roger M. Keesing, *Custom and Confrontation: The Kwaio Struggle for Cultural Autonomy* (Chicago, 1992) and Bronwen Douglas, *Across the Great Divide: Journeys in History and Anthropology* (Amsterdam, 1998). More recent examples include Helen Bethea Gardner, *Gathering for God: George Brown in Oceania* (Dunedin, NZ, 2006) and Tracey Banivanua-Mar, *Violence and Colonial Dialogue: The Australian-Pacific Indentured Labor Trade* (Honolulu, 2007). That scholarship also informs Nicholas Thomas, *Entangled Objects: Exchange, Material Culture, and Colonialism in the Pacific* (Cambridge, MA, 1991), Thomas, *Colonialism's Culture: Anthropology, Travel and Government* (Princeton, 1994) and Thomas, *Islanders: The Pacific in the Age of Empire* (New Haven, 2010).

A series of books by Anne Salmond, from *Two Worlds: First Meetings between Maori and Europeans, 1642–1772* (Auckland, NZ, 1991) to *Aphrodite's Island: The European Discovery of Tahiti* (Berkeley, 2009), has been vital in strengthening this anthropologically informed history and taking it to wider audiences, especially in New Zealand. The state of play was reviewed in Nicholas Thomas, 'Partial Texts: Representation, Colonialism and Agency in Pacific History', *Journal of Pacific History* 25 (1990), 139–58, which was reprinted in Thomas, *In Oceania: Visions, Artefacts, Histories* (Durham, NC, 1997), pp. 23–49. Epeli Hau'ofa's rethinking of the region was inspirational and continues to have reverberations today. His most influential essays appeared as Hau'ofa, *We Are the Ocean: Selected Works* (Honolulu, 2008). The field has continued to diversify. Jonathan Kay Kamakawiwo'ole Osorio, *Dismembering Lāhui: A History of the Hawaiian Nation to 1887* (Honolulu, 2002) exemplifies increasingly strong work by scholars based more in the emerging field of Native Studies than Pacific History as it was formerly constituted. Very different in scope and scale are several new overviews from the vantage point of world history, including notably Matt K. Matsuda's *Pacific Worlds: A History of Seas, Peoples, and Cultures* (Cambridge, 2012).

## 5   A Pacific Century?

There is a vast amount of literature on the international history of the Asia-Pacific region in the twentieth century. On the emergence of the United States as a Pacific empire, the two standard accounts by Ernest R. May, *Imperial Democracy: The Emergence of America as a Great Power* (New York, 1961) and *American Imperialism: A Speculative Essay* (New York, 1968), should be supplemented by such subsequent works as Kristin L. Hoganson, *Fighting for American Manhood: How Gender Politics Provoked the Spanish–American and Philippine–American Wars* (New Haven, 1998), and Paul Kramer, *The Blood of Government: Race, Empire, the United States, and the Philippines* (Chapel Hill, 2006). The former adds the dimension of gender considerations, and the latter that of race relations, to the discussion of US. expansion into the Pacific. On the rise of Japan as an empire and early rivalry with the United States, see Akira Iriye, *Pacific Estrangement: Japanese and American Expansion, 1897–1911* (Cambridge,

MA, 1972). The Pacific aspect of the First World War is chronicled by Hermann Joseph Hiery, *The Neglected War: The German South Pacific and World War I* (Honolulu, 1995), which describes battles fought in the German colonial islands and their transfer as mandates to Japan and the British Dominions after the war. Xu Guoqi's *China and the Great War: China's Pursuit of a New National Identity and Internationalization* (New York, 2005) and *Strangers on the Western Front: Chinese Workers in the Great War* (Cambridge, MA, 2011) connect China to Europe during the war through the former's US-educated leaders as well as labourers who crossed the Pacific to get to Britain and France.

On the 'interwar' (1919–39) period, see Akira Iriye, *After Imperialism: The Search for a New Order in the Far East, 1921–1931* (Cambridge, MA, 1965) and William Roger Louis, *British Strategy in the Far East, 1919–1939* (Oxford, 1971) on the naval rivalry in the Pacific. The 'road to war' that began with the Japanese invasion of Manchuria in 1931 and culminated in the Pearl Harbor attack, is summarised in Akira Iriye, *The Origins of the Second World War in Asia and the Pacific* (New York, 1987), but it is amply supplemented by more detailed accounts of the naval rivalry in the Pacific, such as Stephen E. Pelz, *Race to Pearl Harbor: The Failure of the Second London Naval Congress and the Onset of World War II* (Cambridge, MA, 1974), Gordon Prange, *At Dawn We Slept: The Untold Story of Pearl Harbor* (New York, 1981) and Waldo H. Heinrichs, *Threshold of War: Franklin D. Roosevelt and American Entry into World War II* (New York, 1988). Japan's quest for natural resources in the Pacific and the consequent collision with the US, British and Dutch empires is well treated in Jonathan G. Utley, *Going to War with Japan, 1937–1941* (Knoxville, 1985) and Daniel Yergin, *The Prize: The Epic Quest for Oil, Money, and Power* (New York, 1991).

The Pacific War (1941–5) has been extensively covered by such books as Peter Calvocoressi and Guy Wint, *Total War: The Story of World War II* (New York, 1972) and Christopher Thorne, *Allies of a Kind: The United States, Britain, and the War Against Japan, 1941–1945* (New York, 1978), while the transition from war to Cold War is described by Martin J. Sherwin, *A World Destroyed: The Atomic Bomb and the Grand Alliance* (New York, 1975), Daniel Yergin, *Shattered Peace: The Origins of the Cold War and the National Security State* (Boston, 1977) and Marc S. Gallicchio, *The Cold War Begins in Asia: American East Asian Policy and the Fall of the Japanese Empire* (New York, 1988), among others. The Pacific Ocean became a site of the Cold War through the nuclear testing carried out by the United States, a subject treated in Robert A. Divine, *Blowing on the Wind: The Nuclear Test Ban Debate, 1954–1960* (New York, 1979). The most up-to-date history of the Korean War is Sheila Miyoshi Jager, *Brothers at War: The Unending Conflict in Korea* (New York, 2013).

As the chapter notes, it is important to broaden our inquiry into Pacific History by examining such transnational aspects as economic globalisation, migrations, human rights, cultural exchanges and environmental disasters. These are less geopolitical than social and cultural phenomena, and historians have been paying increasing attention to them. Regarding globalisation, particularly in the Asia-Pacific region, sociologist Ezra Vogel's studies, for instance *The Four Little Dragons: The Spread of Industrialization in East Asia* (Cambridge,

MA, 1991) and *Deng Xiaoping and the Transformation of China* (Cambridge, MA, 2011), are very valuable. On migrations, in addition to works cited in Adam McKeown's chapter in this volume, broad historical perspectives offered by such accounts as Dirk Hoerder, 'Migrations and Belongings', in Emily S. Rosenberg, ed., *A World Connecting, 1870–1945* (Cambridge, MA, 2012), pp. 433–89, and Ian Goldin, Geoffrey Cameron and Meera Balarajan, *Exceptional People: How Migration Shaped Our World and Will Define Our Future* (Princeton, 2011), should be consulted.

On cultural relations, a theme that is given particular emphasis in the chapter, a broad survey is offered by Akira Iriye, *Cultural Internationalism and World Order* (Baltimore, 1997), tracing various efforts around the world to promote intercultural communication and understanding as a foundation of a peaceful world order. More specific to Pacific History are such works as Warren I. Cohen, *The Chinese Connection: Roger S. Greene, Thomas W. Lamont, George E. Sokolsky and American East-Asian Relations* (New York, 1978), Jane Hunter, *The Gospel of Gentility: American Women Missionaries in Turn-of-the-Century China* (New Haven, 1984), and Tomoko Akami, *Internationalizing the Pacific: The United States, Japan, and the Institute of Pacific Relations in War and Peace, 1919–1945* (London, 2002). The first book describes three Americans who played crucial roles in establishing economic and social connections between China and the United States, the second deals with American women missionaries in China at the turn of the twentieth century, and the third discusses how the Institute of Pacific Relations sought to maintain trans-Pacific intellectual dialogue all the way to the eve of the war. The best studies of non-geopolitical phenomena during the Cold War are those that focus on human rights development globally and regionally. Among the most-up-to-date and useful are the essays in Akira Iriye, Petra Goedde and William I. Hitchcock, eds., *The Human Rights Revolution: An International History* (Oxford, 2012). The global (and successful) struggle against imperialism and racism is a key component of Pacific History, as can be seen in such accounts as Marilyn Lake and Henry Reynolds, *Drawing the Global Colour Line: White Men's Countries and the International Challenge of Racial Equality* (Cambridge, 2008), and Nico Slate, *Colored Cosmopolitanism: The Shared struggle for Freedom in the United States and India* (Cambridge, MA, 2012). Environmental history, another transnational subject, is given a masterful summary in J. R. McNeill and Peter Engelke, 'Into the Anthropocene', in Akira Iriye, ed., *Global Interdependence since 1945* (Cambridge, MA, 2013), pp. 363–533.

## 6 The Environment

The literature on the Pacific's environmental history is still mainly to be found in the natural sciences and anthropology, but several recent works have begun to integrate the ocean into the human past. The best of these is Donald Freeman, *The Pacific* (London, 2010), especially the first several chapters. The tropical Pacific has received the most attention, and useful and eloquent summaries are found in J. R. McNeill, 'Of Rats and Men: A Synoptic Environmental History of the Island Pacific', *Journal of World History* 5 (1994),

299–349, and Paul D'Arcy, 'Oceania: The Environmental History of One-Third of the Globe', in J. R. McNeill and Erin Steward Mauldin, eds., *A Companion to Global Environmental History* (Chichester, 2012), pp. 196–221. Classic works from anthropologists include Marshall Sahlins and Patrick Vinton Kirch, *Anahulu: The Anthropology of History in the Kingdom of Hawaii* (Chicago, 1994) and William Alkire, *Coral Islanders* (Arlington Heights, 1978). These can be supplemented by the more recent (and more historical) Paul D'Arcy, *Peoples of the Sea: Environment, Identity, and History in Oceania* (Honolulu, 2008) and Jennifer Newell, *Trading Nature: Tahitians, Europeans and Ecological Exchange* (Honolulu, 2010). A very readable survey of Hawaiian environmental history, though marked by a strong declensionist streak, is John Culliney, *Islands in a Far Sea: The Fate of Nature in Hawaii* (Honolulu, 2006). Judith Bennett's *Natives and Exotics: World War II and the Environment in the South Pacific* (Honolulu, 2009) is one of the few works to examine the all-important wartime developments.

California's environmental history is nearly as well served as the South Pacific's. One excellent documentary collection is Carolyn Merchant, ed., *Green Versus Gold: Sources in California's Environmental History* (Washington, DC, 1998), while David Igler's *The Great Ocean: Pacific Worlds from Captain Cook to the Gold Rush* (Oxford, 2013) tells the maritime environmental history of the state (and far beyond) better than it has been since the superb Arthur McEvoy, *The Fisherman's Problem: Ecology and Law in the California Fisheries, 1850–1900* (Cambridge, 1990).

By comparison, environmental historians have neglected the rest of the Pacific, though, again, anthropologists and archaeologists have produced an array of studies on Arctic cultures that closely consider the natural world. Most innovative amongst these include Herbert Maschner, et al., 'An Introduction to the Biocomplexity of Sanak Island, Western Gulf of Alaska', *Pacific Science* 63 (2009), 673–709, and Todd Braje and Torben Rick, eds., *Human Impacts on Seals, Sea Lions, and Sea Otters: Integrating Archaeology and Ecology in the Northeast Pacific* (Berkeley, 2011). Both this last work and a similar volume on whales, James Estes, et al., eds., *Whales, Whaling, and Ocean Ecosystems* (Berkeley, 2007), introduced intriguing, but still disputed ideas about the ways in which marine-mammal hunting in the Pacific permanently reshaped those ecosystems. American whaling is covered best in Eric Dolin, *Leviathan: The History of Whaling in America* (New York, 2008). My own *Empire of Extinction: Russians and the Strange Beasts of the Sea in the North Pacific, 1709–1867* (Oxford, 2014) examines the development of environmentalism in that region during the imperial era. Katherine Reedy-Maschner, *Aleut Identities: Tradition and Modernity in an Indigenous Fishery* (Montreal, 2010) describes the way Alaskan indigenous cultures have negotiated modern conservation.

On the other side of the ocean, New Zealand and Australian environmental history focus mainly on the land, though Lyndall Ryan's *The Aboriginal Tasmanians* (Vancouver, BC, 1981) and Lynette Russell's *Roving Mariners: Australian Aboriginal Whalers and Sealers in the Southern Oceans, 1790–1870* (Albany, NY, 2012) are changing views of maritime history. Alfred W. Crosby, *Ecological Imperialism: The Biological Expansion of Europe, 900–1900*, new edn

(Cambridge, 2004), ch. 10, 'New Zealand', gives the reader a very quick summary of how those islands' environments impacted European imperialism. Literature on Latin America's Pacific environmental history is lacking, but Edward D. Melillo, 'The First Green Revolution: Debt Peonage and the Making of the Nitrogen Fertilizer Trade, 1840–1930', *American Historical Review* (2012), 1028–60, is a good start. Similar histories for China are still difficult to find, but Japan is covered in several works including Brett Walker, *The Conquest of Ainu Lands: Ecology and Culture in Japanese Expansion, 1590– 1800* (Berkeley, 2006) as well as Arne Kalland, *Fishing Villages in Tokugawa Japan* (Honolulu, 1995).

A classic study of indigenous environmental knowledge is R. E. Johannes, *Worlds of the Lagoon: Fishing and Marine Lore in the Palau District of Micronesia* (Berkeley, 1992), which describes the incredibly detailed knowledge of fish behaviour Palauan fishermen have gained. For similar themes in Melanesia see Edvard Hviding, *Guardians of Marovo Lagoon: Practice, Place, and Politics in Maritime Melanesia* (Honolulu, 1996). Finally, an excellent film on South Pacific responses to global warming is Briar March, *There Once Was an Island: Te Henua e Nnoho* (On the Level Productions, 2010).

# 7 Movement

Peter Bellwood has written extensively on ancient migrations into Southeast Asia, and the movement of Austronesian speakers throughout the Pacific and Indian Oceans: see his *Prehistory of the Indo-Malaysian Archipelago* (Honolulu, 1997) and *Man's Conquest of the Pacific: The Prehistory of Southeast Asia and Oceania* (Oxford, 1979). K. R. Howe has written engagingly on the settlement of the Pacific and the history of ideas about that settlement: see his *Vaka Moana: Voyages of the Ancestors* (Honolulu, 2007) and *The Quest for Origins: Who First Discovered and Settled the Pacific Islands?* (Honolulu, 2003).

On the history of maritime Southeast Asia, see Anthony Reid, *Southeast Asia in the Age of Commerce, 1450–1680*, II: *Expansion and Crisis* (New Haven, 1995) and Eric Tagliacozzo and Wen-chin Chang, eds., *Chinese Circulations: Capital, Commodities and Networks in Southeast Asia* (Durham, NC, 2011).

O. H. K. Spate's trilogy, *The Pacific Since Magellan*, is the most thorough work on European exploration and trade across the Pacific until the early nineteenth century. The three volumes are *The Spanish Lake* (London, 1979), *Monopolists and Freebooters* (London, 1983) and *Paradise Found and Lost* (London, 1989). Several articles about the galleon trade and the importance of American silver in the Pacific are collected in Dennis Flynn and Arturo Giráldez, eds. *Metals and Moneys in an Emerging Global Economy* (Aldershot, 1997), and in Flynn, Giráldez and James Sobredo, eds., *European Entry into the Pacific: Spain and the Acapulco–Manila Galleons* (Aldershot, 2001).

Much has been written about the European voyages of exploration of the late eighteenth century, especially Captain Cook. See Anne Salmond, *The Trial of the Cannibal Dog: The Remarkable Story of Captain Cook's Encounters in the South Seas* (New Haven, 2003), and Nicholas Thomas, *Cook: The Extraordinary Voyages of Captain Cook* (New York, 2004). An interesting study of how the early China trade linked culturally diverse parts of the Pacific is Marshall Sahlins, 'Cosmologies of Capitalism: The Trans-Pacific Sector of "The World System"', *Proceedings of the British Academy* 74 (1989), 1–51.

On multicultural ships and island communities in the early nineteenth century, see David A. Chappell, *Double Ghosts: Oceanian Voyagers on Early Euroamerican Ships* (Armonk, NY, 1997) and Caroline Ralston, *Grass Huts and Warehouses: Pacific Beach Communities in the Nineteenth Century* (Honolulu, 1978). Alistair Couper, *Sailors and Traders: A Maritime History of the Pacific Peoples* (Honolulu, 2009) brings these concerns up to the present.

On the Pacific economy of the nineteenth century (and beyond), see essays in Dennis Flynn, Lionel Frost and A. J. H. Latham, eds., *Pacific Centuries: Pacific and Pacific Rim History since the Sixteenth Century* (London, 1998); Sally Miller, A. J. H. Latham and Dennis Flynn, eds., *Studies in the Economic History of the Pacific Rim* (London, 1998); and A. J. H. Latham and Heita Kawakatsu, eds., *Asia–Pacific Dynamism 1550–2000* (London, 2000). The history of Pacific shipping is still not well-developed. A good place to start is William Wray, *Mitsubishi and the N.Y.K., 1870–1914: Business Strategy in the Japanese Shipping Industry* (Cambridge, MA, 1984).

On patterns of Chinese emigration, see Adam McKeown, 'Chinese Emigration in Global Context, 1850–1940', *Journal of Global History* 5 (2010), 95–124. On the spread of Chinese exclusion and immigration control, see Adam McKeown, *Melancholy Order: Asian Migration and the Globalization of Borders* (New York, 2008). On the spread of racial ideas throughout the Pacific, see Marilyn Lake and Henry Reynolds, *Drawing the Global Colour Line: White Men's Countries and the International Challenge of Racial Equality* (Cambridge, 2008), Andrew Markus, *Fear and Hatred: Purifying Australia and California 1850–1901* (Sydney, 1974) and Charles Price, *The Great White Walls Are Built: Restrictive Immigration to North America and Australia, 1836–1888* (Canberra, 1974).

Histories of Japanese–American relations in the early twentieth century include Eiichiro Azuma, *Between Two Empires: Race, History and Transnationalism in Japanese America* (Oxford, 2005), Akira Iriye, *After Imperialism: The Search for a New Order in the Far East, 1921–1931* (Cambridge, MA, 1965) and Iriye, *Pacific Estrangement: Japanese and American Expansion, 1897–1911* (Cambridge, MA, 1972). These are extended to include Australia and other Asian countries in Sean Brawley, *The White Peril: Foreign Relations and Asian Immigration into Australasia and North America, 1919–78* (Sydney, 1995).

Histories of the American Pacific are often the most wide-ranging in time and space. Three such works are Warren I. Cohen, *The Asian–American Century* (Cambridge, MA, 2002), Bruce Cumings, *Dominion from the Sea: Pacific Ascendancy and American Power* (New Haven, 2009) and Arthur Dudden, *The American Pacific: From the Old China Trade to the Present* (Oxford, 1994). Finally, for a criticism of the contemporary idea of the Pacific Rim, see Arif Dirlik, ed., *What Is In a Rim? Critical Perspectives on the Pacific Region Idea*, 2nd edn (Lanham, MD, 1998).

## 8   The Pacific Economy since 1800

There is no comprehensive volume on the economic history of the Pacific since 1800. *The Pacific World: Lands, Peoples and History of the Pacific, 1500–1900*, 17 vols. (Aldershot, 2001–9), a 17-volume collection of essays published under the general editorship of Dennis O. Flynn and Arturo Giráldez, mainly explores early modern themes and perspectives, but some volumes cover the early phase of industrialisation. Kenneth Pomeranz, ed., *The Pacific in the Age of Early Industrialization* (Farnham, 2009) comprises essays on trade, technology, industrialisation and the role of the state in Japan, China, Korea, Taiwan, Southeast Asia and Chile, with a full introduction on the theme of the title. Debin Ma, ed., *Textiles in the Pacific, 1500–1900* (Aldershot, 2005), includes essays on trade, technology and institutions relating to silk, cotton and wool industries in Japan, China, Korea, Southeast Asia, California and Australia, also with a brief but useful introduction. In the same vein, Sally M. Miller, A. J. H. Latham and Dennis O. Flynn, eds., *Studies in the Economic History of the Pacific Rim* (London, 1998), contains a useful introduction by Flynn and Arturo Giráldez, 'The Pacific Rim's Past Deserves a Future' (ibid., pp. 1–18), along with essays relating to trade and industry across the Pacific.

Three strands of literature are relevant to the methodological focus of this chapter, though none of them is explicitly concerned with the Pacific. W. Arthur Lewis studied tropical development, the growth of exports of primary products and factoral terms of trade, to discuss how the North–South divide emerged and how it should be overcome through industrialisation. Lewis effectively used the distinction between the tropics and the temperate zones to delineate the divergent paths of the Pacific economies: see Lewis, ed., *Tropical Development, 1880–1913: Studies in Economic Progress* (London, 1970), Lewis, *Growth and Fluctuations, 1870–1913* (London, 1978) and Lewis, *The Evolution of the International Economic Order* (Princeton, 1978).

Giovanni Arrighi, Takeshi Hamashita and Mark Seldon, eds., *The Resurgence of East Asia: 500, 150 and 50 Year Perspectives* (London, 2003) and Gareth Austin and Kaoru Sugihara, eds., *Labour-intensive Industrialization in Global History* (London, 2013), summarize recent discussion on the long-term path of economic development in East Asia. My chapter in the latter volume brings the story to the post-war phase of the 'East Asian miracle', extending the discussion to other parts of East and Southeast Asia.

The literature on the success and failure of international regimes of trade, currency and investment, and the institutional convergence for deeper integration, are important for Pacific economic history. Anne O. Krueger describes changes in developing countries' policies from import-substitution industrialisation to the more open, export-oriented stance, resulting in both the rise of East Asian Newly Industrialised Economies and debt crises in Latin America, in her *Trade Policies and Developing Nations* (Washington, DC, 1995). Ross Garnaut and Peter Drysdale, eds., *Asia Pacific Regionalism: Readings in International Economic Relations* (Pymble, 1994) contains a short introduction, which describes the emergence of 'open regionalism' in the western Pacific. Historians' works with a useful angle to the Pacific include Steven Topik, Carlos Marichal and Zephyr Frank, eds., *From Silver to Cocaine: Latin American Commodity Chains and the Building of the World Economy, 1500–2000* (Durham, NC, 2006), and Kenneth Pomeranz and Steven Topik, *The World That Trade Created: Society, Culture and the World Economy, 1400 to the Present*, 3rd edn (New York, 2013).

Turning to the more specific recent trends in Asian economic history, Eric Tagliacozzo and Wen-Chin Chang, eds., *Chinese Circulations: Capital, Commodities and Networks in Southeast Asia* (Durham, NC, 2011) shows the importance of China-centred demand and trading networks. A. J. H. Latham and Heita Kawakatsu have edited a series of volumes – among them *Japanese Industrialization and the Asian Economy* (London, 1994), *Asia Pacific Dynamism, 1550–2000* (London, 2000) and *Intra-Asian Trade and Industrialization: Essays in Memory of Yasukichi Yasuba* (London, 2009) – which, along with Kaoru Sugihara, ed., *Japan, China and the Growth of the Asian International Economy, 1850–1949* (Oxford, 2005) and Takeshi Hamashita, *China, East Asia and the Global Economy: Regional and Historical Perspectives*, ed. Linda Grove and Mark Selden (London, 2008), represent Japanese-led research on the evolution of intra-Asian trade and East and Southeast Asian trade networks. Billy K. L. So and Ramon H. Myers, eds., *The Treaty Port Economy in Modern China: Empirical Studies of Institutional Change and Economic Performance* (Berkeley, 2011) takes into account the new emphasis on institutions in economics. For the 1930s, Tomoko Shiroyama, *China during the Great Depression: Market, State and the World Economy* (Cambridge, MA, 2008), and Shigeru Akita and Nicholas J. White, eds., *The International Order of Asia in the 1930s and 1950s* (Farnham, 2010) are important recent additions to the literature.

Finally, academic discussion played a role in policy recommendation and assessment. Asian Development Bank, *Southeast Asia's Economy in the 1970s* (New York, 1971) marked the beginning of academic discussion on the export-oriented development strategy. *The East Asian Miracle: Economic Growth and Public Policy* (Washington DC, 1993), a World Bank Policy Research Report, has been widely read and debated, mainly in the context of assessment of the role of the state.

## 9   Religion

For general histories of Hindu, Islamic, and Christian movements into Indonesia and the Philippines and conversions to Islam and Christianity, see M. C. Ricklefs, *A History of Modern Indonesia since c. 1200* (Stanford, 2008) and Anthony Reid, 'Islamization and Christianization in Southeast Asia: The Critical Phase, 1550–1650', in Reid, ed., *Southeast Asia in the Early Modern Era: Trade, Power, and Belief* (Ithaca, NY, 1993), pp. 151–79. John Garrett published a useful series of general histories of Christianity in the Pacific Islands from a theological perspective: *To Live among the Stars: Christian Origins in Oceania* (Geneva, 1982); *Footsteps in the Sea: Christianity in Oceania to World War II* (Suva, 1992); and *Where Nets Were Cast: Christianity in Oceania since World War II* (Suva, 1977). Niel Gunson's *Messengers of Grace: Evangelical Missionaries in the South Seas 1797–1860*

(Melbourne, 1978) is the best general history of early Evangelical missionary work in the Pacific Islands. For Catholic missionary activity in the Pacific, see Ralph M. Wiltgen, *The Founding of the Roman Catholic Church in Oceania, 1825–1850* (Canberra, 1979) and Wiltgen, *The Founding of the Roman Catholic Church in Melanesia and Micronesia, 1850–1875* (Eugene, OR, 2008).

From the 16th century, missionaries in Oceania published myriad histories, ethnographies, dictionaries, and grammars, many available for download on Google Books or Internet Archive. See George Brown, *Melanesians and Polynesians their Life-histories Described and Compared* (London, 1910); James Calvert and Thomas Williams, *Fiji and the Fijians*, 2 vols. (London, 1858); Pedro Chirino, *Relación de las Islas Filipinas. The Philippines in 1600*, trans. Ramón Echeverria (Manila, 1969); R. H. Codrington, *The Melanesians: Studies in their Anthropology and Folk-lore* (Oxford, 1891); [John Davies], *A Tahitian and English Dictionary* (1851) (New York, 1978); William Ellis, *Polynesian Researche During a Residence of Nearly Six Years in the South Sea Islands*, 4 vols. (London, 1831); John Inglis, *In the New Hebrides: Reminiscences of Missionary Life and Work* (London, 1887); [Thomas Kendall], *A Grammar and Vocabulary of the Language of New Zealand* (London, 1820); W. G. Lawes, *Grammar and Vocabulary of Language Spoken by Motu Tribe (New Guinea)*, 2nd edn (Sydney 1888); L. E. Threlkeld, *An Australian Language as Spoken by the Awabakal, the People of Awaba* (Sydney, 1892); C. M. Léopold Verguet, *Histoire de la première mission catholique au Vicariat de Mélanésie* (Carcassonne, 1854); and John Williams, *A Narrative of Missionary Enterprises in the South Sea Islands* (London, 1837).

Important general reflections on the concept of Christian conversion include Kenelm Burridge, *In the Way: A Study of Christian Missionary Endeavors* (Vancouver, BC, 1991) and Robert W. Hefner, ed., *Conversion to Christianity: Historical and Anthropological Perspectives on a Great Transformation* (Berkeley, 1993). Histories of Christian missions, missionaries and conversion in Oceania and of indigenous encounters with Christianity are legion: for example, Ron Adams, *In the Land of Strangers: A Century of European Contact with Tanna, 1774–1874* (Canberra, 1984); Judith Binney, *The Legacy of Guilt: A Life of Thomas Kendall* (Auckland, 1968); James Clifford, *Person and Myth: Maurice Leenhardt in the Melanesian World* (Berkeley, 1982); Vicente M. Diaz, *Repositioning the Missionary: Rewriting the Histories of Colonialism, Native Catholicism, and Indigeneity in Guam* (Honolulu, 2010); Helen Bethea Gardner, *Gathering for God: George Brown in Oceania* (Dunedin, NZ, 2006); Robert Kenny, *The Lamb Enters the Dreaming: Nathanael Pepper and the Ruptured World* (Melbourne, 2007); Sione Lātūkefu, *Church and State in Tonga: The Wesleyan Methodist Missionaries and Political Development, 1822–1875* (Canberra, 1974); Vicente L. Rafael, *Contracting Colonialism: Translation and Christian Conversion in Tagalog Society under Early Spanish Rule* (Durham, NC, 1988); and Tony Swain and Deborah Bird Rose, eds., *Aboriginal Australians and Christian Missions: Ethnographic and Historical Studies* (Bedford Park, 1988).

Histories of Islander missionaries were published by Raeburn Lange, *Island Ministers: Indigenous Leadership in Nineteenth Century Pacific Islands Christianity* (Christchurch, NZ, 2006), and Doug Munro and Andrew Thornley, eds., *The*

*Covenant Makers: Islander Missionaries in the Pacific* (Suva, 1996). On Island churches, see Charles W. Forman, *The Island Churches of the South Pacific: Emergence in the Twentieth Century* (Maryknoll, 1982) and Manfred Ernst, *Winds of Change: Rapidly Growing Religious Groups in the Pacific Islands* (Suva, 1994) for a study of evangelical, pentecostal and charismatic Christianities in Oceania.

The themes of women missionaries and women and Christianity in the Pacific are addressed by Margaret Jolly and Martha Macintyre, eds., *Family and Gender in the Pacific: Domestic Contradictions and the Colonial Impact* (Cambridge, 1989); Patricia Grimshaw, *Paths of Duty: American Missionary Wives in Nineteenth-Century Hawaii* (Honolulu, 1989); Bronwen Douglas, ed., *Women's Groups and Everyday Modernity in Melanesia*, Special Issue, *Oceania* 74, 1–2 (September–December 2003); and Gwendoline Malogne-Fer, *Les femmes dans l'Eglise protestante mâ'ohi: religion, genre et pouvoir en Polynésie française* (Paris, 2007).

For a sample of recent ethnographies of Oceanian Christianities, see John Barker, ed., *Christianity in Oceania: Ethnographic Perspectives* (Lanham, MD, 1990); Annelin Eriksen, *Gender, Christianity and Change in Vanuatu: An Analysis of Social Movements in North Ambrym* (Farnham, 2007); Charles E. Farhadian, *Christianity, Islam, and Nationalism in Indonesia* (New York, 2005); Jacqueline Ryle, *My God, My Land: Interwoven Paths of Christianity and Tradition in Fiji* (Farnham, 2010); and Geoffrey M. White, *Identity Through History: Living Stories in a Solomon Islands Society* (Cambridge, 1991).

## 10   Law

The peoples of the Pacific region produced rich and varied systems of law. Much of the best recent work on Islander law and statecraft is contained in the footnotes of Damon Salesa's and Bronwen Douglas's chapters. Though it focuses on political and economic, rather than legal history, the *Cambridge History of Southeast Asia* (Cambridge 1994–9) has very useful essays on state-making and colonialism in that region. J. S. Furnivall's 80-year-old book, *Colonial Policy and Practice: A Comparative Study of Burma and Netherlands India* (Cambridge, 1938), usefully compares Dutch and British colonisation in Southeast Asia; while M. B. Hooker's *A Concise Legal History of South-East Asia* (Oxford, 1978) is another old, but still cited source, on the legal history of the region. English language sources on the modern legal history of China include Philip C. C. Huang's *Code, Custom, and Legal Practice in China: The Qing and the Republic Compared* (Stanford, 2001). Adam McKeown's *Melancholy Order: Asian Migration and the Globalization of Borders* (New York, 2008) is the leading text on legal regimes of border control among Japan, China, the United States, Canada and Australia. Akira Iriye's *Pacific Estrangement: Japanese and American Expansion, 1897–1911* (Cambridge, MA, 1972), meanwhile, is a good starting point for students interested in the role of Japanese and US expansion in the articulation of conflicts about the Pacific in the late nineteenth and early twentieth centuries. For a more detailed case study of Japanese expansion, see Alexis Dudden, *Japan's Colonization of Korea: Discourse and Power* (Honolulu, 2005).

Lauren Benton, with collaborators, has produced the most concise, recent analysis of the legal toolkit of European explorers in the early modern period – for example, Benton, 'Possessing Empire: Iberian Claims and Interpolity Law', in Saliha Belmessous, ed., *Native Claims: Indigenous Law Against Empire, 1500–1920* (New York, 2012), pp. 19–40. She has worked to dissolve distinctions between Iberian and later protestant claims to the New World posited by Patricia Seed, *Ceremonies of Possession in Europe's Conquest of the New World, 1492–1640* (Cambridge, 1995). Legal history of company engagement in the Pacific is a growing field: see, for example, forthcoming work from Arthur Weststeijn, Adam Clulow and Edward Cavanagh. For a good example of older work, see H. J. Leue, 'Legal Expansion in the Age of Companies: Aspects of the Administration of Justice in the English and Dutch Settlements of Maritime Asia, c. 1600–1750', in W. J. Mommsen and J. A. de Moor, eds., *European Expansion and Law: The Encounter of European and Indigenous Law in 19th- and 20th-Century Africa and Asia* (Oxford, 1992), pp. 129–58.

On European engagements with Pacific land tenures from the islands to Australia and Canada, see Stuart Banner's excellent *Possessing the Pacific: Land, Settlers, and Indigenous People from Australia to Alaska* (Cambridge, MA, 2007). On the legal complexities of regulating European trade in the nineteenth-century Islands, J. M. Ward, *British Policy in the South Pacific, 1786–1893: A Study in British Policy towards the South Pacific Islands Prior to the Establishment of Governments by the Great Powers* (Sydney, 1948), is still unsurpassed, though see also Jane Samson, *Imperial Benevolence: Making British Authority in the Pacific Islands* (Honolulu, 1998). Pär Cassel's recent book, *Grounds of Judgment: Extraterritoriality and Imperial Power in Nineteenth-century China and Japan* (Oxford, 2011), based in European, Chinese and Japanese archives, gives a nuanced account of the Opium War era treaties in East Asia; Eileen Scully's *Bargaining with the State from Afar: American Citizenship in Treaty Port China, 1844–1942* (New York, 2001), deals with treaties between the United States and China. Students interested in China's interactions with the law of nations and international law more generally should also read Lydia H. Liu, 'Legislating the Universal: The Circulation of International Law in the Nineteenth Century', in Liu, ed, *Tokens of Exchange: The Problem of Translation in Global Circulations* (Durham, NC, 1999), pp. 127–64, and, on Japan, John Peter Stern, *The Japanese Interpretation of the 'Laws of Nations', 1854–1874* (Princeton, NJ, 1979).

M. F. Lindley, *The Acquisition and Government of Backward Territory in International Law, Being a Treatise on the Law and Practice relating to Colonial Expansion* (London, 1926) remains the key Eurocentric statement of the relationship of early twentieth-century international law with Pacific (and African) peoples. The logic of protection in international law, meanwhile, has been thoughtfully analysed (though not necessarily in Pacific contexts), by Martti Koskenniemi, *The Gentle Civilizer of Nations: The Rise and Fall of International Law 1870–1960* (Cambridge, 2004) and Antony Anghie, *Imperialism, Sovereignty and the Making of International Law* (Cambridge, 2004).

My treatment of post-war debates about sovereignty, jurisdiction and the law of the sea is based largely on law journals. However, students interested in the late twentieth-century legal history of the Pacific should start with Philip

E. Steinberg's brief and imaginative *The Social Construction of the Ocean* (Cambridge, 2001). Robert Cribb and Michele Ford, eds., *Indonesia beyond the Water's Edge: Managing an Archipelagic State* (Singapore, 2009), is one of the few books to look meaningfully at the engagement of a Southeast Asian polity with the sea. Yash Ghai, ed., *Law, Government and Politics in the Pacific Island States* (Suva, Fiji, 1988), though aging, is still an excellent overview of the postcolonial island states. There is a multitude of scholarly work on indigenous claims in Anglophone settler polities: Paul Havemann, ed., *Indigenous Peoples' Rights in Australia, Canada and New Zealand* (Auckland, 1999), Diane Kirkby and Catharine Coleborne, eds., *Law, History, Colonialism: The Reach of Empire* (Manchester, 2001) and Lisa Ford and Tim Rowse, eds., *Between Settler and Indigenous Governance* (London, 2012), provide three very different sets of perspectives relevant to the subject. Jane McAdam, ed., *Climate Change and Displacement: Multidisciplinary Perspectives* (Oxford, 2010), meanwhile, provides a useful overview of the legal ramifications of climate change around the globe.

## 11   Science

The history of science is currently in the midst of a wave of work on global interactions: for indicative surveys and historiographical interventions, see Lissa Roberts, ed., 'Situating Science in Global History: Local Exchanges and Networks of Circulation', *Itinerario* 33 (2009), 5–95, and Sujit Sivasundaram, ed., 'Global Histories of Science', *Isis* 110 (2010), 95–158. For Pacific historians, this global turn serves as a call to place the region in relation to its neighbours such as the Atlantic and Indian Oceans, for example Kate Fullagar, ed., *The Atlantic World in the Antipodes: Effects and Transformations since the Eighteenth Century* (Newcastle upon Tyne, 2012), and South Asia, for example, Tony Ballantyne, *Orientalism and Race: Aryanism in the British Empire* (Basingstoke, 2001). Pacific historians might also attend to recent work on science in the Arctic, for example, Michael Bravo and Sverker Sörlin, eds., *Narrating the Arctic: A Cultural History of Nordic Scientific Practice* (Canton, MA, 2002). Historians of science in Russia are also now attending to engagements with the Pacific: see, for instance, Simon Werrett, 'Russian Responses to the Voyages of Captain Cook', in Glyn Williams, ed., *Captain Cook: Explorations and Reassessments* (New York, 2004), pp. 179–200, and Werrett, 'Technology on Display: Instruments and Identities on Russian Voyages of Exploration', *Russian Review* 70 (2011), 380–96. For the transnational dimensions of science in the twentieth century, drawing in multiple nations, including Australia- and New Zealand-based scientists, see Roy Macleod, ed., *Science and the Pacific War: Science and Survival in the Pacific, 1939–1945* (Dordrecht, 1999).

The need to contextualise the Pacific in a more variegated and non-Eurocentric history also becomes urgent in taking on board recent work on brokerage and intermediation in giving rise to science: see Simon Schaffer, Lissa Roberts, Kapil Raj and James Delbourgo, eds., *The Brokered World: Go-betweens and Global Intelligence, 1770–1820* (Sagamore, Beach, MA, 2009). Work on brokerage in the Pacific context has paid attention in particular to the status of indigenous knowledge traditions with respect to navigation, as in David Turnbull, *Mapping the World in the Mind: An Investigation of the Unwritten Knowledge of Micronesian Navigators* (Geelong, 1990) and Turnbull, 'Pacific Navigation: An Alternative Scientific Tradition', in Turnbull, *Masons, Tricksters and Cartographers: Comparative Studies in the Sociology of Scientific and Indigenous Knowledge* (Amsterdam, 2000), pp. 131–60. For cartography more generally, see Paul Carter, *The Road to Botany Bay: An Essay in Spatial History* (London, 1987). For early work on natural history, which was beginning to pay attention to the role of intermediaries and indigenous knowledges, see David Philip Miller and Peter Hans Reill, eds., *Visions of Empire: Voyages, Botany and Representations of Nature* (Cambridge, 1996). For a reconsideration of Cook's explorations in relation to intermediation, see Anne Salmond, *The Trial of the Cannibal Dog: The Remarkable Story of Captain Cook's Encounters in the South Seas* (London, 2003). For the role of encounter in giving rise to racial ideas, see Bronwen Douglas and Chris Ballard, eds., *Foreign Bodies: Oceania and the Science of Race, 1750–1940* (Canberra, 2008) and Douglas, *Science, Voyages and Encounters in Oceania, 1511–1850* (Basingstoke, 2014). For the role of exchange in giving rise to anthropology see Amiria Salmond, *Museums, Anthropology and Imperial Exchange* (Cambridge, 2005). A new line of analysis pertains to the medical history of the Pacific, notably Alison Bashford, *Imperial Hygiene: A Critical History of Colonialism, Nationalism and Public Health* (Basingstoke, 2004) and Rod Edmond, *Leprosy and Empire: A Medical and Cultural History* (Cambridge, 2006). Twentieth-century American public health in the Pacific is treated in Anne Perez Hattori, *Colonial Dis-ease: US Navy Policy and the Chamorros of Guam, 1898–1941* (Honolulu, 2004), Warwick Anderson, *Colonial Pathologies: American Tropical Medicine, Race and Hygiene in the Philippines* (Durham, NC, 2006) and Anderson, 'Pacific Crossings: Imperial Logics in U.S. Public Health Programs', in Alfred W. McCoy and Francisco Scarano, eds., *Colonial Crucible: Empire in the Making of the Modern American State* (Madison, WI, 2009), pp. 277–87.

These more recent reconsiderations of medical history follow in the wake of major work on the relationship between science and empire in the Pacific Ocean, which made the claim that this tract of the earth was critical to the emergence of new disciplines, methods and styles of representation in Europe. In many ways the groundwork for this tradition was laid in 1960 by Bernard Smith, *European Vision and the South Pacific, 1768–1850*, 2nd edn (New Haven, 1985); for an excellent collection of some of the classic articles in this field, see Tony Ballantyne, ed., *Science, Empire and the European Exploration of the Pacific* (Aldershot, 2004). For other collections which consider relations of science and empire, see Margarette Lincoln, ed., *Science and Exploration in the Pacific* (Woodbridge, 1998), Roy Macleod and Philip Rehbock, eds., *Darwin's Laboratory: Evolutionary Theory and Natural History in the Pacific* (Honolulu, 1994) and MacLeod and Rehbock, eds., *Nature in its Greatest Extent: Western Science in the Pacific* (Honolulu, 1988). This interest also veered into maritime and naval history: for a classic example, see Richard Sorrenson, 'The Ship as Scientific Instrument', *Osiris* 11 (1996), 221–36, and for a newer work, Helen

Rozwadowski, *Fathoming the Ocean: The Discovery and Exploration of the Deep Sea* (Cambridge, MA, 2005). The nature of empire and imperial agencies is becoming more fragmented and multi-sited in the more recent literature. For the role of missionaries as scientific thinkers, see Sujit Sivasundaram, *Nature and the Godly Empire: Science and Evangelical Mission in the South Pacific, 1795–1850* (Cambridge, 2005). For the role of New Zealand as generative of scientific debates in its own terms, see John Stenhouse 'Darwinism in New Zealand, 1859–1900', in Ronald L. Numbers and Stenhouse, eds., *Disseminating Darwinism: The Role of Place, Race, Religion, and Gender* (Cambridge, 1999), pp. 61–89.

## 12   Race

The accounts of explorers are still useful for understanding peoples' perceptions of each other in the Pacific. Most explorers were European, but they did include a few indigenous pilots and interpreters, such as the Tahitian priest and pilot Tupaia, who had firm views on the inferiority of other island cultures: see, most recently, Joan Druett, *Tupaia: Captain Cook's Polynesian Navigator* (Santa Barbara, CA, 2011). The definitive edition of Cook's own journals is *The Journals of Captain James Cook on his Voyages of Discovery*, ed. J. C. Beaglehole, 4 vols. (London 1955). *The Resolution Journal of Johann Reinhold Forster, 1772–1775*, ed. M. E. Hoare, 4 vols. (London, 1982), complete with reflections on race, make an interesting counterpoint. Charles Darwin's *Voyage of the Beagle*, of which there are many editions, is a prime example of how ideas of race and the Pacific helped constitute each other. An intriguing take on explorer mentality is Anne Salmond, *The Trial of the Cannibal Dog: Captain Cook in the South Seas* (London 2003), while Bernard Smith's classic, *European Vision and the South Pacific, 1768–1850*, 2nd edn (New Haven, 1985) remains well worth reading.

Racial mixing and its myths around the Pacific littoral are discussed in Adele Perry, *On the Edge of Empire: Gender, Race, and the Making of British Columbia 1849–1871* (Toronto, 2001); Damon Salesa, *Racial Crossings: Race, Intermarriage, and the Victorian British Empire* (Oxford 2011); and Gwenn A. Miller, *Kodiak Kreol: Communities of Empire in Early Russian America* (Ithaca, NY, 2010). Mexico is a good point of entry into the myriad complexities of race in Pacific Latin America: see María Elena Martínez, *Genealogical Fictions: Limpieza de Sangre, Religion, and Gender in Colonial Mexico* (Stanford, 2008) and Ilona Katzew and Susan Deans-Smith, eds., *Race and Classification: The Case of Mexican America* (Stanford, 2009). On the Aryan myth in the Pacific and Indian Oceans, see Tony Ballantyne, *Orientalism and Race: Aryanism in the British Empire* (Basingstoke, 2002).

There is a large and commendably transnational literature on 'White Pacific' immigration policies. Standard examples are Charles Price, *The Great White Walls are Built: Restrictive Immigration to North America and Australasia, 1836–1888* (Canberra, 1974); Robert A. Huttenback, *Racism and Empire: White Settlers and Colored Immigrants in the British Self-governing Colonies, 1830–1910* (Ithaca, NY, 1976) and, more recently, Erika Lee, 'The "Yellow Peril" and Asian Exclusion in the Americas', *Pacific Historical Review* 76 (2007), 537–52 and Marilyn Lake and Henry Reynolds , *Drawing the Global Colour Line: White Men's Countries and the International Challenge of Racial Equality* (Cambridge, 2008).

The interplay of Pacific exploration and the development of modern racial thought is investigated in various works by Bronwen Douglas and others, including Douglas and Chris Ballard, eds., *Foreign Bodies: Oceania and the Science of Race 1750–1940* (Canberra 2008) and Douglas, *Science, Voyages and Encounters in Oceania, 1511–1850* (Basingstoke, 2014). For alternative views of the origins of racism see James H. Sweet, 'The Iberian Roots of American Racist Thought', *William and Mary Quarterly* 3rd ser., 54 (1997), 143–66; Joyce E. Chaplin, 'Race', in David Armitage and Michael J. Braddick, eds., *The British Atlantic World, 1500–1800*, 2nd edn (Basingstoke, 2009), pp. 173–90; and Miriam Eliav-Feldon, Benjamin Isaac and Joseph Ziegler, eds., *The Origins of Racism in the West* (Cambridge, 2009). For the notion that non-Europeans sometimes developed racism independently see Jonathon Glassman, 'Slower Than a Massacre: The Multiple Sources of Racial Thought in Colonial Africa', *American Historical Review* 109 (2004), 720–55, and S. B. Miles, 'Imperial Discourse, Regional Elite, and Local Landscape on the South China Frontier, 1577–1722', *Journal of Early Modern History* 12 (2008), 99–136. For racism in East Asia more generally see Frank Dikötter, ed., *The Construction of Racial Identities in China and Japan: Historical and Contemporary Perspectives* (London 1997). For racism towards East Asians, see Michael Keevak, *Becoming Yellow: A Short History of Racial Thinking* (Princeton, 2011).

# 13 Gender

On masculinities and homosexualities in the Pacific, see Eric McCormick, *Omai: Pacific Envoy* (Auckland, NZ, 1977), Lee Wallace, *Sexual Encounters: Pacific Texts, Modern Sexualities* (Ithaca, NY, 2003), Sabrina Ramet, *Gender Reversals and Gender Cultures: Anthropological and Historical Perspectives* (London 1996), Patty O'Brien, 'Exotic Primitivism and the Baudin Voyage to Tasmania in 1802', *Journal of Australian Studies* 23 (1999), 13–21, and Shino Konishi, *The Aboriginal Male in the Enlightenment World* (London, 2012). On mythologies of Pacific women, see Matt Matsuda, *Empire of Love: Histories of France and the Pacific* (Oxford 2005), Jane Desmond, *Staging Tourism: Bodies on Display form Waikiki to Sea World* (Chicago, 1999), Tamasailau Suaalii, 'Deconstructing the "Exotic" Female Beauty of the Pacific Islands', in Alison Jones, Phyllis Herda and Suaalii, eds., *Bitter Sweet: Indigenous Women in the Pacific* (Dunedin, NZ, 2000), pp. 93–108, and A. Marata Tamaira, 'From Full Dusk to Full Tusk: Reimagining the Dusky Maiden through the Visual Arts', *The Contemporary Pacific* 22 (2010), 1–35. On historical anthropology, encounters, race and representation see Margaret Jolly, Serge Tcherkézoff and Darrell Tryon, eds., *Oceanic Encounters: Exchange, Desire, Violence* (Canberra, 2009) and Bronwen Douglas and Chris Ballard eds., *Foreign Bodies: Oceania and the Science of Race 1750–1940* (Canberra, 2008). Works by Harriet Guest explore the gendered dimensions of art generated during Pacific exploration, especially her *Empire, Barbarism, and Civilisation: James Cook, William Hodges, and the Return to the Pacific* (Cambridge, 2007).

For literature on convict women Anne Summers, *Damned Whores and God's Police: The Colonization of Women in Australia* (Melbourne, 1975), Miriam Dixson, *Real Matilda: Women and Identity in Australia from 1788 to the Present* (Sydney, 1976), Portia Robinson, *The Women of Botany Bay: A Reinterpretation of the Role of Women in the Origins of Australian Society* (Ringwood, 1993), Deborah Oxley, *Convict Maids: The Forced Migration of Women to Australia* (Cambridge, 1996), Kay Daniels, *Convict Women* (St Leonards, NSW, 1998) and Sian Rees, *The Floating Brothel: The Extraordinary True Story of Female Convicts Bound for Botany Bay* (Sydney, 2001). For white women in empire see Chilla Bulbeck, *Australian Women in Papua New Guinea: Colonial Passages, 1920–1960* (Cambridge, 1992) and Fiona Paisley, *Glamour in the Pacific: Cultural Internationalism and Race Politics in the Women's Pan-Pacific* (Honolulu, 2009).

Regarding gender in Asian history, see Carol Benedict's *Golden-Silk Smoke: A History of Tobacco in China, 1550–2010* (Berkeley, 2011) for a gendered social history of tobacco, Yoshimi Yoshiaki's *Comfort Women: Sexual Slavery in the Japanese Military During World War II* (New York, 2000) and numerous works by Louise Edwards and Mina Roces that explore gender in the Philippines, women's lives, dress and Asian women's migration. On gender and war, see Sean Brawley and Chris Dixon, *Hollywood's South Seas and the Pacific War: Searching for Dorothy Lamour* (New York, 2012) and Gabriel Koureas, 'Where the Boys Are: Militarization, Sexuality and Red Cross Donut Dollies in the Vietnam War', in Ana Carden Coyne, ed., *Gender and Conflict since 1914: Historical and Interdisciplinary Perspectives* (New York, 2012), pp. 138–53.

## 14    Politics

Most works on individual countries and cultures provide detailed material on political systems and the changes they have undergone. Some volumes also provide useful transnational and cross-cultural perspectives. David C. Kang, *East Asia before the West: Five Centuries of Trade and Tribute* (New York, 2010), offers a good introduction to the Chinese system of tributary states, and O. W. Wolters, *History, Culture and Region in Southeast Asian Perspective*, rev. edn (Ithaca, NY, 1999) develops the idea of political 'mandalas' in Buddhist states. Anthony Milner, *The Malays* (Oxford, 2011) is a recent overview of that cultural zone. Douglas L. Oliver, *Oceania: The Native Cultures of Australia and the Pacific Islands* (Honolulu, 1989) remains an authoritative source on the indigenous societies of the southern Pacific. An interpretive introduction to politics in South America is David Bushnell and Neil Macaulay, *The Emergence of Latin America in the Nineteenth Century* (Oxford, 1994).

Among the countless books on colonialism, John Darwin, *After Tamerlane: The Rise and Fall of Global Empire, 1400–2000* (London, 2007) is a good wide-angle approach. One of the most insightful comparative studies of the transformation of governance under colonialism, and the survival of precolonial institutions, is Colin Newbury, *Patrons, Clients and Empire: Chieftaincy and Over-Rule in Asia, Africa, and the Pacific* (Oxford, 2003).

Works on settler colonialism frequently use particular cases to suggest comparative perspectives. A recent example is Fiona Bateman and Lionel Pilkington, eds., *Studies in Settler Colonialism: Politics, Identity, and Culture* (New York, 2011), with chapters on Hawai'i, Canada and Australasia as well as non-Pacific examples. Studies of indigenous rights have developed rapidly in recent years; Adolfo de Oliveira, ed., *Decolonising Indigenous Rights* (New York, 2009) includes cases from the United States, Canada, Chile and Australia. James Curran and Stuart Ward, *The Unknown Nation: Australia after Empire* (Melbourne, 2010) traces Australia's disengagement from the British imperial mantle. David Hackett Fischer, *Fairness and Freedom: A History of Two Open Societies–New Zealand and the United States* (Oxford, 2012), provides a rare and welcome sustained comparison of the history of two Pacific countries.

For the political ferment in Asia in the late 1800s and early 1900s, Benedict Anderson, *Under Three Flags: Anarchism and the Anti-Colonial Imagination* (London, 2008), is especially interesting in linking the Philippines with ideological ferment in Europe and the Americas. Peter Zarrow, *After Empire: The Conceptual Transformation of the Chinese State, 1885–1924* (Stanford, 2012), offers an excellent study of the ideology and strategy of government and opposition there. Pankaj Mishra, *From the Ruins of Empire: The Revolt against the West and the Remaking of Asia* (London, 2012), stresses the role of Asian theorists and the importance of Japan as a meeting-place for nationalists. Donald Keene, *Emperor of Japan: Meiji and His World, 1852–1912* (New York, 2002) is a wide-ranging study of personalities and politics in Japan itself.

Anti-colonial movements are well covered in the literature, and collections of the writings of such figures as Mao Zedong, Ho Chi Minh and Sukarno are invaluable for understanding their ideology and tactics. Biographies of individual leaders, past and present, provide a good lens through which to view political developments. For the Francophone areas, for instance, there is Pierre Brocheux, *Ho Chi Minh: A Biography*, trans. Claire Dulker (Cambridge, 2007), and on the later leader of New Caledonia's independence movement, Eric Waddell, *Jean-Marie Tjibaou: Kanak Witness to the World – An Intellectual Biography* (Honolulu, 2008).

Alfred W. McCoy, Josep M. Fradera and Stephen Jacobson, eds., *Endless Empire: Spain's Retreat, Europe's Eclipse, America's Decline* (Madison, WI, 2012), discusses the rise and fall of Pacific empires. The four volumes of Shaun Breslin and Richard Higgott, eds., *International Relations of the Asia-Pacific* (London, 2010), comprise a compendium of scholarly articles and provide a *tour d'horizon* of security, development and regional issues, as well as the theorising of international politics.

# Index